DISTRIBUTION CLERK, MACHINE

U.S. Postal Service

E. P. Steinberg

ARCO
New York

ARCO

Simon & Schuster, Inc.
Gulf + Western Building
One Gulf + Western Plaza
New York, NY 10023

DISTRIBUTED BY PRENTICE HALL TRADE

Manufactured in the United States of America

1 2 3 4 5 6 7 8 9 10

Library of Congress Cataloging in Publication Data
Steinberg, Eve P.
  Distribution clerk, machine, U.S. Postal Service.

  1. Postal service—United States—Examinations,
questions, etc. 2. Postal service—United States
—Employees. I. Title.
HE6499.S749 1988   383′.145   88-26271
ISBN 0-13-216698-4 (pbk.)

CONTENTS

INTRODUCTION

HOW TO USE THIS BOOK

The Postal Service examination for Distribution Clerk, Machine, may be the most important exam you ever take. It can be your ticket to a rewarding career that offers good pay, excellent working conditions and a secure future. The very things that make the job appealing to you, though, make it appealing to many others too, and often hundreds of applicants compete for a single job opening. The only way to get the job you seek is to earn the highest possible score on the Distribution Clerk, Machine, Exam. That's where this book can help. If you follow its advice and take advantage of the training and practice it offers, you will be well prepared to earn high scores on the postal exam and a spot near the top of the list of eligibles for jobs with the postal service.

Ideally, you should start your preparation two or three months before the exam. That gives you plenty of time to complete all of the Model Exams, and to decide on and practice the memory scheme that works best for you. If you begin early enough, you will be able to leave a few days between each Model Exam so that your memory of one sorting scheme does not interfere with your memorizing of another scheme. No matter how much time you have, start *now*. Work your way through the entire book, and give it all the time and attention you can.

Read the first two chapters to find out all about the work of the letter sorting machine operator and the process of applying for the job.

Next, take the Diagnostic Exam to discover where you stand at this moment. Choose a quiet, well-lighted spot for your work. Clear away all distractions from your desk or tabletop. Bring two sharpened pencils with erasers and a stop watch or kitchen timer to your work area. Tear out the answer sheet for the Diagnostic Exam. Read the directions and begin.

When you have completed the Diagnostic Exam, check your answers against the correct answers at the end of the exam. Study the explanations for the Number Series questions so that you can learn from your mistakes and gain new insights into the answering of these questions. Note the instructions for analyzing your errors on the Address Checking Test. Follow these instructions and learn what kinds of errors you made most often. If you understand the type of error you are most likely to make, you will be able to avoid that type of error on future tests.

Calculate your score on the score sheet provided, considering only those questions you answered within the time limit. You will notice that the scoring instructions for the various parts of the exam are different. Follow the instructions for each separate part in calculating your score. Then look at the Self-Evaluation Chart to see how well you did. Plot your scores on the Progress Chart so that you can follow your improvement as you complete further exams in this book.

Do not be discouraged by low scores on the Diagnostic Exam. You still have plenty of time to improve your scores with the instruction and practice that follow.

The three chapters following the Diagnostic Exam contain concrete advice about the techniques for answering postal exam questions quickly and accurately. Read these chapters carefully and follow through on all suggestions before taking the remaining Model Exams. It's a good idea to come back to these chapters between exams or just before the actual exam to refresh yourself on ways to improve your scores.

Leaving ample time between them, take the remaining Model Exams just the way you took the Diagnostic Exam. Time yourself accurately and score yourself honestly. Study and learn from the explanations that accompany the correct answers to Number Series questions. Analyze the errors you made on each Address Checking Test so that you can try to avoid making the same mistakes in the future. After you complete each Model Exam, fill in the graph to check your progress and locate your score on the Self-Evaluation Chart to see how your ranking improves.

By the time you have completed this book, you should be well prepared for your examination.

SUGGESTIONS FOR EXAM DAY

- Get a good night's sleep.

- Get up in time to eat breakfast and do whatever you have to do to insure that you are fully alert.

- Dress comfortably.

- Allow yourself plenty of time to get to the exam.

- Remember to bring your admission card and identification that has your picture or your signature.

- Choose a comfortable seat that is as free as possible from drafts, noise, and traffic.

- Follow the directions of the test administrator. If you don't understand what you are to do, *ask questions*.

- Take a deep breath, relax, and resolve to do your best. Your preparation and practice should pay off in high scores on the exam.

WORKING FOR THE POST OFFICE

The United States Postal Service is an independent agency of the Federal Government. As such, employees of the Postal Service are federal employees who enjoy the very generous benefits offered by the government. These benefits include an automatic raise at least once a year, regular cost of living adjustments, liberal paid vacation and sick leave, life insurance, hospitalization, and the opportunity to join a credit union. At the same time, the operation of the Postal Service is businesslike and independent of politics. A postal worker's job is secure even though administrations may change. An examination system is used to fill vacancies. The examination system provides opportunities for those who are able and motivated to enter the Postal Service and to move within it.

Since postal employment is so popular, entry is very competitive. In most areas the Distribution Clerk, Machine, Exam is administered only once every three years. The resulting list is used to fill vacancies as they occur in the next three years. An individual who is already employed by the Postal Service, however, may request to take an exam during those intervening years. Any person who works for the Postal Service may ask to take the exam for any position and, if properly qualified, may fill a vacancy ahead of a person whose name is on the regular list. It is even possible to change careers within the Postal Service. A custodian, for instance, might take the Clerk-Carrier Exam; a stenographer might choose to become a letter sorting machine operator; or a mail handler might take an exam to enter personnel work. If the exam for the precise position that you want will not be administered for some time, it might be worthwhile to take the exam for another position in hopes of entering the Postal Service and then moving from within.

One very common "instant progression" within the Postal Service is that from clerk-carrier, a salary level 5 position, to distribution clerk, machine (also known as letter sorting machine operator), a level 6 position. Anyone who qualifies as a clerk-carrier is automatically offered the opportunity to take the machine exam. The advantages of becoming a letter sorting machine operator include not only higher salary, but also increased employment possibilities. Mechanization is the wave of the future. The field is expanding, and there are far more openings for machine operators than there are for clerks or carriers. Of course, the desirability of the job leads to a greater number of applicants and a still more competitive position for you. This fact should further motivate you to study hard for your exam.

Salaries, hours, and some other working conditions as well are subject to frequent change. The postal workers have a very effective union that bargains for them and gains increasingly better conditions. At the time of your employment, you should make your own inquiry as to salary, hours, and other conditions as they apply to you. Job descriptions and requirements are less subject to change. In the next few pages we quote job descriptions as provided by the government.

OCCUPATIONS IN THE POSTAL SERVICE

The U.S. Postal Service handles billions of pieces of mail a year, including letters, magazines, and parcels. Close to a million workers are required to process and deliver this mail. The vast majority of Postal Service jobs are open to workers with 4 years of high school or less. The work is steady. Some of the jobs, such as mail carrier, offer a good deal of personal freedom. Other jobs, however, are more closely supervised and more routine.

WHO WORKS FOR THE POSTAL SERVICE?

Most people are familiar with the duties of the mail carrier and the post office window clerk. Yet few are aware of the many different tasks required in processing mail and of the variety of occupations in the Postal Service.

At all hours of the day and night, a steady stream of letters, packages, magazines, and papers moves through the typical large post office. Mail carriers have collected some of this mail from neighborhood mailboxes; some has been trucked in from surrounding towns or from the airport. When a truck arrives at the post office, mail handlers unload the mail. Postal clerks then sort it according to destination. After being sorted, outgoing mail is loaded into trucks for delivery to the airport or nearby towns. Local mail is left for carriers to deliver the next morning.

To keep buildings and equipment clean and in good working order, the Postal Service employs a variety of service and maintenance workers, including janitors, laborers, truck mechanics, electricians, carpenters, and painters. Some workers specialize in repairing machines that process mail.

Postal inspectors audit the operations of post offices to see that they are run efficiently, that funds are spent properly, and that postal laws and regulations are observed. They also prevent and detect crimes such as theft, forgery, and fraud involving use of the mail.

Postmasters and supervisors are responsible for the day-to-day operation of the post office, for hiring and promoting employees, and for setting up work schedules.

The Postal Service also contracts with private businesses to transport mail. There are more than 12,500 of these "Star" route contracts. Most "Star" route carriers use trucks to haul mail, but in some remote areas horses or boats are used instead.

Almost 85 percent of all postal workers are in jobs directly related to processing and delivering mail. This group includes postal clerks, mail carriers, mail handlers, and truck drivers. Postmasters and supervisors make up nearly 10 percent of total employment and maintenance workers about 4 percent. The remainder includes such workers as postal inspectors, guards, personnel workers, and secretaries.

WHERE ARE THE JOBS?

The Postal Service operates more than 41,000 installations. Most are post offices, but some serve special purposes such as handling payroll records or supplying equipment.

Although every community receives mail service, employment is concentrated in large metropolitan areas. Post offices in cities such as New York, Chicago, and Los Angeles employ a great number of workers because they not only process huge amounts of mail for their own populations but also serve as mail processing points for the smaller communities that surround them. These large city post offices have sophisticated machines for sorting the mail. In these post offices, distribution clerks who have qualified as machine operators quickly scan addresses and send letters on their way automatically by pushing the proper button. These clerks must be able to read addresses quickly and accurately, must be able to memorize codes and sorting schemes and must demonstrate machine aptitude by the performance on the Number Series part of the exam.

TRAINING, OTHER QUALIFICATIONS, AND ADVANCEMENT

An applicant for a Postal Service job must pass an examination and meet minimum age requirements. Generally, the minimum age is 18 years, but a high school graduate may begin work at 16 years if the job is not hazardous and does not require use of a motor vehicle. Many Postal Service jobs do not require formal education or special training. Applicants for these jobs are hired on the basis of their examination scores.

Applicants should apply at the post office where they wish to work and take the entrance examination for the job they want. Examinations for most jobs include a written test. A physical examination is required as well. Applicants for jobs that require strength and stamina are sometimes given a special test. For example, mail handlers must be able to lift mail sacks weighing up to 70 pounds. The names of applicants who pass the examinations are placed on a list in the order of their scores. Separate eligibility lists are maintained for each post office. Five extra points are added to the score of an honorably discharged veteran and 10 extra points to the score of a veteran wounded in combat or disabled. Disabled veterans who have a compensable, service-connected disability of 10 percent or more are placed at the top of the eligibility list. When a job opens, the appointing officer chooses one of the top three applicants. Others are left on the list so that they can be considered for future openings.

New employees are trained either on the job by supervisors and other experienced employees or in local training centers. Training ranges from a few days to several months, depending on the job. For example, mail handlers and mechanics' helpers can learn their jobs in a relatively short time. Postal inspectors, on the other hand, need months of training.

Advancement opportunities are available for most postal workers because there is a management commitment to provide career development. Also, employees can get preferred assignments, such as the day shift or a more desirable delivery route, as their seniority increases. When an opening occurs, employees may submit written requests, called "bids," for assignment to the vacancy. The bidder who meets the qualifications and has the most seniority gets the job.

In addition, postal workers can advance to better paying positions by learning new skills. Training programs are available for low-skilled workers who wish to become technicians or mechanics.

Applicants for supervisory jobs must pass an examination. Additional requirements for promotion may include training or education, a satisfactory work record, and appropriate personal characteristics such as leadership ability. If the leading candidates are equally qualified, length of service also is considered.

Although opportunities for promotion to supervisory positions in smaller post offices are limited, workers may apply for vacancies in a larger post office and thus increase their chances.

EMPLOYMENT OUTLOOK

Employment in the Postal Service is expected to grow more slowly than the average for all industries through the mid-1980's. Mechanization of mail processing and more efficient delivery should allow the Postal Service to handle increasing amounts of mail without corresponding increases in employment. Nevertheless, thousands of job openings will result as workers retire, die, or transfer to other fields.

EARNINGS AND WORKING CONDITIONS

Postal Service employees are paid under several separate pay schedules depending upon the duties of the job and the knowledge, experience, or skill required. For example, there are separate schedules for production workers such as clerks and mail handlers, for rural carriers, for postal managers, and for postal executives. In all pay schedules, except that of executives, employees receive periodic "step" increases up to a specified maximum if their job performance is satisfactory.

The conditions that follow are subject to collective bargaining and may well be different by the time you are employed by the Postal Service.

Full-time employees work an 8-hour day, 5 days a week. Both full-time and part-time employees who work more than 8 hours a day or 40 hours a week receive overtime pay of one and one-half times their hourly rates. In addition, pay is higher for those on the night shift.

Postal employees earn 13 days of annual leave (vacation) during each of their first 3 years of service, including prior Federal civilian and military service; 20 days each year for 3 to 15 years of service; and 26 days after 15 years. In addition, they earn 13 days of paid sick leave a year regardless of length of service.

Other benefits include retirement and survivorship annuities, free group life insurance, and optional participation in health insurance programs supported in part by the Postal Service.

Most post office buildings are clean and well-lighted, but some of the older ones are not. The Postal Service is in the process of replacing and remodeling its outmoded buildings, and conditions are expected to improve.

Most postal workers are members of unions and are covered by a national agreement between the Postal Service and the unions.

APPLYING FOR POSTAL POSITIONS

The Post Office Distribution Clerk, Machine, Exam is not a regularly scheduled exam given on the same date all over the country. Rather, the exam is scheduled separately in each postal geographic area. An area may comprise a number of states or, in densely populated regions, may consist of only a portion of one county. The frequency of administration also varies, though generally the exam is offered every two or three years.

When an exam is about to open in a postal area, the postal examiner for the area sends notices to all the post offices serviced by that area. The examiner also places ads in local newspapers and commercials over local radio stations. State employment offices receive and post copies of the announcement, and Civil Service newspapers carry the information as well. The announcement that you can pick up at your post office looks like this:

The Opportunity: Applications are now being accepted, and examinations will be given to establish a register of eligibles or to expand the current register of eligibles from which future vacancies in this Post Office will be filled. All interested persons who meet the requirements described in this announcement are urged to apply.

Qualification Requirements: No experience is required. All applicants will be required to take a written examination designed to test aptitude for learning and performing the duties of the position. The test will consist of 4 parts: (A) Number Series (B) Address Coding (C) Address Code Memory (D) Address Checking. The test and completion of the forms will require approximately 2½ hours.

Duties: Distribution clerks work indoors. Often clerks must handle sacks of mail weighing as much as 70 pounds. They sort mail and distribute it by using a complicated scheme which must be memorized. Machine distribution clerks must learn computer codes for the automatic routing of mail. Clerks may be on their feet all day. They also have to stretch, reach, and throw mail. As representatives of the Postal Service, they must maintain pleasant and effective public relations with patrons and others, requiring a general familiarity with postal laws, regulations, and procedures commonly used.

Employees may be assigned to work in places exposed to public view. Their appearance influences the general public's confidence and attitude toward the entire Postal Service.

Employees appointed under this standard are, therefore, expected to maintain neat and proper personal attire and grooming appropriate to conducting public business, including the wearing of a uniform when required.

Physical Requirements: Applicants must be physically able to perform the duties described elsewhere in this announcement. Any physical condition which would cause the applicant to be a hazard to himself or to others will be disqualifying for appointment.

The distant vision for clerk and carrier positions not involving driving duties must test at least 20/30 (Snellen) in one eye, glasses permitted, and applicants generally must be able to hear ordinary conversation with or without a hearing aid, but some clerk positions may be filled by the deaf.

A physical examination will be required before appointment.

Age Requirement: The general age requirement is 18 years or 16 years for high school graduates, except for those for whom age limits are waived. For carrier positions which require driving, applicants must be 18 years of age or over. In general, there is no maximum age limit.

Citizenship: All applicants must be citizens of or owe allegiance to the United States of America or have been granted permanent resident alien status in the United States.

Salary: Results from collective bargaining.

Consideration: Consideration to fill these positions will be made of the highest eligibles on the register who are available.

How to Apply: Submit application Form 2479-AB to the postmaster of this office or place designated by him.

Opening date for application: _____

                                         Month   Day   Year

Closing date for application: _____

                                         Month   Day   Year

Written Examination: Applicants will be notified of date, time, and place of examination and will be sent sample questions.

POST OFFICE JOBS OFFER:

Job Security	Liberal Retirement	Cash for Suggestions
Paid Vacations	Sick Leave with Pay	Promotion Opportunities
On the Job Training	Low Cost Life Insurance	Paid Holidays
	Low Cost Health Insurance	

Ask for an application card at your local post office. The card is bright yellow and is in two sections joined at a perforation. Do NOT separate the two sections. The section on the left is called the Application Card, that on the right the Admission Card. Instructions for filling out both sections are printed on the back of the card. Follow these directions precisely, and carefully fill out both sections of the card. Hand in or mail the completed application as instructed.

The application and admission card look like this:

APPLICATION CARD

Name (Last, First, Middle Initials)

Address (House/Apt. No. & Street)

City, State, ZIP Code

Birthdate (Month, Date, Year)

	Do Not Write In This Space

Telephone Number | Today's Date

Title of Examination

Post Office Applied For

PS Form 2479-A, April 1983

(Front)

PS Form 2479-A, April 1983 (Reverse)

Instructions to Applicants

Furnish all the information requested on these cards. The attached card will be returned to you with sample questions and necessary instructions, including the time and place of the written test.

TYPEWRITE OR PRINT IN INK. DO NOT SEPARATE THESE CARDS. FOLD ONLY AT PERFORATION.

Mail or Take This Form—Both Parts—to The Postmaster of the Post Office Where You Wish to Be Employed.

✪ U.S. G.P.O. 1983-655-793

(Back)

ADMISSION CARD

Title of Examination

Social Security No. ___ ___ ___ — ___ ___ — ___ ___ ___ ___

Do Not Write In This Space

Date of Birth | Today's Date | Post Office Applied For

If you have performed active duty in the Armed Forces of the United States and were separated under honorable conditions indicate periods of service

From (Mo., Day, Yr.) ___ to (Mo., Day, Yr.) ___

DO YOU CLAIM VETERAN PREFERENCE?   NO   YES   IF YES, BASED ON
(1) Active duty in the Armed Forces of the U.S. during World War I or the period December 7, 1941, through July 1, 1955.
(2) More than 180 consecutive days of active duty (other than for training) in the Armed Forces of the U.S. any part of which occurred between Jan. 31, 1955 and Oct. 14, 1976, or (3) Award of a campaign badge or service medal

Your status as (1) a disabled veteran or a veteran who was awarded the purple heart for wounds or injuries received in action, (2) a veteran's widow who has not remarried, (3) the wife of an ex serviceman who has a service connected disability which disqualifies him for civil service appointment, or (4) the widowed, divorced or separated mother of an ex-service son or daughter who died in action or who is totally and permanently disabled

Print or Type Your Name and Address ➤

Name (First, Middle, Last)

Address (House, Apt. No. & Street)

City, State, ZIP Code (ZIP Code must be included)

This card will be returned to you. Bring it, along with personal identification bearing your picture or description, with you when you report for the test. ID's will be checked, and a fingerprint or signature specimen may be required.

PS Form 2479-B, April 1983

(Front)

PS Form 2479-B, April 1983 (Reverse)

Final Eligibility in This Examination is Subject to Suitability Determination

The collection of information on this form is authorized by 39 U.S.C. 401.1001; completion of this form is voluntary. This information will be used to determine qualification, suitability, and availability of applicants for USPS employment, and may be disclosed to relevant Federal Agencies regarding eligibility and suitability for employment, law enforcement activities when there is an indication of a potential violation of law, in connection with private relief legislation (to Office of Management and Budget); to a congressional office at your request, to a labor organization as required by the NLRA, and where pertinent, in a legal proceeding to which the Postal Service is a party. If this information is not provided, you may not receive full consideration for a position.

Disclosure by you of your Social Security Number (SSN) is mandatory to obtain the services, benefits, or processes that you are seeking. Solicitation of the SSN by the United States Postal Service is authorized under provisions of Executive Order 9397, dated November 22, 1943. The information gathered through the use of the number will be used only as necessary in authorized personnel administration processes.

Applicant	Fingerprint
Make no marks on this side of the card unless so instructed by examiner.	
Signature of Applicant	

Political Recommendations Prohibited

The law (39 U.S. Code 1002) prohibits political and certain other recommendations for appointments, promotions, assignments, transfers, or designations of persons in the Postal Service. Statements relating solely to character and residence are permitted, but every other kind of statement or recommendation is prohibited unless it either is requested by the Postal Service and consists solely of an evaluation of the work performance, ability, aptitude, and general qualifications of an individual or is requested by a Government representative investigating the individual's loyalty, suitability, and character. Anyone who requests or solicits a prohibited statement or recommendation is subject to disqualification from the Postal Service and anyone in the Postal Service who accepts such a statement may be suspended or removed from office.

Have You Answered All Questions on the Reverse of This Form?

(Back)

When the examination date, time and place have been set, your post office will return to you by mail the Admission Card portion of the application form 2479-B that you filled out (see page 9). In the area that says "Do Not Write In This Space," the post office will have filled in "Report to Room _____ , at such and such address at 8:00 A.M. on a specific date." In addition, you will receive a set of sample questions for your examination, instructions for filling out the long, detailed application form which follows on pages 11 to 16, and the application form itself.

Look over the application form right now. It may well require information that you do not have at your fingertips. In fact, why not fill out the form in this book? Then, when you receive the application form from your post office, you can just transfer the information that you have compiled at your leisure and need not borrow time from your study schedule.

Begin your study with the official U.S. Postal Service Sample Questions beginning on page 17. Don't just look over these questions. Plunge right in by attempting to answer them. The correct answers accompany the questions.

INSTRUCTIONS FOR APPLICATION FORM

Read all instructions carefully and follow them closely. It is important that you give **full** and **truthful answers** on all application forms. The application forms must be **filled out completely** and presented to the Examiner with your admission card when reporting for the written test. The examination starts **promptly** at the hour shown on your admission card. **Latecomers cannot be admitted.**

If you are entitled to 10-point preference as a disabled veteran, or have been awarded the Purple Heart Medal, fill out the enclosed Form 15, and take it to the examination together with the proof of preference required. Letters of proof can be obtained from the Veterans Administration Office.

U.S. POSTAL SERVICE **APPLICATION FOR EMPLOYMENT**	ENTRANCE EXAMINATION SCORE

First Name, Middle Name, Last Name

THIS SECTION ONLY TO BE COMPLETED IN EXAMINATION ROOM IF APPLYING FOR POST OFFICE CLERK-CARRIER OR MAIL HANDLER POSITIONS

NAME OF POST OFFICE APPLIED FOR *(City and State)* — DATE OF TEST — Month Day Year

Number and Street

Examination applied for: *(Check one)*
☐ CLERK-CARRIER   ☐ MAIL HANDLER

City, State, ZIP Code

If you are applying for a Clerk-Carrier position, do you wish to be considered for: *(Check one)*
☐ CLERK   ☐ CARRIER   ☐ CLERK-CARRIER

1. SOCIAL SECURITY NO.

2.a. BIRTH DATE *(Mo., Day, Yr.)*

b. BIRTH PLACE

3. PHONE *(Area Code and Number)*
a. HOME   b. BUSINESS

4. KIND OF JOB YOU ARE FILING FOR AND LOCATION

5. LOWEST GRADE AND/OR SALARY YOU WILL ACCEPT
GRADE:
$ _____ Per

6. WILL YOU ACCEPT
a. TEMPORARY WORK ☐ YES ☐ NO
b. LESS THAN FULL TIME ☐ YES ☐ NO

7. WHEN WILL YOU BE AVAILABLE?

8. WHERE WILL YOU ACCEPT A JOB?
Washington, D.C.? ☐ YES ☐ NO
Any place in the United States? ☐ YES ☐ NO
Outside of the United States? ☐ YES ☐ NO
Only in: *(Specify)*

9. ARE YOU WILLING TO TRAVEL? *(Check one)*
☐ NO   ☐ SOME   ☐ OFTEN

10.a. ARE YOU A HIGH SCHOOL GRADUATE? If you expect to graduate within 9 months or have an official equivalency certificate of graduation, also answer "yes" to this question.

b. NAME AND LOCATION *(City and State)* OF LAST HIGH SCHOOL ATTENDED

YES	MONTH/YEAR	NO	HIGHEST GRADE COMPLETED

c. NAME AND LOCATION *(City, State and ZIP Code if known)* OF COLLEGE OR UNIVERSITY. *(If you expect to graduate within 9 months, give month and year you expect degree.)*

	Dates attended		Years completed		No. of credits completed		Type of degree *(B.A., etc.)*	Year of degree
	From	To	Day	Night	Semester hours	Quarter hours		

d. CHIEF UNDERGRADUATE COLLEGE SUBJECTS	No. of credits completed		e. CHIEF GRADUATE COLLEGE SUBJECTS	No. of credits completed	
	Semester hours	Quarter hours		Semester hours	Quarter hours

f. MAJOR FIELD OF STUDY AT HIGHEST LEVEL OF COLLEGE WORK

g. OTHER SCHOOLS OR TRAINING (for example, trade, vocational, armed forces, or business). (Give for each the name and location *(City, State, and ZIP Code if known)* of school, dates attended, subjects studied, number of classroom hours of instruction per week, certificates, and any other pertinent data.

h. HONORS, AWARDS, AND FELLOWSHIPS RECEIVED

i. SPECIAL QUALIFICATIONS AND SKILLS (Licenses; skills with machines, patents or inventions; publications—do not submit copies unless requested; public speaking; memberships in professional or scientific societies; typing or shorthand speed; etc.)

PS Form 2591 June 1977

The United States Postal Service is an Equal Opportunity Employer

11 EXPERIENCE *(Start with your PRESENT position and work back. Account for periods of unemployment in separate blocks in order. Include Military Experiences.)*

May inquiry be made of your present employer regarding your character, qualifications, and record of employment? *(A "NO" will not affect your consideration for employment opportunities.)*　　YES　NO

A.
Dates of employment *(month, year)*　　Exact title of position　　If Federal service, civilian or military grade.
From　　To PRESENT TIME

Salary or earnings　　Avg. hrs. per week　　Place of employment　　Number and kind of employees supervised　　Kind of business or organization *(manufacturing, accounting, insurance, etc.)*
Starting $ per　　City:
Present $ per　　State:

Name of immediate supervisor　　Name of employer *(firm, organization, etc.)* and address *(including ZIP Code, if known)*

Area Code and phone No. if known

Reason for wanting to leave

Description of duties, responsibilities, and accomplishments

For USPS use *(skill codes, etc.)*

B.
Dates of employment *(month, year)*　　Exact title of position　　If Federal service, civilian or military grade.
From　　To

Salary or earnings　　Avg. hrs. per week　　Place of employment　　Number and kind of employees supervised　　Kind of business or organization *(manufacturing, accounting, insurance, etc.)*
Starting $ per　　City:
Final $ per　　State:

Name of immediate supervisor　　Name of employer *(firm, organization, etc.)* and address *(including ZIP Code, if known)*

Area Code and phone No. if known

Reason for leaving

Description of duties, responsibilities, and accomplishments

For USPS use *(skill codes, etc.)*

C.
Dates of employment *(month, year)*　　Exact title of position　　If Federal service, civilian or military grade.
From　　To

Salary or earnings　　Avg. hrs. per week　　Place of employment　　Number and kind of employees supervised　　Kind of business or organization *(manufacturing, accounting, insurance, etc.)*
Starting $ per　　City:
Final $ per　　State:

Name of immediate supervisor　　Name of employer *(firm, organization, etc.)* and address *(including ZIP Code, if known)*

Area Code and phone No. if known

Reason for leaving

Description of duties, responsibilities, and accomplishments

For USPS use *(skill codes, etc.)*

D.

Dates of employment *(month, year)*		Exact title of position		If Federal service, civilian or military grade.
From	To			

Salary or earnings	Avg. hrs. per week	Place of employment	Number and kind of employees supervised	Kind of business or organization *(manufacturing, accounting, insurance, etc.)*
Starting $ per		City:		
Final $ per		State:		

Name of immediate supervisor | Name of employer *(firm, organization, etc.)* and address *(including ZIP Code, if known)*

Area Code and phone No. if known

Reason for leaving

Description of duties, responsibilities, and accomplishments

For USPS use *(skill codes, etc.)*

E.

Dates of employment *(month, year)*		Exact title of position		If Federal service, civilian or military grade.
From	To			

Salary or earnings	Avg. hrs. per week	Place of employment	Number and kind of employees supervised	Kind of business or organization *(manufacturing, accounting, insurance, etc.)*
Starting $ per		City:		
Final $ per		State:		

Name of immediate supervisor | Name of employer *(firm, organization, etc.)* and address *(including ZIP Code, if known)*

Area Code and phone No. if known

Reason for leaving

Description of duties, responsibilities, and accomplishments

For USPS use *(skill codes, etc.)*

F.

Dates of employment *(month, year)*		Exact title of position		If Federal service, civilian or military grade.
From	To			

Salary or earnings	Avg. hrs. per week	Place of employment	Number and kind of employees supervised	Kind of business or organization *(manufacturing, accounting, insurance, etc.)*
Starting $ per		City:		
Final $ per		State:		

Name of immediate supervisor | Name of employer *(firm, organization, etc.)* and address *(including ZIP Code, if known)*

Area Code and phone No. if known

Reason for leaving

Description of duties, responsibilities, and accomplishments

For USPS use *(skill codes, etc.)*

IF YOU NEED ADDITIONAL EXPERIENCE BLOCKS USE BLANK SHEETS.

12. VETERAN PREFERENCE. *Answer all parts. If a part does not apply to you, answer "NO."*

	YES	NO

A. Have you ever served on active duty in the United States military service? *(Exclude tours of active duty for training as a reservist or Guardsman.)* . . . .

B. Have you ever been discharged from the armed services under other than honorable conditions? *(You may omit any such discharge changed to honorable by a Discharge Review Board or similar authority.)* . . . .
If "YES," give details in Item 22.

C. Do you claim 5-point preference based on active duty in the armed forces? . . . .
If "YES," you will be required to furnish records to support your claim if employed.

D. Do you claim 10-point preference? . . . .
If "Yes," Check type of preference claimed and complete and attach Standard Form 15, Claim for 10-point Veteran Preference, together with the proof called for in that form.

TYPE: ☐ COMPENSABLE DISABILITY ☐ DISABILITY ☐ WIFE/HUSBAND ☐ WIDOW/WIDOWER ☐ MOTHER ☐ OTHER

E. List for all active military service: *(Enter "N/A" if not applicable)*

DATES *(From-To)*	Serial or Service Number	Branch of Service	Type of Discharge

FOR OFFICE USE ONLY

RATED FOR	RATING	DATE RECEIVED	PREFERENCE HAS BEEN VERIFIED THROUGH PROOF THAT THE SEPARATION WAS UNDER HONORABLE CONDITIONS, AND OTHER PROOF AS REQUIRED
		TIME RECEIVED	TITLE
SIGNATURE AND DATE		SIGNATURE AND DATE	

13. REFERENCES. List three persons who are NOT related to you and who have definite knowledge of your qualifications and fitness for the position for which you are applying. Do not repeat names of supervisors listed above.

FULL NAME	PRESENT BUSINESS OR HOME ADDRESS *(Number, street, city, state and ZIP code)*	BUSINESS OR OCCUPATION

THE LAW (39 U.S. CODE 1002) PROHIBITS POLITICAL AND CERTAIN OTHER RECOMMENDATIONS FOR APPOINTMENTS, PROMOTIONS, ASSIGNMENTS, TRANSFERS, OR DESIGNATIONS OF PERSONS IN THE POSTAL SERVICE. Statements relating solely to character and residence are permitted, but every other kind of statement or recommendation is prohibited unless it either is requested by the Postal Service and consists solely of an evaluation of the work performance, ability, aptitude, and general qualifications of an individual or is requested by a Government representative investigating the individual's loyalty, suitability, and character. Anyone who requests or solicits a prohibited statement or recommendation is subject to disqualification from the Postal Service and anyone in the Postal Service who accepts such a statement may be suspended or removed from office.

14. ARE YOU:

	YES	NO

A. A citizen of the United States? . . . .

B. A citizen of American Samoa or any other territory owing allegiance to the United States? . . . .

C. An alien with permanent residence status? . . . .

15. WITHIN THE LAST FIVE YEARS HAVE YOU BEEN FIRED FROM ANY JOB FOR ANY REASON? . . . .

16. WITHIN THE LAST FIVE YEARS HAVE YOU QUIT A JOB AFTER BEING NOTIFIED THAT YOU WOULD BE FIRED? . . . .

If your answer to 15 or 16 above is "Yes," give details in Item 22. Show the name and address *(including ZIP Code)* of employer, approximate date, and reasons in each case.

17. DO YOU RECEIVE OR HAVE YOU APPLIED FOR RETIREMENT PAY, PENSION, OR OTHER COMPENSATION BASED UPON MILITARY OR FEDERAL CIVILIAN SERVICE?
If your answer is "Yes," give details in Item 22.

18. HAVE YOU EVER BEEN CONVICTED OF AN OFFENSE AGAINST THE LAW OR FORFEITED COLLATERAL, OR ARE YOU NOW UNDER CHARGES FOR ANY OFFENSE AGAINST THE LAW? (You may omit: (1) traffic violations for which you paid a fine of $30.00 or less; and (2) any offense finally adjudicated in a juvenile court.) . . . .

While in the military service were you ever convicted by special or general court-martial? . . . .

If your answer to either question is "Yes," give details in Item 22. Show for each offense: (1) date; (2) charge; (3) place; (4) court; and (5) action taken. NOTE – A conviction does not automatically mean you cannot be appointed. What you were convicted of, and how long ago, are important. Give all of the facts so that a decision can be made.

19. ARE YOU A FORMER FEDERAL CIVILIAN EMPLOYEE NOT NOW EMPLOYED BY THE U.S. GOVERNMENT? . . . .

20. A Federal official *(civilian or military)* may not appoint any of his relatives or recommend them for appointment in his agency, and a relative who is appointed in violation of this restriction can not be paid. Thus it is necessary to have information about your relatives who are working for the Government. This includes: father, mother, son, daughter, brother, sister, uncle, aunt, first cousin, nephew, niece, husband, wife, father-in-law, mother-in-law, son-in-law, daughter-in-law, brother-in-law, sister-in-law, stepfather, stepmother, stepson, stepdaughter, setpbrother, stepsister, half brother, and half sister. (5 U.S. Code 3110)

DOES THE UNITED STATES GOVERNMENT EMPLOY IN A CIVILIAN CAPACITY OR AS A MEMBER OF THE ARMED FORCES ANY RELATIVE OF YOURS BY BLOOD OR MARRIAGE? . . . .

If "YES," give in Item 22 for such relatives: (1) full name; (2) present address *(including ZIP Code)*; (3) relationship; (4) department, agency, or branch of the Armed Forces.

	YES	NO

21a. Have you, within the past forty-eight months, because of use of drugs, been a patient of any hospital, institution, or rehabilitation center for diagnosis or treatment, or otherwise received treatment? . . . .

21b. Are you now, or have you within the past forty-eight (48) months been dependent upon, or a habitual user of ANY addictive or hallucinogenic drug, including amphetamines, barbiturates, heroin, morphine, cocaine, mescaline, LSD, STP, hashish, or methadone, other than for medical treatment under the supervision of a doctor? . . . .

If your answer to either question is "Yes," give details in Item 22: (Include Name and complete address of attending physician or counselor, hospital, institution, or rehabilitation center.)

If your answer to 21a or 21b above is "YES," in order to establish your employability the following RELEASE must be signed because it may be necessary to obtain evaluations from drug abuse treatment programs in which you have participated during the past forty-eight (48) months. If this RELEASE is not signed, your application will not be processed and you will not be considered for employment because the Postal Service will not have complete information necessary to make a decision.

RELEASE FOR DRUG ABUSE TREATMENT PROGRAM EVALUATION

I hereby authorize and request any qualified physician or counselor employed by or associated with any program of drug abuse rehabilitation treatment in which I have participated in the past or am participating at present to furnish to *(Postmaster, Appointing Officer, or to his representative)*:

a summary or evaluation of my progress or status in such treatment program within the past forty-eight *(48)* months insofar as such information is reasonably necessary to the determination by the Postal Service of my suitability for employment.

This Release shall not be construed to authorize the disclosure to or use by the Postal Service of any actual records in connection with any such treatment program.

I authorize and request the disclosure to the Postal Service of the information described herein for the limited purpose of determining my suitability for employment by the Postal Service and for no other purpose.

I understand that the use of any information obtained pursuant to this authorization shall be strictly limited by the Postal Service to the purpose for which it was requested and that the Postal Service will take all steps reasonable to protect the confidentiality of any information so obtained.

I understand that this report shall be made without cost to the United States Postal Service.

A photostat of this authorization shall be as effective as the original.

SIGNATURE OF APPLICANT

DATE SIGNED

22. THIS SPACE IS FOR DETAILED ANSWERS (Indicate item numbers to which answers apply)

ATTENTION

BEFORE SIGNING THIS FORM CAREFULLY READ THE PARAGRAPHS BELOW

The collection of information on this form is authorized by 39 U.S.C. 401, 1001; completion of this form is voluntary. This information will be used to determine qualifications, suitability, and availability of applicants for USPS employment, and may be disclosed to relevant Federal Agencies regarding; eligibility and suitability for employment, law enforcement activities when there is an indication of a potential violation of law, in connection with private relief legislation (to Office of Management and Budget), to a congressional office at your request, to a labor organization as required by the NLRA, and where pertinent, in a legal proceeding to which the Postal Service is a party. If this information is not provided, you may not receive full consideration for a position.

Disclosure by you of your Social Security Number (SSN) is mandatory to obtain the services, benefits, or processes that you are seeking. Solicitation of the SSN by the United States Postal Service is authorized under provisions of Executive Order 9397, dated November 22, 1943. The information gathered through the use of the number will be used only as necessary in authorized personnel administration processes.

A false or dishonest answer to any question in this Statement may be grounds for not employing you or for dismissing you after you begin work, and may be punishable by fine or imprisonment. *(U.S. Code, Title 18, Sec 1001).* All the information you give will be considered in reviewing your Statement and is subject to investigation.

CERTIFICATION	SIGNATURE OF APPLICANT	DATE SIGNED
I certify that all of the statements made in this application are true, complete, and correct to the best of my knowledge and belief and are made in good faith.		

TO BE COMPLETED AFTER APPOINTMENT

I, _____ , do solemnly swear (or affirm) that I will support and defend the Constitution of the United States against all enemies, foreign and domestic, that I will bear true faith and allegiance to the same that I take this obligation freely, without any mental reservation or purpose of evasion; and that I will well and faithfully discharge the duties of the office on which I am about to enter.

A. AFFIDAVIT AS TO STRIKING AGAINST THE FEDERAL GOVERNMENT: I am not participating in any strike against the Government of the United States of any agency thereof, and I will not so participate while an employee of the Government of the United States or any agency thereof.

B. AFFIDAVIT AS TO PURCHASE AND SALE OF OFFICE: I have not, nor has anyone acting in my behalf, given, transferred, promised or paid any consideration for or in expectation or hope of receiving assistance in securing such appointment.

C. AFFIDAVIT AS TO TRUTH OF APPLICATION: All items and statements in this application are true as of this date except for the following changes:

_____
(Date of entrance on duty)

_____
(Signature of appointee)

Subscribed and sworn (or affirmed) before me this _____ day of _____

_____ A.D. 19 _____

at _____
(City, State and ZIP Code)

_____
(Signature of officer)

(SEAL)

_____
(Title)

☆U.S. GOVERNMENT PRINTING OFFICE: 1978— 753-777

U.S. POSTAL SERVICE
SAMPLE QUESTIONS

The following sample questions show the types of questions that will be used in the test. They also show the method of answering the questions.

PART A—NUMBER SERIES

For each Number Series question there is at the left a series of numbers which follow some definite order and at the right five sets of two numbers each. You are to look at the numbers in the series at the left and find out what order they follow. Then decide what the next two numbers in that series would be if the same order were continued. Mark your answers on the Sample Answer Sheet.

1. 1 2 3 4 5 6 7 .... (A) 1 2 (B) 5 6 (C) 8 9 (D) 4 5 (E) 7 8

The numbers in this series are increasing by 1. If the series were continued for two more numbers, it would read: 1 2 3 4 5 6 7 8 9. Therefore the correct answer is 8 and 9, and you should have darkened C for question 1.

2. 15 14 13 12 11 10 9 .... (A) 2 1 (B) 17 16 (C) 8 9 (D) 8 7 (E) 9 8

The numbers in this series are decreasing by 1. If the series were continued for two more numbers, it would read: 15 14 13 12 11 10 9 8 7. Therefore the correct answer is 8 and 7 and you should have darkened D for question 2.

3. 20 20 21 21 22 22 23 ..... (A) 23 23 (B) 23 24 (C) 19 19 (D) 22 23 (E) 21 22

Each number in this series is repeated and then increased by 1. If the series were continued for two more numbers it would read: 20 20 21 21 22 22 23 23 24. Therefore the correct answer is 23 and 24, and you should have darkened B for question 3.

4. 17 3 17 4 17 5 17 .... (A) 6 17 (B) 6 7 (C) 17 6 (D) 5 6 (E) 17 7

This series is the number 17 separated by numbers increasing by 1, beginning with the number 3. If the series were continued for two more numbers, it would read: 17 3 17 4 17 5 17 6 17. Therefore the correct answer is 6 and 17, and you should have darkened A for question 4.

5. 1 2 4 5 7 8 10 .... (A) 11 12 (B) 12 14 (C) 10 13 (D) 12 13 (E) 11 13

The numbers in this series are increasing first by 1 (plus 1) and then by 2 (plus 2). If the series were continued for two more numbers, it would read: 1 2 4 5 7 8 10 (plus 1) 11 (plus 2) 13. Therefore the correct answer is 11 and 13, and you should have darkened E for question 5.

Now read and work sample questions 6 through 10 and mark your answers on the Sample Answer Sheet.

6. 21 21 20 20 19 19 18 ..... (A) 18 18 (B) 18 17 (C) 17 18 (D) 17 17 (E) 18 19

7. 1 22 1 23 1 24 1 .... (A) 26 1 (B) 25 26 (C) 25 1 (D) 1 26 (E) 1 25

8. 1 20 3 19 5 18 7 .... (A) 8 9 (B) 8 17 (C) 17 10 (D) 17 9 (E) 9 18

9. 4 7 10 13 16 19 22 .... (A) 23 26 (B) 25 27 (C) 25 26 (D) 25 28 (E) 24 27

10. 30 2 28 4 26 6 24 .... (A) 23 9 (B) 26 8 (C) 8 9 (D) 26 22 (E) 8 22

SAMPLE ANSWER SHEET		CORRECT ANSWERS	
1. Ⓐ Ⓑ Ⓒ Ⓓ Ⓔ	6. Ⓐ Ⓑ Ⓒ Ⓓ Ⓔ	1. C	6. B
2. Ⓐ Ⓑ Ⓒ Ⓓ Ⓔ	7. Ⓐ Ⓑ Ⓒ Ⓓ Ⓔ	2. D	7. C
3. Ⓐ Ⓑ Ⓒ Ⓓ Ⓔ	8. Ⓐ Ⓑ Ⓒ Ⓓ Ⓔ	3. B	8. D
4. Ⓐ Ⓑ Ⓒ Ⓓ Ⓔ	9. Ⓐ Ⓑ Ⓒ Ⓓ Ⓔ	4. A	9. D
5. Ⓐ Ⓑ Ⓒ Ⓓ Ⓔ	10. Ⓐ Ⓑ Ⓒ Ⓓ Ⓔ	5. E	10. E

PART B—ADDRESS CODING

In this test, you will find boxes labeled A, B, C, D, and E. Each box contains five addresses. For each of the addresses in the list, you are to decide in which lettered box (A, B, C, D, or E) it belongs and then mark that letter on the answer sheet.

A	B	C	D	E
4700-5599 Table Lismore 4800-5199 West Hesper 5500-6399 Blake	6800-6999 Table Kelford 5200-5799 West Musella 4800-5499 Blake	5600-6499 Table Joel 3200-3499 West Sardis 6400-7299 Blake	6500-6799 Table Tatum 3500-4299 West Porter 4300-4799 Blake	4400-4699 Table Ruskin 4300-4799 West Somers 7300-7499 Blake

For Part B of the test, the boxes will be shown on the same page with the addresses, but for Part C, you will not have the boxes to look at. Therefore, it is important that you memorize each of the addresses in a box, and letter for that box. You will have 5 minutes to memorize the locations of the addresses.

Now complete the questions for Part B. Mark your answers for each question by darkening the space as was done for questions 1 and 2.

1. Musella
2. 4300-4799 Blake
3. 4700-5599 Table
4. Tatum
5. 5500-6399 Blake
6. Hesper
7. Kelford

8. Somers
9. 6400-7299 Blake
10. Joel
11. 5500-6399 Blake
12. 5200-5799 West
13. Porter
14. 7300-7499 Blake

SAMPLE ANSWER SHEET

1. Ⓐ ● Ⓒ Ⓓ Ⓔ   8. Ⓐ Ⓑ Ⓒ Ⓓ Ⓔ
2. Ⓐ Ⓑ Ⓒ ● Ⓔ   9. Ⓐ Ⓑ Ⓒ Ⓓ Ⓔ
3. Ⓐ Ⓑ Ⓒ Ⓓ Ⓔ   10. Ⓐ Ⓑ Ⓒ Ⓓ Ⓔ
4. Ⓐ Ⓑ Ⓒ Ⓓ Ⓔ   11. Ⓐ Ⓑ Ⓒ Ⓓ Ⓔ
5. Ⓐ Ⓑ Ⓒ Ⓓ Ⓔ   12. Ⓐ Ⓑ Ⓒ Ⓓ Ⓔ
6. Ⓐ Ⓑ Ⓒ Ⓓ Ⓔ   13. Ⓐ Ⓑ Ⓒ Ⓓ Ⓔ
7. Ⓐ Ⓑ Ⓒ Ⓓ Ⓔ   14. Ⓐ Ⓑ Ⓒ Ⓓ Ⓔ

CORRECT ANSWERS

1. B		8. E	
2. D		9. C	
3. A		10. C	
4. D		11. A	
5. A		12. B	
6. A		13. D	
7. B		14. E	

PART C—ADDRESS CODE MEMORY

In this test you will be performing the same task as in the test of ADDRESS CODING; however, you will not be allowed to refer to the address boxes. You must identify an address and recall the correct code from memory. Select the appropriate code for each of the addresses below. DO NOT REFER TO THE ADDRESS BOXES ON THE PREVIOUS PAGE. Mark your answers for each question by darkening the space as you did for the previous questions.

1. 4800-5199 West
2. Ruskin
3. 6800-6999 Table
4. 4800-5499 Blake
5. Tatum
6. 3200-3499 West
7. Lismore

8. Musella
9. Sardis
10. Joel
11. 7300-7499 Blake
12. 3500-4299 West
13. Hesper
14. Kelford

SAMPLE ANSWER SHEET		CORRECT ANSWERS	
1. Ⓐ Ⓑ Ⓒ Ⓓ Ⓔ	8. Ⓐ Ⓑ Ⓒ Ⓓ Ⓔ	1. A	8. B
2. Ⓐ Ⓑ Ⓒ Ⓓ Ⓔ	9. Ⓐ Ⓑ Ⓒ Ⓓ Ⓔ	2. E	9. C
3. Ⓐ Ⓑ Ⓒ Ⓓ Ⓔ	10. Ⓐ Ⓑ Ⓒ Ⓓ Ⓔ	3. B	10. C
4. Ⓐ Ⓑ Ⓒ Ⓓ Ⓔ	11. Ⓐ Ⓑ Ⓒ Ⓓ Ⓔ	4. B	11. E
5. Ⓐ Ⓑ Ⓒ Ⓓ Ⓔ	12. Ⓐ Ⓑ Ⓒ Ⓓ Ⓔ	5. D	12. D
6. Ⓐ Ⓑ Ⓒ Ⓓ Ⓔ	13. Ⓐ Ⓑ Ⓒ Ⓓ Ⓔ	6. C	13. A
7. Ⓐ Ⓑ Ⓒ Ⓓ Ⓔ	14. Ⓐ Ⓑ Ⓒ Ⓓ Ⓔ	7. A	14. B

PART D—ADDRESS CHECKING TEST

In this test you will have to decide whether two addresses are alike or different. If the two addresses are exactly ALIKE in every way, darken space Ⓐ for the question. If the two addresses are DIFFERENT in any way, darken space Ⓓ for the question.

Mark your answers to these sample questions on the Sample Answer Sheet.

1 . . . 213 S 20th St   213 S 20th St

Since the two addresses are exactly alike, mark A for question 1 on the Sample Answer Sheet.

2 . . . 4608 N Warnock St   4806 N Warnock St
3 . . . 1202 W Girard Dr   1202 W Girard Rd
4 . . . Chappaqua NY 10514   Chappaqua NY 10514
5 . . . 2207 Markland Ave   2207 Markham Ave

SAMPLE ANSWER SHEET		CORRECT ANSWERS	
1. Ⓐ Ⓓ	4. Ⓐ Ⓓ	1. A	4. A
2. Ⓐ Ⓓ	5. Ⓐ Ⓓ	2. D	5. D
3. Ⓐ Ⓓ		3. D	

By the time you receive the sample questions, you should be well along in your studies. Compare the sample questions with the question styles detailed in this book. This comparison should reassure you that this book is preparing you correctly for the exam. Continue preparing yourself for the exam so that you complete the book at least a week before the actual examination. You want to take your exam with a clear head so that you can memorize box locations without interference from any previous memorization.

ON EXAMINATION DAY

On the examination day assigned to you, allow the test itself to be the main attraction of the day. Do not squeeze it in between other activities. Arrive rested, relaxed, and on time. In fact, plan to arrive a little bit early. Leave plenty of time for traffic tie-ups or other complications which might upset you and interfere with your test performance.

In the test room the examiner will hand out forms for you to fill out. He or she will give you the instructions that you must follow in taking the examination. The examiner will distribute the pencils to be used for marking the answer sheet and will tell you how to fill in the grids on the forms. Time limits and timing signals will be explained. If you do not understand any of the examiner's instructions, ASK QUESTIONS. Make sure that you know exactly what to do.

During the testing session you will answer both sample questions and actual test questions. The examiner will do the first five Number Series sample questions with you. After those five questions, you will answer all other questions, sample and actual, on your own, within the given time limits. You will see the answers to the sample questions. You will not be given the answers to the actual test questions, even after the test is over. The examination which you will take will look exactly like the model exams in this book. The only exception is that number series sample questions 6 to 14 will not be explained. We have explained all number series questions in this book so that you can learn from them.

At the examination, you must follow instructions exactly. Use only the Postal Service pencils issued to you. Fill in the grids on the forms carefully and accurately. Filling in the wrong grid may lead to loss of veterans' credits to which you may be entitled or to an incorrect address for your test results. Do not begin until you are told to begin. Stop as soon as the examiner tells you to stop. Do not turn pages until you are told to. Do not go back to parts you have already completed. Any infraction of the rules is considered cheating. If you cheat, your test paper will not be scored, and you will not be eligible for appointment.

USING THE ANSWER SHEET

The answer sheet for your postal exam is machine scored. You cannot give any explanations to the machine, so you must fill out the answer sheet clearly and correctly.

1. Blacken your answer space firmly and completely. ● is the only correct way to mark the answer sheet. ◑, ⊗, ⊘, and ∅ are all unacceptable. The machine might not read them at all.
2. Mark only one answer for each question. If you mark more than one answer you will be considered wrong even if one of the answers is correct.

3. If you change your mind, you must erase your mark. Attempting to cross out an incorrect answer like this ● will not work. You must erase any incorrect answer completely. An incomplete erasure might be read as a second answer.

4. All of your answering should be in the form of blackened spaces. The machine cannot read English. Do not write any notes in the margins.

5. MOST IMPORTANT: Answer each question in the right place. Question 1 must be answered in space 1; question 52 in space 52. If you should skip an answer space and mark a series of answers in the wrong places, you must erase all those answers and do the questions over, marking your answers in the proper places. You cannot afford to use the limited time in this way. Therefore, as you answer *each* question, look at its number and check that you are marking your answer in the space with the same number.

6. You may be wondering whether or not it is wise to guess when you are not sure of an answer, or whether it is better to skip a question when you are not certain of the answer. In general, because of the risk of getting out of line on the answer sheet, we recommend that you answer every question in order, even if you have to guess. However, not all parts of the exam are scored in the same way. On some parts guessing can do no harm, while on other parts there is a penalty for a wrong guess.

Part A—Your score on the Number Series part is based upon the number of questions you answer correctly. A wrong answer simply is not counted. Obviously, it is to your advantage to answer every question, even if you must take a wild guess. In fact, you should keep track of your time while answering Part A so that you can be sure to finish. In the last few seconds, you should mark answers to the remaining questions and to the hard questions that you skipped even if you do not have time to read the questions. Mark any answer. It cannot hurt, and it might help.

Parts B and C—Your scores on Address Coding and Address Code Memory are based upon the number of questions you answer correctly minus ¼ point for each wrong answer. While answering Part B you can look at the boxes, so there is nothing to guess at. Just work as quickly as you can. Do not skip any questions; the danger of losing your place is too great. Use all the time allowed for Part B to answer questions according to directions. Do not rush to answer all the questions at the end. Do not make random guesses.

The decision as to whether or not to guess in Part C is entirely up to you. A correct answer gives you one point; a skipped question gives you nothing at all, but costs you nothing except the chance of getting the answer right; a wrong answer costs you ¼ point. If you are really stuck on a question and decide to skip it, be sure to skip its answer space as well. In reaching your decision as to whether or not to guess on Part C, consider the time you would lose if you slipped out of line and had to erase and re-mark a series of answers. We recommend against skipping questions in the middle of this part. On the other hand, do not guess at the remaining questions as you near the end of the time limit. Keep answering questions in order and stop when time is up.

Part D—Your score on Address Checking is calculated by subtracting the number of questions you answered wrong from the number of questions you answered right. Obviously, the penalty for a wrong answer is severe. But, in Address Checking there is nothing to guess. You look at both addresses and make a decision, *alike* or *different*. Answer every question in order; there is no reason to skip questions. Work as quickly as you can, but do not rush. Most certainly do not make any random guesses for questions that you do not have time to look at. Work steadily until time is up.

The complaint most frequently heard about the Distribution Clerk, Machine, Exam is, "There are too many questions and too little time." Very few people are able to finish. Do your best and do not worry about the questions that you were unable to get to.

HOW IS THE EXAM SCORED?

When the exam is over, the examiner will collect test booklets and answer sheets. The answer sheets will be sent to the test center in California where a machine will scan your answers and mark them right or wrong. Then your raw score will be calculated. Your raw score is the score we described in our discussion of guessing. On Number Series your raw score is the number right. On Address Coding and Address Code Memory your raw score is the number right minus ¼ the number wrong. On Address Checking the raw score is number right minus number wrong.

Your raw score is not your final score. The Postal Service takes the four raw scores, combines them according to a formula of its own, and converts them to a scaled score, on a scale of 1 to 100. The entire process of conversion from raw to scaled score is confidential information. The score you receive is not your number right, is not your raw score, and is not a percent. The score you receive is a *scaled score*. Before reporting any scaled scores, the Postal Service adds any veterans' service points or any other advantages to which the applicant might be entitled. Veterans' service points are added only to passing scaled scores of 70 or more. A failing score cannot be brought to passing level by veterans' points. The score earned plus veterans' service points results in the final scaled score that finds it place onto the eligibility list.

A total scaled score of 70 is a passing score. The names of all persons with scaled scores of 70 or more are placed on the list sent to the local post office. Those names are placed on the list in order, with the highest scorer at the top of the list. Hiring then takes place from the top of the list as vacancies occur.

The scoring process may take six to ten weeks or even longer. Be patient. If you pass the exam, you will receive notice of your scaled score. Applicants who fail the exam are not told their score. They are simply notified that they will not be considered eligible.

PART I

Diagnostic Model Exam

BEFORE YOU TAKE THE DIAGNOSTIC MODEL EXAM

The purpose of the Diagnostic Exam is to start you in your studies for the Distribution Clerk, Machine, Exam and to establish a base upon which you can build. The diagnostic exam will give you an idea of where you are now and of how far you need to go. By starting out with a full-length exam, you see from the beginning how many questions you must answer and how quickly you must work to score high on this exam.

DIRECTIONS FOR TAKING THE DIAGNOSTIC EXAM

- Choose a work space that is quiet and well-lit.

- Clear the desk or tabletop of all clutter.

- Bring a stopwatch or kitchen timer and two or three number two pencils with good erasers to your work area.

- While the pencils should have plenty of exposed lead, you will find that you fill in answer circles more quickly if the pencils are not razor sharp. The little circles on the answer sheet must be completely filled in, and the fewer strokes needed to fill them, the faster you work.

  At the actual exam, where pencils are provided, do some scribbling to dull the point while you are waiting for the exam to begin.

- Tear out the answer sheets for the Diagnostic Exam and place them on the desk or table beside your book, to the right if you are right-handed, to the left if you are left-handed.

- Read the directions and first five sample Number Series questions. Set the timer for five minutes and try to answer sample questions 6 to 14. Check your answers and study the explanations. Then reset the timer for twenty minutes and answer the twenty-four questions in Part A.

- Stop as soon as time is up.

- Go directly to the Address Coding sample questions. Answer the questions as directed. Then proceed to Part B, adhering to the time limits as indicated.

- Stop as soon as time is up, set the timer for five minutes and proceed immediately with the questions in Part C.

- Stop as soon as time is up.

- Turn to the sample questions for the Address Checking test and set the timer for three minutes before even reading the directions. Read and answer as directed.

- Go on to Part D, answering as indicated and adhering strictly to the six-minute time limit.

DIRECTIONS FOR SCORING YOUR EXAM

- When you have completed all parts of the Diagnostic Exam, check your answers against the correct answers on page 46.

- Study the explanations of the correct answers to the Number Series questions.

- Follow the directions for analyzing your Address Checking errors.

- Calculate your raw score for each part of the exam as instructed on the Score Sheet on page 49.

- Check to see where your scores fall on the Self-Examination Chart.

- Plot your scores on the Progress Graph.

After you have completed the Diagnostic Exam and have analyzed your results, you will have a good picture of where you stand. Then you may start learning how to add valuable points to your score by increasing your speed and accuracy and by memorizing more effectively. The seven additional Model Exams will give you plenty of practice in applying these new-found skills.

ANSWER SHEET
DIAGNOSTIC MODEL EXAM

Tear out this Answer Sheet and use it to mark your answers for the exam that follows.

PART A—NUMBER SERIES

1. Ⓐ Ⓑ Ⓒ Ⓓ Ⓔ	6. Ⓐ Ⓑ Ⓒ Ⓓ Ⓔ	11. Ⓐ Ⓑ Ⓒ Ⓓ Ⓔ	16. Ⓐ Ⓑ Ⓒ Ⓓ Ⓔ	21. Ⓐ Ⓑ Ⓒ Ⓓ Ⓔ
2. Ⓐ Ⓑ Ⓒ Ⓓ Ⓔ	7. Ⓐ Ⓑ Ⓒ Ⓓ Ⓔ	12. Ⓐ Ⓑ Ⓒ Ⓓ Ⓔ	17. Ⓐ Ⓑ Ⓒ Ⓓ Ⓔ	22. Ⓐ Ⓑ Ⓒ Ⓓ Ⓔ
3. Ⓐ Ⓑ Ⓒ Ⓓ Ⓔ	8. Ⓐ Ⓑ Ⓒ Ⓓ Ⓔ	13. Ⓐ Ⓑ Ⓒ Ⓓ Ⓔ	18. Ⓐ Ⓑ Ⓒ Ⓓ Ⓔ	23. Ⓐ Ⓑ Ⓒ Ⓓ Ⓔ
4. Ⓐ Ⓑ Ⓒ Ⓓ Ⓔ	9. Ⓐ Ⓑ Ⓒ Ⓓ Ⓔ	14. Ⓐ Ⓑ Ⓒ Ⓓ Ⓔ	19. Ⓐ Ⓑ Ⓒ Ⓓ Ⓔ	24. Ⓐ Ⓑ Ⓒ Ⓓ Ⓔ
5. Ⓐ Ⓑ Ⓒ Ⓓ Ⓔ	10. Ⓐ Ⓑ Ⓒ Ⓓ Ⓔ	15. Ⓐ Ⓑ Ⓒ Ⓓ Ⓔ	20. Ⓐ Ⓑ Ⓒ Ⓓ Ⓔ	

PART B—ADDRESS CODING

1. Ⓐ Ⓑ Ⓒ Ⓓ Ⓔ	19. Ⓐ Ⓑ Ⓒ Ⓓ Ⓔ	37. Ⓐ Ⓑ Ⓒ Ⓓ Ⓔ	55. Ⓐ Ⓑ Ⓒ Ⓓ Ⓔ	73. Ⓐ Ⓑ Ⓒ Ⓓ Ⓔ
2. Ⓐ Ⓑ Ⓒ Ⓓ Ⓔ	20. Ⓐ Ⓑ Ⓒ Ⓓ Ⓔ	38. Ⓐ Ⓑ Ⓒ Ⓓ Ⓔ	56. Ⓐ Ⓑ Ⓒ Ⓓ Ⓔ	74. Ⓐ Ⓑ Ⓒ Ⓓ Ⓔ
3. Ⓐ Ⓑ Ⓒ Ⓓ Ⓔ	21. Ⓐ Ⓑ Ⓒ Ⓓ Ⓔ	39. Ⓐ Ⓑ Ⓒ Ⓓ Ⓔ	57. Ⓐ Ⓑ Ⓒ Ⓓ Ⓔ	75. Ⓐ Ⓑ Ⓒ Ⓓ Ⓔ
4. Ⓐ Ⓑ Ⓒ Ⓓ Ⓔ	22. Ⓐ Ⓑ Ⓒ Ⓓ Ⓔ	40. Ⓐ Ⓑ Ⓒ Ⓓ Ⓔ	58. Ⓐ Ⓑ Ⓒ Ⓓ Ⓔ	76. Ⓐ Ⓑ Ⓒ Ⓓ Ⓔ
5. Ⓐ Ⓑ Ⓒ Ⓓ Ⓔ	23. Ⓐ Ⓑ Ⓒ Ⓓ Ⓔ	41. Ⓐ Ⓑ Ⓒ Ⓓ Ⓔ	59. Ⓐ Ⓑ Ⓒ Ⓓ Ⓔ	77. Ⓐ Ⓑ Ⓒ Ⓓ Ⓔ
6. Ⓐ Ⓑ Ⓒ Ⓓ Ⓔ	24. Ⓐ Ⓑ Ⓒ Ⓓ Ⓔ	42. Ⓐ Ⓑ Ⓒ Ⓓ Ⓔ	60. Ⓐ Ⓑ Ⓒ Ⓓ Ⓔ	78. Ⓐ Ⓑ Ⓒ Ⓓ Ⓔ
7. Ⓐ Ⓑ Ⓒ Ⓓ Ⓔ	25. Ⓐ Ⓑ Ⓒ Ⓓ Ⓔ	43. Ⓐ Ⓑ Ⓒ Ⓓ Ⓔ	61. Ⓐ Ⓑ Ⓒ Ⓓ Ⓔ	79. Ⓐ Ⓑ Ⓒ Ⓓ Ⓔ
8. Ⓐ Ⓑ Ⓒ Ⓓ Ⓔ	26. Ⓐ Ⓑ Ⓒ Ⓓ Ⓔ	44. Ⓐ Ⓑ Ⓒ Ⓓ Ⓔ	62. Ⓐ Ⓑ Ⓒ Ⓓ Ⓔ	80. Ⓐ Ⓑ Ⓒ Ⓓ Ⓔ
9. Ⓐ Ⓑ Ⓒ Ⓓ Ⓔ	27. Ⓐ Ⓑ Ⓒ Ⓓ Ⓔ	45. Ⓐ Ⓑ Ⓒ Ⓓ Ⓔ	63. Ⓐ Ⓑ Ⓒ Ⓓ Ⓔ	81. Ⓐ Ⓑ Ⓒ Ⓓ Ⓔ
10. Ⓐ Ⓑ Ⓒ Ⓓ Ⓔ	28. Ⓐ Ⓑ Ⓒ Ⓓ Ⓔ	46. Ⓐ Ⓑ Ⓒ Ⓓ Ⓔ	64. Ⓐ Ⓑ Ⓒ Ⓓ Ⓔ	82. Ⓐ Ⓑ Ⓒ Ⓓ Ⓔ
11. Ⓐ Ⓑ Ⓒ Ⓓ Ⓔ	29. Ⓐ Ⓑ Ⓒ Ⓓ Ⓔ	47. Ⓐ Ⓑ Ⓒ Ⓓ Ⓔ	65. Ⓐ Ⓑ Ⓒ Ⓓ Ⓔ	83. Ⓐ Ⓑ Ⓒ Ⓓ Ⓔ
12. Ⓐ Ⓑ Ⓒ Ⓓ Ⓔ	30. Ⓐ Ⓑ Ⓒ Ⓓ Ⓔ	48. Ⓐ Ⓑ Ⓒ Ⓓ Ⓔ	66. Ⓐ Ⓑ Ⓒ Ⓓ Ⓔ	84. Ⓐ Ⓑ Ⓒ Ⓓ Ⓔ
13. Ⓐ Ⓑ Ⓒ Ⓓ Ⓔ	31. Ⓐ Ⓑ Ⓒ Ⓓ Ⓔ	49. Ⓐ Ⓑ Ⓒ Ⓓ Ⓔ	67. Ⓐ Ⓑ Ⓒ Ⓓ Ⓔ	85. Ⓐ Ⓑ Ⓒ Ⓓ Ⓔ
14. Ⓐ Ⓑ Ⓒ Ⓓ Ⓔ	32. Ⓐ Ⓑ Ⓒ Ⓓ Ⓔ	50. Ⓐ Ⓑ Ⓒ Ⓓ Ⓔ	68. Ⓐ Ⓑ Ⓒ Ⓓ Ⓔ	86. Ⓐ Ⓑ Ⓒ Ⓓ Ⓔ
15. Ⓐ Ⓑ Ⓒ Ⓓ Ⓔ	33. Ⓐ Ⓑ Ⓒ Ⓓ Ⓔ	51. Ⓐ Ⓑ Ⓒ Ⓓ Ⓔ	69. Ⓐ Ⓑ Ⓒ Ⓓ Ⓔ	87. Ⓐ Ⓑ Ⓒ Ⓓ Ⓔ
16. Ⓐ Ⓑ Ⓒ Ⓓ Ⓔ	34. Ⓐ Ⓑ Ⓒ Ⓓ Ⓔ	52. Ⓐ Ⓑ Ⓒ Ⓓ Ⓔ	70. Ⓐ Ⓑ Ⓒ Ⓓ Ⓔ	88. Ⓐ Ⓑ Ⓒ Ⓓ Ⓔ
17. Ⓐ Ⓑ Ⓒ Ⓓ Ⓔ	35. Ⓐ Ⓑ Ⓒ Ⓓ Ⓔ	53. Ⓐ Ⓑ Ⓒ Ⓓ Ⓔ	71. Ⓐ Ⓑ Ⓒ Ⓓ Ⓔ	
18. Ⓐ Ⓑ Ⓒ Ⓓ Ⓔ	36. Ⓐ Ⓑ Ⓒ Ⓓ Ⓔ	54. Ⓐ Ⓑ Ⓒ Ⓓ Ⓔ	72. Ⓐ Ⓑ Ⓒ Ⓓ Ⓔ	

Tear here

PART C—ADDRESS CODE MEMORY

1. Ⓐ Ⓑ Ⓒ Ⓓ Ⓔ
2. Ⓐ Ⓑ Ⓒ Ⓓ Ⓔ
3. Ⓐ Ⓑ Ⓒ Ⓓ Ⓔ
4. Ⓐ Ⓑ Ⓒ Ⓓ Ⓔ
5. Ⓐ Ⓑ Ⓒ Ⓓ Ⓔ
6. Ⓐ Ⓑ Ⓒ Ⓓ Ⓔ
7. Ⓐ Ⓑ Ⓒ Ⓓ Ⓔ
8. Ⓐ Ⓑ Ⓒ Ⓓ Ⓔ
9. Ⓐ Ⓑ Ⓒ Ⓓ Ⓔ
10. Ⓐ Ⓑ Ⓒ Ⓓ Ⓔ
11. Ⓐ Ⓑ Ⓒ Ⓓ Ⓔ
12. Ⓐ Ⓑ Ⓒ Ⓓ Ⓔ
13. Ⓐ Ⓑ Ⓒ Ⓓ Ⓔ
14. Ⓐ Ⓑ Ⓒ Ⓓ Ⓔ
15. Ⓐ Ⓑ Ⓒ Ⓓ Ⓔ
16. Ⓐ Ⓑ Ⓒ Ⓓ Ⓔ
17. Ⓐ Ⓑ Ⓒ Ⓓ Ⓔ
18. Ⓐ Ⓑ Ⓒ Ⓓ Ⓔ

19. Ⓐ Ⓑ Ⓒ Ⓓ Ⓔ
20. Ⓐ Ⓑ Ⓒ Ⓓ Ⓔ
21. Ⓐ Ⓑ Ⓒ Ⓓ Ⓔ
22. Ⓐ Ⓑ Ⓒ Ⓓ Ⓔ
23. Ⓐ Ⓑ Ⓒ Ⓓ Ⓔ
24. Ⓐ Ⓑ Ⓒ Ⓓ Ⓔ
25. Ⓐ Ⓑ Ⓒ Ⓓ Ⓔ
26. Ⓐ Ⓑ Ⓒ Ⓓ Ⓔ
27. Ⓐ Ⓑ Ⓒ Ⓓ Ⓔ
28. Ⓐ Ⓑ Ⓒ Ⓓ Ⓔ
29. Ⓐ Ⓑ Ⓒ Ⓓ Ⓔ
30. Ⓐ Ⓑ Ⓒ Ⓓ Ⓔ
31. Ⓐ Ⓑ Ⓒ Ⓓ Ⓔ
32. Ⓐ Ⓑ Ⓒ Ⓓ Ⓔ
33. Ⓐ Ⓑ Ⓒ Ⓓ Ⓔ
34. Ⓐ Ⓑ Ⓒ Ⓓ Ⓔ
35. Ⓐ Ⓑ Ⓒ Ⓓ Ⓔ
36. Ⓐ Ⓑ Ⓒ Ⓓ Ⓔ

37. Ⓐ Ⓑ Ⓒ Ⓓ Ⓔ
38. Ⓐ Ⓑ Ⓒ Ⓓ Ⓔ
39. Ⓐ Ⓑ Ⓒ Ⓓ Ⓔ
40. Ⓐ Ⓑ Ⓒ Ⓓ Ⓔ
41. Ⓐ Ⓑ Ⓒ Ⓓ Ⓔ
42. Ⓐ Ⓑ Ⓒ Ⓓ Ⓔ
43. Ⓐ Ⓑ Ⓒ Ⓓ Ⓔ
44. Ⓐ Ⓑ Ⓒ Ⓓ Ⓔ
45. Ⓐ Ⓑ Ⓒ Ⓓ Ⓔ
46. Ⓐ Ⓑ Ⓒ Ⓓ Ⓔ
47. Ⓐ Ⓑ Ⓒ Ⓓ Ⓔ
48. Ⓐ Ⓑ Ⓒ Ⓓ Ⓔ
49. Ⓐ Ⓑ Ⓒ Ⓓ Ⓔ
50. Ⓐ Ⓑ Ⓒ Ⓓ Ⓔ
51. Ⓐ Ⓑ Ⓒ Ⓓ Ⓔ
52. Ⓐ Ⓑ Ⓒ Ⓓ Ⓔ
53. Ⓐ Ⓑ Ⓒ Ⓓ Ⓔ
54. Ⓐ Ⓑ Ⓒ Ⓓ Ⓔ

55. Ⓐ Ⓑ Ⓒ Ⓓ Ⓔ
56. Ⓐ Ⓑ Ⓒ Ⓓ Ⓔ
57. Ⓐ Ⓑ Ⓒ Ⓓ Ⓔ
58. Ⓐ Ⓑ Ⓒ Ⓓ Ⓔ
59. Ⓐ Ⓑ Ⓒ Ⓓ Ⓔ
60. Ⓐ Ⓑ Ⓒ Ⓓ Ⓔ
61. Ⓐ Ⓑ Ⓒ Ⓓ Ⓔ
62. Ⓐ Ⓑ Ⓒ Ⓓ Ⓔ
63. Ⓐ Ⓑ Ⓒ Ⓓ Ⓔ
64. Ⓐ Ⓑ Ⓒ Ⓓ Ⓔ
65. Ⓐ Ⓑ Ⓒ Ⓓ Ⓔ
66. Ⓐ Ⓑ Ⓒ Ⓓ Ⓔ
67. Ⓐ Ⓑ Ⓒ Ⓓ Ⓔ
68. Ⓐ Ⓑ Ⓒ Ⓓ Ⓔ
69. Ⓐ Ⓑ Ⓒ Ⓓ Ⓔ
70. Ⓐ Ⓑ Ⓒ Ⓓ Ⓔ
71. Ⓐ Ⓑ Ⓒ Ⓓ Ⓔ
72. Ⓐ Ⓑ Ⓒ Ⓓ Ⓔ

73. Ⓐ Ⓑ Ⓒ Ⓓ Ⓔ
74. Ⓐ Ⓑ Ⓒ Ⓓ Ⓔ
75. Ⓐ Ⓑ Ⓒ Ⓓ Ⓔ
76. Ⓐ Ⓑ Ⓒ Ⓓ Ⓔ
77. Ⓐ Ⓑ Ⓒ Ⓓ Ⓔ
78. Ⓐ Ⓑ Ⓒ Ⓓ Ⓔ
79. Ⓐ Ⓑ Ⓒ Ⓓ Ⓔ
80. Ⓐ Ⓑ Ⓒ Ⓓ Ⓔ
81. Ⓐ Ⓑ Ⓒ Ⓓ Ⓔ
82. Ⓐ Ⓑ Ⓒ Ⓓ Ⓔ
83. Ⓐ Ⓑ Ⓒ Ⓓ Ⓔ
84. Ⓐ Ⓑ Ⓒ Ⓓ Ⓔ
85. Ⓐ Ⓑ Ⓒ Ⓓ Ⓔ
86. Ⓐ Ⓑ Ⓒ Ⓓ Ⓔ
87. Ⓐ Ⓑ Ⓒ Ⓓ Ⓔ
88. Ⓐ Ⓑ Ⓒ Ⓓ Ⓔ

PART D—ADDRESS CHECKING

1. Ⓐ Ⓓ   20. Ⓐ Ⓓ   39. Ⓐ Ⓓ   58. Ⓐ Ⓓ   77. Ⓐ Ⓓ

2. Ⓐ Ⓓ   21. Ⓐ Ⓓ   40. Ⓐ Ⓓ   59. Ⓐ Ⓓ   78. Ⓐ Ⓓ

3. Ⓐ Ⓓ   22. Ⓐ Ⓓ   41. Ⓐ Ⓓ   60. Ⓐ Ⓓ   79. Ⓐ Ⓓ

4. Ⓐ Ⓓ   23. Ⓐ Ⓓ   42. Ⓐ Ⓓ   61. Ⓐ Ⓓ   80. Ⓐ Ⓓ

5. Ⓐ Ⓓ   24. Ⓐ Ⓓ   43. Ⓐ Ⓓ   62. Ⓐ Ⓓ   81. Ⓐ Ⓓ

6. Ⓐ Ⓓ   25. Ⓐ Ⓓ   44. Ⓐ Ⓓ   63. Ⓐ Ⓓ   82. Ⓐ Ⓓ

7. Ⓐ Ⓓ   26. Ⓐ Ⓓ   45. Ⓐ Ⓓ   64. Ⓐ Ⓓ   83. Ⓐ Ⓓ

8. Ⓐ Ⓓ   27. Ⓐ Ⓓ   46. Ⓐ Ⓓ   65. Ⓐ Ⓓ   84. Ⓐ Ⓓ

9. Ⓐ Ⓓ   28. Ⓐ Ⓓ   47. Ⓐ Ⓓ   66. Ⓐ Ⓓ   85. Ⓐ Ⓓ

10. Ⓐ Ⓓ   29. Ⓐ Ⓓ   48. Ⓐ Ⓓ   67. Ⓐ Ⓓ   86. Ⓐ Ⓓ

11. Ⓐ Ⓓ   30. Ⓐ Ⓓ   49. Ⓐ Ⓓ   68. Ⓐ Ⓓ   87. Ⓐ Ⓓ

12. Ⓐ Ⓓ   31. Ⓐ Ⓓ   50. Ⓐ Ⓓ   69. Ⓐ Ⓓ   88. Ⓐ Ⓓ

13. Ⓐ Ⓓ   32. Ⓐ Ⓓ   51. Ⓐ Ⓓ   70. Ⓐ Ⓓ   89. Ⓐ Ⓓ

14. Ⓐ Ⓓ   33. Ⓐ Ⓓ   52. Ⓐ Ⓓ   71. Ⓐ Ⓓ   90. Ⓐ Ⓓ

15. Ⓐ Ⓓ   34. Ⓐ Ⓓ   53. Ⓐ Ⓓ   72. Ⓐ Ⓓ   91. Ⓐ Ⓓ

16. Ⓐ Ⓓ   35. Ⓐ Ⓓ   54. Ⓐ Ⓓ   73. Ⓐ Ⓓ   92. Ⓐ Ⓓ

17. Ⓐ Ⓓ   36. Ⓐ Ⓓ   55. Ⓐ Ⓓ   74. Ⓐ Ⓓ   93. Ⓐ Ⓓ

18. Ⓐ Ⓓ   37. Ⓐ Ⓓ   56. Ⓐ Ⓓ   75. Ⓐ Ⓓ   94. Ⓐ Ⓓ

19. Ⓐ Ⓓ   38. Ⓐ Ⓓ   57. Ⓐ Ⓓ   76. Ⓐ Ⓓ   95. Ⓐ Ⓓ

DIAGNOSTIC MODEL EXAM

PART A—NUMBER SERIES

SAMPLE QUESTIONS

The following sample questions show you the type of question that will be used in Part A. Since this type of question may be new and unfamiliar to you, the examiner will work through the first five questions with you. Once you understand the task, you will have five minutes to answer sample questions 6 to 14 on your own. Correct answers and explanations follow.

Directions: Each number series question consists of a series of numbers which follows some definite order. The numbers progress from left to right according to some rule. One pair of numbers to the right of the series comprises the next two numbers in the series. Study each series to try to find a pattern to the series and to figure out the rule which governs the progression. Choose the answer pair which continues the series according to the pattern established and mark its letter on your answer sheet.

1. 21 21 19 17 17 15 13 ...... (A) 11 11 (B) 13 11 (C) 11 9 (D) 9 7 (E) 13 13

   The pattern of this series is: repeat the number, then subtract 2 and subtract 2 again; repeat the number, then subtract 2 and subtract 2 again and so on. Following the pattern, the series should continue with **(B)** 13 11 and then go on 9 9 7 5 5 3 1 1.

2. 23 22 20 19 16 15 11 ..... (A) 6 5 (B) 10 9 (C) 6 1 (D) 10 6 (E) 10 5

   If you write in the changes between the numbers of the series, you can see that the pattern being established is: −1, −2, −1, −3, −1, −4, −1, −5 . . . Fitting the pattern to the remaining numbers, it is apparent that **(E)** is the answer because 11 − 1 = 10 and 10 − 5 = 5.

3. 5 6 8 9 11 12 14 .... (A) 15 16 (B) 16 17 (C) 15 17 (D) 16 18 (E) 17 19

   The pattern here is: +1, +2; +1, +2; +1, +2 and so on. The answer is **(C)** because 14 + 1 = 15 and 15 + 2 = 17.

4. 7 10 8 13 16 8 19 .... (A) 22 8 (B) 8 22 (C) 20 21 (D) 22 25 (E) 8 25

   Marking the changes between numbers is not sufficient for solving this series. You first must notice that the number 8 is repeated after each two numbers. If you disregard the 8's, you can see that the series is increasing by a factor of +3. With this information, you can choose **(A)** as the correct answer because 19 + 3 = 22, and the two numbers, 19 and 22, are then followed by 8.

33

5. 1   35   2   34   3   33   4 .... (A) 4   5   (B) 32   31 (C) 32   5   (D) 5   32   (E) 31   6

This series is, in reality, two alternating series. One series, beginning with 1, increases at the rate of + 1. The other series alternates with the first. It begins with 35 and decreases by − 1. The answer is **(C)** because the next number in the decreasing series is 32 and the next number in the increasing series is 5. You will now have five minutes to complete the remaining sample number series questions.

6. 3   3   9   9   15   15   21 .... (A) 21   21   (B) 21   27   (C) 27   27   (D) 27   33   (E) 33   33

7. 95   90   86   83   78   74   71 ..... (A) 68   65   (B) 67   63   (C) 66   61   (D) 66   62   (E) 69   67

8. 12   13   14   12   13   14   12 ...... (A) 13   14   (B) 12   13   (C) 14   12   (D) 14   13   (E) 14   15

9. 48   17   45   22   42   27   39 ..... (A) 44   41   (B) 44   24   (C) 24   44   (D) 36   32   (E) 32   36

10. 50   52   48   50   46   48   44 ..... (A) 46   48   (B) 48   42   (C) 46   42   (D) 42   46   (E) 48   50

11. 1   3   3   9   9   27   27 .... (A) 36   36   (B) 27   36   (C) 45   45   (D) 54   54   (E) 81   81

12. 5   6   8   11   15   20   26 .... (A) 32   40   (B) 32   38   (C) 30   36   (D) 33   41   (E) 33   40

13. 4   5   10   11   22   23   46 .... (A) 47   94   (B) 92   93   (C) 93   94   (D) 47   48   (E) 47   49

14. 79   77   75   73   71   69   67 ..... (A) 66   65   (B) 65   64   (C) 65   63   (D) 68   69   (E) 67   65

SAMPLE ANSWER SHEET	
1. Ⓐ Ⓑ Ⓒ Ⓓ Ⓔ	8. Ⓐ Ⓑ Ⓒ Ⓓ Ⓔ
2. Ⓐ Ⓑ Ⓒ Ⓓ Ⓔ	9. Ⓐ Ⓑ Ⓒ Ⓓ Ⓔ
3. Ⓐ Ⓑ Ⓒ Ⓓ Ⓔ	10. Ⓐ Ⓑ Ⓒ Ⓓ Ⓔ
4. Ⓐ Ⓑ Ⓒ Ⓓ Ⓔ	11. Ⓐ Ⓑ Ⓒ Ⓓ Ⓔ
5. Ⓐ Ⓑ Ⓒ Ⓓ Ⓔ	12. Ⓐ Ⓑ Ⓒ Ⓓ Ⓔ
6. Ⓐ Ⓑ Ⓒ Ⓓ Ⓔ	13. Ⓐ Ⓑ Ⓒ Ⓓ Ⓔ
7. Ⓐ Ⓑ Ⓒ Ⓓ Ⓔ	14. Ⓐ Ⓑ Ⓒ Ⓓ Ⓔ

CORRECT ANSWERS	
1. B	8. A
2. E	9. E
3. C	10. C
4. A	11. E
5. C	12. D
6. B	13. A
7. D	14. C

EXPLANATIONS

6. **(B)** The pattern is: repeat the number, +6, repeat the number, +6 and so on. Repeat 21 + 6 = 27.

7. **(D)** The pattern is: −5, −4, −3; −5, −4, −3. 71 − 5 = 66 − 4 = 62.

8. **(A)** The series is simply a repetition of the sequence: 12 13 14; 12 13 14, 12 13 14 . . .

9. **(E)** There are two alternating series. The first series begins with 48 and descends at the rate of −3. The alternating series begins with 17 and ascends at the rate of +5. The next number in the series is 27 + 5, which is 32. It is followed by the next number of the alternating series, 39 − 3, which is 36.

10. **(C)** The simplest pattern to see here is +2, −4; +2, −4 and so on. If you do not see that pattern, you will still get the correct answer if you see two alternating series, one beginning with 50, the other beginning with 52 and both descending at the rate of −2.

11. **(E)** The pattern is ×3, repeat the number, ×3, repeat the number; ×3, repeat the number.

12. **(D)** The pattern is: +1, +2, +3, +4, +5, +6, +7, +8. 26 + 7 = 33 + 8 = 41.

13. **(A)** The pattern is: +1, ×2; +1, ×2; +1 ×2 . . . 46 + 1 = 47 × 2 = 94.

14. **(C)** The pattern is a very simple: −2; −2; −2 . . .

PART A—NUMBER SERIES

TIME 20 Minutes. 24 Questions.

Directions: Each number series question consists of a series of numbers which follows some definite order. The numbers progress from left to right according to some rule. One pair of numbers to the right of the series comprises the next two numbers in the series. Study each series to try to find a pattern to the series and to figure out the rule which governs the progression. Choose the answer pair which continues the series according to the pattern established and mark its letter on your answer sheet. Correct answers are on page 46.

1. 8 9 10 8 9 10 8 .... (A) 8 9 (B) 9 10 (C) 9 8 (D) 10 8 (E) 8 10

2. 3 4 4 3 5 5 3 .... (A) 3 3 (B) 6 3 (C) 3 6 (D) 6 6 (E) 6 7

3. 7 7 3 7 7 4 7 .... (A) 7 7 (B) 7 8 (C) 5 7 (D) 8 7 (E) 7 5

4. 18 18 19 20 20 21 22 ..... (A) 22 23 (B) 23 24 (C) 23 23 (D) 22 22 (E) 21 22

5. 2 6 10 3 7 11 4 .... (A) 12 16 (B) 5 9 (C) 8 5 (D) 12 5 (E) 8 12

6. 11 8 15 12 19 16 23 .... (A) 27 20 (B) 24 20 (C) 27 24 (D) 20 24 (E) 20 27

7. 16 8 15 9 14 10 13 .... (A) 12 11 (B) 13 12 (C) 11 13 (D) 11 12 (E) 11 14

8. 4 5 13 6 7 12 8 .... (A) 9 11 (B) 13 9 (C) 9 13 (D) 11 9 (E) 11 10

9. 19 24 20 25 21 26 22 ..... (A) 18 27 (B) 22 24 (C) 23 29 (D) 27 23 (E) 28 32

10. 25 25 22 22 19 19 16 ..... (A) 18 18 (B) 16 16 (C) 16 13 (D) 15 15 (E) 15 13

11. 1 1 2 3 5 8 13 .... (A) 21 29 (B) 21 34 (C) 18 27 (D) 21 27 (E) 24 32

12. 1 3 2 4 3 5 4 .... (A) 6 5 (B) 5 6 (C) 3 1 (D) 3 5 (E) 4 3

13. 1 2 2 3 3 3 4 .... (A) 4 5 (B) 5 5 (C) 3 5 (D) 4 4 (E) 4 3

14. 9 17 24 30 35 39 42 ..... (A) 43 44 (B) 44 46 (C) 44 45 (D) 45 49 (E) 46 50

15. 1 4 9 16 25 36 49 .... (A) 56 64 (B) 60 65 (C) 62 75 (D) 64 80 (E) 64 81

16. 8 12 17 24 28 33 40 ..... (A) 47 53 (B) 45 50 (C) 43 49 (D) 48 54 (E) 44 49

17. 28 31 34 37 40 43 46 ..... (A) 49 52 (B) 47 49 (C) 50 54 (D) 49 53 (E) 51 55

18. 17 17 24 24 31 31 38 ..... (A) 38 39 (B) 38 17 (C) 38 45 (D) 38 44 (E) 39 50

19. 3 12 6 24 12 48 24 .... (A) 96 48 (B) 56 23 (C) 64 12 (D) 52 36 (E) 64 48

20. 87 83 79 75 71 67 63 ..... (A) 62 61 (B) 63 59 (C) 60 56 (D) 59 55 (E) 59 54

21. 10 2 8 2 6 2 4 .... (A) 4 4 (B) 2 2 (C) 3 3 (D) 4 2 (E) 5 2

22. 8 9 11 14 18 23 29 .... (A) 35 45 (B) 32 33 (C) 38 48 (D) 34 40 (E) 36 44

23. 11 14 12 15 13 16 14 ...... (A) 14 17 (B) 15 16 (C) 16 20 (D) 17 15 (E) 18 13

24. 14 2 12 4 10 6 8 .... (A) 10 12 (B) 6 8 (C) 12 10 (D) 8 6 (E) 10 14

END OF PART A

If you finish this part before time is up, check over your answers. Do not turn the page until you are told to do so.

PART B—ADDRESS CODING

SAMPLE QUESTIONS

The seven sample questions for this part are based upon the addresses in the five boxes below. Your task is to mark on your answer sheet the letter of the box in which each address belongs. When you answer the questions in Part B, you may look at the boxes if you cannot remember in which box an address belongs. The same instruction applies to these sample questions. The questions in Part C will be based upon the same boxes as the questions in Part B, but in answering Part C you may NOT look at the boxes. There will be no sample questions before Part C.

A	B	C	D	E
3200-4199 Burns	5000-5399 Burns	2900-3199 Burns	5400-5599 Burns	4200-4999 Burns
Nelson	Barry	Sprain	Essex	Grand
6900-7599 Sage	6600-6899 Sage	6100-6499 Sage	4800-6099 Sage	6500-6599 Sage
Webster	Tudor	Cornell	Dell	Brown
2900-3699 Aspen	3800-4199 Aspen	4200-5199 Aspen	3700-3799 Aspen	5200-5699 Aspen

1. 6600-6899 Sage
2. 5200-5699 Aspen
3. Webster
4. 5400-5599 Burns

5. Cornell
6. Barry
7. 4200-4999 Burns

SAMPLE ANSWER SHEET		CORRECT ANSWERS	
1. Ⓐ Ⓑ Ⓒ Ⓓ Ⓔ	5. Ⓐ Ⓑ Ⓒ Ⓓ Ⓔ	1. B	5. C
2. Ⓐ Ⓑ Ⓒ Ⓓ Ⓔ	6. Ⓐ Ⓑ Ⓒ Ⓓ Ⓔ	2. E	6. B
3. Ⓐ Ⓑ Ⓒ Ⓓ Ⓔ	7. Ⓐ Ⓑ Ⓒ Ⓓ Ⓔ	3. A	7. E
4. Ⓐ Ⓑ Ⓒ Ⓓ Ⓔ		4. D	

PART B—ADDRESS CODING

Directions: There are five boxes, labeled A, B, C, D, and E. In each box are five addresses, three of which include a number span and a name, two of which are names alone. You will have five (5) minutes to memorize the locations of all twenty-five addresses. Then you will have three (3) minutes to mark your answer sheet with the letter of the box in which each address in the question list belongs. For Part B you may refer to the boxes while answering, though you will lose speed by doing so. For Part C you may NOT look at the boxes, so do your best to memorize in the five minutes allowed you now. Correct answers are on page 47.

MEMORIZING TIME: 5 Minutes.

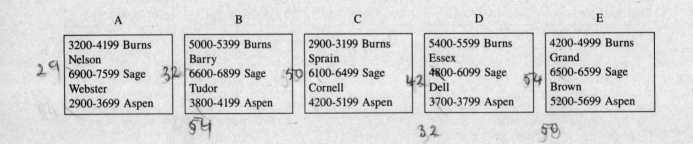

A	B	C	D	E
3200-4199 Burns	5000-5399 Burns	2900-3199 Burns	5400-5599 Burns	4200-4999 Burns
Nelson	Barry	Sprain	Essex	Grand
6900-7599 Sage	6600-6899 Sage	6100-6499 Sage	4800-6099 Sage	6500-6599 Sage
Webster	Tudor	Cornell	Dell	Brown
2900-3699 Aspen	3800-4199 Aspen	4200-5199 Aspen	3700-3799 Aspen	5200-5699 Aspen

ANSWERING TIME: 3 Minutes. 88 Questions.

1. 3800-4199 Aspen
2. Sprain
3. 4800-6099 Sage
4. Dell
5. 4200-5199 Aspen
6. 5000-5399 Burns
7. Webster
8. Cornell
9. 3200-4199 Burns
10. 4200-5199 Aspen
11. Tudor
12. Barry
13. 6600-6899 Sage
14. Nelson
15. 5200-5699 Aspen

16. 5400-5699 Burns
17. 2900-3199 Burns
18. 6500-6599 Sage
19. Grand
20. Essex
21. 6900-7599 Sage
22. 6100-6499 Sage
23. Dell
24. Brown
25. 4200-4999 Burns
26. 4800-6099 Sage
27. 4200-5199 Aspen
28. Tudor
29. 6900-7599 Sage
30. 2900-3699 Aspen

31. Cornell
32. Essex
33. Barry
34. 3800-4199 Aspen
35. 4200-5199 Aspen
36. 4200-4999 Burns
37. 3200-4199 Burns
38. Brown
39. 5200-5699 Aspen
40. 4800-6099 Sage
41. Nelson
42. Grand
43. Webster
44. 5400-5599 Burns
45. 6100-6499 Sage
46. 2900-3699 Aspen
47. 5000-5399 Burns
48. 6100-6499 Sage
49. 4200-4999 Burns
50. Essex
51. Sprain
52. Tudor
53. 5200-5699 Aspen
54. 6900-7599 Sage
55. 5400-5599 Burns
56. 3700-3799 Aspen
57. Barry
58. Dell
59. 2900-3199 Burns

60. 6500-6599 Sage
61. 2900-3699 Aspen
62. Brown
63. 3200-4199 Burns
64. 5400-5599 Burns
65. 6100-6499 Sage
66. Tudor
67. Webster
68. 4200-5199 Aspen
69. 4800-6099 Sage
70. Nelson
71. 4200-4999 Burns
72. 6900-7599 Sage
73. Grand
74. Sprain
75. 5000-5399 Burns
76. 3700-3799 Aspen
77. 5200-5699 Aspen
78. Cornell
79. Essex
80. 6600-6899 Sage
81. 3800-4199 Aspen
82. 6900-7599 Sage
83. Cornell
84. 4200-5199 Aspen
85. 5400-5599 Burns
86. 6500-6599 Sage
87. Tudor
88. 2900-3699 Aspen

END OF PART B

If you finish before time is up, use the spare time to continue memorizing the address locations. Do not turn the page until you are told to do so.

PART C—ADDRESS CODE MEMORY

TIME: 5 Minutes. 88 Questions.

Directions: Relying entirely upon your memory, mark your answer sheet with the letter of the box in which each address belongs. Correct answers are on page 47.

1. 6600-6899 Sage
2. 2900-3699 Aspen
3. Cornell   C
4. 5200-5699 Aspen
5. Nelson   A
6. Essex   D
7. 5400-5599 Burns
8. 3800-4199 Aspen
9. Grand   E
10. Webster   A
11. 2900-3199 Burns
12. 6900-7599 Sage
13. 6500-6599 Sage
14. 3200-4199 Burns
15. 4200-5199 Aspen
16. Barry   B
17. Essex   D
18. 4200-4999 Burns
19. 3700-3799 Aspen
20. Dell   D
21. Sprain   C
22. 6100-6499 Sage
23. 4800-6099 Sage
24. Brown   E
25. Grand   E
26. 2900-3699 Aspen
27. Tudor   B
28. 4200-4999 Burns
29. 3700-3799 Aspen
30. 6900-7599 Sage
31. Sprain   C
32. Dell   D
33. Webster   A
34. Cornell   C
35. 5200-5699 Aspen

36. 5400-5599 Burns
37. 6600-6899 Sage
38. 6100-6499 Sage
39. 5000-5399 Burns
40. 3800-4199 Aspen
41. Nelson   A
42. Barry   B
43. Grand   E
44. 3700-3799 Aspen
45. 6500-6599 Sage
46. 4200-5199 Aspen
47. 5400-5599 Burns
48. Brown   E
49. Essex   D
50. Tudor   B
51. 6100-6499 Sage
52. 3200-4199 Burns
53. 2900-3199 Burns
54. 4800-6099 Sage
55. 3700-3799 Aspen
56. 6900-7599 Sage
57. Webster   A
58. 2900-3699 Aspen
59. 6100-6499 Sage
60. Sprain   C
61. 4200-5199 Aspen
62. Dell   D
63. 5200-5699 Aspen
64. 4200-4999 Burns
65. Barry   B
66. Brown   E
67. 3800-4199 Aspen
68. 4800-6099 Sage
69. Cornell   C
70. 3200-4199 Burns

71. 5400-5599 Burns
72. 4200-4999 Burns
73. Nelson
74. 6600-6899 Sage
75. 3800-4199 Aspen
76. 4800-6099 Sage
77. 6500-6599 Sage
78. 2900-3699 Aspen
79. Sprain

80. Essex
81. 5200-5699 Aspen
82. 3700-3799 Aspen
83. Brown
84. Webster
85. Dell
86. Tudor
87. 5000-5399 Burns
88. 4200-5199 Aspen

END OF PART C

If you finish before time is up, check your answers on this part only. Do not turn the page until you are told to do so.

PART D—ADDRESS CHECKING TEST

SAMPLE QUESTIONS

You will be allowed three minutes to read the directions and answer the five sample questions which follow. On the actual test, however, you will have only six minutes to answer 95 questions, so see how quickly you can compare addresses and still get the correct answer.

> **Directions:** *Each question consists of two addresses. If the two addresses are* alike in EVERY *way, mark* Ⓐ *on your answer sheet. If the two addresses are* different in ANY *way, mark* Ⓓ *on your answer sheet.*

1 . . . 3380 Federal Street	3380 S Federal Street
2 . . . 1618 Highland Way	1816 Highland Way
3 . . . Greenvale NY 11548	Greenvale NY 11548
4 . . . Ft. Collins CO 80523	Ft. Collings CO 80523
5 . . . 7214 NW 83rd St	7214 NW 83rd St

SAMPLE ANSWER SHEET	
1. Ⓐ Ⓓ	4. Ⓐ Ⓓ
2. Ⓐ Ⓓ	5. Ⓐ Ⓓ
3. Ⓐ Ⓓ	

CORRECT ANSWERS	
1. D	4. D
2. D	5. A
3. A	

PART D—ADDRESS CHECKING

TIME: 6 Minutes. 95 Questions.

Directions: For each question, compare the address in the left column with the address in the right column. If the two addresses are alike in EVERY way, blacken space Ⓐ on your answer sheet. If the two addresses are different in ANY way, blacken space Ⓓ on your answer sheet. Correct answers for this test are on page 48.

1 . . . 462 Midland Ave	462 Midland Ave
2 . . . 2319 Sherry Dr	3219 Sherry Dr
3 . . . 1015 Kimball Ave	1015 Kimball Av
4 . . . Wappinger Falls NY 12590	Wappinger Falls NY 12590
5 . . . 1255 North Ave	1225 North Ave
6 . . . 1826 Tibbets Rd	1826 Tibetts Rd
7 . . . 603 N Division St	603 N Division St
8 . . . 2304 Manhattan Ave	2034 Manhattan Ave
9 . . . Worcester MA 01610	Worcester ME 01610
10 . . . 1186 Vernon Drive	1186 Vernon Drive
11 . . . 209 Peter Bont Rd	209 Peter Bent Rd
12 . . . Miami Beach FL 33139	Miami Beach FL 33193
13 . . . 1100 West Ave	1100 East Ave
14 . . . 2063 Winyah Ter	2036 Winyah Ter
15 . . . 3483 Suncrest Ave	3483 Suncrest Dr
16 . . . 234 Rochambeau Rd	234 Roshambeau Rd
17 . . . 306 N. Terrace Blvd	306 N Terrace Blvd
18 . . . 1632 Paine St	1632 Pain St
19 . . . Palm Springs CA 92262	Palm Spring CA 92262
20 . . . 286 Marietta Ave	286 Marrietta Ave
21 . . . 2445 Pigott Rd	2445 Pigott Rd
22 . . . 2204 PineBrook Blvd	2204 Pinebrook Blvd
23 . . . Buffalo NY 42113	Buffulo NY 42113
24 . . . 487 Warburton Ave	487 Warburton Ave
25 . . . 9386 North St	9386 North Ave
26 . . . 2272 Glandale Rd	2772 Glandale Rd
27 . . . 9236 Puritan Dr	9236 Puritan Pl
28 . . . Watertown MA 02172	Watertown MA 02172
29 . . . 7803 Kimball Ave	7803 Kimbal Ave
30 . . . 1362 Colonial Pkwy	1362 Colonial Pkwy
31 . . . 115 Rolling Hills Rd	115 Rolling Hills Rd
32 . . . 218 Rockledge Rd	2181 Rockledge Rd

33 . . . 8346 N Broadway	8346 W Broadway
34 . . . West Chester PA 19380	West Chester PA 19830
35 . . . 9224 Highland Way	9244 Highland Way
36 . . . 8383 Mamaroneck Ave	8383 Mamaroneck Ave
37 . . . 276 Furnace Dock Rd	276 Furnace Dock Rd
38 . . . 4137 Loockerman St	4137 Lockerman St
39 . . . 532 Broadhollow Rd	532 Broadhollow Rd
40 . . . Sunrise FL 33313	Sunrise FL 33133
41 . . . 148 Cortlandt Rd	148 Cortland Rd
42 . . . 5951 W Hartsdale Rd	5951 W Hartsdale Ave
43 . . . 5231 Alta Vista Cir	5321 Alta Vista Cir
44 . . . 6459 Chippewa Rd	6459 Chippewa Rd
45 . . . 1171 S Highland Rd	1771 S Highland Rd
46 . . . Dover DE 19901	Dover DL 19901
47 . . . 2363 Old Farm Ln	2363 Old Farm Ln
48 . . . 1001 Hemingway Dr	1001 Hemmingway Dr
49 . . . 1555 Morningside Ave	1555 Morningslide Ave
50 . . . Purchase NY 10577	Purchase NY 10577
51 . . . 1189 E 9th St	1189 E 9th St
52 . . . 168 Old Lyme Rd	186 Old Lyme Rd
53 . . . 106 Notingham Rd	106 Nottingham Rd
54 . . . 1428 Midland Ave	1428 Midland Ave
55 . . . Elmhurst NY 11373	Elmherst NY 11373
56 . . . 1450 West Chester Pike	1450 West Chester Pike
57 . . . 3357 NW Main St	3357 NE Main St
58 . . . 5062 Marietta Ave	5062 Marrietta Ave
59 . . . 1890 NE 3rd Ct	1980 NE 3rd Ct
60 . . . Wilmington DE 19810	Wilmington DE 19810
61 . . . 1075 Central Park Av	1075 Central Park W
62 . . . 672 Bacon Hill Rd	672 Beacon Hill Rd
63 . . . 1725 W 17th St	1725 W 17th St
64 . . . Bronxville NY 10708	Bronxville NJ 10708
65 . . . 2066 Old Wilmot Rd	2066 Old Wilmont Rd
66 . . . 3333 S State St	3333 S State St
67 . . . 1483 Meritoria Dr	1438 Meritoria Dr
68 . . . 2327 E 23rd St	2327 E 27th St
69 . . . Baltimore MD 21215	Baltimore MD 21215
70 . . . 137 Clarence Rd	137 Claremont Rd
71 . . . 3516 N Ely Ave	3516 N Ely Ave
72 . . . 111 Beechwood St	1111 Beechwood St
73 . . . 143 N Highland Ave	143 N Highland Ave
74 . . . Miami Beach FL 33179	Miami FL 33179
75 . . . 6430 Spring Mill Rd	6340 Spring Mill Rd
76 . . . 1416 87th Ave	1416 78th Ave
77 . . . 4204 S Lexington Ave	4204 Lexington Ave
78 . . . 3601 Clarks Lane	3601 Clark Lane
79 . . . Indianapolis IN 46260	Indianapolis IN 46260
80 . . . 4256 Fairfield Ave	4256 Fairfield Ave
81 . . . Jamaica NY 11435	Jamiaca NY 11435
82 . . . 1809 83rd St	1809 83rd St
83 . . . 3288 Page Ct	3288 Paige Ct

84 . . . 2436 S Broadway

2436 S Broadway

85 . . . 6309 The Green

6309 The Green

86 . . . Kew Gardens NY 11415

Kew Garden NY 11415

87 . . . 4370 W 158th St

4370 W 158th St

88 . . . 4263 3rd Ave

4623 3rd Ave

89 . . . 1737 Fisher Ave

1737 Fischer Ave

90 . . . Bronx NY 10475

Bronx NY 10475

91 . . . 5148 West End Ave

5184 West End Ave

92 . . . 1011 Ocean Ave

1011 Ocean Ave

93 . . . 1593 Webster Dr

1593 Webster Dr

94 . . . Darien CT 06820

Darien CT 06820

95 . . . 1626 E 115th St

1662 E 115th St

END OF EXAM

*If you finish Part D before time is up, check your answers
on this part only. Do not return to any previous part.*

CORRECT ANSWERS FOR DIAGNOSTIC MODEL EXAM

PART A—NUMBER SERIES

1. B	4. A	7. D	10. C	13. D	16. E	19. A	22. E
2. D	5. E	8. A	11. B	14. C	17. A	20. D	23. D
3. E	6. E	9. D	12. A	15. E	18. C	21. B	24. D

EXPLANATIONS—NUMBER SERIES

1. **(B)** The series is simply a repetition of the sequence 8 9 10.

2. **(D)** You can feel the rhythm of this series if you read it aloud. Beginning with 4, doubled numbers are progressing upwards by +1, separated by the number 3.

3. **(E)** In this series two 7's separate numbers which are increasing by +1.

4. **(A)** In this series the numbers are increasing by +1. Every other number is repeated before it increases.

5. **(E)** This series is made up of a number of mini-series. In each mini-series the numbers increase by +4. After each mini-series of three numbers, a new mini-series begins, each time with a number one higher than the beginning number of the previous mini-series.

6. **(E)** This pattern is not as easy to spot as the ones in the previous questions. If you write in the direction and degree of change between each number, you can see that the rule is −3, +7, −3, +7 and so on.

7. **(D)** This series consists of two alternating series. One series begins with 16 and decreases by −1. The alternating series begins with 8 and increases by +1.

8. **(A)** Again we have alternating series. This time the ascending series consists of two numbers increasing by +1 before being interrupted by one number of the descending series which is decreasing by −1.

9. **(D)** You may see this series as following the rule: +5, −4, +5, −4 . . . or you may see two alternating series, one beginning with 19, the other with 24.

10. **(C)** Repeat, −3, repeat, −3, repeat, −3. . . . . .

11. **(B)** Each number is reached by adding together the two previous numbers. Thus, 1 + 1 = 2; 1 + 2 = 3; 2 + 3 = 5; 5 + 8 = 13; 8 + 13 = 21; 13 + 21 = 34.

12. **(A)** You might see two alternating series increasing by +1, or you might see a rule: +2, −1, +2, −1.

13. **(D)** In this series, each number appears as often as its name implies: one 1, two 2's, three 3's, four 4's.

46

14. **(C)** The rule here is: $+8, +7, +6, +5, +4, +3, +2$.

15. **(E)** The elements of this series are the squares of successive numbers: $1^2, 2^2, 3^2, 4^2$, etc.

16. **(E)** The rule is $+4, +5, +7$ and repeat $+4, +5, +7$.

17. **(A)** A simple $+3$ rule.

18. **(C)** Each number repeats itself, then increases by $+7$.

19. **(A)** You might see this as two alternating parallel series. If this is how you see the problem, then you see that in each series, the next number is the previous number multiplied by 2. Another pattern you might see is $\times 4, \div 2, \times 4, \div 2$.

20. **(D)** Here the rule is -4.

21. **(B)** Basically the series descends by -2: 10 8 6 4 2. The number $\underline{2}$ appears between terms of the series.

22. **(E)** The rule is: $+1, +2, +3, +4, +5, +6, +7, +8$.

23. **(D)** Parallel ascending series alternate or the series follows the rule: $+3, -2, +3, -2, +3$.

24. **(D)** The first series decreases by -2. The alternating series increases by $+2$.

PART B—ADDRESS CODING

1. B	12. B	23. D	34. B	45. C	56. D	67. A	78. C
2. C	13. B	24. E	35. C	46. A	57. B	68. C	79. D
3. D	14. A	25. E	36. E	47. B	58. D	69. D	80. B
4. D	15. E	26. D	37. A	48. C	59. C	70. A	81. B
5. C	16. D	27. C	38. E	49. E	60. E	71. E	82. A
6. B	17. C	28. B	39. E	50. D	61. A	72. A	83. C
7. A	18. E	29. A	40. D	51. C	62. E	73. E	84. C
8. C	19. E	30. A	41. A	52. B	63. A	74. C	85. D
9. A	20. D	31. C	42. E	53. E	64. D	75. B	86. E
10. C	21. A	32. D	43. A	54. A	65. C	76. D	87. B
11. B	22. C	33. B	44. D	55. D	66. B	77. E	88. A

PART C—ADDRESS CODE MEMORY

1. B	12. A	23. D	34. C	45. E	56. A	67. B	78. A
2. A	13. E	24. E	35. E	46. C	57. A	68. D	79. C
3. C	14. A	25. E	36. D	47. D	58. A	69. C	80. D
4. E	15. C	26. A	37. B	48. E	59. C	70. A	81. E
5. A	16. B	27. B	38. C	49. D	60. C	71. D	82. D
6. D	17. D	28. E	39. B	50. B	61. C	72. E	83. E
7. D	18. E	29. D	40. B	51. C	62. D	73. A	84. A
8. B	19. D	30. A	41. A	52. A	63. E	74. B	85. D
9. E	20. D	31. C	42. B	53. C	64. E	75. B	86. B
10. A	21. C	32. D	43. E	54. D	65. B	76. D	87. B
11. C	22. C	33. A	44. D	55. D	66. E	77. E	88. C

PART D—ADDRESS CHECKING

1. A	13. D	25. D	37. A	49. D	61. D	73. A	85. A
2. D	14. D	26. D	38. D	50. A	62. D	74. D	86. D
3. D	15. D	27. D	39. A	51. A	63. A	75. D	87. A
4. A	16. D	28. A	40. D	52. D	64. D	76. D	88. D
5. D	17. A	29. D	41. D	53. D	65. D	77. D	89. D
6. D	18. D	30. A	42. D	54. A	66. A	78. D	90. A
7. A	19. D	31. A	43. D	55. D	67. D	79. A	91. D
8. D	20. D	32. D	44. A	56. A	68. D	80. A	92. A
9. D	21. A	33. D	45. D	57. D	69. A	81. D	93. A
10. A	22. D	34. D	46. D	58. D	70. D	82. A	94. A
11. D	23. D	35. D	47. A	59. D	71. A	83. D	95. D
12. D	24. A	36. A	48. D	60. A	72. D	84. A	

ANALYZING YOUR
ADDRESS CHECKING ERRORS

The Address Checking Test of the Diagnostic Exam contains 35 addresses that are exactly alike and 60 addresses that are different. The chart below shows what kind of difference occurs in each of the addresses that contains a difference. Check your answers against this chart to see which kind of difference you missed most often. Note also the questions in which you thought you saw a difference but in which there really was none. Becoming aware of your errors will help you to eliminate those errors on future model exams and on the actual exam.

Type of Difference	Question Numbers	Number of Questions You Missed
Difference in NUMBERS	2, 5, 8, 12, 14, 26, 32, 34, 35, 40, 43, 45, 52, 59, 67, 68, 72, 75, 76, 88, 91, 95	
Difference in ABBREVIATIONS	3, 9, 15, 25, 27, 33, 42, 46, 57, 61, 64, 77	
Difference in NAMES	6, 11, 13, 16, 18, 19, 20, 22, 23, 29, 38, 41, 48, 49, 53, 55, 58, 62, 65, 70, 74, 78, 81, 83, 86, 89	
No Difference	1, 4, 7, 10, 17, 21, 24, 28, 30, 31, 36, 37, 39, 44, 47, 50, 51, 54, 56, 60, 63, 66, 69, 71, 73, 79, 80, 82, 84, 85, 87, 90, 92, 93, 94	

SCORE SHEET FOR DIAGNOSTIC MODEL EXAM

PART A—NUMBER SERIES

Number Right equals Score

_____ = _____

PART B—ADDRESS CODING

Number Right minus (Number Wrong ÷ 4) equals   Score

_____ - _____ = _____

PART C—ADDRESS CODE MEMORY

Number Right minus (Number Wrong ÷ 4) equals   Score

_____ - _____ = _____

PART D—ADDRESS CHECKING

Number Right minus Number Wrong equals   Score

_____ - _____ = _____

SELF-EVALUATION CHART

The Self-Evaluation Chart will help you to rate yourself on the Diagnostic Model Exam and on all other Model Exams that follow. Calculate your score for each test as shown above. Then check to see where score falls on the scale from Poor to Excellent. Lightly shade in the boxes in which your scores fall.

Part	Excellent	Good	Average	Fair	Poor
Number Series	21–24	18–20	14–17	11–13	1–10
Address Coding	75–88	63–74	52–62	40–51	1–39
Address Code Memory	75–88	60–74	45–59	30–44	1–29
Address Checking	80–95	65–79	50–64	35–49	1–34

PROGRESS CHART

A Progress Chart like this one accompanies each Model Exam. After you score each exam, blacken the bar for each test part to the score closest to the score you earned. The SAMPLE PROGRESS CHART below illustrates how to fill in the graph for scores of 14 on Part A, Number Series; 62 on Part B, Address Coding; 50 on Part C, Address Code Memory; and 70 on Part D, Address Checking. Use the graph entitled YOUR PROGRESS CHART to record your scores for the Diagnostic Model Exam. Later, you may wish to transfer these scores to the Progress Charts for succeeding Model Exams so that you can see at a glance how much you are improving.

SAMPLE PROGRESS CHART

Blacken to the closest score to chart your progress.

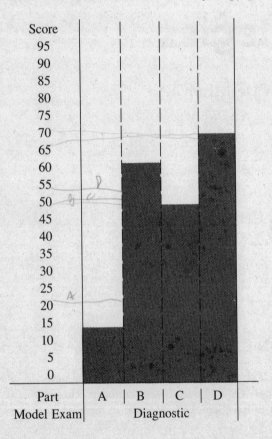

YOUR PROGRESS CHART

Blacken to the closest score to chart your progress.

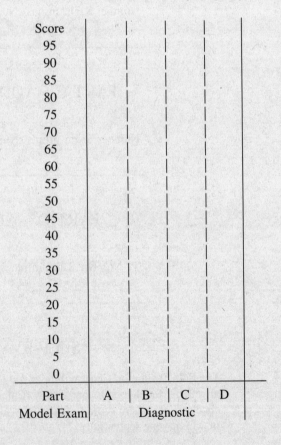

PART II

Test Strategies

HOW TO ANSWER NUMBER SERIES QUESTIONS

The Number Series part of your exam is designed to test your aptitude for working with the letter sorting machine. This part of the exam measures your ability to think with numbers and to see the relationship between elements of a series. While this type of task may be new and unfamiliar to you, the actual mathematics of number series questions is not complicated. The problems involve nothing more than simple addition, subtraction, multiplication and division. What the questions do require of you is concentration. You must be able to see how the numbers in a series are related so that you can supply the next two numbers in that series. You must be flexible enough in your thinking so that if the first pattern you consider for a series turns out to invalid, you can shift gears and try a different pattern.

There is a system with which to approach number series questions.

SOLVE AT A GLANCE

First, look hard at the series. The pattern may be obvious to you upon inspection. A series such as: 1 2 3 1 2 3 1 should not require any deep thought. Clearly, the sequence 1   2   3 is repeating itself over and over. The next two numbers in the series must be: 2   3. You might also instantly recognize the pattern of a simple series into which one number periodically intrudes. An example of such a series is: 1   2   15   3   4   15   5 . . . The number 15 appears after each set of two numbers in a simple + 1 series. The next two numbers in this series are 6 and 15. Can you see why?

Here are five series questions which you should be able to answer by inspection. Circle the letter of the next two numbers in each series.

1. 12 10 13 10 14 10 15   . . . (A) 15 10 (B) 10 15 (C) 10 16 (D) 10 10 (E) 15 16
2. 20 40 60 20 40 60 20 ..... (A) 20 40 (B) 40 60 (C) 60 40 (D) 60 20 (E) 60 40
3. 9 2 9 4 9 6 9 .... (A) 9 9 (B) 9 8 (C) 8 10 (D) 10 8 (E) 8 9
4. 5 8 5 8 5 8 5 .... (A) 8 5 (B) 5 8 (C) 5 5 (D) 5 6 (E) 8 8
5. 10 9 8 7 6 5 4 .... (A) 4 3 (B) 4 2 (C) 3 2 (D) 5 6 (E) 2 1

Answers:

1. **(C)** The series is a simple + 1 series with the number 10 inserted after each step of the series.

2. **(B)** The sequence 20 40 60 repeats itself over and over again.

3. **(E)** This is a simple + 2 series with the number 9 appearing before each member of the series.

4. **(A)** In this series the sequence 5   8 repeats itself.

5. **(C)** You should be able to see that this is a descending series, each number one lower than the one before it. You can call this a − 1 series.

SAY IT ALOUD

Sometimes you may find that your ear is more adept than your eye. You may be able to "hear" a pattern or "feel" a rhythm more easily than you can "see" it. If you cannot immediately spot a pattern, try saying the series softly to yourself. First read the series through. If that does not help, try accenting the printed numbers and speaking the missing intervening numbers even more softly. Try grouping the numbers within the series into twos or threes. After grouping, try accenting the last number, or the first. If you read aloud: 2   4   6   8   10   12   14, you will hear that the next two numbers are 16 and 18. Likewise, if you see the series: 31   32   33   32   33   34   34, and you group that series: 31   32   33; 32   33   34; 34, you will "feel" the rhythm. The series consists of three-number mini-series. Each mini-series begins with a number one higher than the first number of the previous mini-series. The next two numbers of the series are 35 and 36 to be followed by: 35   36   37.

You may be able to answer the next five series questions by inspection. If you cannot, then try sounding them out.

1. 1   2   5   6   9   10   13 .... (A) 15   17   (B) 14   15   (C) 14   16   (D) 15   16   (E) 14   17

2. 2   3   4   3   4   5   4 .... (A) 4   3   (B) 3   5   (C) 5   6   (D) 3   2   (E) 5   4

3. 10   10   12   14   14   16   18 ...... (A) 18   20   (B) 20   20   (C) 20   22   (D) 18   22   (E) 18   18

4. 1   2   3   2   2   3   3   2   3 .... (A) 2   3   (B) 3   2   (C) 3   4   (D) 4   2   (E) 4   3

5. 10   9   8   9   8   7   8 .... (A) 8   7   (B) 7   6   (C) 9   10   (D) 7   8   (E) 8   9

Answers:

1. **(E)** Read aloud (softly): 1   2   5   6   9   10   13
    whisper: 3   4   7   8   11   12
    The next number to read aloud is 14, to be followed by a whispered 15, 16, and then aloud again 17.

2. **(C)** If you group the numbers into threes and read them aloud, accenting either the first or last number of each group, you should "feel" that each group of three begins and ends with a number one higher than the previous series. Read 2, 3 4; 3 4 5; 4 5 6 or 2 3 4; 3 4 5; 4 5 6.

3. **(A)** Once more group into threes. This time be certain to accent the third number in each group in order to sense the rhythm and thereby the pattern of the series. 10 10 12; 14 14 16; 18 18 20 . . .

4. **(D)** In this series the rhythm emerges when you accent the first number in each group: 1 2 3; 2 2 3; 3 2 3.

5. **(B)** After you have seen a number of series of this type, you may very well be able to spot the pattern by inspection alone. If not, read aloud, group and read again.

MARK THE DIFFERENCE

If you cannot see or hear the pattern of a series, the next step to take is marking the degree and direction of change between numbers. Most series progress either + (plus) or − (minus) or a combination of both directions, so first try marking your changes in terms of + and − . If you cannot make sense of a series in terms of + and − , try × (times) and ÷ (divided by). You may mark the changes between numbers right on your exam paper, but be sure to mark the letter of the answer on your answer sheet when you figure it out. Only your answer sheet will be scored. The exam booklet will be collected, but it will not be scored. You do not need to erase markings you make in the exam booklet.

Try this next set of practice questions. If you cannot ''see'' or ''hear'' the pattern, mark the differences between the numbers to establish the pattern. Then continue the pattern to determine the next two numbers of the series.

1. 9 10 12 15 19 24 30 .... (A) 35 40 (B) 36 42 (C) 30 36 (D) 30 37 (E) 37 45

2. 35 34 31 30 27 26 23 ..... (A) 22 19 (B) 22 20 (C) 23 22 (D) 20 19 (E) 20 17

3. 16 21 19 24 22 27 25 ..... (A) 28 30 (B) 30 28 (C) 29 24 (D) 30 27 (E) 26 29

4. 48 44 40 36 32 28 24 ..... (A) 22 20 (B) 24 22 (C) 23 22 (D) 20 18 (E) 20 16

5. 20 30 39 47 54 60 65 ..... (A) 70 75 (B) 68 70 (C) 69 72 (D) 66 67 (E) 68 71

Answers:

1. **(E)** $9 \overset{+1}{} 10 \overset{+2}{} 12 \overset{+3}{} 15 \overset{+4}{} 19 \overset{+5}{} 24 \overset{+6}{} 30 \overset{+7}{} 37 \overset{+8}{} 45$

2. **(A)** $35 \overset{-1}{} 34 \overset{-3}{} 31 \overset{-1}{} 30 \overset{-3}{} 27 \overset{-1}{} 26 \overset{-3}{} 23 \overset{-1}{} 22 \overset{-3}{} 19$

3. **(B)** $16 \overset{+5}{} 21 \overset{-2}{} 19 \overset{+5}{} 24 \overset{-2}{} 22 \overset{+5}{} 27 \overset{-2}{} 25 \overset{+5}{} 30 \overset{-2}{} 28$

4. **(E)** $48 \overset{-4}{} 44 \overset{-4}{} 40 \overset{-4}{} 36 \overset{-4}{} 32 \overset{-4}{} 28 \overset{-4}{} 24 \overset{-4}{} 20 \overset{-4}{} 16$

5. **(C)** $20 \overset{+10}{} 30 \overset{+9}{} 39 \overset{+8}{} 47 \overset{+7}{} 54 \overset{+6}{} 60 \overset{+5}{} 65 \overset{+4}{} 69 \overset{+3}{} 72$

LOOK FOR REPEATED NUMBERS

Arithmetical series such as the ones above may be interrupted by a particular number that appears periodically or by repetition of numbers according to a pattern. For example: 3 6 25 9 12 25 15 18 25 . . . and 50 50 35 40 40 35 30 30 35 . . . In these cases you must search a bit harder to spot both the arithmetic pattern and the pattern of repetition. When choosing your answer you must be alert to the point at which the pattern was interrupted. Do not further repeat a number that has already been repeated; do not forget to repeat before continuing the arithmetical pattern if repetition is called for at this point in the series.

1. 10 13 13 16 16 19 19 ...... (A) 19 19 (B) 19 22 (C) 22 22 (D) 22 25 (E) 22 24

2. 2 4 25 8 16 25 32 .... (A) 32 35 (B) 25 64 (C) 48 25 (D) 25 48 (E) 64 25

3. 80 80 75 75 70 70 65 ..... (A) 65 60 (B) 65 65 (C) 60 60 (D) 60 55 (E) 55 55

4. 35 35 32 30 30 27 25 ..... (A) 22 20 (B) 25 25 (C) 22 22 (D) 25 22 (E) 25 23

5. 76 70 12 65 61 12 58 ..... (A) 55 12 (B) 56 12 (C) 12 54 (D) 12 55 (E) 54 51

Answers:

r = repeat. O = extraneous number repeated periodically.

1. **(C)** $10 \overset{+3}{} 13^r \ 13 \overset{+3}{} 16^r \ 16 \overset{+3}{} 19^r \ 19 \overset{+3}{} 22^r \ 22$

2. **(E)** $2 \overset{\times 2}{} 4 \overset{\times 2}{} \ ⓐ \ 8 \overset{\times 2}{} 16 \overset{\times 2}{} \ ㉕ \ 32 \overset{\times 2}{} 64 \overset{\times 2}{}; \ ㉕ \ . . . 128 \overset{\times 2}{}$

3. **(A)** $80^r \ 80 \overset{-5}{} 75^r \ 75 \overset{-5}{} 70^r \ 70 \overset{-5}{} 65^r \ 65 \overset{-5}{} 60$

4. **(D)** $35^r \ 35 \overset{-3}{} 32 \overset{-2}{} 30^r \ 30 \overset{-3}{} 27 \overset{-2}{} 25^r \ 25 \overset{-3}{} 22$

5. **(B)** $76 \overset{-6}{} 70 \overset{-5}{} \ ⑫ \ 65 \overset{-4}{} 61 \overset{-3}{} \ ⑫ \ 58 \overset{-2}{} 56 \overset{-1}{} \ ⑫ \ . . . 55$

LOOK FOR ALTERNATING SERIES

If you still cannot determine the pattern of a series by inspection, sounding out or marking the differences, you may have to shift gears and try a totally new tactic. First check to see whether the numbers within the series combine to create the following numbers. For instance: 2 0 0 2 1 2 2 2 4, which must be interpreted: $2 \times 0 = 0; 2 \times 1 = 2; 2 \times 2 = 4$. The next few numbers of this series would be 2 3 6 2 4 8. Or look for two alternating series. Each of the two series which alternate will follow a pattern, but they may not necessarily follow the same pattern. A series that encompasses two series might look like this: 5 37 10 36 15 35 20. With practice you should be able to solve a series of this variety without diagramming and writing lots of little numbers. Until you get used to alternating series questions, you might work them out this way:

```
    +5      +5      +5           +5           +5
5   37   10   36   15   35   20 followed by 34   25   33   30 . . .
      -1      -1           -1           -1
```

The next five questions represent series which are just a little more complicated than the series described earlier in this chapter. Try to figure these out.

1. 38 15 32 17 27 19 23 ..... (A) 20 20 (B) 21 26 (C) 20 21 (D) 21 20 (E) 21 25

2. 3 2 5 2 7 2 9 .... (A) 11 13 (B) 9 2   (C) 2 11 (D) 11 2 (E) 2 13

3. 90 83 92 86 94 89 96 ..... (A) 92 98 (B) 98 100 (C) 90 99 (D) 98 92 (E) 98 99

4. 80 12 40 17 20 22 10 ..... (A) 25 15 (B) 15 25 (C) 24 5 (D) 25 5 (E) 27 5

5. 5 6 20 21 34 35 47 .... (A) 48 49 (B) 48 59 (C) 48 36 (D) 36 48 (E) 48 55

Answers:

1. **(D)**
```
          -6        -5        -4        -3
38     15   32   17   27   19   23   21   20
         +2        +2        +2
```

2. **(C)** 3 + 2 = 5 + 2 = 7 + 2 = 9 + 2 = 11
or
$3 \overset{+2}{} ② \ 5 \overset{+2}{} ② \ 7 \overset{+2}{} ② \ 9 \overset{+2}{} ② \ 11$

3. **(A)**
```
          +2        +2        +2        +2
90     83   92   86   94   89   96   92   98
         +3        +3        +3
```

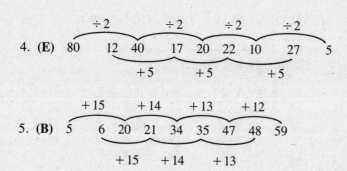

In answering the Number Series questions on your exam, be careful and methodical. You are allowed twenty minutes in which to answer twenty-four questions. That should be enough time. Once you have completed this book, you should be skillful enough to handle any kind of number series question.

NUMBER SERIES TACTICS

1. Do first the questions that seem easiest for you. The questions are not necessarily arranged in order of difficulty, so answer quickly the questions which require little time and leave yourself extra time for the more difficult questions.

    When you skip a question, put a mark before the question number on the question sheet and SKIP ITS ANSWER SPACE. When you return to a question that you have skipped, be sure to mark its answer in the correct space. The time you spend checking to make sure that question and answer number are alike is time well spent.
2. Follow the procedures outlined in this chapter. First, look for an obvious pattern. Second, sound out the series; if necessary, group the numbers and sound out again. Third, write the direction and amount of change between numbers. If you still have not found the rule, look for two alternating series and for uncommon types of progressions.

    If you do any figuring on the question sheet, be sure to mark the letter of the correct answer on your answer sheet. All answers must be marked on the answer sheet.
3. If none of the answers given fits the rule you have figured out, try again. Try to figure out a rule that makes one of the five answers a correct one.
4. Do not spend too much time on any one question. If a question seems impossible, skip it and come back later. A fresh look will sometimes help you find the answer. If you still cannot figure out the answer, guess. There is no scoring penalty for a wrong answer on this part of your exam, so by all means guess.
5. Keep track of time. Since there is no penalty for a wrong answer, you will want to answer every question. Leave yourself time to go back to the questions you skipped to give them a second look. If you are a slow worker and have not quite finished this part, leave a few seconds to mark random answers for the questions you cannot reach.

Apply everthing you have learned as you answer the practice questions that follow. Build up your skill. Do not worry about time as you work on these practice questions. You will have plenty of chance to build up speed in the model exams. All of the questions are explained at the end of the set.

NUMBER SERIES PRACTICE QUESTIONS

```
┌─────────────────────────────────────────────────────────────────────────────┐
│                          Sample Answer Sheet                                  │
│                                                                               │
│  1. Ⓐ Ⓑ Ⓒ Ⓓ Ⓔ      6. Ⓐ Ⓑ Ⓒ Ⓓ Ⓔ     11. Ⓐ Ⓑ Ⓒ Ⓓ Ⓔ     16. Ⓐ Ⓑ Ⓒ Ⓓ Ⓔ    21. Ⓐ Ⓑ Ⓒ Ⓓ Ⓔ │
│  2. Ⓐ Ⓑ Ⓒ Ⓓ Ⓔ      7. Ⓐ Ⓑ Ⓒ Ⓓ Ⓔ     12. Ⓐ Ⓑ Ⓒ Ⓓ Ⓔ     17. Ⓐ Ⓑ Ⓒ Ⓓ Ⓔ    22. Ⓐ Ⓑ Ⓒ Ⓓ Ⓔ │
│  3. Ⓐ Ⓑ Ⓒ Ⓓ Ⓔ      8. Ⓐ Ⓑ Ⓒ Ⓓ Ⓔ     13. Ⓐ Ⓑ Ⓒ Ⓓ Ⓔ     18. Ⓐ Ⓑ Ⓒ Ⓓ Ⓔ    23. Ⓐ Ⓑ Ⓒ Ⓓ Ⓔ │
│  4. Ⓐ Ⓑ Ⓒ Ⓓ Ⓔ      9. Ⓐ Ⓑ Ⓒ Ⓓ Ⓔ     14. Ⓐ Ⓑ Ⓒ Ⓓ Ⓔ     19. Ⓐ Ⓑ Ⓒ Ⓓ Ⓔ    24. Ⓐ Ⓑ Ⓒ Ⓓ Ⓔ │
│  5. Ⓐ Ⓑ Ⓒ Ⓓ Ⓔ     10. Ⓐ Ⓑ Ⓒ Ⓓ Ⓔ     15. Ⓐ Ⓑ Ⓒ Ⓓ Ⓔ     20. Ⓐ Ⓑ Ⓒ Ⓓ Ⓔ                  │
└─────────────────────────────────────────────────────────────────────────────┘
```

1. 12 26 15 26 18 26 21 ...... (A) 21 24 (B) 24 26 (C) 21 26 (D) 26 24 (E) 26 25

2. 72 67 69 64 66 61 63 ..... (A) 58 60 (B) 65 62 (C) 60 58 (D) 65 60 (E) 60 65

3. 81 10 29 81 10 29 81 ..... (A) 29 10 (B) 81 29 (C) 10 29 (D) 81 10 (E) 29 81

4. 91 91 90 88 85 81 76 ..... (A) 71 66 (B) 70 64 (C) 75 74 (D) 70 65 (E) 70 63

5. 22 44 29 37 36 30 43 ..... (A) 50 23 (B) 23 50 (C) 53 40 (D) 40 53 (E) 50 57

6. 0 1 1 0 2 2 0 .... (A) 0 0 (B) 0 3 (C) 3 3 (D) 3 4 (E) 2 3

7. 32 34 36 34 36 38 36 ..... (A) 34 32 (B) 36 34 (C) 36 38 (D) 38 40 (E) 38 36

8. 26 36 36 46 46 56 56 ..... (A) 66 66 (B) 56 66 (C) 57 57 (D) 46 56 (E) 26 66

9. 64 63 61 58 57 55 52 ..... (A) 51 50 (B) 52 49 (C) 50 58 (D) 50 47 (E) 51 49

10. 4 6 8 7 6 8 10 9 8 ..... (A) 7 9 (B) 11 12 (C) 12 14 (D) 7 10 (E) 10 12

11. 57 57 52 47 47 42 37 ..... (A) 32 32 (B) 37 32 (C) 37 37 (D) 32 27 (E) 27 27

12. 13 26 14 25 16 23 19 ...... (A) 20 21 (B) 20 22 (C) 20 23 (D) 20 24 (E) 22 25

13. 15 27 39 51 63 75 87 ..... (A) 97 112 (B) 99 111 (C) 88 99 (D) 89 99 (E) 90 99

14. 2 0 2 2 2 4 2 6 2 8 ... (A) 2 2 (B) 2 8 (C) 2 10 (D) 2 12 (E) 2 16

15. 19 18 18 17 17 17 16 ...... (A) 16 16 (B) 16 15 (C) 15 15 (D) 15 14 (E) 16 17

16. 55 53 44 51 49 44 47 ..... (A) 45 43 (B) 46 45 (C) 46 44 (D) 44 44 (E) 45 44

17. 100 81 64 49 36 25 16 ..... (A) 8 4 (B) 8 2 (C) 9 5 (D) 9 4 (E) 9 3

18. 2 2 4 6 8 18 16 .... (A) 32 64 (B) 32 28 (C) 54 32 (D) 32 54 (E) 54 30

19. 47 43 52 48 57 53 62 ..... (A) 58 54 (B) 67 58 (C) 71 67 (D) 58 67 (E) 49 58

20. 38 38 53 48 48 63 58 ..... (A) 58 58 (B) 58 73 (C) 73 73 (D) 58 68 (E) 73 83

21. 12 14 16 13 15 17 14 ...... (A) 17 15 (B) 15 18 (C) 17 19 (D) 15 16 (E) 16 18

22. 30 30 30 37 37 37 30 ..... (A) 30 30 (B) 30 37 (C) 37 37 (D) 37 30 (E) 31 31

23. 75 52 69 56 63 59 57 ..... (A) 58 62 (B) 55 65 (C) 51 61 (D) 61 51 (E) 63 55

24. 176 88 88 44 44 22 22 .... (A) 22 11 (B) 11 11 (C) 11 10 (D) 11 5 (E) 22 10

Answers:

1. D	4. E	7. D	10. E	13. B	16. E	19. D	22. A
2. A	5. B	8. A	11. B	14. C	17. D	20. B	23. D
3. C	6. C	9. E	12. C	15. A	18. C	21. E	24. B

Explanations:

1. **(D)** A + 3 series with the number 26 between terms.

   $12 \overset{+3}{} \enspace ㉖ \enspace 15 \overset{+3}{} \enspace ㉖ \enspace 18 \overset{+3}{} \enspace ㉖ \enspace 21 \overset{+3}{} \enspace ㉖ \enspace 24$

2. **(A)** You may read this as a −5, +2 series

   $72 \overset{-5}{} 67 \overset{+2}{} 69 \overset{-5}{} 64 \overset{+2}{} 66 \overset{-5}{} 61 \overset{+2}{} 63 \overset{-5}{} 58 \overset{+2}{} 60$

   or as two alternating −3 series

   $$72 \quad 67 \quad 69 \quad 64 \quad 66 \quad 61 \quad 63 \quad 58 \quad 60$$

   (top brackets: −3, −3, −3, −3; bottom brackets: −3, −3, −3)

3. **(C)** By inspection or grouping, the sequence 81 10 29 repeats itself over and over.

4. **(E)** Write in the numbers for this one.

   $91 \overset{-0}{} 91 \overset{-1}{} 90 \overset{-2}{} 88 \overset{-3}{} 85 \overset{-4}{} 81 \overset{-5}{} 76 \overset{-6}{} 70 \overset{-7}{} 63$

5. **(B)** Here we have two distinct alternating series.

   $$22 \quad 44 \quad 29 \quad 37 \quad 36 \quad 30 \quad 43 \quad 23 \quad 50$$

   (top brackets: +7, +7, +7, +7; bottom brackets: −7, −7, −7)

6. **(C)** The digit 0 intervenes after each repeating number of a simple + 1 and repeat series.

   $⓪ \enspace 1^r \enspace 1 \overset{+1}{} ⓪ \enspace 2^r \enspace 2 \overset{+1}{} ⓪ \enspace 3^r \enspace 3$

7. **(D)** Group the numbers into threes. Each succeeding group of three begins with a number two higher than the first number of the preceding group of three. Within each group the pattern is +2, +2.

8. **(A)** The pattern is + 10, repeat the number, + 10, repeat the number.

   $26 \overset{+10}{} 36^r \enspace 36 \overset{+10}{} 46^r \enspace 46 \overset{+10}{} 56^r \enspace 56 \overset{+10}{} 66^r \enspace 66$

9. **(E)** The pattern is −1, −2, −3; −1, −2, −3 and so on. If you can't see it, write it in for yourself.

10. **(E)** Here the pattern is +2, +2, −1, −1; +2, +2, −1, −1.

    $4 \overset{+2}{} 6 \overset{+2}{} 8 \overset{-1}{} 7 \overset{-1}{} 6 \overset{+2}{} 8 \overset{+2}{} 10 \overset{-1}{} 9 \overset{-1}{} 8 \overset{+2}{} 10 \overset{+2}{} 12$

    The series which is given to you is a little bit longer than most to better assist you in establishing this extra long pattern.

11. **(B)** This is a −5 pattern with every other term repeated.

    $57^r \enspace 57 \overset{-5}{} 52 \overset{-5}{} 47^r \enspace 47 \overset{-5}{} 42 \overset{-5}{} 37^r \enspace 37 \overset{-5}{} 32$

12. **(C)**. This series consists of two alternating series.

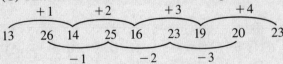

13. **(B)** This is a simple +12 series.

14. **(C)** Even with the extra length, you may have trouble with this one. You might have to change your approach a couple of times to figure it out.
$$2^{\times 0}\, 0;\; 2^{\times 1}\, 2;\; 2^{\times 2}\, 4;\; 2^{\times 3}\, 6;\; 2^{\times 4}\, 8;\; 2^{\times 5}\, 10$$

15. **(A)** Each number is repeated one tine more than the number before it. 19 appears only once, 18 twice, 17 three times and, if the series were extended beyond the question, 16 would appear four times.

16. **(E)** This is a −2 series with the number 44 appearing after every two numbers of the series. You probably can see this now without writing it out.

17. **(D)** The series consists of the squares of the numbers from two to ten in descending order.

18. **(C)** This is a tricky alternating series question.

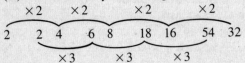

19. **(D)** The progress of this series is −4, +9; −4, +9.

20. **(B)** This series is not really difficult, but you may have to write it out to see it.
$$38^{r}\quad 38^{+15}\, 53^{-5}\, 48^{r}\, 48^{+15}\, 63^{-5}\, 58^{r}\, 58^{+15}\, 73$$
You may also see this as two alternating +10 series with the numbers ending in 8 repeated.

21. **(E)** Group into sets of three numbers. Each +2 mini-series begins one step up from the previous mini-series.

22. **(A)** By inspection you can see that this series is nothing more than the number 30 repeated three times and the number 37 repeated three times. Since you have no further clues, you must assume that the series continues with the number 30 repeated three times.

23. **(D)** Here are two alternating series.

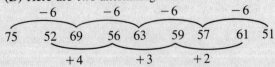

24. **(B)** The pattern is ÷2 and repeat the number, ÷2 and repeat the number.
$$176^{\div 2}\, 88^{r}\, 88^{\div 2}\, 44^{r}\, 44^{\div 2}\, 22^{r}\, 22^{\div 2}\, 11^{r}\, 11$$

HOW TO ANSWER ADDRESS
CODING AND ADDRESS
CODE MEMORY QUESTIONS

Parts B and C of your exam are so interrelated that they must be treated as a unit. Preparation for Part C should be invaluable to you as you tackle Part B as well. This chapter will deal with memorizing. You must concentrate on memorizing before you answer the questions in Part B even though you are permitted to look at the addresses while answering Part B. The time limit for Part B is even shorter than the time limit for Part C. The more address locations you have committed to memory, the more quickly you can answer the questions in Part B. Searching for addresses takes time, but if you must look back while you are answering the Part B questions. concentrate hard and try to memorize as you look.

On your exam, the address boxes which accompany the sample questions before Part B will be the same as the address boxes on the exam itself. Answer the seven sample questions. Use any extra time that the examiner may allow to begin memorizing address locations.

Memorizing is a special skill, simple for some few people, a chore for most. If you are one of the lucky ones with a good visual memory—that is, if you can look at a page and remember not only what was on the page but how the page looked—you will find this task very easy. You need only picture the spot on the page where each item is located. If, however, you do not have this gift, then Address Coding and Address Code Memory may appear to be frighteningly difficult. This chapter contains suggestions to help you memorize more efficiently and tips to help you cope with this particular memorizing test.

The first thing you must do in this test is to memorize the location of 25 addresses which are presented in five different boxes labeled A, B, C, D, and E. Here is a typical set of addresses. Look at it carefully and commit it to memory, following the step-by-step analysis that follows.

A	B	C	D	E
3200-3499 Apple Book 7400-7699 Tripp Silver 5900-6499 Budd	1000-2199 Apple Taxter 7900-8499 Tripp Bloom 6800-7199 Budd	3500-3599 Apple Superior 7700-7799 Tripp Malter 4500-5199 Budd	2200-2899 Apple Brayton 6800-7399 Tripp Moore 5500-6799 Budd	2900-3199 Apple Miller 7800-7899 Tripp Clayton 5200-5499 Budd

Step One: The fewer items you have to memorize, the easier your job will be. Therefore, the first step is to eliminate any unnecessary items. Concentrate on the number spans. In this case, every one is different. This means there is no need to remember the street names associated with the number spans, so you can immediately narrow down the information to be memorized to this:

A	B	C	D	E
3200-3499	1000-2199	3500-3599	2200-2899	2900-3199
Book	Taxter	Superior	Brayton	Miller
7400-7699	7900-8499	7700-7799	6800-7399	7800-7899
Silver	Bloom	Malter	Moore	Clayton
5900-6499	6800-7199	4500-5199	5500-6799	5200-5499

Step Two: Close examination of each number span reveals that the first number of each span always ends in *00* and the second number always ends in *99*. With this knowledge, you can ignore half of each number, reducing your memorization to the following:

A	B	C	D	E
32-34	10-21	35-35	22-28	29-31
Book	Taxter	Superior	Brayton	Miller
74-76	79-84	77-77	68-73	78-78
Silver	Bloom	Malter	Moore	Clayton
59-64	68-71	45-51	55-67	52-54

Step Three: Now look only at the first number in each span. Only two spans begin with the same number (68-71 in box B and 68-73 in box D). This means that you can eliminate the second number from all but these two spans. Thus, you have narrowed down the information be to memorized from 30 four-digit numbers and 25 names to 17 two-digit numbers and 10 names. You can answer every question on the test by remembering only this information:

A	B	C	D	E
32	10	35	22	29
Book	Taxter	Superior	Brayton	Miller
74	79	77	68-73	78
Silver	Bloom	Malter	Moore	Clayton
59	68-71	45	55	52

Of course, each exam offers a different set of names and numbers. You must mentally go through all these steps with each exam, blocking out all unnecessary material and memorizing only what you need to know. On the actual exam, you cannot use scratch paper and cannot learn the names and numbers by writing them down.

You must be certain to memorize enough to differentiate the addresses from box to box. If by any chance you find an exact duplication of number spans, you must memorize the names that go with those number spans.

To simplify your task still further, consider that if you memorize which addresses belong in each of four boxes, those addresses that you have not memorized automatically belong in the fifth box. And so, you really need memorize the locations of only twenty items. Suddenly, the Address Code Memory Test does not seem so hard after all.

DECIDING WHAT TO MEMORIZE

You must practice the narrowing down process so that you can decide very quickly what it is that you must memorize in order to answer the questions on the Address Code Memory Test. The exercise that follows presents two sorting schemes. Examine the boxes in each row. Then fill in the empty boxes with the information you must memorize for each scheme.

1.

A	B	C	D	E
2300-2599 Hall River 7500-8199 Elm Court 8500-8999 Macy	1500-1799 Hall Division 2400-2899 Elm Beach 6800-6999 Macy	3200-3599 Hall Lake 4200-4499 Elm Church 5600-5899 Macy	1200-1399 Hall Post 3500-3799 Elm Maple 9100-9299 Macy	4400-4699 Hall Ellis 6100-6399 Elm Dale 7200-7599 Macy

A	B	C	D	E

2.

A	B	C	D	E
6200-6399 Main Salem 8000-8499 Long Amherst 5500-6399 Oak	5600-5899 Main Forest 9400-9599 Long Saratoga 4800-5499 Oak	6400-6599 Main Harbor 8500-8699 Long Avondale 6600-7299 Oak	5000-5599 Main Ridge 9600-9799 Long Hewitt 4300-4799 Oak	4700-4999 Main Palmer 8700-8999 Long Union 7300-7499 Oak

A	B	C	D	E

Answers:

1.

A	B	C	D	E
23 River 75 Court 85	15 Division 24 Beach 68	32 Lake 42 Church 56	12 Post 35 Maple 91	

2.

A	B	C	D	E
62 Salem 80 Amherst 55	56 Forest 94 Saratoga 48	64 Harbor 85 Avondale 66	50 Ridge 96 Hewitt 43	

TECHNIQUES FOR MEMORIZING

You can use many different methods to do the actual memorizing of the sorting scheme. Since people are different, the same method does not work for everyone. You may choose to learn the locations of the names first, or you may find it easier to learn the numbers first. Or you may find that you learn most quickly if you concentrate on one box at a time, read the items over and over, and then cover the box and try to repeat those items. Even while learning the contents of a box, you might prefer to either learn one item at a time or to learn the items in groups of two or three. Remember that you do not have to memorize the items in any particular order. You may mentally rearrange the items within any box if the rearrangement helps you learn.

Here is one memory strategy that works for many people:

- First, narrow down the information in each box to the bare essentials.

- Next, group together all the necessary numbers and names in each box.

- Then, combine the names in such a way that they form a word or an image that helps you fix each box in your mind.

Let's try this strategy on the sorting scheme that follows:

A	B	C	D	E
5500-5899 Town Marshall 2200-2499 Park Endicott 1700-1999 Grand	6300-6500 Town Needham 1800-2199 Park Haymarket 1100-1299 Grand	5900-6299 Town Prescott 2600-2899 Park Draper 4200-4499 Grand	4800-5299 Town Whitehall 1500-1699 Park Houseman 6200-6399 Grand	3700-3999 Town Rider 1300-1499 Park Carthage 3100-3399 Grand

Step One: Narrow down the information to the barest essentials. Of course you may eliminate whichever box threatens to be hardest to learn.

A	B	C	D	E
55 Marshall 22 Endicott 17	63 Needham 18 Haymarket 11	59 Prescott 26 Draper 42	48 Whitehall 15 Houseman 62	

Step Two: Group together the numbers and the names in each box.

A	B	C	D	E
55 22 17 Marshall Endicott	63 18 11 Needham Haymarket	59 26 42 Prescott Draper	48 15 62 Whitehall Houseman	

Step Three: Combine the names to form a word or an image that will help you fix each box in your mind.

A	B	C	D	E
55 22 17 A *Marshal* at the *End* of a parade	63 18 11 *Needle* buried in the *Hay*stack	59 26 42 See the man *Pressing Drapes*	48 15 62 De*White House*	

NOTE: The image you choose may be different from the one given. The object is to choose an image that helps you to remember what is in each box. Use an image that works for you.

Step Four: Group the numbers with the box letters in some fashion that helps you to memorize them together. You might set the numbers up as a telephone number: A55-2217 or, perhaps, as a building and apartment number: 6318 11B. You may also rearrange the numbers if doing so will create a date that is meaningful to you, as, for instance, 1548. Remember: You do not need to remember the order of the words and numbers within any box, only the letter of the box in which they appear.

Alternatively you can combine Steps 3 and 4 by making up a single silly sentence that provides all the clues you need to identify the contents of each box. For example, using the boxes above you might come up with sentences like these:

55 Marshals at the End of A parade of 2217 men.

63 Needles Buried in a Haystack in 1811.

59 men Pressing Drapes on the Corner of 26th and 42nd Streets.

48 White Houses Designed in 1562.

The time you spend developing an image that helps you to remember the names and numbers in the boxes is, of course, a part of the time allotted for memorization. For this reason, it is essential that you experiment with memory schemes to find the one that works best for you. Start with the memory strategies suggested here. Or, invent another memory strategy that suits you better. Anything that is fast and effective is acceptable. Try a different memory strategy on each of the first few model exams in this book. Once you decide which strategy is best for you, develop your skill and speed in using it on the remaining model exams.

While working on questions in this chapter, forget about time limits. The time pressure in the actual exam is very real, but use the model exams to develop your speed. In this chapter concentrate on skills. Look again now at the addresses for Practice Exercise 1. Try to memorize as little information as possible, but memorize it thoroughly. When you feel that you are ready, answer the following questions. While you are answering the questions in Set 1, you may refer to the address boxes whenever you need to. Do not look back at the address boxes when you answer the questions in Set 2. Correct answers to these questions are on page 72.

PRACTICE EXERCISE 1

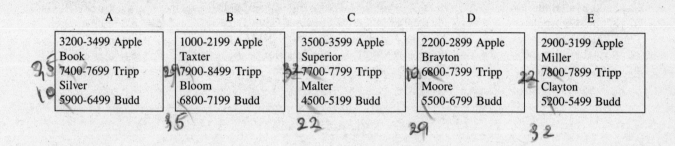

A	B	C	D	E
3200-3499 Apple Book 7400-7699 Tripp Silver 5900-6499 Budd	1000-2199 Apple Taxter 7900-8499 Tripp Bloom 6800-7199 Budd	3500-3599 Apple Superior 7700-7799 Tripp Malter 4500-5199 Budd	2200-2899 Apple Brayton 6800-7399 Tripp Moore 5500-6799 Budd	2900-3199 Apple Miller 7800-7899 Tripp Clayton 5200-5499 Budd

SET 1

1. 7900-8499 Tripp
2. 5500-6799 Budd
3. Silver
4. Miller
5. Superior
6. 4500-5199 Budd
7. 3200-3499 Apple
8. 7800-7899 Tripp
9. 5900-6499 Budd
10. Book
11. Brayton
12. 2900-3199 Apple
13. 1000-2199 Apple
14. Taxter
15. 5200-5499 Budd
16. Clayton
17. 7400-7699 Tripp
18. 6800-7199 Budd
19. 3500-3599 Apple
20. Moore
21. 2200-2899 Apple
22. Bloom
23. Malter
24. 5900-6499 Budd
25. 7700-7799 Tripp
26. 6800-7199 Budd
27. 3200-3499 Apple
28. Miller
29. Silver
30. 6800-7399 Tripp
31. 7200-7699 Tripp
32. Superior
33. Clayton
34. 1000-2199 Apple
35. 5500-6799 Budd

1. Ⓐ Ⓑ Ⓒ Ⓓ Ⓔ
2. Ⓐ Ⓑ Ⓒ Ⓓ Ⓔ
3. Ⓐ Ⓑ Ⓒ Ⓓ Ⓔ
4. Ⓐ Ⓑ Ⓒ Ⓓ Ⓔ
5. Ⓐ Ⓑ Ⓒ Ⓓ Ⓔ
6. Ⓐ Ⓑ Ⓒ Ⓓ Ⓔ
7. Ⓐ Ⓑ Ⓒ Ⓓ Ⓔ
8. Ⓐ Ⓑ Ⓒ Ⓓ Ⓔ
9. Ⓐ Ⓑ Ⓒ Ⓓ Ⓔ
10. Ⓐ Ⓑ Ⓒ Ⓓ Ⓔ
11. Ⓐ Ⓑ Ⓒ Ⓓ Ⓔ
12. Ⓐ Ⓑ Ⓒ Ⓓ Ⓔ
13. Ⓐ Ⓑ Ⓒ Ⓓ Ⓔ
14. Ⓐ Ⓑ Ⓒ Ⓓ Ⓔ
15. Ⓐ Ⓑ Ⓒ Ⓓ Ⓔ
16. Ⓐ Ⓑ Ⓒ Ⓓ Ⓔ
17. Ⓐ Ⓑ Ⓒ Ⓓ Ⓔ
18. Ⓐ Ⓑ Ⓒ Ⓓ Ⓔ
19. Ⓐ Ⓑ Ⓒ Ⓓ Ⓔ
20. Ⓐ Ⓑ Ⓒ Ⓓ Ⓔ
21. Ⓐ Ⓑ Ⓒ Ⓓ Ⓔ
22. Ⓐ Ⓑ Ⓒ Ⓓ Ⓔ
23. Ⓐ Ⓑ Ⓒ Ⓓ Ⓔ
24. Ⓐ Ⓑ Ⓒ Ⓓ Ⓔ
25. Ⓐ Ⓑ Ⓒ Ⓓ Ⓔ
26. Ⓐ Ⓑ Ⓒ Ⓓ Ⓔ
27. Ⓐ Ⓑ Ⓒ Ⓓ Ⓔ
28. Ⓐ Ⓑ Ⓒ Ⓓ Ⓔ
29. Ⓐ Ⓑ Ⓒ Ⓓ Ⓔ
30. Ⓐ Ⓑ Ⓒ Ⓓ Ⓔ
31. Ⓐ Ⓑ Ⓒ Ⓓ Ⓔ
32. Ⓐ Ⓑ Ⓒ Ⓓ Ⓔ
33. Ⓐ Ⓑ Ⓒ Ⓓ Ⓔ
34. Ⓐ Ⓑ Ⓒ Ⓓ Ⓔ
35. Ⓐ Ⓑ Ⓒ Ⓓ Ⓔ

36. 5200-5499 Budd
37. Book
38. Brayton
39. 2900-3199 Apple
40. 7900-8499 Tripp
41. 4500-5199 Budd
42. Taxter
43. 7800-7899 Tripp
44. 3500-3599 Apple
45. 7400-7699 Tripp
46. 5200-5499 Budd
47. Silver
48. Brayton
49. 3200-3499 Apple
50. 7900-8499 Tripp
51. 4500-5199 Budd
52. Moore
53. Miller
54. 5200-5499 Budd
55. 6800-7399 Tripp
56. 3500-3599 Apple
57. Taxter
58. Silver
59. 5900-6499 Budd
60. Bloom
61. 7700-7799 Tripp
62. Brayton
63. 2900-3199 Apple
64. Book
65. 7800-7899 Tripp
66. Clayton
67. 6800-7199 Budd
68. 2200-2899 Apple
69. Superior
70. Malter

36. Ⓐ Ⓑ Ⓒ Ⓓ Ⓔ
37. Ⓐ Ⓑ Ⓒ Ⓓ Ⓔ
38. Ⓐ Ⓑ Ⓒ Ⓓ Ⓔ
39. Ⓐ Ⓑ Ⓒ Ⓓ Ⓔ
40. Ⓐ Ⓑ Ⓒ Ⓓ Ⓔ
41. Ⓐ Ⓑ Ⓒ Ⓓ Ⓔ
42. Ⓐ Ⓑ Ⓒ Ⓓ Ⓔ
43. Ⓐ Ⓑ Ⓒ Ⓓ Ⓔ
44. Ⓐ Ⓑ Ⓒ Ⓓ Ⓔ
45. Ⓐ Ⓑ Ⓒ Ⓓ Ⓔ
46. Ⓐ Ⓑ Ⓒ Ⓓ Ⓔ
47. Ⓐ Ⓑ Ⓒ Ⓓ Ⓔ
48. Ⓐ Ⓑ Ⓒ Ⓓ Ⓔ
49. Ⓐ Ⓑ Ⓒ Ⓓ Ⓔ
50. Ⓐ Ⓑ Ⓒ Ⓓ Ⓔ
51. Ⓐ Ⓑ Ⓒ Ⓓ Ⓔ
52. Ⓐ Ⓑ Ⓒ Ⓓ Ⓔ
53. Ⓐ Ⓑ Ⓒ Ⓓ Ⓔ
54. Ⓐ Ⓑ Ⓒ Ⓓ Ⓔ
55. Ⓐ Ⓑ Ⓒ Ⓓ Ⓔ
56. Ⓐ Ⓑ Ⓒ Ⓓ Ⓔ
57. Ⓐ Ⓑ Ⓒ Ⓓ Ⓔ
58. Ⓐ Ⓑ Ⓒ Ⓓ Ⓔ
59. Ⓐ Ⓑ Ⓒ Ⓓ Ⓔ
60. Ⓐ Ⓑ Ⓒ Ⓓ Ⓔ
61. Ⓐ Ⓑ Ⓒ Ⓓ Ⓔ
62. Ⓐ Ⓑ Ⓒ Ⓓ Ⓔ
63. Ⓐ Ⓑ Ⓒ Ⓓ Ⓔ
64. Ⓐ Ⓑ Ⓒ Ⓓ Ⓔ
65. Ⓐ Ⓑ Ⓒ Ⓓ Ⓔ
66. Ⓐ Ⓑ Ⓒ Ⓓ Ⓔ
67. Ⓐ Ⓑ Ⓒ Ⓓ Ⓔ
68. Ⓐ Ⓑ Ⓒ Ⓓ Ⓔ
69. Ⓐ Ⓑ Ⓒ Ⓓ Ⓔ
70. Ⓐ Ⓑ Ⓒ Ⓓ Ⓔ

71. 1000-2199 Apple	71. Ⓐ Ⓑ Ⓒ Ⓓ Ⓔ	80. Clayton	80. Ⓐ Ⓑ Ⓒ Ⓓ Ⓔ
72. 7400-7699 Tripp	72. Ⓐ Ⓑ Ⓒ Ⓓ Ⓔ	81. Bloom	81. Ⓐ Ⓑ Ⓒ Ⓓ Ⓔ
73. 5500-6799 Budd	73. Ⓐ Ⓑ Ⓒ Ⓓ Ⓔ	82. Brayton	82. Ⓐ Ⓑ Ⓒ Ⓓ Ⓔ
74. 7900-8499 Tripp	74. Ⓐ Ⓑ Ⓒ Ⓓ Ⓔ	83. 6800-7199 Budd	83. Ⓐ Ⓑ Ⓒ Ⓓ Ⓔ
75. 5200-5499 Budd	75. Ⓐ Ⓑ Ⓒ Ⓓ Ⓔ	84. 1000-2199 Apple	84. Ⓐ Ⓑ Ⓒ Ⓓ Ⓔ
76. 3200-3499 Apple	76. Ⓐ Ⓑ Ⓒ Ⓓ Ⓔ	85. 6800-7399 Tripp	85. Ⓐ Ⓑ Ⓒ Ⓓ Ⓔ
77. 7700-7799 Tripp	77. Ⓐ Ⓑ Ⓒ Ⓓ Ⓔ	86. 7800-7899 Tripp	86. Ⓐ Ⓑ Ⓒ Ⓓ Ⓔ
78. Silver	78. Ⓐ Ⓑ Ⓒ Ⓓ Ⓔ	87. Superior	87. Ⓐ Ⓑ Ⓒ Ⓓ Ⓔ
79. 2200-2899 Apple	79. Ⓐ Ⓑ Ⓒ Ⓓ Ⓔ	88. Taxter	88. Ⓐ Ⓑ Ⓒ Ⓓ Ⓔ

SET 2

Mark as your answer the letter of the box in which each address appears. Do *not* look back at the address boxes while answering these questions.

1. 7900-8499 Tripp	1. Ⓐ Ⓑ Ⓒ Ⓓ Ⓔ	35. Silver	35. Ⓐ Ⓑ Ⓒ Ⓓ Ⓔ
2. Bloom	2. Ⓐ Ⓑ Ⓒ Ⓓ Ⓔ	36. 2900-3199 Apple	36. Ⓐ Ⓑ Ⓒ Ⓓ Ⓔ
3. Book	3. Ⓐ Ⓑ Ⓒ Ⓓ Ⓔ	37. 5500-6799 Budd	37. Ⓐ Ⓑ Ⓒ Ⓓ Ⓔ
4. 3500-3599 Apple	4. Ⓐ Ⓑ Ⓒ Ⓓ Ⓔ	38. 7700-7799 Tripp	38. Ⓐ Ⓑ Ⓒ Ⓓ Ⓔ
5. 5900-6499 Budd	5. Ⓐ Ⓑ Ⓒ Ⓓ Ⓔ	39. Bloom	39. Ⓐ Ⓑ Ⓒ Ⓓ Ⓔ
6. 7400-7699 Tripp	6. Ⓐ Ⓑ Ⓒ Ⓓ Ⓔ	40. Brayton	40. Ⓐ Ⓑ Ⓒ Ⓓ Ⓔ
7. Miller	7. Ⓐ Ⓑ Ⓒ Ⓓ Ⓔ	41. 7800-7899 Tripp	41. Ⓐ Ⓑ Ⓒ Ⓓ Ⓔ
8. Malter	8. Ⓐ Ⓑ Ⓒ Ⓓ Ⓔ	42. 6800-7199 Budd	42. Ⓐ Ⓑ Ⓒ Ⓓ Ⓔ
9. 1000-2199 Apple	9. Ⓐ Ⓑ Ⓒ Ⓓ Ⓔ	43. 2200-2899 Apple	43. Ⓐ Ⓑ Ⓒ Ⓓ Ⓔ
10. 5500-6799 Budd	10. Ⓐ Ⓑ Ⓒ Ⓓ Ⓔ	44. Taxter	44. Ⓐ Ⓑ Ⓒ Ⓓ Ⓔ
11. 2900-3199 Apple	11. Ⓐ Ⓑ Ⓒ Ⓓ Ⓔ	45. Moore	45. Ⓐ Ⓑ Ⓒ Ⓓ Ⓔ
12. 5200-5499 Budd	12. Ⓐ Ⓑ Ⓒ Ⓓ Ⓔ	46. 5500-6799 Budd	46. Ⓐ Ⓑ Ⓒ Ⓓ Ⓔ
13. Taxter	13. Ⓐ Ⓑ Ⓒ Ⓓ Ⓔ	47. 7900-8499 Tripp	47. Ⓐ Ⓑ Ⓒ Ⓓ Ⓔ
14. Clayton	14. Ⓐ Ⓑ Ⓒ Ⓓ Ⓔ	48. 1000-2199 Apple	48. Ⓐ Ⓑ Ⓒ Ⓓ Ⓔ
15. Silver	15. Ⓐ Ⓑ Ⓒ Ⓓ Ⓔ	49. Malter	49. Ⓐ Ⓑ Ⓒ Ⓓ Ⓔ
16. 3200-3499 Apple	16. Ⓐ Ⓑ Ⓒ Ⓓ Ⓔ	50. 5900-6499 Budd	50. Ⓐ Ⓑ Ⓒ Ⓓ Ⓔ
17. 7900-8499 Tripp	17. Ⓐ Ⓑ Ⓒ Ⓓ Ⓔ	51. 6800-7199 Budd	51. Ⓐ Ⓑ Ⓒ Ⓓ Ⓔ
18. 5500-6799 Budd	18. Ⓐ Ⓑ Ⓒ Ⓓ Ⓔ	52. 7800-7899 Tripp	52. Ⓐ Ⓑ Ⓒ Ⓓ Ⓔ
19. Brayton	19. Ⓐ Ⓑ Ⓒ Ⓓ Ⓔ	53. Silver	53. Ⓐ Ⓑ Ⓒ Ⓓ Ⓔ
20. Bloom	20. Ⓐ Ⓑ Ⓒ Ⓓ Ⓔ	54. Superior	54. Ⓐ Ⓑ Ⓒ Ⓓ Ⓔ
21. 7400-7699 Tripp	21. Ⓐ Ⓑ Ⓒ Ⓓ Ⓔ	55. Malter	55. Ⓐ Ⓑ Ⓒ Ⓓ Ⓔ
22. 3500-3599 Apple	22. Ⓐ Ⓑ Ⓒ Ⓓ Ⓔ	56. 3200-3499 Apple	56. Ⓐ Ⓑ Ⓒ Ⓓ Ⓔ
23. 5200-5499 Budd	23. Ⓐ Ⓑ Ⓒ Ⓓ Ⓔ	57. 2900-3199 Apple	57. Ⓐ Ⓑ Ⓒ Ⓓ Ⓔ
24. Malter	24. Ⓐ Ⓑ Ⓒ Ⓓ Ⓔ	58. 3500-3599 Apple	58. Ⓐ Ⓑ Ⓒ Ⓓ Ⓔ
25. Clayton	25. Ⓐ Ⓑ Ⓒ Ⓓ Ⓔ	59. 7900-8499 Tripp	59. Ⓐ Ⓑ Ⓒ Ⓓ Ⓔ
26. 3200-3499 Apple	26. Ⓐ Ⓑ Ⓒ Ⓓ Ⓔ	60. 5500-6799 Budd	60. Ⓐ Ⓑ Ⓒ Ⓓ Ⓔ
27. 6800-7399 Tripp	27. Ⓐ Ⓑ Ⓒ Ⓓ Ⓔ	61. 6800-7199 Budd	61. Ⓐ Ⓑ Ⓒ Ⓓ Ⓔ
28. 4500-5199 Budd	28. Ⓐ Ⓑ Ⓒ Ⓓ Ⓔ	62. Bloom	62. Ⓐ Ⓑ Ⓒ Ⓓ Ⓔ
29. Book	29. Ⓐ Ⓑ Ⓒ Ⓓ Ⓔ	63. Brayton	63. Ⓐ Ⓑ Ⓒ Ⓓ Ⓔ
30. Superior	30. Ⓐ Ⓑ Ⓒ Ⓓ Ⓔ	64. 2200-2899 Apple	64. Ⓐ Ⓑ Ⓒ Ⓓ Ⓔ
31. 5900-6499 Budd	31. Ⓐ Ⓑ Ⓒ Ⓓ Ⓔ	65. 7400-7699 Tripp	65. Ⓐ Ⓑ Ⓒ Ⓓ Ⓔ
32. 1000-2199 Apple	32. Ⓐ Ⓑ Ⓒ Ⓓ Ⓔ	66. 6800-7399 Tripp	66. Ⓐ Ⓑ Ⓒ Ⓓ Ⓔ
33. 7900-8499 Tripp	33. Ⓐ Ⓑ Ⓒ Ⓓ Ⓔ	67. Clayton	67. Ⓐ Ⓑ Ⓒ Ⓓ Ⓔ
34. Miller	34. Ⓐ Ⓑ Ⓒ Ⓓ Ⓔ	68. 7700-7799 Tripp	68. Ⓐ Ⓑ Ⓒ Ⓓ Ⓔ

69. 5500-6799 Budd	69. Ⓐ Ⓑ Ⓒ Ⓓ Ⓔ	79. 6800-7199 Budd	79. Ⓐ Ⓑ Ⓒ Ⓓ Ⓔ
70. 4500-5199 Budd	70. Ⓐ Ⓑ Ⓒ Ⓓ Ⓔ	80. 2900-3199 Apple	80. Ⓐ Ⓑ Ⓒ Ⓓ Ⓔ
71. Taxter	71. Ⓐ Ⓑ Ⓒ Ⓓ Ⓔ	81. 5900-6499 Budd	81. Ⓐ Ⓑ Ⓒ Ⓓ Ⓔ
72. Moore	72. Ⓐ Ⓑ Ⓒ Ⓓ Ⓔ	82. 7700-7799 Tripp	82. Ⓐ Ⓑ Ⓒ Ⓓ Ⓔ
73. 1000-2199 Apple	73. Ⓐ Ⓑ Ⓒ Ⓓ Ⓔ	83. Taxter	83. Ⓐ Ⓑ Ⓒ Ⓓ Ⓔ
74. 6800-7399 Tripp	74. Ⓐ Ⓑ Ⓒ Ⓓ Ⓔ	84. Moore	84. Ⓐ Ⓑ Ⓒ Ⓓ Ⓔ
75. 5900-6499 Budd	75. Ⓐ Ⓑ Ⓒ Ⓓ Ⓔ	85. Clayton	85. Ⓐ Ⓑ Ⓒ Ⓓ Ⓔ
76. 4500-5199 Budd	76. Ⓐ Ⓑ Ⓒ Ⓓ Ⓔ	86. 3200-3499 Apple	86. Ⓐ Ⓑ Ⓒ Ⓓ Ⓔ
77. 3200-3499 Apple	77. Ⓐ Ⓑ Ⓒ Ⓓ Ⓔ	87. 6800-7399 Tripp	87. Ⓐ Ⓑ Ⓒ Ⓓ Ⓔ
78. 5200-5499 Budd	78. Ⓐ Ⓑ Ⓒ Ⓓ Ⓔ	88. 7800-7899 Tripp	88. Ⓐ Ⓑ Ⓒ Ⓓ Ⓔ

ANSWERS TO PRACTICE EXERCISE 1

SET 1

1. B	12. E	23. C	34. B	45. A	56. C	67. B	78. A
2. D	13. B	24. A	35. D	46. E	57. B	68. D	79. D
3. A	14. B	25. C	36. E	47. A	58. A	69. C	80. E
4. E	15. E	26. B	37. A	48. D	59. A	70. C	81. B
5. C	16. E	27. A	38. D	49. A	60. B	71. B	82. D
6. C	17. A	28. E	39. E	50. B	61. C	72. A	83. B
7. A	18. B	29. A	40. B	51. C	62. D	73. D	84. B
8. E	19. C	30. D	41. C	52. D	63. E	74. B	85. D
9. A	20. D	31. A	42. B	53. E	64. A	75. E	86. E
10. A	21. D	32. C	43. E	54. E	65. E	76. A	87. C
11. D	22. B	33. E	44. C	55. D	66. E	77. C	88. B

SET 2

1. B	12. E	23. E	34. E	45. D	56. A	67. E	78. E
2. B	13. B	24. C	35. A	46. D	57. E	68. C	79. B
3. A	14. E	25. E	36. E	47. B	58. C	69. D	80. E
4. C	15. A	26. A	37. D	48. B	59. B	70. C	81. A
5. A	16. A	27. D	38. C	49. C	60. D	71. B	82. C
6. A	17. B	28. C	39. B	50. A	61. B	72. D	83. B
7. E	18. D	29. A	40. D	51. B	62. B	73. B	84. D
8. C	19. D	30. C	41. E	52. E	63. D	74. D	85. E
9. B	20. B	31. A	42. B	53. A	64. D	75. A	86. A
10. D	21. A	32. B	43. D	54. C	65. A	76. C	87. D
11. E	22. C	33. B	44. B	55. C	66. D	77. A	88. E

Here is another set of boxes for you to try out the techniques you have just learned. Begin by narrowing the memorizing task to the fewest and simplest possible items. Then try to memorize the box in which each item is located. Finally, see how well you can do with identifying the box location of each practice question. Mark your answer by blackening the space that contains the letter of the box in which each address is found. If necessary, you may look at the boxes for the first set of practice questions. Answer the second set of practice questions without looking at the boxes. Once again, take as much time as you need to memorize before you begin answering questions. Work to perfect your technique. Correct answers for these questions are on page 73.

PRACTICE EXERCISE 2

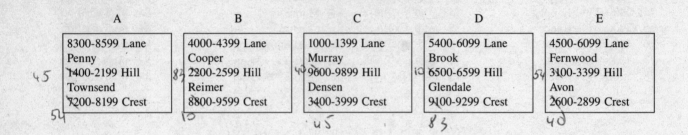

A	B	C	D	E
8300-8599 Lane Penny 1400-2199 Hill Townsend 7200-8199 Crest	4000-4399 Lane Cooper 2200-2599 Hill Reimer 8800-9599 Crest	1000-1399 Lane Murray 9600-9899 Hill Densen 3400-3999 Crest	5400-6099 Lane Brook 6500-6599 Hill Glendale 9100-9299 Crest	4500-6099 Lane Fernwood 3100-3399 Hill Avon 2600-2899 Crest

SET 1

You may refer to the address boxes while answering these questions.

1. 9600-9899 Hill
2. Reimer
3. 2600-2899 Crest
4. 8300-8599 Lane
5. 8800-9599 Crest
6. Densen
7. Avon
8. 6500-6599 Hill
9. 5400-6099 Lane
10. 1400-2199 Hill
11. Glendale
12. Cooper
13. 7200-8199 Crest
14. 4500-6099 Lane
15. 4000-4399 Lane
16. Murray
17. Penny
18. 9100-9299 Crest
19. 2200-2599 Hill
20. 3100-3399 Hill
21. Brook
22. Townsend
23. 1000-1399 Lane
24. 3400-3999 Crest
25. Fernwood
26. 8800-9599 Crest
27. 1400-2199 Hill
28. Glendale
29. 4500-6099 Lane
30. 3400-3999 Crest
31. Avon

1. (A)(B)(C)(D)(E)
2. (A)(B)(C)(D)(E)
3. (A)(B)(C)(D)(E)
4. (A)(B)(C)(D)(E)
5. (A)(B)(C)(D)(E)
6. (A)(B)(C)(D)(E)
7. (A)(B)(C)(D)(E)
8. (A)(B)(C)(D)(E)
9. (A)(B)(C)(D)(E)
10. (A)(B)(C)(D)(E)
11. (A)(B)(C)(D)(E)
12. (A)(B)(C)(D)(E)
13. (A)(B)(C)(D)(E)
14. (A)(B)(C)(D)(E)
15. (A)(B)(C)(D)(E)
16. (A)(B)(C)(D)(E)
17. (A)(B)(C)(D)(E)
18. (A)(B)(C)(D)(E)
19. (A)(B)(C)(D)(E)
20. (A)(B)(C)(D)(E)
21. (A)(B)(C)(D)(E)
22. (A)(B)(C)(D)(E)
23. (A)(B)(C)(D)(E)
24. (A)(B)(C)(D)(E)
25. (A)(B)(C)(D)(E)
26. (A)(B)(C)(D)(E)
27. (A)(B)(C)(D)(E)
28. (A)(B)(C)(D)(E)
29. (A)(B)(C)(D)(E)
30. (A)(B)(C)(D)(E)
31. (A)(B)(C)(D)(E)

32. Densen
33. 2200-2599 Hill
34. 8300-8599 Lane
35. 7200-8199 Crest
36. 4000-4399 Lane
37. Reimer
38. Cooper
39. 6500-6599 Hill
40. 2600-2899 Crest
41. 1000-1399 Lane
42. Townsend
43. Brook
44. 9100-9299 Crest
45. 3100-3399 Hill
46. 4500-6099 Lane
47. Penny
48. Murray
49. 9600-9899 Hill
50. Fernwood
51. 1400-2199 Hill
52. 8800-9599 Crest
53. 4500-6099 Lane
54. Brook
55. 8300-8599 Lane
56. 2600-2899 Crest
57. Fernwood
58. Densen
59. 9600-9899 Hill
60. 8800-9599 Crest
61. 7200-8199 Crest
62. 1400-2199 Hill

32. (A)(B)(C)(D)(E)
33. (A)(B)(C)(D)(E)
34. (A)(B)(C)(D)(E)
35. (A)(B)(C)(D)(E)
36. (A)(B)(C)(D)(E)
37. (A)(B)(C)(D)(E)
38. (A)(B)(C)(D)(E)
39. (A)(B)(C)(D)(E)
40. (A)(B)(C)(D)(E)
41. (A)(B)(C)(D)(E)
42. (A)(B)(C)(D)(E)
43. (A)(B)(C)(D)(E)
44. (A)(B)(C)(D)(E)
45. (A)(B)(C)(D)(E)
46. (A)(B)(C)(D)(E)
47. (A)(B)(C)(D)(E)
48. (A)(B)(C)(D)(E)
49. (A)(B)(C)(D)(E)
50. (A)(B)(C)(D)(E)
51. (A)(B)(C)(D)(E)
52. (A)(B)(C)(D)(E)
53. (A)(B)(C)(D)(E)
54. (A)(B)(C)(D)(E)
55. (A)(B)(C)(D)(E)
56. (A)(B)(C)(D)(E)
57. (A)(B)(C)(D)(E)
58. (A)(B)(C)(D)(E)
59. (A)(B)(C)(D)(E)
60. (A)(B)(C)(D)(E)
61. (A)(B)(C)(D)(E)
62. (A)(B)(C)(D)(E)

63.	Cooper	63. Ⓐ Ⓑ Ⓒ Ⓓ Ⓔ		76.	1000-1399 Lane	76. Ⓐ Ⓑ Ⓒ Ⓓ Ⓔ
64.	Glendale	64. Ⓐ Ⓑ Ⓒ Ⓓ Ⓔ		77.	4000-4399 Lane	77. Ⓐ Ⓑ Ⓒ Ⓓ Ⓔ
65.	Avon	65. Ⓐ Ⓑ Ⓒ Ⓓ Ⓔ		78.	Reimer	78. Ⓐ Ⓑ Ⓒ Ⓓ Ⓔ
66.	3100-3399 Hill	66. Ⓐ Ⓑ Ⓒ Ⓓ Ⓔ		79.	Brook	79. Ⓐ Ⓑ Ⓒ Ⓓ Ⓔ
67.	4500-6099 Lane	67. Ⓐ Ⓑ Ⓒ Ⓓ Ⓔ		80.	3100-3399 Hill	80. Ⓐ Ⓑ Ⓒ Ⓓ Ⓔ
68.	5400-6099 Lane	68. Ⓐ Ⓑ Ⓒ Ⓓ Ⓔ		81.	8300-8599 Lane	81. Ⓐ Ⓑ Ⓒ Ⓓ Ⓔ
69.	2200-2599 Hill	69. Ⓐ Ⓑ Ⓒ Ⓓ Ⓔ		82.	5400-6099 Lane	82. Ⓐ Ⓑ Ⓒ Ⓓ Ⓔ
70.	3400-3999 Crest	70. Ⓐ Ⓑ Ⓒ Ⓓ Ⓔ		83.	Fernwood	83. Ⓐ Ⓑ Ⓒ Ⓓ Ⓔ
71.	Townsend	71. Ⓐ Ⓑ Ⓒ Ⓓ Ⓔ		84.	9600-9899 Hill	84. Ⓐ Ⓑ Ⓒ Ⓓ Ⓔ
72.	Penny	72. Ⓐ Ⓑ Ⓒ Ⓓ Ⓔ		85.	8800-9599 Crest	85. Ⓐ Ⓑ Ⓒ Ⓓ Ⓔ
73.	Murray	73. Ⓐ Ⓑ Ⓒ Ⓓ Ⓔ		86.	2600-2899 Crest	86. Ⓐ Ⓑ Ⓒ Ⓓ Ⓔ
74.	9100-9299 Crest	74. Ⓐ Ⓑ Ⓒ Ⓓ Ⓔ		87.	Brook	87. Ⓐ Ⓑ Ⓒ Ⓓ Ⓔ
75.	6500-6599 Hill	75. Ⓐ Ⓑ Ⓒ Ⓓ Ⓔ		88.	Avon	88. Ⓐ Ⓑ Ⓒ Ⓓ Ⓔ

SET 2

Do *not* look back at the address boxes while answering these questions.

#	Address		#	Address
1.	1400-2199 Hill		45.	Densen
2.	9600-9899 Hill		46.	2200-2599 Hill
3.	3400-3999 Crest		47.	7200-8199 Crest
4.	4500-6099 Lane		48.	8800-9599 Crest
5.	Reimer		49.	Murray
6.	Fernwood		50.	Townsend
7.	6500-6599 Hill		51.	4500-6099 Lane
8.	5400-6099 Lane		52.	6500-6599 Hill
9.	2600-2899 Crest		53.	4000-4399 Lane
10.	9100-9299 Crest		54.	7200-8199 Crest
11.	Avon		55.	8300-8599 Lane
12.	Densen		56.	3400-3999 Crest
13.	Penny		57.	Densen
14.	4000-4399 Lane		58.	Glendale
15.	7200-8199 Crest		59.	Fernwood
16.	2200-2599 Hill		60.	2200-2599 Hill
17.	Townsend		61.	9600-9899 Hill
18.	Murray		62.	2600-2899 Crest
19.	8300-8599 Lane		63.	8300-8599 Lane
20.	1000-1399 Lane		64.	7200-8199 Crest
21.	Cooper		65.	4500-6099 Lane
22.	3100-3399 Hill		66.	Avon
23.	8800-9599 Crest		67.	Penny
24.	Glendale		68.	3100-3399 Hill
25.	Brook		69.	5400-6099 Lane
26.	6500-6599 Hill		70.	8800-9599 Crest
27.	2600-2899 Crest		71.	Murray
28.	4000-4399 Lane		72.	1400-2199 Hill
29.	3400-3999 Crest		73.	1000-1399 Lane
30.	Cooper		74.	9100-9299 Crest
31.	Glendale		75.	3400-3999 Crest
32.	4500-6099 Lane		76.	Townsend
33.	1400-2199 Hill		77.	Cooper
34.	1000-1399 Lane		78.	6500-6599 Hill
35.	Avon		79.	4000-4399 Lane
36.	Reimer		80.	Reimer
37.	8300-8599 Lane		81.	Brook
38.	9600-9899 Hill		82.	3100-3399 Hill
39.	9100-9299 Crest		83.	8800-9599 Crest
40.	5400-6099 Lane		84.	5400-6099 Lane
41.	3100-3399 Hill		85.	6500-6599 Hill
42.	Fernwood		86.	9100-9299 Crest
43.	Brook		87.	8300-8599 Lane
44.	Penny		88.	Fernwood

Answer bubbles (A B C D E) for items 1–44 and 45–88.

ANSWERS TO PRACTICE EXERCISE 2

SET 1

1. C	12. B	23. C	34. A	45. E	56. E	67. E	78. B
2. B	13. A	24. C	35. A	46. E	57. E	68. D	79. D
3. E	14. E	25. E	36. B	47. A	58. C	69. B	80. E
4. A	15. B	26. B	37. B	48. C	59. C	70. C	81. A
5. B	16. C	27. A	38. B	49. C	60. B	71. A	82. D
6. C	17. A	28. D	39. D	50. E	61. A	72. A	83. E
7. E	18. D	29. E	40. E	51. A	62. A	73. C	84. C
8. D	19. B	30. C	41. C	52. B	63. B	74. D	85. B
9. D	20. E	31. E	42. A	53. E	64. D	75. D	86. E
10. A	21. D	32. C	43. D	54. D	65. E	76. C	87. D
11. D	22. A	33. B	44. D	55. A	66. E	77. B	88. E

SET 2

1. A	12. C	23. B	34. C	45. C	56. C	67. A	78. D
2. C	13. A	24. D	35. E	46. B	57. C	68. E	79. B
3. C	14. B	25. D	36. B	47. A	58. D	69. D	80. B
4. E	15. A	26. D	37. A	48. B	59. E	70. B	81. D
5. B	16. B	27. E	38. C	49. C	60. B	71. C	82. E
6. E	17. A	28. B	39. D	50. A	61. C	72. A	83. B
7. D	18. C	29. C	40. D	51. E	62. E	73. C	84. D
8. D	19. A	30. B	41. E	52. D	63. A	74. D	85. D
9. E	20. C	31. D	42. E	53. B	64. A	75. C	86. D
10. D	21. B	32. E	43. D	54. A	65. E	76. A	87. A
11. E	22. E	33. A	44. A	55. A	66. E	77. B	88. E

As you go through the model exams in this book, remember all the tricks and techniques you have learned, and apply them. Also, work to develop your own memory scheme. Try to leave enough time between model exams so that your memory of a previous set of boxes does not interfere with the task at hand. Come back to this chapter to brush up whenever necessary. Reread the chapter the day before your exam, but do NOT try any practice exercises and do NOT do a model exam that day. You want your mind to be like a clean slate in order to learn the sorting scheme on your actual Distribution Clerk, Machine, Exam.

HOW TO ANSWER ADDRESS CHECKING QUESTIONS

The Address Checking Test is not difficult, but it requires great speed and it carries a heavy penalty for inaccuracy. You must learn to spot differences very quickly and to make firm, fast decisions about addresses that are exactly alike. This chapter will help you to develop a system for comparing addresses. Once you have a system, practice with that system will help you to build up speed.

The directions make it very clear that if there is *any difference at all* between the two addresses they are to be marked as different. This means that once you spot a difference, mark the answer as Ⓓ and go immediately to the next question. There is no point in looking at the remainder of an address once you have found a difference. You will be amazed at how much time you can save by not reading the whole of every address.

READ EXACTLY WHAT YOU SEE

The best way to read addresses being compared is to read exactly what you see and to sound out words by syllables. For example:

Ⅰf you see "St," read "es tee" not "street."
Ⅰf you see "NH," read "en aitch" not "New Hampshire."
Ⅰf you see "1035," read "one oh three five" not "one thousand thirty-five."
Read "sassafrass" as "sas-sa-frass."

Psychologists have discovered that the human mind always tries to complete a figure. If you read "Pky" as "Parkway," you will probably read "Pkwy" as "Parkway," and will never notice the difference. You mind will complete the word without allowing you to focus on the letters. If, however, you read the abbreviation as an abbreviation, you will notice that the two abbreviations are different. If you read "Kansas City MO" as "Kansas City Missouri," you are unlikely to catch the difference with "Kansas City MD." But if you read "Kansas City em oh," you will readily pick up on "Kansas City em dee."

USE YOUR HANDS

Since speed is so important in answering Address Checking questions and since it is so easy to lose your place, you must use both hands during your work on this part. In the hand with which you write, hold your pencil poised at the number on your answer sheet. Run the index finger of your other hand under the addresses being compared. The finger will help you to focus on one line at a time, will keep your eyes from jumping up or down a line. By holding your place on both question and answer sheet, you are less likely to skip a question or an answer space.

One effective way to tackle address checking questions quickly and accurately is to look for differences in only one area at a time. Every address consists of both numbers and words. If you narrow your focus to compare only the numbers or only the words, you are more likely to notice differences and less apt to see what you expect to see rather than what is actually printed on the page.

LOOK FOR DIFFERENCES IN NUMBERS

Look first at the numbers. Read the number in the left column, then skip immediately to the number in the right column. Do the two numbers contain the same number of digits?

A difference of this type should be easy to see. In questions that follow, blacken Ⓐ if the two numbers are exactly alike and Ⓓ if the numbers are different in any way.

IS THE NUMBER OF DIGITS THE SAME?

1 . . . 2003	2003	1.	ⒶⒹ
2 . . . 75864	75864	2.	ⒶⒹ
3 . . . 7300	730	3.	ⒶⒹ
4 . . . 50106	5016	4.	ⒶⒹ
5 . . . 2184	2184	5.	ⒶⒹ

Answers: 1. A   2. A   3. D   4. D   5. A

Did you spot the differences? Train your eye to count digits rapidly.

IS THE ORDER OF DIGITS THE SAME?

1 . . . 7516	7561	1.	ⒶⒹ
2 . . . 80302	80302	2.	ⒶⒹ
3 . . . 19832	18932	3.	ⒶⒹ
4 . . . 6186	6186	4.	ⒶⒹ
5 . . . 54601	54610	5.	ⒶⒹ

Answers: 1. D   2. A   3. D   4. A   5. D

Did you get these all correct? If not, look again right now. See where you made your mistakes.

IS THERE A SUBSTITUTION OF ONE DIGIT FOR ANOTHER?

1 . . . 16830	16830	1.	ⒶⒹ
2 . . . 94936	94636	2.	ⒶⒹ
3 . . . 3287	3285	3.	ⒶⒹ
4 . . . 54216	54216	4.	ⒶⒹ
5 . . . 32341	33341	5.	ⒶⒹ

Answers: 1. A   2. D   3. D   4. A   5. D

Did you catch all the differences? Were you able to mark Ⓐ with confidence when there was no difference?

PRACTICE FINDING DIFFERENCES IN NUMBERS

In the following set of practice questions, all differences are in the numbers. Work quickly, focusing only on the numbers. You may find any of the three varieties of differences just described.

1 . . . 3685 Brite Ave	3865 Brite Ave.	1.	Ⓐ Ⓓ
2 . . . Ware MA 08215	Ware MA 08215	2.	Ⓐ Ⓓ
3 . . . 4001 Webster Rd	401 Webster Rd	3.	Ⓐ Ⓓ
4 . . . 9789 Bell Rd	9786 Bell Rd	4.	Ⓐ Ⓓ
5 . . . Scarsdale NY 10583	Scarsdale NY 10583	5.	Ⓐ Ⓓ
6 . . . 1482 Grand Blvd	1482 Grand Blvd	6.	Ⓐ Ⓓ
7 . . . Milwaukee WI 53202	Milwaukee WI 52302	7.	Ⓐ Ⓓ
8 . . . 3542 W 48th St	3542 W 84th St	8.	Ⓐ Ⓓ
9 . . . 9461 Hansen St	9461 Hansen St	9.	Ⓐ Ⓓ
10 . . . 32322 Florence Pkwy	3232 Florence Pkwy	10.	Ⓐ Ⓓ
11 . . . Portland OR 97208	Portland OR 99208	11.	Ⓐ Ⓓ
12 . . . 3999 Thompson Dr	3999 Thompson Dr	12.	Ⓐ Ⓓ
13 . . . 1672 Sutton Pl	1972 Sutton Pl	13.	Ⓐ Ⓓ
14 . . . Omaha NE 68127	Omaha NE 68127	14.	Ⓐ Ⓓ
15 . . . 1473 S 96th St	1743 S 96th St	15.	Ⓐ Ⓓ
16 . . . 3425 Geary St	3425 Geary St	16.	Ⓐ Ⓓ
17 . . . Dallas TX 75234	Dallas TX 75234	17.	Ⓐ Ⓓ
18 . . . 4094 Horchow Rd	4904 Horchow Rd	18.	Ⓐ Ⓓ
19 . . . San Francisco CA 94108	San Francisco CA 94108	19.	Ⓐ Ⓓ
20 . . . 1410 Broadway	141 Broadway	20.	Ⓐ Ⓓ
21 . . . 424 Fifth Ave	4240 Fifth Ave	21.	Ⓐ Ⓓ
22 . . . Westport CT 06880	Westport CT 06880	22.	Ⓐ Ⓓ
23 . . . 1932 Wilton Rd	1923 Wilton Rd	23.	Ⓐ Ⓓ
24 . . . 2052 Victoria Sta	2502 Victoria Sta	24.	Ⓐ Ⓓ
25 . . . 1982 Carlton Pl	1982 Carlton Pl	25.	Ⓐ Ⓓ

Answers:

1. D	6. A	11. D	16. A	21. D
2. A	7. D	12. A	17. A	22. A
3. D	8. D	13. D	18. D	23. D
4. D	9. A	14. A	19. A	24. D
5. A	10. D	15. D	20. D	25. A

Were you able to focus on the numbers? Were you able to spot the differences quickly? Could you make a rapid decision when there was no difference? If you got any of these questions wrong, look now to see why.

If you find a difference between the two numbers, mark Ⓓ and go on to the next question. Do not bother to look at the words in any pair of addresses in which you find a difference between the numbers.

If, while concentrating on numbers, you happen to catch a difference in spelling or abbreviations, by all means mark Ⓓ and go on to the next question. In other words, if you spot *any* difference between the addresses, even while you are looking for a specific type of difference, mark Ⓓ at once. A system may be useful, but do not stick to it slavishly when an answer is obvious.

LOOK FOR DIFFERENCES IN ABBREVIATIONS

When you are satisfied that the numbers are alike, and if no other difference has "struck you between the eyes," turn your attention to the abbreviations. Keep alert for differences such as:

Rd	Dr
Wy	Way
NH	NM

In comparing numbers, you began by looking at the numbers in the left column, then moved your eyes to focus on the right column. If you found a difference, you marked Ⓓ on your answer sheet, moved pencil and hand down one line and began again with the numbers of the next question. If you found no difference between the numbers, your eyes should have stopped at the right column. Look now at the abbreviations in the right column, then move your eyes to the left column to see if there are any differences. A difference is a difference, left to right or right to left, so do not waste time going back to the left column when you are focusing on the right. Try the next group of practice questions holding your place with the pencil and finger and comparing the first question from left to right, the next question from right to left, and so on down the list. Remember to sound out the abbreviations exactly as you see them.

1	3238 NW 3rd St	3238 NE 3rd St	1. Ⓐ Ⓓ
2	7865 Harkness Blvd	7865 Harkness Blvd	2. Ⓐ Ⓓ
3	Seattle WA 98102	Seattle WY 98102	3. Ⓐ Ⓓ
4	342 Madison Ave	342 Madison St	4. Ⓐ Ⓓ
5	723 Broadway E	723 Broadway E	5. Ⓐ Ⓓ
6	4731 W 88th Dr	4731 W 88th Rd	6. Ⓐ Ⓓ
7	Boiceville NY 12412	Boiceville NY 12412	7. Ⓐ Ⓓ
8	9021 Rodeo Dr	9021 Rodeo St	8. Ⓐ Ⓓ
9	2093 Post St	2093 Post Rd	9. Ⓐ Ⓓ
10	New Orleans LA 70153	New Orleans LA 70153	10. Ⓐ Ⓓ
11	5332 SW Bombay St	5332 SW Bombay St	11. Ⓐ Ⓓ
12	416 Wellington Pkwy	416 Wellington Hwy	12. Ⓐ Ⓓ
13	2096 Garden Ln	2096 Garden Wy	13. Ⓐ Ⓓ
14	3220 W Grant Ave	3220 W Grant Ave	14. Ⓐ Ⓓ
15	Charlotte VT 05445	Charlotte VA 05445	15. Ⓐ Ⓓ
16	4415 Oriental Blvd	4415 Oriental Blvd	16. Ⓐ Ⓓ
17	6876 Raffles Rd	6876 Raffles Dr	17. Ⓐ Ⓓ
18	891 S Hotel Hwy	891 E Hotel Hwy	18. Ⓐ Ⓓ
19	9500 London Br	9500 London Br	19. Ⓐ Ⓓ
20	24A Motcomb St	24A Motcomb St	20. Ⓐ Ⓓ
21	801 S Erleigh Ln	801 S Erleigh Dr	21. Ⓐ Ⓓ
22	839 Casco St	839 Casco St	22. Ⓐ Ⓓ
23	Freeport ME 04033	Freeport NE 04033	23. Ⓐ Ⓓ
24	3535 Island Ave	3535 Island Rd	24. Ⓐ Ⓓ
25	2186 Missouri Ave NE	2186 Missouri Ave NW	25. Ⓐ Ⓓ

Answers:

1. D	6. D	11. A	16. A	21. D
2. A	7. A	12. D	17. D	22. A
3. D	8. D	13. D	18. D	23. D
4. D	9. D	14. A	19. A	24. D
5. A	10. A	15. D	20. A	25. D

LOOK FOR DIFFERENCES IN STREET OR CITY NAMES

If, after you have compared the numbers and the abbreviations, you have still not spotted any differences, you must look at the main words of the address. First of all, are the words in the two addresses really the same words? Look hard to determine whether the words are alike or different. The determination is, of course, made on the basis of the letters. Try not to notice the words themselves. Some streets and towns have very odd names. Do not allow yourself to notice or to be amused. You cannot spare the time.

1 . . . Brookfield	Brookville	1. Ⓐ Ⓓ
2 . . . Wayland	Wayland	2. Ⓐ Ⓓ
3 . . . Ferncliff	Farmcliff	3. Ⓐ Ⓓ
4 . . . Spring	Springs	4. Ⓐ Ⓓ
5 . . . New City	New City	5. Ⓐ Ⓓ

Answers: 1. D   2. A   3. D   4. D   5. A

Sound out the words by syllables or spell them out. Is the spelling exactly the same? Are the same letters doubled? Are two letters reversed?

1 . . . Beech	Beach	1. Ⓐ Ⓓ
2 . . . Torrington	Torington	2. Ⓐ Ⓓ
3 . . . Brayton	Brayton	3. Ⓐ Ⓓ
4 . . . Collegiate	Collegaite	4. Ⓐ Ⓓ
5 . . . Weston	Wetson	5. Ⓐ Ⓓ

Answers: 1. D   2. D   3. A   4. D   5. D

PRACTICE FINDING DIFFERENCES IN NAMES

Now try some practice questions in which differences may be found between the main words. Remember, you can save precious time by scanning for differences first from the left column to the right column and then from the right column to the left.

1 . . . 5254 Shaeffer St	5254 Schaeffer St	1. Ⓐ Ⓓ
2 . . . 8003 Sheraton Wy	8003 Sheraton Wy	2. Ⓐ Ⓓ
3 . . . 1937 Cordelia Terr	1937 Cordelia Terr	3. Ⓐ Ⓓ
4 . . 392 Kauai Hwy	392 Kauaui Hwy	4. Ⓐ Ⓓ
5 . . . 7500 Preferred Rd	7500 Preffered Rd	5. Ⓐ Ⓓ
6 . . . Natick MA 01760	Natick MA 01760	6. Ⓐ Ⓓ
7 . . . 727 Stockbridge Rd	727 Stockbridge Rd	7. Ⓐ Ⓓ
8 . . . 294 Friend St	294 Freind St	8. Ⓐ Ⓓ
9 . . . 4550 Munching St	4550 Munchkin St	9. Ⓐ Ⓓ
10 . . . Gt Barrington MA 01230	Gt Barnington MA 01230	10. Ⓐ Ⓓ
11 . . . 7070 Baltic Wy	7070 Baltic Wy	11. Ⓐ Ⓓ
12 . . . 889 Safari St	889 Seafari St	12. Ⓐ Ⓓ
13 . . . Irvington NY 10533	Irvington NY 10533	13. Ⓐ Ⓓ
14 . . . 475 Ghirardelli Sq	475 Ghirardelli Sq	14. Ⓐ Ⓓ
15 . . . Sea Island GA 31561	Sea Inland GA 31561	15. Ⓐ Ⓓ
16 . . . 8486 Massachusetts Tpke	8486 Massachusetts Tpke	16. Ⓐ Ⓓ

17 . . . 6874 Cloister St	6874 Cloister St	17. Ⓐ Ⓓ
18 . . . 292 Westminster MI	292 Westminster MI	18. Ⓐ Ⓓ
19 . . . Providence RI 02903	Providence RI 02903	19. Ⓐ Ⓓ
20 . . . Arundel ME 04046	Anurdel ME 04046	20. Ⓐ Ⓓ
21 . . . 1000 Cadiz St	1000 Cadiz St	21. Ⓐ Ⓓ
22 . . . 821 Calphalon Wy	821 Caphalon Wy	22. Ⓐ Ⓓ
23 . . . Oakland CA 94604	Oakland CA 94604	23. Ⓐ Ⓓ
24 . . . 371 Himalaya St	371 Himalaya St	24. Ⓐ Ⓓ
25 . . . 1053 Columbus Cir	1053 Columbia Cir	25. Ⓐ Ⓓ

Answers:

1. D	6. A	11. A	16. A	21. A
2. A	7. A	12. D	17. A	22. D
3. A	8. D	13. A	18. D	23. A
4. D	9. D	14. A	19. A	24. A
5. D	10. D	15. D	20. D	25. D

Check your answers. Then look at the questions to see where you made your mistakes. If your mistakes fall into any sort of pattern—missing letter reversals, doubling of letters or real differences between words, or, conversely, if you often think that you have noticed a difference where there really is none—guard against those errors in the future. If your mistakes seem to be random, then practice and care should help you to improve.

Comparing first the numbers, then the little words and abbreviations, and finally the main words must be done in a flash. If you have gone through this process and have spotted no errors, mark Ⓐ on your answer sheet and go on to the next question. In order to complete the Address Checking Test, you can allow only *four seconds* for each question. That means you cannot afford to reread a single address. Make your decision based on your first check and go right on.

Keeping these suggestions in mind, try the practice questions that follow. In these questions, you may find differences between numbers, abbreviations or main words, or you may find no difference at all. Work quickly, but do not time yourself on these practice questions.

ADDRESS CHECKING PRACTICE TEST

1 . . . 8690 W 134 St	8960 W 143th St	1. Ⓐ Ⓓ
2 . . . 1912 Berkshire Wy	1912 Berkshire Wy	2. Ⓐ Ⓓ
3 . . . 5331 W Professor St	5331 W Proffesor St	3. Ⓐ Ⓓ
4 . . . Philadelphia PA 19124	Philadephia PN 19124	4. Ⓐ Ⓓ
5 . . . 7450 Saguenay St	7450 Saguenay St	5. Ⓐ Ⓓ
6 . . . 8650 Christy St	8650 Christey St	6. Ⓐ Ⓓ
7 . . . Lumberville PA 18933	Lumberville PA 19833	7. Ⓐ Ⓓ
8 . . . 114 Alabama Ave NW	114 Alabama Rd NW	8. Ⓐ Ⓓ
9 . . . 1756 Waterford St	1756 Waterville St	9. Ⓐ Ⓓ
10 . . . 2214 Wister Wy	2214 Wister Wy	10. Ⓐ Ⓓ
11 . . . 2974 Repplier Rd	2974 Repplier Dr	11. Ⓐ Ⓓ
12 . . . Essex CT 06426	Essex CT 06426	12. Ⓐ Ⓓ
13 . . . 7676 N Bourbon St	7616 N Bourbon St	13. Ⓐ Ⓓ
14 . . . 2762 Rosengarten Wy	2762 Rosengarden Wy	14. Ⓐ Ⓓ
15 . . . 239 Windell Ave	239 Windell Ave	15. Ⓐ Ⓓ
16 . . . 4667 Edgeworth Rd	4677 Edgeworth Rd	16. Ⓐ Ⓓ
17 . . . 2661 Kennel St SE	2661 Kennel St SW	17. Ⓐ Ⓓ

18 . . . Alamo TX 78516	Alamo TX 78516	18. Ⓐ Ⓓ
19 . . . 3709 Columbine St	3709 Columbine St	19. Ⓐ Ⓓ
20 . . . 9699 W 14th St	9699 W 14th Rd	20. Ⓐ Ⓓ
21 . . . 2207 Markland Ave	2207 Markham Ave	21. Ⓐ Ⓓ
22 . . . Los Angeles Ca 90013	Los Angeles CA 90018	22. Ⓐ Ⓓ
23 . . . 4608 N Warnock St	4806 N Warnock St	23. Ⓐ Ⓓ
24 . . . 7718 S Summer St	7718 S Sumner St	24. Ⓐ Ⓓ
25 . . . New York, NY 10016	New York, NY 10016	25. Ⓐ Ⓓ
26 . . . 4514 Ft Hamilton Pk	4514 Ft Hamilton Pk	26. Ⓐ Ⓓ
27 . . . 5701 Kosciusko St	5701 Koscusko St	27. Ⓐ Ⓓ
28 . . . 5422 Evergreen St	4522 Evergreen St	28. Ⓐ Ⓓ
29 . . . Gainsville FL 32611	Gainsville FL 32611	29. Ⓐ Ⓓ
30 . . . 5018 Church St	5018 Church Ave	30. Ⓐ Ⓓ
31 . . . 1079 N Blake St	1097 N Blake St	31. Ⓐ Ⓓ
32 . . . 8072 W 20th Rd	8072 W 20th Dr	32. Ⓐ Ⓓ
33 . . . Onoro ME 04473	Orono ME 04473	33. Ⓐ Ⓓ
34 . . . 2175 Kimbell Rd	2175 Kimball Rd	34. Ⓐ Ⓓ
35 . . . 1243 Mermaid St	1243 Mermaid St	35. Ⓐ Ⓓ
36 . . . 4904 SW 134th St	4904 SW 134th St	36. Ⓐ Ⓓ
37 . . . 1094 Hancock St	1049 Hancock St	37. Ⓐ Ⓓ
38 . . . Des Moines IA 50311	Des Moines IA 50311	38. Ⓐ Ⓓ
39 . . . 4832 S Rinaldi Rd	4832 S Rinaldo Rd	39. Ⓐ Ⓓ
40 . . . 2015 Dorchester Rd	2015 Dorchester Rd	40. Ⓐ Ⓓ
41 . . . 5216 Woodbine St	5216 Woodburn St	41. Ⓐ Ⓓ
42 . . . Boulder CO 80302	Boulder CA 80302	42. Ⓐ Ⓓ
43 . . . 4739 N Marion St	479 N Marion St	43. Ⓐ Ⓓ
44 . . . 3720 Nautilus Wy	3720 Nautilus Dr	44. Ⓐ Ⓓ
45 . . . 3636 Gramercy Pk	3636 Gramercy Pk	45. Ⓐ Ⓓ
46 . . . 757 Johnson Ave	757 Johnston Ave	46. Ⓐ Ⓓ
47 . . . 3045 Brighton 12th St	3054 Brighton 12th St	47. Ⓐ Ⓓ
48 . . . 237 Ovington Ave	237 Ovington Ave	48. Ⓐ Ⓓ
49 . . . Kalamazoo MI 49007	Kalamazoo MI 49007	49. Ⓐ Ⓓ
50 . . . Missoula MT 59812	Missoula MS 59812	50. Ⓐ Ⓓ
51 . . . Stillwater OK 74704	Stillwater OK 47404	51. Ⓐ Ⓓ
52 . . . 4746 Empire Blvd	4746 Empire Bldg	52. Ⓐ Ⓓ
53 . . . 6321 St Johns Pl	6321 St Johns Pl	53. Ⓐ Ⓓ
54 . . . 2242 Vanderbilt Ave	2242 Vanderbilt Ave	54. Ⓐ Ⓓ
55 . . . 542 Ditmas Blvd	542 Ditmars Blvd	55. Ⓐ Ⓓ
56 . . . 4603 W Argyle Rd	4603 W Argyle Rd	56. Ⓐ Ⓓ
57 . . . 653 Knickerbocker Ave NE	653 Knickerbocker Ave NE	57. Ⓐ Ⓓ
58 . . . 3651 Midwood Terr	3651 Midwood Terr	58. Ⓐ Ⓓ
59 . . . Chapel Hill NC 27514	Chaple Hill NC 27514	59. Ⓐ Ⓓ
60 . . . 3217 Vernon Pl NW	3217 Vernon Dr NW	60. Ⓐ Ⓓ

61 . . . 1094 Rednor Pkwy	1049 Rednor Pkwy	61. Ⓐ Ⓓ
62 . . . 986 S Doughty Blvd	986 S Douty Blvd	62. Ⓐ Ⓓ
63 . . . Lincoln NE 68508	Lincoln NE 65808	63. Ⓐ Ⓓ
64 . . . 1517 LaSalle Ave	1517 LaSalle Ave	64. Ⓐ Ⓓ
65 . . . 3857 S Morris St	3857 S Morriss St	65. Ⓐ Ⓓ
66 . . . 6104 Saunders Expy	614 Saunders Expy	66. Ⓐ Ⓓ
67 . . . 2541 Appleton St	2541 Appleton Rd	67. Ⓐ Ⓓ
68 . . . Washington DC 20052	Washington DC 20052	68. Ⓐ Ⓓ
69 . . . 6439 Kessler Blvd S	6439 Kessler Blvd S	69. Ⓐ Ⓓ
70 . . . 4786 Catalina Dr	4786 Catalana Dr	70. Ⓐ Ⓓ
71 . . . 132 E Hampton Pkwy	1322 Hampton Pkwy	71. Ⓐ Ⓓ
72 . . . 1066 Goethe Sq S	1066 Geothe Sq S	72. Ⓐ Ⓓ
73 . . . 1118 Jerriman Wy	1218 Jerriman Wy	73. Ⓐ Ⓓ
74 . . . 5798 Gd Central Pkwy	5798 Gd Central Pkwy	74. Ⓐ Ⓓ
75 . . . Delaware OH 43015	Delaware OK 43015	75. Ⓐ Ⓓ
76 . . . Corvallis OR 97331	Corvallis OR 97331	76. Ⓐ Ⓓ
77 . . . 4231 Keating Ave N	4231 Keating Av N	77. Ⓐ Ⓓ
78 . . . 5689 Central Pk Pl	5869 Central Pk Pl	78. Ⓐ Ⓓ
79 . . . 1108 Lyndhurst Dr	1108 Lyndhurst Dr	79. Ⓐ Ⓓ
80 . . . 842 Chambers Ct	842 Chamber Ct	80. Ⓐ Ⓓ
81 . . . Athens OH 45701	Athens GA 45701	81. Ⓐ Ⓓ
82 . . . Tulsa OK 74171	Tulsa OK 71471	82. Ⓐ Ⓓ
83 . . . 6892 Beech Grove Ave	6892 Beech Grove Ave	83. Ⓐ Ⓓ
84 . . . 2939 E Division St	2939 W Division St	84. Ⓐ Ⓓ
85 . . . 1554 Pitkin Ave	1554 Pitkin Ave	85. Ⓐ Ⓓ
86 . . . 905 St Edwards Plz	950 St Edwards Plz	86. Ⓐ Ⓓ
87 . . . 1906 W 152nd St	1906 W 152nd St	87. Ⓐ Ⓓ
88 . . . 3466 Glenmore Ave	3466 Glenville Ave	88. Ⓐ Ⓓ
89 . . . Middlebury VT 05753	Middlebery VT 05753	89. Ⓐ Ⓓ
90 . . . Evanston IL 60201	Evanston IN 60201	90. Ⓐ Ⓓ
91 . . . 9401 W McDonald Ave	9401 W MacDonald Ave	91. Ⓐ Ⓓ
92 . . . 5527 Albermarle Rd	5527 Albermarle Rd	92. Ⓐ Ⓓ
93 . . . 9055 Carter Dr	9055 Carter Rd	93. Ⓐ Ⓓ
94 . . . Greenvale NY 11548	Greenvale NY 11458	94. Ⓐ Ⓓ
95 . . . 1149 Cherry Gr S	1149 Cherry Gr S	95. Ⓐ Ⓓ

ANSWERS TO PRACTICE TEST

1. D	13. D	25. A	37. D	49. A	61. D	73. D	85. A
2. A	14. D	26. A	38. A	50. D	62. D	74. A	86. D
3. D	15. A	27. D	39. D	51. D	63. D	75. D	87. A
4. D	16. D	28. D	40. A	52. D	64. A	76. A	88. D
5. A	17. D	29. A	41. D	53. A	65. D	77. D	89. D
6. D	18. A	30. D	42. D	54. A	66. D	78. D	90. D
7. D	19. A	31. D	43. D	55. D	67. D	79. A	91. D
8. D	20. D	32. D	44. D	56. A	68. A	80. D	92. A
9. D	21. D	33. D	45. A	57. A	69. A	81. D	93. D
10. A	22. D	34. D	46. D	58. A	70. D	82. D	94. D
11. D	23. D	35. A	47. D	59. D	71. D	83. A	95. A
12. A	24. D	36. A	48. A	60. D	72. D	84. D	

Use the chart below to analyze your errors on the Practice Test.

ANALYSIS OF DIFFERENCES

Type of Difference	Question Numbers	Number of Questions You Missed
Difference in NUMBERS	1, 7, 13, 16, 22, 23, 28, 31, 37, 43, 47, 51, 61, 63, 66, 71, 73, 78, 82, 86, 94	
Difference in ABBREVIATIONS	4, 8, 11, 17, 20, 22, 30, 32, 42, 44, 50, 52, 60, 67, 75, 77, 81, 84, 90, 93	
Difference in NAMES	3, 6, 9, 14, 21, 24, 27, 33, 34, 39, 41, 46, 55, 59, 62, 65, 70, 80, 88, 89, 91.	
No Difference	2, 5, 10, 12, 15, 18, 19, 25, 26, 29, 35, 36, 38, 40, 45, 48, 49, 53, 54, 56, 57, 58, 64, 68, 69, 72, 74, 76, 79, 83, 85, 87, 92, 95	

The Model Exams that follow will offer you plenty of practice with Address Checking questions. Flip back to this chapter between Model Exams as you work through the book. Reread the chapter the day before your exam for a quick refresher.

REMEMBER: Look first for differences between numbers.

Next, look at the abbreviations and little words.

Read what is written, as it is written.

Finally, sound out or spell out the main words.

When you find any difference, mark Ⓓ and go immediately to the next question.

If you find no difference, do not linger. Mark Ⓐ and move right on to the next question.

Do NOT read the whole address as a unit.

PART III

Seven Model Exams

ANSWER SHEET
SECOND MODEL EXAM

Tear out this Answer Sheet and use it to mark your answers for the exam that follows.

PART A—NUMBER SERIES

1. Ⓐ Ⓑ Ⓒ Ⓓ Ⓔ	6. Ⓐ Ⓑ Ⓒ Ⓓ Ⓔ	11. Ⓐ Ⓑ Ⓒ Ⓓ Ⓔ	16. Ⓐ Ⓑ Ⓒ Ⓓ Ⓔ	21. Ⓐ Ⓑ Ⓒ Ⓓ Ⓔ
2. Ⓐ Ⓑ Ⓒ Ⓓ Ⓔ	7. Ⓐ Ⓑ Ⓒ Ⓓ Ⓔ	12. Ⓐ Ⓑ Ⓒ Ⓓ Ⓔ	17. Ⓐ Ⓑ Ⓒ Ⓓ Ⓔ	22. Ⓐ Ⓑ Ⓒ Ⓓ Ⓔ
3. Ⓐ Ⓑ Ⓒ Ⓓ Ⓔ	8. Ⓐ Ⓑ Ⓒ Ⓓ Ⓔ	13. Ⓐ Ⓑ Ⓒ Ⓓ Ⓔ	18. Ⓐ Ⓑ Ⓒ Ⓓ Ⓔ	23. Ⓐ Ⓑ Ⓒ Ⓓ Ⓔ
4. Ⓐ Ⓑ Ⓒ Ⓓ Ⓔ	9. Ⓐ Ⓑ Ⓒ Ⓓ Ⓔ	14. Ⓐ Ⓑ Ⓒ Ⓓ Ⓔ	19. Ⓐ Ⓑ Ⓒ Ⓓ Ⓔ	24. Ⓐ Ⓑ Ⓒ Ⓓ Ⓔ
5. Ⓐ Ⓑ Ⓒ Ⓓ Ⓔ	10. Ⓐ Ⓑ Ⓒ Ⓓ Ⓔ	15. Ⓐ Ⓑ Ⓒ Ⓓ Ⓔ	20. Ⓐ Ⓑ Ⓒ Ⓓ Ⓔ	

PART B—ADDRESS CODING

1. Ⓐ Ⓑ Ⓒ Ⓓ Ⓔ	19. Ⓐ Ⓑ Ⓒ Ⓓ Ⓔ	37. Ⓐ Ⓑ Ⓒ Ⓓ Ⓔ	55. Ⓐ Ⓑ Ⓒ Ⓓ Ⓔ	73. Ⓐ Ⓑ Ⓒ Ⓓ Ⓔ
2. Ⓐ Ⓑ Ⓒ Ⓓ Ⓔ	20. Ⓐ Ⓑ Ⓒ Ⓓ Ⓔ	38. Ⓐ Ⓑ Ⓒ Ⓓ Ⓔ	56. Ⓐ Ⓑ Ⓒ Ⓓ Ⓔ	74. Ⓐ Ⓑ Ⓒ Ⓓ Ⓔ
3. Ⓐ Ⓑ Ⓒ Ⓓ Ⓔ	21. Ⓐ Ⓑ Ⓒ Ⓓ Ⓔ	39. Ⓐ Ⓑ Ⓒ Ⓓ Ⓔ	57. Ⓐ Ⓑ Ⓒ Ⓓ Ⓔ	75. Ⓐ Ⓑ Ⓒ Ⓓ Ⓔ
4. Ⓐ Ⓑ Ⓒ Ⓓ Ⓔ	22. Ⓐ Ⓑ Ⓒ Ⓓ Ⓔ	40. Ⓐ Ⓑ Ⓒ Ⓓ Ⓔ	58. Ⓐ Ⓑ Ⓒ Ⓓ Ⓔ	76. Ⓐ Ⓑ Ⓒ Ⓓ Ⓔ
5. Ⓐ Ⓑ Ⓒ Ⓓ Ⓔ	23. Ⓐ Ⓑ Ⓒ Ⓓ Ⓔ	41. Ⓐ Ⓑ Ⓒ Ⓓ Ⓔ	59. Ⓐ Ⓑ Ⓒ Ⓓ Ⓔ	77. Ⓐ Ⓑ Ⓒ Ⓓ Ⓔ
6. Ⓐ Ⓑ Ⓒ Ⓓ Ⓔ	24. Ⓐ Ⓑ Ⓒ Ⓓ Ⓔ	42. Ⓐ Ⓑ Ⓒ Ⓓ Ⓔ	60. Ⓐ Ⓑ Ⓒ Ⓓ Ⓔ	78. Ⓐ Ⓑ Ⓒ Ⓓ Ⓔ
7. Ⓐ Ⓑ Ⓒ Ⓓ Ⓔ	25. Ⓐ Ⓑ Ⓒ Ⓓ Ⓔ	43. Ⓐ Ⓑ Ⓒ Ⓓ Ⓔ	61. Ⓐ Ⓑ Ⓒ Ⓓ Ⓔ	79. Ⓐ Ⓑ Ⓒ Ⓓ Ⓔ
8. Ⓐ Ⓑ Ⓒ Ⓓ Ⓔ	26. Ⓐ Ⓑ Ⓒ Ⓓ Ⓔ	44. Ⓐ Ⓑ Ⓒ Ⓓ Ⓔ	62. Ⓐ Ⓑ Ⓒ Ⓓ Ⓔ	80. Ⓐ Ⓑ Ⓒ Ⓓ Ⓔ
9. Ⓐ Ⓑ Ⓒ Ⓓ Ⓔ	27. Ⓐ Ⓑ Ⓒ Ⓓ Ⓔ	45. Ⓐ Ⓑ Ⓒ Ⓓ Ⓔ	63. Ⓐ Ⓑ Ⓒ Ⓓ Ⓔ	81. Ⓐ Ⓑ Ⓒ Ⓓ Ⓔ
10. Ⓐ Ⓑ Ⓒ Ⓓ Ⓔ	28. Ⓐ Ⓑ Ⓒ Ⓓ Ⓔ	46. Ⓐ Ⓑ Ⓒ Ⓓ Ⓔ	64. Ⓐ Ⓑ Ⓒ Ⓓ Ⓔ	82. Ⓐ Ⓑ Ⓒ Ⓓ Ⓔ
11. Ⓐ Ⓑ Ⓒ Ⓓ Ⓔ	29. Ⓐ Ⓑ Ⓒ Ⓓ Ⓔ	47. Ⓐ Ⓑ Ⓒ Ⓓ Ⓔ	65. Ⓐ Ⓑ Ⓒ Ⓓ Ⓔ	83. Ⓐ Ⓑ Ⓒ Ⓓ Ⓔ
12. Ⓐ Ⓑ Ⓒ Ⓓ Ⓔ	30. Ⓐ Ⓑ Ⓒ Ⓓ Ⓔ	48. Ⓐ Ⓑ Ⓒ Ⓓ Ⓔ	66. Ⓐ Ⓑ Ⓒ Ⓓ Ⓔ	84. Ⓐ Ⓑ Ⓒ Ⓓ Ⓔ
13. Ⓐ Ⓑ Ⓒ Ⓓ Ⓔ	31. Ⓐ Ⓑ Ⓒ Ⓓ Ⓔ	49. Ⓐ Ⓑ Ⓒ Ⓓ Ⓔ	67. Ⓐ Ⓑ Ⓒ Ⓓ Ⓔ	85. Ⓐ Ⓑ Ⓒ Ⓓ Ⓔ
14. Ⓐ Ⓑ Ⓒ Ⓓ Ⓔ	32. Ⓐ Ⓑ Ⓒ Ⓓ Ⓔ	50. Ⓐ Ⓑ Ⓒ Ⓓ Ⓔ	68. Ⓐ Ⓑ Ⓒ Ⓓ Ⓔ	86. Ⓐ Ⓑ Ⓒ Ⓓ Ⓔ
15. Ⓐ Ⓑ Ⓒ Ⓓ Ⓔ	33. Ⓐ Ⓑ Ⓒ Ⓓ Ⓔ	51. Ⓐ Ⓑ Ⓒ Ⓓ Ⓔ	69. Ⓐ Ⓑ Ⓒ Ⓓ Ⓔ	87. Ⓐ Ⓑ Ⓒ Ⓓ Ⓔ
16. Ⓐ Ⓑ Ⓒ Ⓓ Ⓔ	34. Ⓐ Ⓑ Ⓒ Ⓓ Ⓔ	52. Ⓐ Ⓑ Ⓒ Ⓓ Ⓔ	70. Ⓐ Ⓑ Ⓒ Ⓓ Ⓔ	88. Ⓐ Ⓑ Ⓒ Ⓓ Ⓔ
17. Ⓐ Ⓑ Ⓒ Ⓓ Ⓔ	35. Ⓐ Ⓑ Ⓒ Ⓓ Ⓔ	53. Ⓐ Ⓑ Ⓒ Ⓓ Ⓔ	71. Ⓐ Ⓑ Ⓒ Ⓓ Ⓔ	
18. Ⓐ Ⓑ Ⓒ Ⓓ Ⓔ	36. Ⓐ Ⓑ Ⓒ Ⓓ Ⓔ	54. Ⓐ Ⓑ Ⓒ Ⓓ Ⓔ	72. Ⓐ Ⓑ Ⓒ Ⓓ Ⓔ	

PART C—ADDRESS CODE MEMORY

1. Ⓐ Ⓑ Ⓒ Ⓓ Ⓔ
2. Ⓐ Ⓑ Ⓒ Ⓓ Ⓔ
3. Ⓐ Ⓑ Ⓒ Ⓓ Ⓔ
4. Ⓐ Ⓑ Ⓒ Ⓓ Ⓔ
5. Ⓐ Ⓑ Ⓒ Ⓓ Ⓔ
6. Ⓐ Ⓑ Ⓒ Ⓓ Ⓔ
7. Ⓐ Ⓑ Ⓒ Ⓓ Ⓔ
8. Ⓐ Ⓑ Ⓒ Ⓓ Ⓔ
9. Ⓐ Ⓑ Ⓒ Ⓓ Ⓔ
10. Ⓐ Ⓑ Ⓒ Ⓓ Ⓔ
11. Ⓐ Ⓑ Ⓒ Ⓓ Ⓔ
12. Ⓐ Ⓑ Ⓒ Ⓓ Ⓔ
13. Ⓐ Ⓑ Ⓒ Ⓓ Ⓔ
14. Ⓐ Ⓑ Ⓒ Ⓓ Ⓔ
15. Ⓐ Ⓑ Ⓒ Ⓓ Ⓔ
16. Ⓐ Ⓑ Ⓒ Ⓓ Ⓔ
17. Ⓐ Ⓑ Ⓒ Ⓓ Ⓔ
18. Ⓐ Ⓑ Ⓒ Ⓓ Ⓔ

19. Ⓐ Ⓑ Ⓒ Ⓓ Ⓔ
20. Ⓐ Ⓑ Ⓒ Ⓓ Ⓔ
21. Ⓐ Ⓑ Ⓒ Ⓓ Ⓔ
22. Ⓐ Ⓑ Ⓒ Ⓓ Ⓔ
23. Ⓐ Ⓑ Ⓒ Ⓓ Ⓔ
24. Ⓐ Ⓑ Ⓒ Ⓓ Ⓔ
25. Ⓐ Ⓑ Ⓒ Ⓓ Ⓔ
26. Ⓐ Ⓑ Ⓒ Ⓓ Ⓔ
27. Ⓐ Ⓑ Ⓒ Ⓓ Ⓔ
28. Ⓐ Ⓑ Ⓒ Ⓓ Ⓔ
29. Ⓐ Ⓑ Ⓒ Ⓓ Ⓔ
30. Ⓐ Ⓑ Ⓒ Ⓓ Ⓔ
31. Ⓐ Ⓑ Ⓒ Ⓓ Ⓔ
32. Ⓐ Ⓑ Ⓒ Ⓓ Ⓔ
33. Ⓐ Ⓑ Ⓒ Ⓓ Ⓔ
34. Ⓐ Ⓑ Ⓒ Ⓓ Ⓔ
35. Ⓐ Ⓑ Ⓒ Ⓓ Ⓔ
36. Ⓐ Ⓑ Ⓒ Ⓓ Ⓔ

37. Ⓐ Ⓑ Ⓒ Ⓓ Ⓔ
38. Ⓐ Ⓑ Ⓒ Ⓓ Ⓔ
39. Ⓐ Ⓑ Ⓒ Ⓓ Ⓔ
40. Ⓐ Ⓑ Ⓒ Ⓓ Ⓔ
41. Ⓐ Ⓑ Ⓒ Ⓓ Ⓔ
42. Ⓐ Ⓑ Ⓒ Ⓓ Ⓔ
43. Ⓐ Ⓑ Ⓒ Ⓓ Ⓔ
44. Ⓐ Ⓑ Ⓒ Ⓓ Ⓕ
45. Ⓐ Ⓑ Ⓒ Ⓓ Ⓔ
46. Ⓐ Ⓑ Ⓒ Ⓓ Ⓔ
47. Ⓐ Ⓑ Ⓒ Ⓓ Ⓔ
48. Ⓐ Ⓑ Ⓒ Ⓓ Ⓔ
49. Ⓐ Ⓑ Ⓒ Ⓓ Ⓔ
50. Ⓐ Ⓑ Ⓒ Ⓓ Ⓔ
51. Ⓐ Ⓑ Ⓒ Ⓓ Ⓔ
52. Ⓐ Ⓑ Ⓒ Ⓓ Ⓔ
53. Ⓐ Ⓑ Ⓒ Ⓓ Ⓔ
54. Ⓐ Ⓑ Ⓒ Ⓓ Ⓔ

55. Ⓐ Ⓑ Ⓒ Ⓓ Ⓔ
56. Ⓐ Ⓑ Ⓒ Ⓓ Ⓔ
57. Ⓐ Ⓑ Ⓒ Ⓓ Ⓔ
58. Ⓐ Ⓑ Ⓒ Ⓓ Ⓔ
59. Ⓐ Ⓑ Ⓒ Ⓓ Ⓔ
60. Ⓐ Ⓑ Ⓒ Ⓓ Ⓔ
61. Ⓐ Ⓑ Ⓒ Ⓓ Ⓔ
62. Ⓐ Ⓑ Ⓒ Ⓓ Ⓔ
63. Ⓐ Ⓑ Ⓒ Ⓓ Ⓔ
64. Ⓐ Ⓑ Ⓒ Ⓓ Ⓔ
65. Ⓐ Ⓑ Ⓒ Ⓓ Ⓔ
66. Ⓐ Ⓑ Ⓒ Ⓓ Ⓔ
67. Ⓐ Ⓑ Ⓒ Ⓓ Ⓔ
68. Ⓐ Ⓑ Ⓒ Ⓓ Ⓔ
69. Ⓐ Ⓑ Ⓒ Ⓓ Ⓔ
70. Ⓐ Ⓑ Ⓒ Ⓓ Ⓔ
71. Ⓐ Ⓑ Ⓒ Ⓓ Ⓔ
72. Ⓐ Ⓑ Ⓒ Ⓓ Ⓔ

73. Ⓐ Ⓑ Ⓒ Ⓓ Ⓔ
74. Ⓐ Ⓑ Ⓒ Ⓓ Ⓔ
75. Ⓐ Ⓑ Ⓒ Ⓓ Ⓔ
76. Ⓐ Ⓑ Ⓒ Ⓓ Ⓔ
77. Ⓐ Ⓑ Ⓒ Ⓓ Ⓔ
78. Ⓐ Ⓑ Ⓒ Ⓓ Ⓔ
79. Ⓐ Ⓑ Ⓒ Ⓓ Ⓔ
80. Ⓐ Ⓑ Ⓒ Ⓓ Ⓔ
81. Ⓐ Ⓑ Ⓒ Ⓓ Ⓔ
82. Ⓐ Ⓑ Ⓒ Ⓓ Ⓔ
83. Ⓐ Ⓑ Ⓒ Ⓓ Ⓔ
84. Ⓐ Ⓑ Ⓒ Ⓓ Ⓔ
85. Ⓐ Ⓑ Ⓒ Ⓓ Ⓔ
86. Ⓐ Ⓑ Ⓒ Ⓓ Ⓔ
87. Ⓐ Ⓑ Ⓒ Ⓓ Ⓔ
88. Ⓐ Ⓑ Ⓒ Ⓓ Ⓔ

PART D—ADDRESS CHECKING

1. Ⓐ Ⓓ	20. Ⓐ Ⓓ	39. Ⓐ Ⓓ	58. Ⓐ Ⓓ	77. Ⓐ Ⓓ
2. Ⓐ Ⓓ	21. Ⓐ Ⓓ	40. Ⓐ Ⓓ	59. Ⓐ Ⓓ	78. Ⓐ Ⓓ
3. Ⓐ Ⓓ	22. Ⓐ Ⓓ	41. Ⓐ Ⓓ	60. Ⓐ Ⓓ	79. Ⓐ Ⓓ
4. Ⓐ Ⓓ	23. Ⓐ Ⓓ	42. Ⓐ Ⓓ	61. Ⓐ Ⓓ	80. Ⓐ Ⓓ
5. Ⓐ Ⓓ	24. Ⓐ Ⓓ	43. Ⓐ Ⓓ	62. Ⓐ Ⓓ	81. Ⓐ Ⓓ
6. Ⓐ Ⓓ	25. Ⓐ Ⓓ	44. Ⓐ Ⓓ	63. Ⓐ Ⓓ	82. Ⓐ Ⓓ
7. Ⓐ Ⓓ	26. Ⓐ Ⓓ	45. Ⓐ Ⓓ	64. Ⓐ Ⓓ	83. Ⓐ Ⓓ
8. Ⓐ Ⓓ	27. Ⓐ Ⓓ	46. Ⓐ Ⓓ	65. Ⓐ Ⓓ	84. Ⓐ Ⓓ
9. Ⓐ Ⓓ	28. Ⓐ Ⓓ	47. Ⓐ Ⓓ	66. Ⓐ Ⓓ	85. Ⓐ Ⓓ
10. Ⓐ Ⓓ	29. Ⓐ Ⓓ	48. Ⓐ Ⓓ	67. Ⓐ Ⓓ	86. Ⓐ Ⓓ
11. Ⓐ Ⓓ	30. Ⓐ Ⓓ	49. Ⓐ Ⓓ	68. Ⓐ Ⓓ	87. Ⓐ Ⓓ
12. Ⓐ Ⓓ	31. Ⓐ Ⓓ	50. Ⓐ Ⓓ	69. Ⓐ Ⓓ	88. Ⓐ Ⓓ
13. Ⓐ Ⓓ	32. Ⓐ Ⓓ	51. Ⓐ Ⓓ	70. Ⓐ Ⓓ	89. Ⓐ Ⓓ
14. Ⓐ Ⓓ	33. Ⓐ Ⓓ	52. Ⓐ Ⓓ	71. Ⓐ Ⓓ	90. Ⓐ Ⓓ
15. Ⓐ Ⓓ	34. Ⓐ Ⓓ	53. Ⓐ Ⓓ	72. Ⓐ Ⓓ	91. Ⓐ Ⓓ
16. Ⓐ Ⓓ	35. Ⓐ Ⓓ	54. Ⓐ Ⓓ	73. Ⓐ Ⓓ	92. Ⓐ Ⓓ
17. Ⓐ Ⓓ	36. Ⓐ Ⓓ	55. Ⓐ Ⓓ	74. Ⓐ Ⓓ	93. Ⓐ Ⓓ
18. Ⓐ Ⓓ	37. Ⓐ Ⓓ	56. Ⓐ Ⓓ	75. Ⓐ Ⓓ	94. Ⓐ Ⓓ
19. Ⓐ Ⓓ	38. Ⓐ Ⓓ	57. Ⓐ Ⓓ	76. Ⓐ Ⓓ	95. Ⓐ Ⓓ

SECOND MODEL EXAM

PART A—NUMBER SERIES

The following sample questions show you the type of question that will be used in Part A. Since this type of question may be new and unfamiliar to you, the examiner will work through the first five questions with you. Once you understand the task, you will have five minutes to answer sample questions 6 to 14 on your own. Correct answers and explanations follow.

Directions: Each number series question consists of a series of numbers which follows some definite order. The numbers progress from left to right according to some rule. One pair of numbers to the right of the series comprises the next two numbers in the series. Study each series to figure out the rule which governs the progression. Choose the answer pair which continues the series according to the pattern established and mark its letter on your answer sheet.

1. 17 20 20 23 23 26 26 ..... (A) 26 26 (B) 26 27 (C) 26 29 (D) 29 29 (E) 29 32

    In this series, the pattern is: $+3$, repeat the number, $+3$, repeat the number, $+3$, repeat the number. Since 26 has been repeated, the next number in the series should be 29, which should then be repeated. **(D)** is the correct answer.

2. 76 75 73 70 66 61 55 ..... (A) 50 41 (B) 54 51 (C) 46 40 (D) 45 35 (E) 48 40

    The pattern here is: $-1, -2, -3, -4, -5, -6, -7, -8$ . . . Continuing the series we see that $55 - 7 = 48 - 8 = 40$, so **(E)** is the correct answer.

3. 22 26 31 35 40 44 49 ..... (A) 53 58 (B) 54 58 (C) 54 59 (D) 53 57 (E) 55 61

    Here the pattern is $+4, +5, +4, +5; +4, +5$ . . . **(A)** is the correct answer because $49 + 4 = 53 + 5 = 58$.

4. 12 36 14 33 16 30 18 ..... (A) 20 27 (B) 27 20 (C) 20 22 (D) 28 26 (E) 16 14

    This series is actually two alternating series. The first series begins with 12 and ascends at the rate of $+2$. This series reads: 12 14 16 18 20. The alternating series begins with 36 and descends at the rate of -3. This series reads: 36 33 30 27. The correct answer is **(B)** because the next number in the total series must be the next number in the descending series, which is 27, followed by the text number in the ascending series, 20.

5. 4 12 8 12 12 12 16 12 20 . (A) 16 16 (B) 20 20 (C) 20 24 (D) 24 28 (E) 12 24

    This is a difficult series which has been extended to give you more opportunity to spot the pattern. Actually the basic series is a simple $+4$; 4 8 12 16 20 24. After each number in the basic series, you find the number 12. The problem would be easy if it were not for the coincidence of the number 12 appearing in the series itself. Once you understand the series, you can easily see that **(E)** is the answer. You will now have five minutes to complete the remaining sample number series questions.

6.	14	14	14	17	17	17	20	...... (A) 17	14	(B) 17	20	(C) 20	20	(D) 20	23	(E) 20 21
7.	97	87	78	70	63	57	52	...... (A) 48	45	(B) 50	48	(C) 51	50	(D) 48	46	(E) 47 42
8.	34	36	39	43	45	48	52	...... (A) 54	56	(B) 54	57	(C) 55	57	(D) 55	58	(E) 56 59
9.	3	6	12	12	24	48	48	.... (A) 48	96	(B) 96	96	(C) 144	144	(D) 96	144	(E) 96 192
10.	10	68	20	63	30	58	40	...... (A) 50	53	(B) 48	55	(C) 45	55	(D) 50	56	(E) 53 50
11.	38	32	32	38	38	32	32	...... (A) 32	38	(B) 38	32	(C) 32	32	(D) 38	38	(E) 34 34
12.	15	28	14	30	13	32	12	...... (A) 10	35	(B) 11	34	(C) 34	11	(D) 10	34	(E) 34 10
13.	11	13	16	20	25	31	38	...... (A) 45	51	(B) 48	58	(C) 46	56	(D) 46	55	(E) 46 57
14.	54	52	17	50	48	17	46	...... (A) 44	42	(B) 17	44	(C) 44	17	(D) 43	17	(E) 17 43

SAMPLE ANSWER SHEET

1. Ⓐ Ⓑ Ⓒ Ⓓ Ⓔ   8. Ⓐ Ⓑ Ⓒ Ⓓ Ⓔ
2. Ⓐ Ⓑ Ⓒ Ⓓ Ⓔ   9. Ⓐ Ⓑ Ⓒ Ⓓ Ⓔ
3. Ⓐ Ⓑ Ⓒ Ⓓ Ⓔ   10. Ⓐ Ⓑ Ⓒ Ⓓ Ⓔ
4. Ⓐ Ⓑ Ⓒ Ⓓ Ⓔ   11. Ⓐ Ⓑ Ⓒ Ⓓ Ⓔ
5. Ⓐ Ⓑ Ⓒ Ⓓ Ⓔ   12. Ⓐ Ⓑ Ⓒ Ⓓ Ⓔ
6. Ⓐ Ⓑ Ⓒ Ⓓ Ⓔ   13. Ⓐ Ⓑ Ⓒ Ⓓ Ⓔ
7. Ⓐ Ⓑ Ⓒ Ⓓ Ⓔ   14. Ⓐ Ⓑ Ⓒ Ⓓ Ⓔ

CORRECT ANSWERS

1. D	8. B
2. E	9. E
3. A	10. E
4. B	11. D
5. E	12. C
6. C	13. D
7. A	14. C

EXPLANATIONS

6. **(C)** The pattern is: Repeat the number three times, +3; repeat the number three times, +3 . . . The number 20 must be repeated two more times as in choice **(C)**. If the series were to be extended, the next number would be 23.

7. **(A)** This series follows the descending pattern: −10, −9, −8, −7, −6, −5. Continuing the pattern: 52 − 4 = 48 − 3 = 45.

8. **(B)** The pattern is: +2, +3, +4; +2, +3, +4 . . . Then, 52 + 2 = 54 + 3 = 57.

9. **(E)** The pattern is: × 2, × 2, repeat the number; × 2, × 2, repeat the number . . . . Having just repeated the number, the series continues: 48 × 2 = 96 × 2 = 192.

10. **(E)** There are two alternating series. The first series ascends by +10. The alternating series descends by −5. Thus, the two series are: 10 20 30 40 50 and 68 63 58 53.

11. **(D)** The series consists of a repetition of the sequence: 38 32 32 38; 38 32 32 38; 38 . . .

12. **(C)** There are two alternating series. The first series, 15 14 13 12 11, descends at the rate of −1. The alternating series, 28 30 32 34, ascends at the rate of +2.

13. **(D)** The series ascends: +2, +3, +4, +5, +6, +7. Then, 38 + 8 = 46 + 9 = 55.

14. **(C)** This is a −2 series with the number 17 intervening after each two numbers in the series. Continuing the series: 46 − 2 = 44, then 17 and, if the series were to continue still further, 44 − 2 = 42.

PART A—NUMBER SERIES

TIME: 20 Minutes. 24 Questions.

Directions: Each number series question consists of a series of numbers which follows some definite order. The numbers progress from left to right according to some rule. One lettered pair of numbers comprises the next two numbers in the series. Study each series to try to find a pattern to the series and to figure the rule which governs the progression. Choose the answer pair which continues the series according to the pattern established and mark its letter on your answer sheet. Correct answers are on page 102.

1. 10 11 12 10 11 12 10 ...... (A) 10 11 (B) 12 10 (C) 11 10 (D) 11 12 (E) 10 12

2. 4 6 7 4 6 7 4 .... (A) 6 7 (B) 4 7 (C) 7 6 (D) 7 4 (E) 6 8

3. 10 10 9 11 11 10 12 .... (A) 13 14 (B) 12 11 (C) 13 13 (D) 12 12 (E) 12 13

4. 3 4 10 5 6 10 7 .... (A) 10 8 (B) 9 8 (C) 8 14 (D) 8 9 (E) 8 10

5. 6 6 7 7 8 8 9 .... (A) 10 11 (B) 10 10 (C) 9 10 (D) 9 9 (E) 10 9

6. 3 8 9 4 9 10 5 .... (A) 6 10 (B) 10 11 (C) 9 10 (D) 11 6 (E) 10 6

7. 2 4 3 6 4 8 5 .... (A) 6 10 (B) 10 7 (C) 10 6 (D) 9 6 (E) 6 7

8. 11 5 9 7 7 9 5 .... (A) 11 3 (B) 7 9 (C) 7 11 (D) 9 7 (E) 3 7

9. 7 16 9 15 11 14 13 .... (A) 12 14 (B) 13 15 (C) 17 15 (D) 15 12 (E) 13 12

10. 40 42 39 44 38 46 37 ..... (A) 48 36 (B) 37 46 (C) 36 48 (D) 43 39 (E) 46 40

11. 1 3 6 10 15 21 28 36 .... (A) 40 48 (B) 36 45 (C) 38 52 (D) 45 56 (E) 45 55

12. 1 2 3 3 4 7 5 6 11 7 .. (A) 8 12 (B) 9 15 (C) 8 15 (D) 6 12 (E) 8 7

13. 3 18 4 24 5 30 6 .... (A) 7 40 (B) 7 42 (C) 42 7 (D) 36 7 (E) 40 7

14. 3 3 4 8 10 30 33 132 .... (A) 152 158 (B) 136 680 (C) 165 500 (D) 143 560 (E) 300 900

15. 18 20 22 20 18 20 22 ..... (A) 18 20 (B) 20 18 (C) 22 20 (D) 24 20 (E) 18 22

16. 4 8 8 16 16 32 32 .... (A) 32 64 (B) 36 40 (C) 64 64 (D) 64 128 (E) 64 82

17. 1 2 12 3 4 34 5 .... (A) 6 65 (B) 7 12 (C) 5 6 (D) 6 60 (E) 6 56

18. 8   16   24   32   40   48   56 .... (A) 64   72 (B) 60   64 (C) 70   78 (D) 62   70 (E) 64   68

19. 5   15   18   54   57   171   174 ..... (A) 176 528(B) 522 821(C) 177 531(D) 522 525(E) 525 528

20. 25   20   24   21   23   22   22 ..... (A) 24   20 (B) 23   21 (C) 23   24 (D) 24   21 (E) 22   23

21. 99   88   77   66   55   44   33 ..... (A) 22   11 (B) 33   22 (C) 44   55 (D) 32   22 (E) 30   20

22. 7   5   9   7   11   9   13 .... (A) 9   11 (B) 11   9 (C) 7   11 (D) 9   15 (E) 11   15

23. 47   44   41   38   35   32   29 ..... (A) 28   27 (B) 27   24 (C) 26   23 (D) 25   21 (E) 26   22

24. 99   99   99   33   33   33   11).... (A) 9   7 (B) 22   33 (C) 11   0 (D) 11   33 (E) 11   11

END OF PART A

If you complete your work before time is up, check over your answers on this test only. Do not turn the page until you are told to do so.

PART B—ADDRESS CODING

SAMPLE QUESTIONS

The seven sample questions for this part are based upon the addresses in the five boxes below. Your task is to mark on your answer sheet the letter of the box in which each address belongs. The instructions for Part B permit you to look at the boxes if you cannot remember in which box an address belongs. You may look at the boxes while answering these Part B sample questions. The questions in Part C of the exam will be based upon the same boxes as the questions in Part B, but in answering Part C you may NOT look at the boxes. There will be no sample questions before Part C.

A	B	C	D	E
8300-8499 Oak Hillburn 4300-5199 Secor Abbey 1200-1899 Gilmore	8000-8299 Oak Brambach 5700-6099 Secor Winslow 2700-3199 Gilmore	6200-7599 Oak Woods 3100-4199 Secor Dobbs 3200-3899 Gilmore	7600-7999 Oak Burgess 5200-5699 Secor Plains 1900-2699 Gilmore	4900-6199 Oak Mercer 4200-4299 Secor Clayton 1100-1199 Gilmore

1. 3200-3899 Gilmore
2. Mercer
3. Abbey
4. 8000-8299 Oak

5. 5200-5699 Secor
6. 4300-5199 Secor
7. Dobbs

SAMPLE ANSWER SHEET	
1. Ⓐ Ⓑ Ⓒ Ⓓ Ⓔ	5. Ⓐ Ⓑ Ⓒ Ⓓ Ⓔ
2. Ⓐ Ⓑ Ⓒ Ⓓ Ⓔ	6. Ⓐ Ⓑ Ⓒ Ⓓ Ⓔ
3. Ⓐ Ⓑ Ⓒ Ⓓ Ⓔ	7. Ⓐ Ⓑ Ⓒ Ⓓ Ⓔ
4. Ⓐ Ⓑ Ⓒ Ⓓ Ⓔ	

CORRECT ANSWERS	
1. C	5. D
2. E	6. A
3. A	7. C
4. B	

PART B—ADDRESS CODING

Directions*: There are five boxes labeled A, B, C, D, and E. In each box are five addresses, three of which include a number span and a name and two of which are names alone. You will have five (5) minutes to memorize the locations of all twenty-five addresses. Then you will have three (3) minutes to mark your answer sheet with the letter of the box in which each address in the question list belongs. For Part B you may refer to the boxes while answering, though you will lose speed by doing so. For Part C you may NOT look at the boxes, so do your best to memorize in the five minutes allowed you now. Correct answers are on page 103.*

MEMORIZING TIME: 5 Minutes.

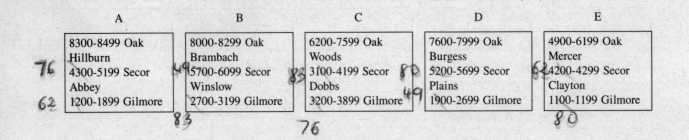

A	B	C	D	E
8300-8499 Oak	8000-8299 Oak	6200-7599 Oak	7600-7999 Oak	4900-6199 Oak
Hillburn	Brambach	Woods	Burgess	Mercer
4300-5199 Secor	5700-6099 Secor	3100-4199 Secor	5200-5699 Secor	4200-4299 Secor
Abbey	Winslow	Dobbs	Plains	Clayton
1200-1899 Gilmore	2700-3199 Gilmore	3200-3899 Gilmore	1900-2699 Gilmore	1100-1199 Gilmore

ANSWERING TIME: 3 Minutes. 88 Questions.

1. 3200-3899 Gilmore
2. 5200-5699 Secor
3. 4900-6199 Oak
4. Hillburn
5. 8300-8499 Oak
6. 2700-3199 Gilmore
7. Mercer
8. 1900-2699 Gilmore
9. 4200-4299 Secor
10. 5700-6099 Secor
11. Dobbs
12. Clayton
13. 7600-7999 Oak
14. 3100-4199 Secor

15. 8000-8299 Oak
16. 1200-1899 Gilmore
17. Brambach
18. Burgess
19. Woods
20. 6200-7599 Oak
21. 4300-5199 Secor
22. Abbey
23. Winslow
24. 1100-1199 Gilmore
25. Plains
26. 5200-5699 Secor
27. Brambach
28. 8000-8299 Oak

29. 4300-5199 Secor
30. 1900-2699 Gilmore
31. Hillburn
32. Dobbs
33. 4900-6199 Oak
34. 4300-5199 Secor
35. 3200-3899 Gilmore
36. Mercer
37. 7600-7999 Oak
38. 8300-8499 Oak
39. Brambach
40. Clayton
41. Abbey
42. 5700-6099 Secor
43. 4200-4299 Secor
44. 1200-1899 Gilmore
45. Winslow
46. Dobbs
47. 6200-7599 Oak
48. Plains
49. 3100-4199 Secor
50. 1100-1199 Gilmore
51. 2700-3199 Gilmore
52. 5200-5699 Secor
53. Hillburn
54. Woods
55. 5700-6099 Secor
56. 6200-7599 Oak
57. 1200-1899 Gilmore
58. 4900-6199 Oak

59. 1900-2699 Gilmore
60. Winslow
61. Dobbs
62. 1100-1199 Gilmore
63. 8300-8499 Oak
64. Clayton
65. Mercer
66. 3100-4199 Secor
67. Brambach
68. 2700-3199 Gilmore
69. 5200-5699 Secor
70. 7600-7999 Oak
71. Burgess
72. Woods
73. 4200-4299 Secor
74. Plains
75. 1900-2699 Gilmore
76. 3200-3899 Gilmore
77. 4200-4299 Secor
78. Abbey
79. Winslow
80. 1200-1899 Gilmore
81. 8000-8299 Oak
82. 7600-7999 Oak
83. Hillburn
84. Clayton
85. 8300-8499 Oak
86. 4300-5199 Secor
87. 5200-5699 Secor
88. Woods

END OF PART B

If you finish before time is up, use the remaining seconds to continue memorizing the locations of the addresses. Do not turn the page until you are told to do so.

PART C—ADDRESS CODE MEMORY

TIME: 5 Minutes. 88 Questions.

Directions: *Relying entirely upon your memory, mark your answer sheet with the letter of the box in which each address belongs. Correct answers are on page 103.*

1. 1900-2699 Gilmore
2. 4900-6199 Oak
3. Dobbs
4. Abbey
5. 4300-5199 Secor
6. 4200-4299 Secor
7. 8300-8499 Oak
8. 3200-3899 Gilmore
9. Brambach
10. Mercer
11. Burgess
12. 1200-1899 Gilmore
13. 5700-6099 Secor
14. 8000-8299 Oak
15. Woods
16. 3100-4199 Secor
17. 7600-7999 Oak
18. 1100-1199 Gilmore
19. Clayton
20. Hillburn
21. 2700-3199 Gilmore
22. 6200-7599 Oak
23. Winslow
24. 5200-5699 Secor
25. Plains
26. 4300-5199 Secor
27. 7600-7999 Oak
28. Hillburn
29. 1100-1199 Gilmore
30. Clayton
31. 8300-8499 Oak
32. 3100-4199 Secor
33. 1900-2699 Gilmore
34. Mercer
35. Abbey
36. Woods
37. 1200-1899 Gilmore
38. 4900-6199 Oak
39. 6200-7599 Oak
40. 8000-8299 Oak
41. 5700-6099 Secor
42. Dobbs
43. Clayton
44. Burgess
45. 2700-3199 Gilmore
46. Plains
47. 4200-4299 Secor
48. 8000-8299 Oak
49. 3100-4199 Secor
50. 1900-2699 Gilmore
51. Hillburn
52. Brambach
53. 3200-3899 Gilmore
54. 4900-6199 Oak
55. 5200-5699 Secor
56. 8300-8499 Oak
57. Winslow
58. Clayton
59. Mercer
60. 1100-1199 Gilmore
61. 8000-8299 Oak
62. 4900-6199 Oak
63. 4300-5199 Secor
64. 3200-3899 Gilmore
65. 4200-4299 Secor
66. Burgess
67. Woods
68. Winslow
69. 7600-7999 Oak
70. 3100-4199 Secor

71. 2700-3199 Gilmore
72. 1900-2699 Gilmore
73. Abbey
74. Winslow
75. 5700-6099 Secor
76. 3200-3899 Gilmore
77. 8300-8499 Oak
78. Dobbs
79. 4200-4299 Secor

80. 4900-6199 Oak
81. Clayton
82. 1200-1899 Gilmore
83. 8000-8299 Oak
84. 5200-5699 Secor
85. Mercer
86. 1100-1199 Gilmore
87. 4300-5199 Secor
88. 6200-7599 Oak

END OF PART C

If you finish before time is up, check your answers on this part only. Do not turn the page until you are told to do so.

PART D—ADDRESS CHECKING TEST

SAMPLE QUESTIONS

You will be allowed three minutes to read the directions and answer the five sample questions which follow. On the actual test, however, you will have only six minutes to answer 95 questions, so see how quickly you can compare addresses and still get the correct answer.

Directions: *Each question consists of two addresses. If the two addresses are* alike in EVERY way, *mark* Ⓐ *on your answer sheet. If the two addresses are* different in ANY way, *mark* Ⓓ *on your answer sheet.*

1 . . .	3969 Ardsley Rd	3696 Ardsley Rd
2 . . .	Bryn Mawr PA 19010	Bryn Mawr PA 19010
3 . . .	1684 Beechwood Rd	1684 Beachwood Rd
4 . . .	1885 Black Birch La	1885 Black Birch La
5 . . .	Indianapolis IN 46208	Indianapollis IN 46208

SAMPLE ANSWER SHEET	
1. Ⓐⓓ	4. Ⓐⓓ
2. Ⓐⓓ	5. Ⓐⓓ
3. Ⓐⓓ	

CORRECT ANSWERS	
1. D	4. A
2. A	5. D
3. D	

PART D—ADDRESS CHECKING

TIME: 6 Minutes. 95 Questions.

Directions: For each question, compare the address in the left column with the address in the right column. If the addresses are alike in EVERY way, blacken space Ⓐ on your answer sheet. If the two addresses are different in ANY way, blacken space Ⓓ on your answer sheet. Correct answers for this test are on page 104.

1	9411 41st Rd	9411 41st St
2	2843 Noe St	2834 Noe St
3	E Williston NY 11596	E Williston NH 11596
4	1151 Girard St	1151 Girard St
5	841 St Francis Rd W	841 St Frances Rd W
6	8001 E Broadway	8001 E Broadway
7	Lake Worth FL 33463	Lake Worth FL 33463
8	1161 Lefferts Blvd	1161 Lefferts Rd
9	444 W 66th St	444 E 66th St
10	1626 Butler Rd	1626 Butler Rd
11	154 Woodside Ave	154 Woodland Ave
12	Mountain Lakes NJ 07046	Mountain Lakes NJ 07064
13	329 B Cranstoun Ct	329 B Cranstown Ct
14	Medford MA 02155	Medford MA 02155
15	148 Meritoria Dr	148 Meritorious Dr
16	6032 Cannon Hill Rd	6032 Canon Hill Rd
17	561 S Atlantic Ave	561 S Atlantic Ave
18	5009 Stuyvesant Oval	5009 Stuyvesant Oval
19	Wilmington DE 19808	Wilmington DE 19888
20	2387 Bayview Ave	2378 Bayview Ave
21	636 Briarcliff Rd	6363 Briarcliff Rd
22	Santa Monica CA 90402	Santa Monica CA 90402
23	5986 Echo Dr	5896 Echo Dr
24	Brooklyn NY 11235	Brooklyn NY 12135
25	132 E 35th St	132 E 35th St
26	1786 W 79th St	1786 W 79th St
27	1155 Central Park W	1155 Central Park S
28	Ft. Washington PA 19034	Ft Washington PN 19034
29	1736 Chatterton Ave	1736 Chaterton Ave
30	666 N Bedford Rd	666 N Bedford Rd
31	7591 Selleck St	7951 Selleck St
32	120 Old Lake Dr	120 Old Lake Dr

33 . . . Scarsdale NY 10583	Scarsdale NY 10585
34 . . . 2907 Columbus Ave	2709 Columbus Ave
35 . . . 693 S Moger Ave	693 S Moger Ave
36 . . . 7557 N Greeley Ave	7557 N Greely Ave
37 . . . 219 Park Ave S	291 Park Ave S
38 . . . New York NY 10003	New York NY 10003
39 . . . 1974 Commerce St	1974 Commerce St
40 . . . 174 Grand St	174 Grand Pl
41 . . . Mahopac Falls NY 10542	Maohpac Falls NY 10542
42 . . . 1320 Stoneybrook Ave	1320 Stoney Brook Ave
43 . . . 160 W 166th St	166 W 166th St
44 . . . 2257 Saw Mill River Rd	257 Saw Mill River Rd
45 . . . 4717 Sherwood Ave	4717 Sherwood Ave
46 . . . Newton Lower Falls MA 02162	Newton Lower Falls MO 02162
47 . . . 5300 Ocean Blvd	5300 Oceana Blvd
48 . . . 1042 Barbary Rd	1024 Barbary Rd
49 . . . 113 Crossways Park Dr	133 Crossways Park Dr
50 . . . Maple Plain MN 55348	Maple Plain NM 55348
51 . . . 790 Bronx River Rd	970 Bronx River Rd
52 . . . 6587 Forest Ave	6587 Forrest Ave
53 . . . Tuckahoe NY 10707	Tuckahoe NY 70707
54 . . . 155 Riverside Dr	155 Riverside Dr
55 . . . Princeton NJ 08541	Princeton NJ 08541
56 . . . 222 Lake Ave	2222 Lake Ave
57 . . . 1127 Hardscrabble Rd	1127 Hardscrable Rd
58 . . . 1776 E 157th St	1776 E 157th St
59 . . . 466 Union Ave	466 Union Ave
60 . . . 4211 Hugunot Ave	4211 Huguenot Ave
61 . . . 3435 DeKalb Ave	3435 Dekalb Ave
62 . . . 4986 Spencer Pl	4986 Spenser Pl
63 . . . Sarasota FL 33581	Saratoga FL 33581
64 . . . 345 Belmore Pk	345 Belmore Pk
65 . . . 1793 Purdy Ave	1973 Purdy Ave
66 . . . 2764 Gaylor Rd	2764 Gaylord Rd
67 . . . 2082 W 83rd Rd	2082 W 83rd Rd
68 . . . 908 Adison Rd	908 Edison Rd
69 . . . Cincinnati OH 45202	Cincinatti OH 45202
70 . . . Alamo TX 78516	Alamo TX 78516
71 . . . 3030 Garth Rd	3030 Garth Rd
72 . . . 9806 NW Main St	9806 NE Main St
73 . . . 615 C North Ave	615C North Ave
74 . . . 5555 N Bedford Rd	5555 Bedford Rd
75 . . . Framingham MA 01701	Farmingham MA 01701
76 . . . 1415 Fiske Pl	1415 Fiske Way
77 . . . 3354 N MacQuesten Pkwy	3354 N McQuesten Pkwy
78 . . . 521 English Pl	521 English Pl
79 . . . 3624 Reeder Ave	3624 Reader Ave
80 . . . New Brunswick NJ 08903	New Brunswick NJ 08903
81 . . . 3763 Kings Hwy E	3763 E Kings Hwy
82 . . . 4573 White Plains Rd	4537 White Plains Rd
83 . . . Miami Beach FL 33139	Miami Beach FL 33139

84 . . . 5978 Putnam Ave	5978 Putnam Ave
85 . . . 2754 Madison Rd	2754 Medison Rd
86 . . . 128½ 4th Ave	128¼ 4th Ave
87 . . . 132 E 35th St	132 E 35th St
88 . . . 705 Kingsland Ave	507 Kingsland Ave
89 . . . Cleveland OH 44106	Cleveland OH 44601
90 . . . 1626 E 115th St	1662 E 115th St
91 . . . Iowa City IA 52243	Iowa City IA 52443
92 . . . 561 S Atlantic Ave	561 S Atlantic Ave
93 . . . 8080 Knightsbridge Rd	8080 Kingsbridge Rd
94 . . . 3292 Rugby Rd	2392 Rugby Rd
95 . . . Mesa AZ 85208	Mesa AR 85208

END OF EXAM

If you finish Part D before time is up, check your answers on this part only. Do not return to any previous part.

CORRECT ANSWERS—SECOND MODEL EXAM

PART A—NUMBER SERIES

1. D	4. E	7. C	10. A	13. D	16. C	19. D	22. E
2. A	5. C	8. A	11. E	14. B	17. E	20. B	23. C
3. B	6. B	9. B	12. C	15. B	18. A	21. A	24. E

EXPLANATIONS—NUMBER SERIES

1. **(D)** The sequence, 10 11 12, repeats itself.

2. **(A)** Another repeating sequence; this one is 4 6 7.

3. **(B)** Two sequences alternate. The first repeats itself, then advances by +1 and repeats again. The alternating sequence proceeds forward one number at a time.

4. **(E)** The sequence consists of numbers proceeding upward from 3, with the number 10 intervening between each set of two numbers in the sequence.

5. **(C)** The numbers proceed upward from 6 by +1, with each number repeating itself.

6. **(B)** One series starts at 3 and proceeds upward by +1. The alternating series consists of two numbers which ascend according to the following rule: +1, repeat; +1, repeat.

7. **(C)** One series proceeds upward by +1. The alternating series proceeds up by +2.

8. **(A)** The first series begins with 11 and descends by −2. The alternating series begins with 5 and ascends by +2.

9. **(B)** There are two alternating series, the first ascending by +2, the other descending one number at a time.

10. **(A)** The first series descends one number at a time while the alternating series ascends at the rate of +2.

11. **(E)** The rule is +2, +3, +4, +5, +6, +7, +8, +9.

12. **(C)** Basically the series ascends 1 2 3 4 5 6 7 8, but there is a twist to this problem. The number which intervenes after each two numbers of the series is the sum of those two numbers. Thus, the series may be read: $1 + 2 = 3$; $3 + 4 = 7$; $5 + 6 = 11$; $7 + 8 = 15$.

13. **(D)** Look carefully. This is a $\times 6$ series. $3 \times 6 = 18$; $4 \times 6 = 24$; $5 \times 6 = 30$; $6 \times 6 = 36$, $7 \ldots$.

14. **(B)** This one is not easy, but if you wrote out the steps between numbers, you should have come up with: $\times 1$, $+1$; $\times 2$, $+2$; $\times 3$, $+3$; $\times 4$, $+4$; $\times 5 \ldots$.

15. **(B)** This series is deceptively simple. The sequence 18 20 22 20 is repeated over and over again.

16. **(C)** The series picks up with the second member of a repeat. The pattern is ×2 and repeat, ×2 and repeat . . . .

17. **(E)** There is no mathematical formula for this series. By inspection you may see that two successive numbers are brought together to form a larger number. Thus 1 2 12; 3 4 34; 5 6 56 . . . .

18. **(A)** Straightforward +8.

19. **(D)** The pattern is ×3, +3; ×3, +3 . . . .

20. **(B)** There are two alternating series. The first begins with 25 and descends, one number at a time. The alternating series begins with 20 and ascends one number at a time.

21. **(A)** A simple descending series of −11.

22. **(E)** You may see this as two alternating series, both ascending in steps of +2. You might also interpret the series as reading −2, +4; −2, +4 . . . With either solution you should reach the correct answer.

23. **(C)** The series is a simple −3 series which begins with an unusual number.

24. **(E)** Repeat, repeat, ÷3, repeat, repeat, ÷ 3 repeat, repeat, ÷ 3.

PART B—ADDRESS CODING

1. C	12. E	23. B	34. A	45. B	56. C	67. B	78. A
2. D	13. D	24. E	35. C	46. C	57. A	68. B	79. B
3. E	14. C	25. D	36. E	47. C	58. E	69. D	80. A
4. A	15. B	26. D	37. D	48. D	59. D	70. D	81. B
5. A	16. A	27. B	38. A	49. C	60. B	71. D	82. D
6. B	17. B	28. B	39. B	50. E	61. C	72. C	83. A
7. E	18. D	29. A	40. E	51. B	62. E	73. E	84. E
8. D	19. C	30. D	41. A	52. D	63. A	74. D	85. A
9. E	20. C	31. A	42. B	53. A	64. E	75. D	86. A
10. B	21. A	32. C	43. E	54. C	65. E	76. C	87. D
11. C	22. A	33. E	44. A	55. B	66. C	77. E	88. C

PART C—ADDRESS CODE MEMORY

1. D	12. A	23. B	34. E	45. B	56. A	67. C	78. C
2. E	13. B	24. D	35. A	46. D	57. B	68. B	79. E
3. C	14. B	25. D	36. C	47. E	58. E	69. D	80. E
4. A	15. C	26. A	37. A	48. B	59. E	70. C	81. E
5. A	16. C	27. D	38. E	49. C	60. E	71. B	82. A
6. E	17. D	28. A	39. C	50. D	61. B	72. D	83. B
7. A	18. E	29. E	40. B	51. A	62. E	73. A	84. D
8. C	19. E	30. E	41. B	52. B	63. A	74. B	85. E
9. B	20. A	31. A	42. C	53. C	64. C	75. B	86. E
10. E	21. B	32. C	43. E	54. E	65. E	76. C	87. A
11. D	22. C	33. D	44. D	55. D	66. D	77. A	88. C

PART D—ADDRESS CHECKING

1. D	13. D	25. A	37. D	49. D	61. D	73. D	85. D
2. D	14. A	26. A	38. A	50. D	62. D	74. D	86. D
3. D	15. D	27. D	39. A	51. D	63. D	75. D	87. A
4. A	16. D	28. D	40. D	52. D	64. ~~D~~A	76. D	88. D
5. D	17. A	29. D	41. D	53. D	65. D	77. D	89. D
6. A	18. A	30. A	42. D	54. A	66. D	78. A	90. D
7. A	19. D	31. D	43. D	55. A	67. A	79. D	91. D
8. D	20. D	32. A	44. D	56. D	68. D	80. A	92. A
9. D	21. D	33. D	45. A	57. D	69. D	81. D	93. D
10. A	22. A	34. D	46. D	58. A	70. A	82. D	94. D
11. D	23. D	35. A	47. D	59. A	71. A	83. A	95. D
12. D	24. D	36. D	48. D	60. D	72. D	84. A	

ADDRESS CHECKING ERROR ANALYSIS CHART

Type of Difference	Question Numbers	Number of Questions You Missed
Difference in NUMBERS	2, 12, 19, 20, 21, 23, 24, 31, 33, 34, 37, 43, 44, 48, 49, 51, 53, 56, 65, 73, 82, 86, 88, 89, 90, 91, 94	
Difference in ABBREVIATIONS	1, 3, 8, 9, 27, 28, 40, 46, 50, 72, 74, 76, 81, 95	
Difference in NAMES	5, 11, 13, 15, 16, 29, 36, 41, 42, 47, 52, 57, 60, 61, 62, 63, 64, 66, 68, 69, 75, 77, 79, 85, 93	
No Difference	4, 6, 7, 10, 14, 17, 18, 22, 25, 26, 30, 32, 35, 38, 39, 45, 54, 55, 58, 59, 67, 70, 71, 78, 80, 83, 84, 87, 92	

SCORE SHEET FOR SECOND MODEL EXAM

PART A—NUMBER SERIES

Number Right equals Score

_____ = _____

PART B—ADDRESS CODING

Number Right minus (Number Wrong ÷ 4) equals Score

_____ − _____ = _____

PART C—ADDRESS CODE MEMORY

Number Right minus (Number Wrong ÷ 4) equals Score

_____ − _____ = _____

PART D—ADDRESS CHECKING

Number Right minus Number Wrong equals Score

_____ − _____ = _____

SELF-EVALUATION CHART

Part	Excellent	Good	Average	Fair	Poor
Number Series	21–24	18–20	14–17	11–13	1–10
Address Coding	75–88	63–74	52–62	40–51	1–39
Address Code Memory	75–88	60–74	45–59	30–44	1–29
Address Checking	80–95	65–79	50–64	35–49	1–34

PROGRESS CHART

Blacken to the closest score to chart your progress.

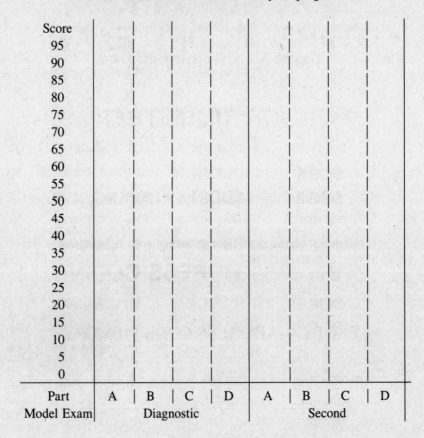

Score								
95								
90								
85								
80								
75								
70								
65								
60								
55								
50								
45								
40								
35								
30								
25								
20								
15								
10								
5								
0								
Part	A	B	C	D	A	B	C	D
Model Exam		Diagnostic				Second		

ANSWER SHEET
THIRD MODEL EXAM

Tear out this Answer Sheet and use it to mark your answers for the exam that follows.

PART A—NUMBER SERIES

1. Ⓐ Ⓑ Ⓒ Ⓓ Ⓔ	6. Ⓐ Ⓑ Ⓒ Ⓓ Ⓔ	11. Ⓐ Ⓑ Ⓒ Ⓓ Ⓔ	16. Ⓐ Ⓑ Ⓒ Ⓓ Ⓔ	21. Ⓐ Ⓑ Ⓒ Ⓓ Ⓔ
2. Ⓐ Ⓑ Ⓒ Ⓓ Ⓔ	7. Ⓐ Ⓑ Ⓒ Ⓓ Ⓔ	12. Ⓐ Ⓑ Ⓒ Ⓓ Ⓔ	17. Ⓐ Ⓑ Ⓒ Ⓓ Ⓔ	22. Ⓐ Ⓑ Ⓒ Ⓓ Ⓔ
3. Ⓐ Ⓑ Ⓒ Ⓓ Ⓔ	8. Ⓐ Ⓑ Ⓒ Ⓓ Ⓔ	13. Ⓐ Ⓑ Ⓒ Ⓓ Ⓔ	18. Ⓐ Ⓑ Ⓒ Ⓓ Ⓔ	23. Ⓐ Ⓑ Ⓒ Ⓓ Ⓔ
4. Ⓐ Ⓑ Ⓒ Ⓓ Ⓔ	9. Ⓐ Ⓑ Ⓒ Ⓓ Ⓔ	14. Ⓐ Ⓑ Ⓒ Ⓓ Ⓔ	19. Ⓐ Ⓑ Ⓒ Ⓓ Ⓔ	24. Ⓐ Ⓑ Ⓒ Ⓓ Ⓔ
5. Ⓐ Ⓑ Ⓒ Ⓓ Ⓔ	10. Ⓐ Ⓑ Ⓒ Ⓓ Ⓔ	15. Ⓐ Ⓑ Ⓒ Ⓓ Ⓔ	20. Ⓐ Ⓑ Ⓒ Ⓓ Ⓔ	

PART B—ADDRESS CODING

1. Ⓐ Ⓑ Ⓒ Ⓓ Ⓔ	19. Ⓐ Ⓑ Ⓒ Ⓓ Ⓔ	37. Ⓐ Ⓑ Ⓒ Ⓓ Ⓔ	55. Ⓐ Ⓑ Ⓒ Ⓓ Ⓔ	73. Ⓐ Ⓑ Ⓒ Ⓓ Ⓔ
2. Ⓐ Ⓑ Ⓒ Ⓓ Ⓔ	20. Ⓐ Ⓑ Ⓒ Ⓓ Ⓔ	38. Ⓐ Ⓑ Ⓒ Ⓓ Ⓔ	56. Ⓐ Ⓑ Ⓒ Ⓓ Ⓔ	74. Ⓐ Ⓑ Ⓒ Ⓓ Ⓔ
3. Ⓐ Ⓑ Ⓒ Ⓓ Ⓔ	21. Ⓐ Ⓑ Ⓒ Ⓓ Ⓔ	39. Ⓐ Ⓑ Ⓒ Ⓓ Ⓔ	57. Ⓐ Ⓑ Ⓒ Ⓓ Ⓔ	75. Ⓐ Ⓑ Ⓒ Ⓓ Ⓔ
4. Ⓐ Ⓑ Ⓒ Ⓓ Ⓔ	22. Ⓐ Ⓑ Ⓒ Ⓓ Ⓔ	40. Ⓐ Ⓑ Ⓒ Ⓓ Ⓔ	58. Ⓐ Ⓑ Ⓒ Ⓓ Ⓔ	76. Ⓐ Ⓑ Ⓒ Ⓓ Ⓔ
5. Ⓐ Ⓑ Ⓒ Ⓓ Ⓔ	23. Ⓐ Ⓑ Ⓒ Ⓓ Ⓔ	41. Ⓐ Ⓑ Ⓒ Ⓓ Ⓔ	59. Ⓐ Ⓑ Ⓒ Ⓓ Ⓔ	77. Ⓐ Ⓑ Ⓒ Ⓓ Ⓔ
6. Ⓐ Ⓑ Ⓒ Ⓓ Ⓔ	24. Ⓐ Ⓑ Ⓒ Ⓓ Ⓔ	42. Ⓐ Ⓑ Ⓒ Ⓓ Ⓔ	60. Ⓐ Ⓑ Ⓒ Ⓓ Ⓔ	78. Ⓐ Ⓑ Ⓒ Ⓓ Ⓔ
7. Ⓐ Ⓑ Ⓒ Ⓓ Ⓔ	25. Ⓐ Ⓑ Ⓒ Ⓓ Ⓔ	43. Ⓐ Ⓑ Ⓒ Ⓓ Ⓔ	61. Ⓐ Ⓑ Ⓒ Ⓓ Ⓔ	79. Ⓐ Ⓑ Ⓒ Ⓓ Ⓔ
8. Ⓐ Ⓑ Ⓒ Ⓓ Ⓔ	26. Ⓐ Ⓑ Ⓒ Ⓓ Ⓔ	44. Ⓐ Ⓑ Ⓒ Ⓓ Ⓔ	62. Ⓐ Ⓑ Ⓒ Ⓓ Ⓔ	80. Ⓐ Ⓑ Ⓒ Ⓓ Ⓔ
9. Ⓐ Ⓑ Ⓒ Ⓓ Ⓔ	27. Ⓐ Ⓑ Ⓒ Ⓓ Ⓔ	45. Ⓐ Ⓑ Ⓒ Ⓓ Ⓔ	63. Ⓐ Ⓑ Ⓒ Ⓓ Ⓔ	81. Ⓐ Ⓑ Ⓒ Ⓓ Ⓔ
10. Ⓐ Ⓑ Ⓒ Ⓓ Ⓔ	28. Ⓐ Ⓑ Ⓒ Ⓓ Ⓔ	46. Ⓐ Ⓑ Ⓒ Ⓓ Ⓔ	64. Ⓐ Ⓑ Ⓒ Ⓓ Ⓔ	82. Ⓐ Ⓑ Ⓒ Ⓓ Ⓔ
11. Ⓐ Ⓑ Ⓒ Ⓓ Ⓔ	29. Ⓐ Ⓑ Ⓒ Ⓓ Ⓔ	47. Ⓐ Ⓑ Ⓒ Ⓓ Ⓔ	65. Ⓐ Ⓑ Ⓒ Ⓓ Ⓔ	83. Ⓐ Ⓑ Ⓒ Ⓓ Ⓔ
12. Ⓐ Ⓑ Ⓒ Ⓓ Ⓔ	30. Ⓐ Ⓑ Ⓒ Ⓓ Ⓔ	48. Ⓐ Ⓑ Ⓒ Ⓓ Ⓔ	66. Ⓐ Ⓑ Ⓒ Ⓓ Ⓔ	84. Ⓐ Ⓑ Ⓒ Ⓓ Ⓔ
13. Ⓐ Ⓑ Ⓒ Ⓓ Ⓔ	31. Ⓐ Ⓑ Ⓒ Ⓓ Ⓔ	49. Ⓐ Ⓑ Ⓒ Ⓓ Ⓔ	67. Ⓐ Ⓑ Ⓒ Ⓓ Ⓔ	85. Ⓐ Ⓑ Ⓒ Ⓓ Ⓔ
14. Ⓐ Ⓑ Ⓒ Ⓓ Ⓔ	32. Ⓐ Ⓑ Ⓒ Ⓓ Ⓔ	50. Ⓐ Ⓑ Ⓒ Ⓓ Ⓔ	68. Ⓐ Ⓑ Ⓒ Ⓓ Ⓔ	86. Ⓐ Ⓑ Ⓒ Ⓓ Ⓔ
15. Ⓐ Ⓑ Ⓒ Ⓓ Ⓔ	33. Ⓐ Ⓑ Ⓒ Ⓓ Ⓔ	51. Ⓐ Ⓑ Ⓒ Ⓓ Ⓔ	69. Ⓐ Ⓑ Ⓒ Ⓓ Ⓔ	87. Ⓐ Ⓑ Ⓒ Ⓓ Ⓔ
16. Ⓐ Ⓑ Ⓒ Ⓓ Ⓔ	34. Ⓐ Ⓑ Ⓒ Ⓓ Ⓔ	52. Ⓐ Ⓑ Ⓒ Ⓓ Ⓔ	70. Ⓐ Ⓑ Ⓒ Ⓓ Ⓔ	88. Ⓐ Ⓑ Ⓒ Ⓓ Ⓔ
17. Ⓐ Ⓑ Ⓒ Ⓓ Ⓔ	35. Ⓐ Ⓑ Ⓒ Ⓓ Ⓔ	53. Ⓐ Ⓑ Ⓒ Ⓓ Ⓔ	71. Ⓐ Ⓑ Ⓒ Ⓓ Ⓔ	
18. Ⓐ Ⓑ Ⓒ Ⓓ Ⓔ	36. Ⓐ Ⓑ Ⓒ Ⓓ Ⓔ	54. Ⓐ Ⓑ Ⓒ Ⓓ Ⓔ	72. Ⓐ Ⓑ Ⓒ Ⓓ Ⓔ	

PART C—ADDRESS CODE MEMORY

1. Ⓐ Ⓑ Ⓒ Ⓓ Ⓔ
2. Ⓐ Ⓑ Ⓒ Ⓓ Ⓔ
3. Ⓐ Ⓑ Ⓒ Ⓓ Ⓔ
4. Ⓐ Ⓑ Ⓒ Ⓓ Ⓔ
5. Ⓐ Ⓑ Ⓒ Ⓓ Ⓔ
6. Ⓐ Ⓑ Ⓒ Ⓓ Ⓔ
7. Ⓐ Ⓑ Ⓒ Ⓓ Ⓔ
8. Ⓐ Ⓑ Ⓒ Ⓓ Ⓔ
9. Ⓐ Ⓑ Ⓒ Ⓓ Ⓔ
10. Ⓐ Ⓑ Ⓒ Ⓓ Ⓔ
11. Ⓐ Ⓑ Ⓒ Ⓓ Ⓔ
12. Ⓐ Ⓑ Ⓒ Ⓓ Ⓔ
13. Ⓐ Ⓑ Ⓒ Ⓓ Ⓔ
14. Ⓐ Ⓑ Ⓒ Ⓓ Ⓔ
15. Ⓐ Ⓑ Ⓒ Ⓓ Ⓔ
16. Ⓐ Ⓑ Ⓒ Ⓓ Ⓔ
17. Ⓐ Ⓑ Ⓒ Ⓓ Ⓔ
18. Ⓐ Ⓑ Ⓒ Ⓓ Ⓔ

19. Ⓐ Ⓑ Ⓒ Ⓓ Ⓔ
20. Ⓐ Ⓑ Ⓒ Ⓓ Ⓔ
21. Ⓐ Ⓑ Ⓒ Ⓓ Ⓔ
22. Ⓐ Ⓑ Ⓒ Ⓓ Ⓔ
23. Ⓐ Ⓑ Ⓒ Ⓓ Ⓔ
24. Ⓐ Ⓑ Ⓒ Ⓓ Ⓔ
25. Ⓐ Ⓑ Ⓒ Ⓓ Ⓔ
26. Ⓐ Ⓑ Ⓒ Ⓓ Ⓔ
27. Ⓐ Ⓑ Ⓒ Ⓓ Ⓔ
28. Ⓐ Ⓑ Ⓒ Ⓓ Ⓔ
29. Ⓐ Ⓑ Ⓒ Ⓓ Ⓔ
30. Ⓐ Ⓑ Ⓒ Ⓓ Ⓔ
31. Ⓐ Ⓑ Ⓒ Ⓓ Ⓔ
32. Ⓐ Ⓑ Ⓒ Ⓓ Ⓔ
33. Ⓐ Ⓑ Ⓒ Ⓓ Ⓔ
34. Ⓐ Ⓑ Ⓒ Ⓓ Ⓔ
35. Ⓐ Ⓑ Ⓒ Ⓓ Ⓔ
36. Ⓐ Ⓑ Ⓒ Ⓓ Ⓔ

37. Ⓐ Ⓑ Ⓒ Ⓓ Ⓔ
38. Ⓐ Ⓑ Ⓒ Ⓓ Ⓔ
39. Ⓐ Ⓑ Ⓒ Ⓓ Ⓔ
40. Ⓐ Ⓑ Ⓒ Ⓓ Ⓔ
41. Ⓐ Ⓑ Ⓒ Ⓓ Ⓔ
42. Ⓐ Ⓑ Ⓒ Ⓓ Ⓔ
43. Ⓐ Ⓑ Ⓒ Ⓓ Ⓔ
44. Ⓐ Ⓑ Ⓒ Ⓓ Ⓔ
45. Ⓐ Ⓑ Ⓒ Ⓓ Ⓔ
46. Ⓐ Ⓑ Ⓒ Ⓓ Ⓔ
47. Ⓐ Ⓑ Ⓒ Ⓓ Ⓔ
48. Ⓐ Ⓑ Ⓒ Ⓓ Ⓔ
49. Ⓐ Ⓑ Ⓒ Ⓓ Ⓔ
50. Ⓐ Ⓑ Ⓒ Ⓓ Ⓔ
51. Ⓐ Ⓑ Ⓒ Ⓓ Ⓔ
52. Ⓐ Ⓑ Ⓒ Ⓓ Ⓔ
53. Ⓐ Ⓑ Ⓒ Ⓓ Ⓔ
54. Ⓐ Ⓑ Ⓒ Ⓓ Ⓔ

55. Ⓐ Ⓑ Ⓒ Ⓓ Ⓔ
56. Ⓐ Ⓑ Ⓒ Ⓓ Ⓔ
57. Ⓐ Ⓑ Ⓒ Ⓓ Ⓔ
58. Ⓐ Ⓑ Ⓒ Ⓓ Ⓔ
59. Ⓐ Ⓑ Ⓒ Ⓓ Ⓔ
60. Ⓐ Ⓑ Ⓒ Ⓓ Ⓔ
61. Ⓐ Ⓑ Ⓒ Ⓓ Ⓔ
62. Ⓐ Ⓑ Ⓒ Ⓓ Ⓔ
63. Ⓐ Ⓑ Ⓒ Ⓓ Ⓔ
64. Ⓐ Ⓑ Ⓒ Ⓓ Ⓔ
65. Ⓐ Ⓑ Ⓒ Ⓓ Ⓔ
66. Ⓐ Ⓑ Ⓒ Ⓓ Ⓔ
67. Ⓐ Ⓑ Ⓒ Ⓓ Ⓔ
68. Ⓐ Ⓑ Ⓒ Ⓓ Ⓔ
69. Ⓐ Ⓑ Ⓒ Ⓓ Ⓔ
70. Ⓐ Ⓑ Ⓒ Ⓓ Ⓔ
71. Ⓐ Ⓑ Ⓒ Ⓓ Ⓔ
72. Ⓐ Ⓑ Ⓒ Ⓓ Ⓔ

73. Ⓐ Ⓑ Ⓒ Ⓓ Ⓔ
74. Ⓐ Ⓑ Ⓒ Ⓓ Ⓔ
75. Ⓐ Ⓑ Ⓒ Ⓓ Ⓔ
76. Ⓐ Ⓑ Ⓒ Ⓓ Ⓔ
77. Ⓐ Ⓑ Ⓒ Ⓓ Ⓔ
78. Ⓐ Ⓑ Ⓒ Ⓓ Ⓔ
79. Ⓐ Ⓑ Ⓒ Ⓓ Ⓔ
80. Ⓐ Ⓑ Ⓒ Ⓓ Ⓔ
81. Ⓐ Ⓑ Ⓒ Ⓓ Ⓔ
82. Ⓐ Ⓑ Ⓒ Ⓓ Ⓔ
83. Ⓐ Ⓑ Ⓒ Ⓓ Ⓔ
84. Ⓐ Ⓑ Ⓒ Ⓓ Ⓔ
85. Ⓐ Ⓑ Ⓒ Ⓓ Ⓔ
86. Ⓐ Ⓑ Ⓒ Ⓓ Ⓔ
87. Ⓐ Ⓑ Ⓒ Ⓓ Ⓔ
88. Ⓐ Ⓑ Ⓒ Ⓓ Ⓔ

Tear here

PART D—ADDRESS CHECKING

Tear here

1. Ⓐ Ⓓ
2. Ⓐ Ⓓ
3. Ⓐ Ⓓ
4. Ⓐ Ⓓ
5. Ⓐ Ⓓ
6. Ⓐ Ⓓ
7. Ⓐ Ⓓ
8. Ⓐ Ⓓ
9. Ⓐ Ⓓ
10. Ⓐ Ⓓ
11. Ⓐ Ⓓ
12. Ⓐ Ⓓ
13. Ⓐ Ⓓ
14. Ⓐ Ⓓ
15. Ⓐ Ⓓ
16. Ⓐ Ⓓ
17. Ⓐ Ⓓ
18. Ⓐ Ⓓ
19. Ⓐ Ⓓ

20. Ⓐ Ⓓ
21. Ⓐ Ⓓ
22. Ⓐ Ⓓ
23. Ⓐ Ⓓ
24. Ⓐ Ⓓ
25. Ⓐ Ⓓ
26. Ⓐ Ⓓ
27. Ⓐ Ⓓ
28. Ⓐ Ⓓ
29. Ⓐ Ⓓ
30. Ⓐ Ⓓ
31. Ⓐ Ⓓ
32. Ⓐ Ⓓ
33. Ⓐ Ⓓ
34. Ⓐ Ⓓ
35. Ⓐ Ⓓ
36. Ⓐ Ⓓ
37. Ⓐ Ⓓ
38. Ⓐ Ⓓ

39. Ⓐ Ⓓ
40. Ⓐ Ⓓ
41. Ⓐ Ⓓ
42. Ⓐ Ⓓ
43. Ⓐ Ⓓ
44. Ⓐ Ⓓ
45. Ⓐ Ⓓ
46. Ⓐ Ⓓ
47. Ⓐ Ⓓ
48. Ⓐ Ⓓ
49. Ⓐ Ⓓ
50. Ⓐ Ⓓ
51. Ⓐ Ⓓ
52. Ⓐ Ⓓ
53. Ⓐ Ⓓ
54. Ⓐ Ⓓ
55. Ⓐ Ⓓ
56. Ⓐ Ⓓ
57. Ⓐ Ⓓ

58. Ⓐ Ⓓ
59. Ⓐ Ⓓ
60. Ⓐ Ⓓ
61. Ⓐ Ⓓ
62. Ⓐ Ⓓ
63. Ⓐ Ⓓ
64. Ⓐ Ⓓ
65. Ⓐ Ⓓ
66. Ⓐ Ⓓ
67. Ⓐ Ⓓ
68. Ⓐ Ⓓ
69. Ⓐ Ⓓ
70. Ⓐ Ⓓ
71. Ⓐ Ⓓ
72. Ⓐ Ⓓ
73. Ⓐ Ⓓ
74. Ⓐ Ⓓ
75. Ⓐ Ⓓ
76. Ⓐ Ⓓ

77. Ⓐ Ⓓ
78. Ⓐ Ⓓ
79. Ⓐ Ⓓ
80. Ⓐ Ⓓ
81. Ⓐ Ⓓ
82. Ⓐ Ⓓ
83. Ⓐ Ⓓ
84. Ⓐ Ⓓ
85. Ⓐ Ⓓ
86. Ⓐ Ⓓ
87. Ⓐ Ⓓ
88. Ⓐ Ⓓ
89. Ⓐ Ⓓ
90. Ⓐ Ⓓ
91. Ⓐ Ⓓ
92. Ⓐ Ⓓ
93. Ⓐ Ⓓ
94. Ⓐ Ⓓ
95. Ⓐ Ⓓ

THIRD MODEL EXAM

PART A—NUMBER SERIES

SAMPLE QUESTIONS

The following sample questions show you the type of question that will be used in Part A. Since this type of question may be new and unfamiliar to you, the examiner will work through the first five questions with you. Once you understand the task, you will have five minutes to answer sample questions 6 to 14 on your own. Correct answers and explanations follow.

Directions: Each number series question consists of a series of numbers which follows some definite order. The numbers progress from left to right according to some rule. One pair of numbers to the right of the series comprises the next two numbers in the series. Study each series to try to find a pattern to the series and to figure out the rule which governs the progression. Choose the answer pair which continues the series according to the pattern established and mark its letter on your answer sheet.

1. 42 40 38 35 32 28 24 ..... (A) 20 18 (B) 18 14 (C) 19 14 (D) 20 16 (E) 19 15

    If you write the steps between the numbers, you will find this pattern emerging: $-2, -2, -3, -3, -4, -4 \ldots$. Since it appears that after each two numbers the number being subtracted increases, it is logical to choose answer **(C)** because $24 - 5 = 19$ and $19 - 5 = 14$.

2. 2 2 4 2 6 2 8 .... (A) 8 2 (B) 2 8 (C) 2 10 (D) 10 2 (E) 10 12

    The series progresses by a factor of $+2$: 2 4 6 8 10. After each number of the advancing series, we find the number 2. The answer is, of course, **(C)**.

3. 88 88 82 82 76 76 70 .... (A) 70 70 (B) 70 65 (C) 64 64 (D) 70 64 (E) 64 48

    The pattern in this series is a simple one: repeat the number, -6; repeat the number, -6 and so on. To complete the series, repeat the 70 and subtract 6 to yield 64. The answer is **(D)**.

4. 35   46   39   43   43   40   47 .... (A) 47   43   (B) 51   40   (C) 43   51   (D) 40   50   (E) 37   51

This is a more complicated problem. There are really two series which alternate. The first series begins with 35 and ascends by +4; 35 39 43 47 51. The alternating series begins with 46 and descends by − 3; 46 43 40 37. The number 43 is not really repeated; the two series simply pass each other at that point. In answering a question of this type, you must be careful to maintain the alternation of series. The answer is **(E)** because 37 continues the descending series and 51 continues the ascending one.

5. 8   10   13   17   22   28   35 .... (A) 43   52   (B) 40   45   (C) 35   42   (D) 42   50   (E) 44   53

The pattern is: +2, +3, +4, +5, +6, +7. Continue the series with: 35 + 8 = 43 + 9 = 52 to choose **(A)** as the correct answer.

You will now have five minutes to complete the remaining sample number series questions.

6. 12   17   14   19   16   21   18 .... (A) 20   22   (B) 16   23   (C) 20   23   (D) 23   20   (E) 25   15

7. 12   4   13   6   14   8   15 .... (A) 10   17   (B) 17   10   (C) 10   12   (D) 16   10   (E) 10   16

8. 21   8   18   20   7   17   19 .... (A) 16   18   (B) 18   6   (C) 6   16   (D) 5   15   (E) 6   18

9. 12   13   14   14   16   18   18 .... (A) 18   20   (B) 20   22   (C) 20   20   (D) 21   24   (E) 22   24

10. 51   22   45   22   40   22   36 .... (A) 38   40   (B) 36   22   (C) 22   33   (D) 22   22   (E) 22   34

11. 19   20   21   22   19   20   21 .... (A) 22   19   (B) 21   22   (C) 20   19   (D) 22   23   (E) 21   19

12. 109   109   89   79   79   59 .... (A) 59   49   (B) 49   49   (C) 39   39   (D) 59   39   (E) 49   39

13. 14   15   15   16   16   16   17 .... (A) 17   18   (B) 18   19   (C) 17   17   (D) 17   16   (E) 18   18

14. 27   33   25   31   23   29   21 .... (A) 30   20   (B) 28   22   (C) 25   18   (D) 19   27   (E) 27   19

SAMPLE ANSWER SHEET		CORRECT ANSWERS	
1. Ⓐ Ⓑ Ⓒ Ⓓ Ⓔ	8. Ⓐ Ⓑ Ⓒ Ⓓ Ⓔ	1. C	8. C
2. Ⓐ Ⓑ Ⓒ Ⓓ Ⓔ	9. Ⓐ Ⓑ Ⓒ Ⓓ Ⓔ	2. C	9. D
3. Ⓐ Ⓑ Ⓒ Ⓓ Ⓔ	10. Ⓐ Ⓑ Ⓒ Ⓓ Ⓔ	3. D	10. C
4. Ⓐ Ⓑ Ⓒ Ⓓ Ⓔ	11. Ⓐ Ⓑ Ⓒ Ⓓ Ⓔ	4. E	11. A
5. Ⓐ Ⓑ Ⓒ Ⓓ Ⓔ	12. Ⓐ Ⓑ Ⓒ Ⓓ Ⓔ	5. A	12. B
6. Ⓐ Ⓑ Ⓒ Ⓓ Ⓔ	13. Ⓐ Ⓑ Ⓒ Ⓓ Ⓔ	6. D	13. C
7. Ⓐ Ⓑ Ⓒ Ⓓ Ⓔ	14. Ⓐ Ⓑ Ⓒ Ⓓ Ⓔ	7. E	14. E

EXPLANATIONS

6. **(D)** There are two interpretations to this series. Both yield the same correct answer. If you mark the steps between numbers, you will find the pattern: $+5$, -3; $+5$, -3 . . . . If you continue with this pattern, you will come up with $18 + 5 = 23 - 3 = 20$. Or, before marking the steps, you might notice two alternating series, both ascending by $+2$. These would read: 12 14 16 18 20 and 17 19 21 23.

7. **(E)** The first series ascends by $+1$. The alternating series ascends by $+2$.

8. **(C)** Group the numbers into threes, and you can see that each group of three is a step down from the group before it: 21 8 18; 20 7 17; 19 6 16.

9. **(D)** The pattern is: $+1$, $+1$, repeat the number, $+2$, $+2$, repeat the number, $+3$, $+3$ . . . .

10. **(C)** The pattern is: -6, -5, -4, -3, -2 . . . . Between each step of the series, we find the number 22.

11. **(A)** The sequence 19 20 21 22 is repeated over and over.

12. **(B)** The pattern is: repeat the number, -20, -10; repeat the number, -20, -10; repeat the number . . . .

13. **(C)** The first number appears only once; the second number twice; the third number three times; and, if the series were to continue, the fourth number would appear four times.

14. **(E)** The simplest way to solve this problem is to see the pattern: $+6$, -8; $+6$, -8 . . . . However, you could also see two alternating series, both descending at the rate of -2, one beginning at 27 and the other at 33.

PART A—NUMBER SERIES

TIME: 20 Minutes. 24 Questions.

Directions: Each number series question consists of a series of numbers which follows some definite order. The numbers progress from left to right according to some rule. One lettered pair of numbers comprises the next two numbers in the series. Study each series to try to find a pattern to the series and to figure the rule which governs the progression. Choose the answer pair which continues the series according to the pattern established and mark its letter on your answer sheet. Correct answers are on page 126.

1. 8   9   9   8   10   10   8   ....   (A) 11   8   (B) 8   13   (C) 8   11   (D) 11   11   (E) 8   8

2. 10   10   11   11   12   12   13   ......   (A) 15   15   (B) 13   13   (C) 14   14   (D) 13   14   (E) 14   15

3. 6   6   10   6   6   12   6   ....   (A) 6   14   (B) 13   6   (C) 14   6   (D) 6   13   (E) 6   6

4. 17   11   5   16   10   4   15   ....   (A) 13   9   (B) 13   11   (C) 8   5   (D) 9   5   (E) 9   3

5. 1   3   2   4   3   5   4   ....   (A) 6   8   (B) 5   6   (C) 6   5   (D) 3   4   (E) 3   5

6. 11   11   10   12   12   11   13   ......   (A) 12   14   (B) 14   12   (C) 14   14   (D) 13   14   (E) 13   12

7. 18   5   6   18   7   8   18   ....   (A) 9   9   (B) 9   10   (C) 18   9   (D) 8   9   (E) 18   7

8. 8   1   9   3   10   5   11   ....   (A) 7   12   (B) 6   12   (C) 12   6   (D) 7   8   (E) 6   7

9. 14   12   10   20   18   16   32   30 .   (A) 60   18   (B) 32   64   (C) 30   28   (D) 28   56   (E) 28   28

10. 67   59   52   44   37   29   22   .....   (A) 15   7   (B) 14   8   (C) 14   7   (D) 15   8   (E) 16   11

11. 17   79   20   74   23   69   26   ......   (A) 64   29   (B) 65   30   (C) 29   64   (D) 23   75   (E) 26   64

12. 3   5   10   8   4   6   12   10   5 ...   (A) 8   16   (B) 7   14   (C) 10   20   (D) 10   5   (E) 7   9

13. 58   52   52   46   46   40   40   .....   (A) 34   28   (B) 28   28   (C) 40   34   (D) 35   35   (E) 34   34

14. 32   37   33   33   38   34   34   .....   (A) 38   43   (B) 34   39   (C) 39   35   (D) 39   39   (E) 34   40

15. 15   17   19   16   18   20   17 ....   (A) 14   16   (B) 19   21   (C) 17   19   (D) 16   18   (E) 19   16

16. 5   15   7   21   13   39   31   ....   (A) 93   85   (B) 62   69   (C) 39   117   (D) 93   87   (E) 31   93

17. 84   76   70   62   56   48   42   .....   (A) 42   36   (B) 34   26   (C) 36   28   (D) 36   24   (E) 34   28

18. 47 23 43 27 39 31 35 . . . . . (A) 31 27 (B) 39 43 (C) 39 35 (D) 35 31 (E) 31 35

19. 14 23 31 38 44 49 53 . . . . . (A) 55 57 (B) 57 61 (C) 56 58 (D) 57 59 (E) 58 62

20. 5 6 8 8 9 11 11 12 . . . . . (A) 12 13 (B) 14 14 (C) 14 15 (D) 14 16 (E) 12 14

21. 9 18 41 41 36 72 41 . . . . . (A) 108 108 (B) 41 108 (C) 41 144 (D) 144 144 (E) 72 41

22. 13 15 17 13 15 17 13 . . . . . (A) 17 15 (B) 13 15 (C) 17 13 (D) 15 13 (E) 15 17

23. 13 92 17 89 21 86 25 . . . . . (A) 83 29 (B) 24 89 (C) 29 83 (D) 25 83 (E) 89 21

24. 10 20 23 13 26 29 19 . . . . . (A) 9 12 (B) 38 41 (C) 22 44 (D) 44 33 (E) 36 39

END OF PART A

If you complete this part before time is up, go over your work on this part only. Do not turn the page until you are told to do so.

PART B—ADDRESS CODING

SAMPLE QUESTIONS

The seven sample questions for this part are based upon the addresses in the five boxes below. Your task is to mark on your answer sheet the letter of the box in which each address belongs. The instructions for Part B permit you to look at the boxes if you cannot remember in which box an address belongs. You may look at the boxes while answering these Part B sample questions. The questions in Part C of the exam will be based upon the same boxes as the questions in Part B, but in answering Part C you may NOT look at the boxes. There will be no sample questions before Part C.

A	B	C	D	E
4000-5099 Delhi Hunter 6100-6199 Lyme Joyce 1300-1699 Keats	3700-3899 Delhi Puritan 8200-8399 Lyme Stonewall 2200-3699 Keats	3900-3999 Delhi Torrance 6200-6899 Lyme Berwick 3900-4199 Keats	5700-5899 Delhi Barker 8400-8599 Lyme Chalford 3700-3899 Keats	5100-5699 Delhi Lockwood 6900-8199 Lyme Kempster 1700-2199 Keats

1. Kempster
2. 6100-6199 Lyme
3. 3900-3999 Delhi
4. Chalford
5. Puritan
6. 1700-2199 Keats
7. 3900-4199 Keats

SAMPLE ANSWER SHEET

1. Ⓐ Ⓑ Ⓒ Ⓓ Ⓔ
2. Ⓐ Ⓑ Ⓒ Ⓓ Ⓔ
3. Ⓐ Ⓑ Ⓒ Ⓓ Ⓔ
4. Ⓐ Ⓑ Ⓒ Ⓓ Ⓔ
5. Ⓐ Ⓑ Ⓒ Ⓓ Ⓔ
6. Ⓐ Ⓑ Ⓒ Ⓓ Ⓔ
7. Ⓐ Ⓑ Ⓒ Ⓓ Ⓔ

CORRECT ANSWERS

1. E
2. A
3. C
4. D
5. B
6. E
7. C

PART B—ADDRESS CODING

Directions: *There are five boxes labeled A, B, C, D, and E. In each box are five addresses, three of which include a number span and a name and two of which are names alone. You will have five (5) minutes to memorize the locations of all twenty-five addresses. Then you will have three (3) minutes to mark your answer sheet with the letter of the box in which each address in the question list belongs. For Part B you may refer to the boxes while answering, though you will lose speed by doing so. For Part C you may NOT look at the boxes, so do your best to memorize in the five minutes allowed you now. Correct answers are on page 127.*

MEMORIZING TIME: 5 Minutes.

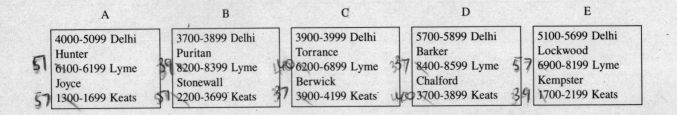

A	B	C	D	E
4000-5099 Delhi Hunter 6100-6199 Lyme Joyce 1300-1699 Keats	3700-3899 Delhi Puritan 8200-8399 Lyme Stonewall 2200-3699 Keats	3900-3999 Delhi Torrance 6200-6899 Lyme Berwick 3900-4199 Keats	5700-5899 Delhi Barker 8400-8599 Lyme Chalford 3700-3899 Keats	5100-5699 Delhi Lockwood 6900-8199 Lyme Kempster 1700-2199 Keats

ANSWERING TIME: 3 Minutes. 88 Questions.

1. Kempster
2. 1300-1699 Keats
3. 8200-8399 Lyme
4. 3900-3999 Delhi
5. 8400-8599 Lyme
6. 1700-2199 Keats
7. Puritan
8. Chalford
9. 4000-5099 Delhi
10. 3700-3899 Keats
11. 6900-8199 Lyme
12. Hunter

13. Barker
14. Berwick
15. 5700-5899 Delhi
16. 6200-6899 Lyme
17. 2200-3699 Keats
18. Kempster
19. Torrance
20. 6100-6199 Lyme
21. 3700-3899 Delhi
22. 3900-4199 Keats
23. Hunter
24. 5100-5699 Delhi

25. Joyce
26. Lockwood
27. Stonewall
28. 2200-3699 Keats
29. 5100-5699 Delhi
30. 8400-8599 Lyme
31. Puritan
32. 4000-5099 Delhi
33. 1700-2199 Keats
34. Torrance
35. Barker
36. 6100-6199 Lyme
37. 3900-3999 Delhi
38. 6900-8199 Lyme
39. Lockwood
40. Joyce
41. 8200-8399 Lyme
42. 5700-5899 Delhi
43. 3700-3899 Delhi
44. Stonewall
45. Berwick
46. 1300-1699 Keats
47. 3700-3899 Keats
48. 8200-8399 Lyme
49. 8400-8599 Lyme
50. Hunter
51. Kempster
52. Chalford
53. 8400-8599 Lyme
54. 3700-3899 Delhi
55. 6100-6199 Lyme
56. Barker

57. 5100-5699 Delhi
58. 1700-2199 Keats
59. 3900-4199 Keats
60. 5700-5899 Delhi
61. Joyce
62. Torrance
63. Kempster
64. 4000-5099 Delhi
65. 2200-3699 Keats
66. 6200-6899 Lyme
67. Berwick
68. Lockwood
69. 6900-8199 Lyme
70. 1300-1699 Keats
71. 5100-5699 Delhi
72. Stonewall
73. Barker
74. 8200-8399 Lyme
75. 3900-4199 Keats
76. 3700-3899 Keats
77. 3700-3899 Delhi
78. Lockwood
79. Berwick
80. Hunter
81. 1700-2199 Keats
82. 8400-8599 Lyme
83. 6100-6199 Lyme
84. Puritan
85. Torrance
86. 6900-8199 Lyme
87. 2200-3699 Keats
88. 5100-5699 Delhi

END OF PART B

If you finish before time is up, use the remaining few seconds to continue memorizing the locations of the addresses. Do not turn the page until you are told to do so.

PART C—ADDRESS CODE MEMORY

TIME: 5 Minutes. 88 Questions.

Directions: *Relying entirely upon your memory, mark your answer sheet with the letter of the box in which each address belongs. Correct answers are on page 127.*

1. 4000-5099 Delhi
2. 6200-6899 Lyme
3. 1700-2199 Keats
4. 1300-1699 Keats
5. Chalford
6. Berwick
7. 3900-3999 Delhi
8. 3700-3899 Keats
9. 6100-6199 Lyme
10. Stonewall
11. Lockwood
12. Kempster
13. Joyce
14. 5100-5699 Delhi
15. 6900-8199 Lyme
16. 5700-5899 Delhi
17. Puritan
18. 8400-8599 Lyme
19. 2200-3699 Keats
20. 3900-4199 Keats
21. Hunter
22. 8200-8399 Lyme
23. Torrance
24. Barker
25. 3700-3899 Delhi
26. Chalford
27. 2200-3699 Keats
28. 4000-5099 Delhi
29. 5100-5699 Delhi
30. 1700-2199 Keats
31. 6100-6199 Lyme
32. 3700-3899 Keats
33. 8200-8399 Lyme
34. Lockwood
35. Hunter

36. 5700-5899 Delhi
37. 6900-8199 Lyme
38. Puritan
39. Kempster
40. 3900-4199 Keats
41. 5100-5699 Delhi
42. 1300-1699 Keats
43. 6200-6899 Lyme
44. Berwick
45. 1700-2199 Keats
46. Stonewall
47. Chalford
48. Hunter
49. 3700-3899 Delhi
50. 3900-4199 Keats
51. 3700-3899 Keats
52. Joyce
53. Lockwood
54. 4000-5099 Delhi
55. 5100-5699 Delhi
56. Puritan
57. Kempster
58. 8400-8599 Lyme
59. 5700-5899 Delhi
60. Berwick
61. 6100-6199 Lyme
62. 6200-6899 Lyme
63. 2200-3699 Keats
64. Torrance
65. Barker
66. 1300-1699 Keats
67. 5100-5699 Delhi
68. 8400-8599 Lyme
69. 3900-4199 Keats
70. Puritan

71. Kempster
72. 6100-6199 Lyme
73. 3700-3899 Delhi
74. 1700-2199 Keats
75. Hunter
76. Berwick
77. 1300-1699 Keats
78. 5700-5899 Delhi
79. 6900-8199 Lyme

80. Chalford
81. Lockwood
82. 4000-5099 Delhi
83. 2200-3699 Lyme
84. 6200-6899 Lyme
85. Torrance
86. Joyce
87. 5700-5899 Delhi
88. 8200-8399 Lyme

END OF PART C

If you finish before time is up, check your answers on this part only. Do not turn the page until you are told to do so.

PART D—ADDRESS CHECKING TEST

SAMPLE QUESTIONS

You will be allowed three minutes to read the directions and answer the five sample questions which follow. On the actual test, however, you will have only six minutes to answer 95 questions, so see how quickly you can compare addresses and still get the correct answer.

Directions: Each question consists of two addresses. If the two addresses are alike in EVERY way, *mark Ⓐ on your answer sheet*. If the two addresses are different in ANY way, *mark Ⓓ on your answer sheet.*

1 . . . 7418 Lehigh Hwy   7418 Lehigh Hwy
2 . . . Santa Barbara CA 93106   Santa Barbra CA 93106
3 . . . 6281 SW 134th St   6821 SW 134th St
4 . . . 9163 Barbados Blvd   9163 Barbados Blvd
5 . . . 6420 Alexandria Ave E   6420 Alexandria Ave S

SAMPLE ANSWER SHEET	
1. Ⓐ Ⓓ	4. Ⓐ Ⓓ
2. Ⓐ Ⓓ	5. Ⓐ Ⓓ
3. Ⓐ Ⓓ	

CORRECT ANSWERS	
1. A	4. A
2. D	5. D
3. D	

PART D—ADDRESS CHECKING

TIME: 6 Minutes. 95 Questions.

Directions: *Look carefully at the two addresses in each question. If the two addresses are* alike *in EVERY way, mark Ⓐ on your answer sheet. If the two addresses are different in ANY way, mark Ⓓ on your answer sheet. Correct answers are on page 128.*

1	7842 Dennison St	7482 Dennison St
2	3286 Sleepy Hlw	3286 Sleepy Hlw
3	New York NY 10027	New York NY 10027
4	New London CT 06320	New London CN 06320
5	1858 Connecticut Ave NW	1858 Connecticut Ave NW
6	2376 Sturgis Blvd	2376 Sturges Blvd
7	1979 S 247th Ave	1979 S 274th Ave
8	3658 Wimpole St	3658 Wimpole St
9	2269 Glengarry Rd	2669 Glengarry Rd
10	Storrs CT 06268	Storrs CT 06268
11	8972 Southern Arty	9872 Southern Arty
12	4162 Avenue D So	4162 Avenue D So
13	9046 Dairylea Wy	9046 Dairylee Wy
14	Ithaca NY 14853	Ithaca NY 14583
15	8824 Festival Pkwy	8824 Festival Pkwy
16	9062 Hollywood Blvd	9062 N Hollywood Blvd
17	1888 Parkchester Tpke	1888 Parkchester Tpke
18	3428 W Rockland Rd	3428 W Rockland Rd
19	Omaha NE 68178	Omaha NB 68178
20	961 SE West St	961 SE West St
21	1794 Chesterfield Rd	1794 Chesterfield Dr
22	7984 Stuyvesant Pl	7984 Stuyvestant Pl
23	Hanover NH 03755	Hangover NH 03755
24	894 Tybouts Cor	894 Tybout Cor
25	4824 S 178th Ave	4824 S 178th Ave
26	1761 Cragswold Apts	1761 Cragswold Apts
27	8423 Scarborough Hl	8423 Scarborough Hl
28	8774 Kentucky Ave SE	8874 Kentucky Ave SE
29	Davidson NC 28036	Davidson NC 28036
30	7568 Brattleboro Hwy	7568 Brattleboro Hwy
31	1426 Bala Cynwyd Hts	1426 Bala Cynwyd Hts
32	135 Paradise Circle	135 S Paradise Circle
33	Dayton OH 45469	Dayton OK 45469
34	9816 School Ln	9816 School Ln
35	5162 W 195th Rd	5163 W 195th Rd

36	4617 Mississippi Ave NW	4617 Mississippi Ave SW
37	6513 Firenze St	6513 Firenze St
38	8651 Ridgeway Crest	8651 Ridgway Crest
39	Newark DE 19711	Newark DE 19771
40	Granville OH 43023	Granville OH 43023
41	219 Park Ave So	2191 Park Ave So
42	8134 Blauvelt Blvd	8134 Blauvelt Blvd
43	3546 Dudley Dr	3546 Dudley Dr
44	8042 Martinson Wy	8402 Martinson Wy
45	4454 Bannister Blvd	4544 Bannister Blvd
46	2862 Blue Ridge Pky	2862 Blue Ridge Pkwy
47	9098 Transcontinental Hwy	9098 Transcontinental Hwy
48	764 Church Ln N	764 Church Ln N
49	2248 S State Rd	2248 S State Dr
50	Denver CO 80208	Denver CO 80208
51	Greencastle IN 46135	Greencastle IN 46135
52	Detroit MI 48221	Detroit MI 48221
53	2252 Tennessee Ave SE	2252 Tennessee Ave SE
54	7416 W 387th Blvd	7416 W 378th Blvd
55	8741 Arundel Arc	8741 Arundle Arc
56	8072 Martine Twr	8072 Martini Twr
57	2236 Heathcote Inn	2236 Heathcote Inn
58	5696 Artillery Ln	5696 Artillery Ln
59	7562 N Needham Rd	7562 N Needham Dr
60	8423 The Buckingham	8432 The Buckingham
61	Carlisle PA 17013	Carlisle PA 17013
62	Des Moines IA 50311	Des Miones IA 50311
63	8432 Bryant Gdn	8432 Bryant Gdns
64	7459 Quaropas St	7459 Quaroppas St
65	842 W Larch Ln	842 W Larch Ln
66	7041 98th Wy	7041 89th Wy
67	4518 Wyoming Ave NW	4518 Wyoming Ave NW
68	9216 S Avenue U	9216 S Avenue U
69	8064 W Fifth St	8064 W Fifth St
70	Madison NJ 07940	Madison NJ 09740
71	Durham NC 27706	Durnam NC 27706
72	7516 Cranberry Hl	7516 Cranberry Hl
73	7568 Cascade Dr	7568 Cascades Dr
74	4181 Chelsea Sta	4181 Chelsea Sta
75	5612 Heatherdell Rd	5612 Heatherdale Rd
76	1286 W 375th Ave	1286 W 375th Ave
77	6238 Rhode Island Ave SE	6283 Rhode Island Ave SE
78	1626 Clarendon Rd	1626 Clarendon Rd
79	3246 W Hartsdale Ave	3246 W Hartsdale Ave
80	Pittsburgh PA 15219	Pittsburgh PA 15219
81	Richmond IN 47374	Richmond IN 47374
82	7416 Coliseum St	7416 Colaseum St
83	1432 Calico Corn	1432 Calico Corn
84	Atlanta GA 30322	Atlanta CA 30322
85	8457 Norumbega Pky	8475 Norumbega Pky
86	9035 Hardscrabble Rd	9035 Hardscramble Rd

87 . . . 6904 Jeffrey Ave		6904 Jeffery Ave
88 . . . Tallahassee FL 32306		Tallahassee FL 32360
89 . . . 8512 Iriquois Ave		8512 Iroquois Ave
90 . . . 7513 Sunrise Hwy		7513 Sunrise Hwy
91 . . . 9563 Schuykill Expy		9563 Schuykill Expy
92 . . . Gainesville FL 32611		Gainsville FL 32611
93 . . . 8672 W Gladstone Rd		8762 Gladstone Rd
94 . . . Bronx NY 10458		Bronx NY 10458
95 . . . 2484 S 423rd Rd		2484 S 423rd Rd

END OF EXAM

*If you finish before time is up, check over your answers on
this part only. Do not return to any previous part.*

CORRECT ANSWERS—THIRD MODEL EXAM

PART A—NUMBER SERIES

1. D	4. E	7. B	10. C	13. E	16. A	19. C	22. E
2. D	5. C	8. A	11. A	14. C	17. E	20. B	23. A
3. A	6. E	9. D	12. B	15. B	18. D	21. C	24. B

EXPLANATIONS—NUMBER SERIES

1. **(D)** The series really begins with 9 and consists of repeated numbers moving upward in order. The number 8 is inserted between each pair of repeated numbers in the series.

2. **(D)** The numbers repeat themselves and move up in order.

3. **(A)** 6 6 is a repetitive theme. Between each set of 6's, the numbers move up by +2.

4. **(E)** The full sequence is a number of sets of mini-series. Each mini-series consists of three numbers decreasing by −6. Each succeeding mini-series begins with a number one lower than the previous mini-series.

5. **(C)** Two alternating series each increase by +1. The first series starts at 1 and the second series starts at 3.

6. **(E)** Two series alternate. The first series consists of repeating numbers that move up by +1. The alternating series consists of numbers that move up by +1 without repeating.

7. **(B)** The series proceeds, 5 6 7 8 9 10 with the number 18 appearing between each two numbers.

8. **(A)** The first series ascends one number at a time starting from 8. The alternating series ascends by +2 starting from 1.

9. **(D)** The pattern is: −2, −2, ×2; −2, −2, ×2 . . . .

10. **(C)** The pattern is: −8, −7; −8, −7; −8, −7 . . . .

11. **(A)** Two series alternate. The first series ascends by +3; the alternating series descends by −5.

12. **(B)** This is a toughie. The pattern is +2, ×2, −2, ÷2; +2, ×2, −2, ÷2 . . . .

13. **(E)** The pattern is: −6, repeat the number; −6, repeat the number . . . .

14. **(C)** The pattern is: +5, −4, repeat the number; +5, −4, repeat the number . . . .

15. **(B)** The pattern is: +2, +2, −3; +2, +2, −3 . . . .

16. **(A)** The pattern is: ×3, −8; ×3, −8; ×3, −8 . . . .

17. **(E)** The pattern is: −8, −6; −8, −6; −8, −6 . . . .

18. **(D)** There are two alternating series. The first series descends by -4 starting from $\underline{47}$; the alternating series ascends by $+4$, starting from $\underline{23}$.

19. **(C)** The pattern is: $+9, +8, +7, +6, +5, +4, +3, +2, +1$.

20. **(B)** The pattern is: $+1, +2$, repeat the number; $+1, +2$, repeat the number . . . .

21. **(C)** This is really a times 2 series with the number 41 appearing twice after each two numbers in the series. Thus: $9 \overset{\times 2}{} 18 \overset{\times 2}{} 36 \overset{\times 2}{} 72 \overset{\times 2}{} 144$.

22. **(E)** The sequence 13 15 17 repeats itself over and over.

23. **(A)** Two series alternate. The first series ascends by $+4$; the alternating series descends by -3.

24. **(B)** The pattern is: $\times 2, +3, -10; \times 2, +3, -10; \times 2, +3, -10$ . . . .

PART B—ADDRESS CODING

1. E	12. A	23. A	34. C	45. C	56. D	67. C	78. E
2. A	13. D	24. E	35. D	46. A	57. E	68. E	79. C
3. B	14. C	25. A	36. A	47. D	58. E	69. E	80. A
4. C	15. D	26. E	37. C	48. B	59. C	70. A	81. E
5. D	16. C	27. B	38. E	49. D	60. D	71. E	82. D
6. E	17. B	28. B	39. E	50. A	61. A	72. B	83. A
7. B	18. E	29. E	40. A	51. E	62. C	73. D	84. B
8. D	19. C	30. D	41. B	52. D	63. E	74. B	85. C
9. A	20. A	31. B	42. D	53. D	64. A	75. C	86. E
10. D	21. B	32. A	43. B	54. B	65. B	76. D	87. B
11. E	22. C	33. E	44. B	55. A	66. C	77. B	88. E

PART C—ADDRESS CODE MEMORY

1. A	12. E	23. C	34. E	45. E	56. B	67. E	78. D
2. C	13. A	24. D	35. A	46. B	57. E	68. D	79. E
3. E	14. E	25. B	36. D	47. D	58. D	69. C	80. D
4. A	15. E	26. D	37. E	48. A	59. D	70. B	81. E
5. D	16. D	27. B	38. B	49. B	60. C	71. E	82. A
6. C	17. B	28. A	39. E	50. C	61. A	72. A	83. B
7. C	18. D	29. E	40. C	51. D	62. C	73. B	84. C
8. D	19. B	30. E	41. E	52. A	63. B	74. E	85. C
9. A	20. C	31. A	42. A	53. E	64. C	75. A	86. A
10. B	21. A	32. D	43. C	54. A	65. D	76. C	87. D
11. E	22. B	33. B	44. C	55. E	66. A	77. A	88. B

PART D—ADDRESS CHECKING

1. D	13. D	25. A	37. A	49. D	61. A	73. D	85. D
2. A	14. D	26. A	38. D	50. A	62. D	74. A	86. D
3. A	15. A	27. A	39. D	51. A	63. D	75. D	87. D
4. D	16. D	28. D	40. A	52. A	64. D	76. A	88. D
5. A	17. A	29. A	41. D	53. A	65. A	77. X D	89. D
6. D	18. A	30. A	42. A	54. D	66. D	78. A	90. A
7. D	19. D	31. A	43. A	55. D	67. A	79. A	91. A
8. A	20. A	32. D	44. D	56. D	68. A	80. A	92. D
9. D	21. D	33. D	45. D	57. A	69. A	81. A	93. D
10. A	22. D	34. A	46. D	58. A	70. D	82. D	94. A
11. D	23. D	35. D	47. A	59. D	71. D	83. A	95. A
12. A	24. D	36. D	48. A	60. D	72. A	84. D	

By now you should be able to analyze your own pattern of errors. Make up a tally sheet by cross-checking your incorrect answers against the correct answers and against the questions themselves. Mark your tally sheet like this | | | | | |.

ADDRESS CHECKING ERROR ANALYSIS CHART

Type of Error	Tally	Total Number
Number of addresses that were alike and you incorrectly marked "different"		
Number of addresses that were different and you incorrectly marked "alike"		
Number of addresses in which you missed a difference in NUMBERS		
Number of addresses in which you missed a difference in ABBREVIATIONS		
Number of addresses in which you missed a difference in NAMES		

SCORE SHEET FOR THIRD MODEL EXAM

PART A—NUMBER SERIES

Number Right equals Score

_____ = _____

PART B—ADDRESS CODING

Number Right minus (Number Wrong ÷ 4) equals Score

_____ − _____ = _____

PART C—ADDRESS CODE MEMORY

Number Right minus (Number Wrong ÷ 4) equals Score

_____ − _____ = _____

PART D—ADDRESS CHECKING

Number Right minus Number Wrong equals Score

_____ − _____ = _____

SELF-EVALUATION CHART

Part	Excellent	Good	Average	Fair	Poor
Number Series	21–24	18–20	14–17	11–13	1–10
Address Coding	75–88	63–74	52–62	40–51	1–39
Address Code Memory	75–88	60–74	45–59	30–44	1–29
Address Checking	80–95	65–79	50–64	35–49	1–34

PROGRESS CHART

Blacken to the closest score to chart your progress.

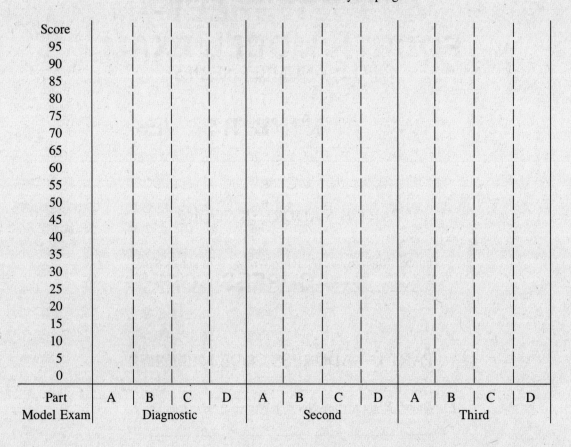

Score												
95												
90												
85												
80												
75												
70												
65												
60												
55												
50												
45												
40												
35												
30												
25												
20												
15												
10												
5												
0												
Part	A	B	C	D	A	B	C	D	A	B	C	D
Model Exam	Diagnostic				Second				Third			

ANSWER SHEET—
FOURTH MODEL EXAM

Tear out this Answer Sheet and use it to mark your answers for the exam that follows.

PART A—NUMBER SERIES

1. Ⓐ Ⓑ Ⓒ Ⓓ Ⓔ   6. Ⓐ Ⓑ Ⓒ Ⓓ Ⓔ   11. Ⓐ Ⓑ Ⓒ Ⓓ Ⓔ   16. Ⓐ Ⓑ Ⓒ Ⓓ Ⓔ   21. Ⓐ Ⓑ Ⓒ Ⓓ Ⓔ
2. Ⓐ Ⓑ Ⓒ Ⓓ Ⓔ   7. Ⓐ Ⓑ Ⓒ Ⓓ Ⓔ   12. Ⓐ Ⓑ Ⓒ Ⓓ Ⓔ   17. Ⓐ Ⓑ Ⓒ Ⓓ Ⓔ   22. Ⓐ Ⓑ Ⓒ Ⓓ Ⓔ
3. Ⓐ Ⓑ Ⓒ Ⓓ Ⓔ   8. Ⓐ Ⓑ Ⓒ Ⓓ Ⓔ   13. Ⓐ Ⓑ Ⓒ Ⓓ Ⓔ   18. Ⓐ Ⓑ Ⓒ Ⓓ Ⓔ   23. Ⓐ Ⓑ Ⓒ Ⓓ Ⓔ
4. Ⓐ Ⓑ Ⓒ Ⓓ Ⓔ   9. Ⓐ Ⓑ Ⓒ Ⓓ Ⓔ   14. Ⓐ Ⓑ Ⓒ Ⓓ Ⓔ   19. Ⓐ Ⓑ Ⓒ Ⓓ Ⓔ   24. Ⓐ Ⓑ Ⓒ Ⓓ Ⓔ
5. Ⓐ Ⓑ Ⓒ Ⓓ Ⓔ   10. Ⓐ Ⓑ Ⓒ Ⓓ Ⓔ   15. Ⓐ Ⓑ Ⓒ Ⓓ Ⓔ   20. Ⓐ Ⓑ Ⓒ Ⓓ Ⓔ

PART B—ADDRESS CODING

1. Ⓐ Ⓑ Ⓒ Ⓓ Ⓔ   19. Ⓐ Ⓑ Ⓒ Ⓓ Ⓔ   37. Ⓐ Ⓑ Ⓒ Ⓓ Ⓔ   55. Ⓐ Ⓑ Ⓒ Ⓓ Ⓔ   73. Ⓐ Ⓑ Ⓒ Ⓓ Ⓔ
2. Ⓐ Ⓑ Ⓒ Ⓓ Ⓔ   20. Ⓐ Ⓑ Ⓒ Ⓓ Ⓔ   38. Ⓐ Ⓑ Ⓒ Ⓓ Ⓔ   56. Ⓐ Ⓑ Ⓒ Ⓓ Ⓔ   74. Ⓐ Ⓑ Ⓒ Ⓓ Ⓔ
3. Ⓐ Ⓑ Ⓒ Ⓓ Ⓔ   21. Ⓐ Ⓑ Ⓒ Ⓓ Ⓔ   39. Ⓐ Ⓑ Ⓒ Ⓓ Ⓔ   57. Ⓐ Ⓑ Ⓒ Ⓓ Ⓔ   75. Ⓐ Ⓑ Ⓒ Ⓓ Ⓔ
4. Ⓐ Ⓑ Ⓒ Ⓓ Ⓔ   22. Ⓐ Ⓑ Ⓒ Ⓓ Ⓔ   40. Ⓐ Ⓑ Ⓒ Ⓓ Ⓔ   58. Ⓐ Ⓑ Ⓒ Ⓓ Ⓔ   76. Ⓐ Ⓑ Ⓒ Ⓓ Ⓔ
5. Ⓐ Ⓑ Ⓒ Ⓓ Ⓔ   23. Ⓐ Ⓑ Ⓒ Ⓓ Ⓔ   41. Ⓐ Ⓑ Ⓒ Ⓓ Ⓔ   59. Ⓐ Ⓑ Ⓒ Ⓓ Ⓔ   77. Ⓐ Ⓑ Ⓒ Ⓓ Ⓔ
6. Ⓐ Ⓑ Ⓒ Ⓓ Ⓔ   24. Ⓐ Ⓑ Ⓒ Ⓓ Ⓔ   42. Ⓐ Ⓑ Ⓒ Ⓓ Ⓔ   60. Ⓐ Ⓑ Ⓒ Ⓓ Ⓔ   78. Ⓐ Ⓑ Ⓒ Ⓓ Ⓔ
7. Ⓐ Ⓑ Ⓒ Ⓓ Ⓔ   25. Ⓐ Ⓑ Ⓒ Ⓓ Ⓔ   43. Ⓐ Ⓑ Ⓒ Ⓓ Ⓔ   61. Ⓐ Ⓑ Ⓒ Ⓓ Ⓔ   79. Ⓐ Ⓑ Ⓒ Ⓓ Ⓔ
8. Ⓐ Ⓑ Ⓒ Ⓓ Ⓔ   26. Ⓐ Ⓑ Ⓒ Ⓓ Ⓔ   44. Ⓐ Ⓑ Ⓒ Ⓓ Ⓔ   62. Ⓐ Ⓑ Ⓒ Ⓓ Ⓔ   80. Ⓐ Ⓑ Ⓒ Ⓓ Ⓔ
9. Ⓐ Ⓑ Ⓒ Ⓓ Ⓔ   27. Ⓐ Ⓑ Ⓒ Ⓓ Ⓔ   45. Ⓐ Ⓑ Ⓒ Ⓓ Ⓔ   63. Ⓐ Ⓑ Ⓒ Ⓓ Ⓔ   81. Ⓐ Ⓑ Ⓒ Ⓓ Ⓔ
10. Ⓐ Ⓑ Ⓒ Ⓓ Ⓔ   28. Ⓐ Ⓑ Ⓒ Ⓓ Ⓔ   46. Ⓐ Ⓑ Ⓒ Ⓓ Ⓔ   64. Ⓐ Ⓑ Ⓒ Ⓓ Ⓔ   82. Ⓐ Ⓑ Ⓒ Ⓓ Ⓔ
11. Ⓐ Ⓑ Ⓒ Ⓓ Ⓔ   29. Ⓐ Ⓑ Ⓒ Ⓓ Ⓔ   47. Ⓐ Ⓑ Ⓒ Ⓓ Ⓔ   65. Ⓐ Ⓑ Ⓒ Ⓓ Ⓔ   83. Ⓐ Ⓑ Ⓒ Ⓓ Ⓔ
12. Ⓐ Ⓑ Ⓒ Ⓓ Ⓔ   30. Ⓐ Ⓑ Ⓒ Ⓓ Ⓔ   48. Ⓐ Ⓑ Ⓒ Ⓓ Ⓔ   66. Ⓐ Ⓑ Ⓒ Ⓓ Ⓔ   84. Ⓐ Ⓑ Ⓒ Ⓓ Ⓔ
13. Ⓐ Ⓑ Ⓒ Ⓓ Ⓔ   31. Ⓐ Ⓑ Ⓒ Ⓓ Ⓔ   49. Ⓐ Ⓑ Ⓒ Ⓓ Ⓔ   67. Ⓐ Ⓑ Ⓒ Ⓓ Ⓔ   85. Ⓐ Ⓑ Ⓒ Ⓓ Ⓔ
14. Ⓐ Ⓑ Ⓒ Ⓓ Ⓔ   32. Ⓐ Ⓑ Ⓒ Ⓓ Ⓔ   50. Ⓐ Ⓑ Ⓒ Ⓓ Ⓔ   68. Ⓐ Ⓑ Ⓒ Ⓓ Ⓔ   86. Ⓐ Ⓑ Ⓒ Ⓓ Ⓔ
15. Ⓐ Ⓑ Ⓒ Ⓓ Ⓔ   33. Ⓐ Ⓑ Ⓒ Ⓓ Ⓔ   51. Ⓐ Ⓑ Ⓒ Ⓓ Ⓔ   69. Ⓐ Ⓑ Ⓒ Ⓓ Ⓔ   87. Ⓐ Ⓑ Ⓒ Ⓓ Ⓔ
16. Ⓐ Ⓑ Ⓒ Ⓓ Ⓔ   34. Ⓐ Ⓑ Ⓒ Ⓓ Ⓔ   52. Ⓐ Ⓑ Ⓒ Ⓓ Ⓔ   70. Ⓐ Ⓑ Ⓒ Ⓓ Ⓔ   88. Ⓐ Ⓑ Ⓒ Ⓓ Ⓔ
17. Ⓐ Ⓑ Ⓒ Ⓓ Ⓔ   35. Ⓐ Ⓑ Ⓒ Ⓓ Ⓔ   53. Ⓐ Ⓑ Ⓒ Ⓓ Ⓔ   71. Ⓐ Ⓑ Ⓒ Ⓓ Ⓔ
18. Ⓐ Ⓑ Ⓒ Ⓓ Ⓔ   36. Ⓐ Ⓑ Ⓒ Ⓓ Ⓔ   54. Ⓐ Ⓑ Ⓒ Ⓓ Ⓔ   72. Ⓐ Ⓑ Ⓒ Ⓓ Ⓔ

Tear here

PART C—ADDRESS CODE MEMORY

1. Ⓐ Ⓑ Ⓒ Ⓓ Ⓔ
2. Ⓐ Ⓑ Ⓒ Ⓓ Ⓔ
3. Ⓐ Ⓑ Ⓒ Ⓓ Ⓔ
4. Ⓐ Ⓑ Ⓒ Ⓓ Ⓔ
5. Ⓐ Ⓑ Ⓒ Ⓓ Ⓔ
6. Ⓐ Ⓑ Ⓒ Ⓓ Ⓔ
7. Ⓐ Ⓑ Ⓒ Ⓓ Ⓔ
8. Ⓐ Ⓑ Ⓒ Ⓓ Ⓔ
9. Ⓐ Ⓑ Ⓒ Ⓓ Ⓔ
10. Ⓐ Ⓑ Ⓒ Ⓓ Ⓔ
11. Ⓐ Ⓑ Ⓒ Ⓓ Ⓔ
12. Ⓐ Ⓑ Ⓒ Ⓓ Ⓔ
13. Ⓐ Ⓑ Ⓒ Ⓓ Ⓔ
14. Ⓐ Ⓑ Ⓒ Ⓓ Ⓔ
15. Ⓐ Ⓑ Ⓒ Ⓓ Ⓔ
16. Ⓐ Ⓑ Ⓒ Ⓓ Ⓔ
17. Ⓐ Ⓑ Ⓒ Ⓓ Ⓔ
18. Ⓐ Ⓑ Ⓒ Ⓓ Ⓔ

19. Ⓐ Ⓑ Ⓒ Ⓓ Ⓔ
20. Ⓐ Ⓑ Ⓒ Ⓓ Ⓔ
21. Ⓐ Ⓑ Ⓒ Ⓓ Ⓔ
22. Ⓐ Ⓑ Ⓒ Ⓓ Ⓔ
23. Ⓐ Ⓑ Ⓒ Ⓓ Ⓔ
24. Ⓐ Ⓑ Ⓒ Ⓓ Ⓔ
25. Ⓐ Ⓑ Ⓒ Ⓓ Ⓔ
26. Ⓐ Ⓑ Ⓒ Ⓓ Ⓔ
27. Ⓐ Ⓑ Ⓒ Ⓓ Ⓔ
28. Ⓐ Ⓑ Ⓒ Ⓓ Ⓔ
29. Ⓐ Ⓑ Ⓒ Ⓓ Ⓔ
30. Ⓐ Ⓑ Ⓒ Ⓓ Ⓔ
31. Ⓐ Ⓑ Ⓒ Ⓓ Ⓔ
32. Ⓐ Ⓑ Ⓒ Ⓓ Ⓔ
33. Ⓐ Ⓑ Ⓒ Ⓓ Ⓔ
34. Ⓐ Ⓑ Ⓒ Ⓓ Ⓔ
35. Ⓐ Ⓑ Ⓒ Ⓓ Ⓔ
36. Ⓐ Ⓑ Ⓒ Ⓓ Ⓔ

37. Ⓐ Ⓑ Ⓒ Ⓓ Ⓔ
38. Ⓐ Ⓑ Ⓒ Ⓓ Ⓔ
39. Ⓐ Ⓑ Ⓒ Ⓓ Ⓔ
40. Ⓐ Ⓑ Ⓒ Ⓓ Ⓔ
41. Ⓐ Ⓑ Ⓒ Ⓓ Ⓔ
42. Ⓐ Ⓑ Ⓒ Ⓓ Ⓔ
43. Ⓐ Ⓑ Ⓒ Ⓓ Ⓔ
44. Ⓐ Ⓑ Ⓒ Ⓓ Ⓔ
45. Ⓐ Ⓑ Ⓒ Ⓓ Ⓔ
46. Ⓐ Ⓑ Ⓒ Ⓓ Ⓔ
47. Ⓐ Ⓑ Ⓒ Ⓓ Ⓔ
48. Ⓐ Ⓑ Ⓒ Ⓓ Ⓔ
49. Ⓐ Ⓑ Ⓒ Ⓓ Ⓔ
50. Ⓐ Ⓑ Ⓒ Ⓓ Ⓔ
51. Ⓐ Ⓑ Ⓒ Ⓓ Ⓔ
52. Ⓐ Ⓑ Ⓒ Ⓓ Ⓔ
53. Ⓐ Ⓑ Ⓒ Ⓓ Ⓔ
54. Ⓐ Ⓑ Ⓒ Ⓓ Ⓔ

55. Ⓐ Ⓑ Ⓒ Ⓓ Ⓔ
56. Ⓐ Ⓑ Ⓒ Ⓓ Ⓔ
57. Ⓐ Ⓑ Ⓒ Ⓓ Ⓔ
58. Ⓐ Ⓑ Ⓒ Ⓓ Ⓔ
59. Ⓐ Ⓑ Ⓒ Ⓓ Ⓔ
60. Ⓐ Ⓑ Ⓒ Ⓓ Ⓔ
61. Ⓐ Ⓑ Ⓒ Ⓓ Ⓔ
62. Ⓐ Ⓑ Ⓒ Ⓓ Ⓔ
63. Ⓐ Ⓑ Ⓒ Ⓓ Ⓔ
64. Ⓐ Ⓑ Ⓒ Ⓓ Ⓔ
65. Ⓐ Ⓑ Ⓒ Ⓓ Ⓔ
66. Ⓐ Ⓑ Ⓒ Ⓓ Ⓔ
67. Ⓐ Ⓑ Ⓒ Ⓓ Ⓔ
68. Ⓐ Ⓑ Ⓒ Ⓓ Ⓔ
69. Ⓐ Ⓑ Ⓒ Ⓓ Ⓔ
70. Ⓐ Ⓑ Ⓒ Ⓓ Ⓔ
71. Ⓐ Ⓑ Ⓒ Ⓓ Ⓔ
72. Ⓐ Ⓑ Ⓒ Ⓓ Ⓔ

73. Ⓐ Ⓑ Ⓒ Ⓓ Ⓔ
74. Ⓐ Ⓑ Ⓒ Ⓓ Ⓔ
75. Ⓐ Ⓑ Ⓒ Ⓓ Ⓔ
76. Ⓐ Ⓑ Ⓒ Ⓓ Ⓔ
77. Ⓐ Ⓑ Ⓒ Ⓓ Ⓔ
78. Ⓐ Ⓑ Ⓒ Ⓓ Ⓔ
79. Ⓐ Ⓑ Ⓒ Ⓓ Ⓔ
80. Ⓐ Ⓑ Ⓒ Ⓓ Ⓔ
81. Ⓐ Ⓑ Ⓒ Ⓓ Ⓔ
82. Ⓐ Ⓑ Ⓒ Ⓓ Ⓔ
83. Ⓐ Ⓑ Ⓒ Ⓓ Ⓔ
84. Ⓐ Ⓑ Ⓒ Ⓓ Ⓔ
85. Ⓐ Ⓑ Ⓒ Ⓓ Ⓔ
86. Ⓐ Ⓑ Ⓒ Ⓓ Ⓔ
87. Ⓐ Ⓑ Ⓒ Ⓓ Ⓔ
88. Ⓐ Ⓑ Ⓒ Ⓓ Ⓔ

Tear here

PART D—ADDRESS CHECKING

Tear here

1. Ⓐ Ⓓ	20. Ⓐ Ⓓ	39. Ⓐ Ⓓ	58. Ⓐ Ⓓ	77. Ⓐ Ⓓ
2. Ⓐ Ⓓ	21. Ⓐ Ⓓ	40. Ⓐ Ⓓ	59. Ⓐ Ⓓ	78. Ⓐ Ⓓ
3. Ⓐ Ⓓ	22. Ⓐ Ⓓ	41. Ⓐ Ⓓ	60. Ⓐ Ⓓ	79. Ⓐ Ⓓ
4. Ⓐ Ⓓ	23. Ⓐ Ⓓ	42. Ⓐ Ⓓ	61. Ⓐ Ⓓ	80. Ⓐ Ⓓ
5. Ⓐ Ⓓ	24. Ⓐ Ⓓ	43. Ⓐ Ⓓ	62. Ⓐ Ⓓ	81. Ⓐ Ⓓ
6. Ⓐ Ⓓ	25. Ⓐ Ⓓ	44. Ⓐ Ⓓ	63. Ⓐ Ⓓ	82. Ⓐ Ⓓ
7. Ⓐ Ⓓ	26. Ⓐ Ⓓ	45. Ⓐ Ⓓ	64. Ⓐ Ⓓ	83. Ⓐ Ⓓ
8. Ⓐ Ⓓ	27. Ⓐ Ⓓ	46. Ⓐ Ⓓ	65. Ⓐ Ⓓ	84. Ⓐ Ⓓ
9. Ⓐ Ⓓ	28. Ⓐ Ⓓ	47. Ⓐ Ⓓ	66. Ⓐ Ⓓ	85. Ⓐ Ⓓ
10. Ⓐ Ⓓ	29. Ⓐ Ⓓ	48. Ⓐ Ⓓ	67. Ⓐ Ⓓ	86. Ⓐ Ⓓ
11. Ⓐ Ⓓ	30. Ⓐ Ⓓ	49. Ⓐ Ⓓ	68. Ⓐ Ⓓ	87. Ⓐ Ⓓ
12. Ⓐ Ⓓ	31. Ⓐ Ⓓ	50. Ⓐ Ⓓ	69. Ⓐ Ⓓ	88. Ⓐ Ⓓ
13. Ⓐ Ⓓ	32. Ⓐ Ⓓ	51. Ⓐ Ⓓ	70. Ⓐ Ⓓ	89. Ⓐ Ⓓ
14. Ⓐ Ⓓ	33. Ⓐ Ⓓ	52. Ⓐ Ⓓ	71. Ⓐ Ⓓ	90. Ⓐ Ⓓ
15. Ⓐ Ⓓ	34. Ⓐ Ⓓ	53. Ⓐ Ⓓ	72. Ⓐ Ⓓ	91. Ⓐ Ⓓ
16. Ⓐ Ⓓ	35. Ⓐ Ⓓ	54. Ⓐ Ⓓ	73. Ⓐ Ⓓ	92. Ⓐ Ⓓ
17. Ⓐ Ⓓ	36. Ⓐ Ⓓ	55. Ⓐ Ⓓ	74. Ⓐ Ⓓ	93. Ⓐ Ⓓ
18. Ⓐ Ⓓ	37. Ⓐ Ⓓ	56. Ⓐ Ⓓ	75. Ⓐ Ⓓ	94. Ⓐ Ⓓ
19. Ⓐ Ⓓ	38. Ⓐ Ⓓ	57. Ⓐ Ⓓ	76. Ⓐ Ⓓ	95. Ⓐ Ⓓ

FOURTH MODEL EXAM

PART A—NUMBER SERIES

SAMPLE QUESTIONS

The following sample questions show you the type of question that will be used in Part A. Since this type of question may be new and unfamiliar to you, the examiner will work through the first five questions with you. Once you understand the task, you will have five minutes to answer sample questions 6 to 14 on your own. Correct answers and explanations follow.

> *Directions: Each number series question consists of a series of numbers which follows some definite order. The numbers progress from left to right according to some rule. One pair of numbers to the right of the series comprises the next two numbers in the series. Study each series to try to find a pattern to the series and to figure out the rule which governs the progression. Choose the answer pair which continues the series according to the pattern established and mark its letter on your answer sheet.*

1. 23 25 27 29 31 33 35 ..... (A) 35 36 (B) 35 37 (C) 36 37 (D) 37 38 (E) 37 39

The answer **(E)** should be easy to see. This series progresses by adding $\underline{2}$. $35 + 2 = 37 + 2 = 39$.

2. 3 3 6 6 12 12 24 .... (A) 24 36 (B) 36 36 (C) 24 24 (D) 24 48 (E) 48 48

The answer is **(D)** because the series requires you to repeat a number, then multiply it by $\underline{2}$.

3. 11 13 16 20 25 31 38 ..... (A) 46 55 (B) 45 55 (C) 40 42 (D) 47 58 (E) 42 46

The easiest way to solve this problem is to write the degree and direction of change between the numbers. By doing this, you see that the pattern is $+2, +3, +4, +5, +6, +7$. Continue the series by continuing the pattern: $38 + 8 = 46 + 9 = 55$. The answer is **(A)**.

4. 76 72 72 68 64 64 60 ..... (A) 60 56 (B) 60 60 (C) 56 56 (D) 56 52 (E) 56 54

Here the pattern is: −4, repeat the number, −4; −4, repeat the number, −4. To find that **(C)** is the answer you must realize that you are at the beginning of the pattern. 60 − 4 = 56, then repeat the number 56.

5. 92 94 96 92 94 96 92 ..... (A) 92 94 (B) 94 96 (C) 96 92 (D) 96 94 (E) 96 98

The series consists of the sequence 92 94 96 repeated over and over again. **(B)** is the answer because 94 96 continues the sequence after 92.

You will now have five minutes to complete the remaining sample number series questions.

6. 10 5 15 5 20 5 25 .... (A) 5 35 (B) 5 5 (C) 30 5 (D) 5 30 (E) 30 35

7. 13 10 11 15 12 13 17 ...... (A) 18 14 (B) 18 15 (C) 15 16 (D) 14 15 (E) 15 18

8. 30 27 24 21 18 15 12 ..... (A) 9 3 (B) 9 6 (C) 6 3 (D) 12 9 (E) 8 5

9. 3 7 10 5 8 10 7 .... (A) 10 11 (B) 10 5 (C) 10 9 (D) 10 10 (E) 9 10

10. 5 3 8 7 6 12 9 9 16 ..... (A) 16 9 (B) 16 16 (C) 11 12 (D) 20 22 (E) 18 20

11. 4 8 10 10 20 22 22 .... (A) 40 44 (B) 44 46 (C) 44 44 (D) 24 40 (E) 24 26

12. 30 30 50 50 70 70 90 ..... (A) 90 90 (B) 70 90 (C) 100 110 (D) 90 110 (E) 110 110

13. 2 3 5 6 11 12 23 .... (A) 24 47 (B) 13 14 (C) 15 17 (D) 24 25 (E) 25 50

14. 26 18 18 12 12 8 8 .... (A) 6 6 (B) 8 8 (C) 8 6 (D) 7 7 (E) 6 4

SAMPLE ANSWER SHEET		CORRECT ANSWERS	
1. A B C D E	8. A B C D E	1. E	8. B
2. A B C D E	9. A B C D E	2. D	9. E
3. A B C D E	10. A B C D E	3. A	10. C
4. A B C D E	11. A B C D E	4. C	11. B
5. A B C D E	12. A B C D E	5. B	12. D
6. A B C D E	13. A B C D E	6. D	13. A
7. A B C D E	14. A B C D E	7. D	14. A

EXPLANATIONS

6. **(D)** You can look at this series either of two ways to get the correct answer. You may see the +5 series, 10 15 20 25 30 with the number 5 appearing between members of the series. Or you may read 10 + 5 = 15 + 5 = 20 + 5 = 25 + 5 = 30.

7. **(D)** There are two series appearing in the ratio of one number of the first series to two numbers of the second series. The first series ascends by +2: 13 15 17 . . . . The second series ascends by +1: 10 11 12 13 14 15 . . . .

8. **(B)** The rule here is −3.

9. **(E)** There are two series with the number 10 appearing each time before the two series ascend. One series begins with 3 and ascends by +2: 3 5 7 . . . The second series begins with 7 and ascends by +1: 7 8 9 . . . Diagrammed, the series looks like this:

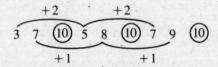

10. **(C)** There are three alternating ascending series. The first series begins with 5 and ascends by +2. The second series begins with 3 and ascends by +3. The third series begins with 8 and ascends by +4. Therefore, the pattern is: +2, +3, +4; +2, +3, +4; +2, +3, +4 . . . .

11. **(B)** The pattern is: ×2, +2, repeat the number; ×2, +2, repeat the number; ×2, +2 . . . .

12. **(D)** The pattern is: repeat the number, +20; repeat the number, +20; repeat the number, +20 . . . .

13. **(A)** This is a difficult problem. Two successive numbers are added together, and their sum becomes the next number, which, in turn is added to the number which follows it to yield another number in the series. The series looks like this: 2 + 3 = 5 + 6 = 11 + 12 = 23 + 24 = 47.

14. **(A)** The pattern is: −8, repeat the number, −6, repeat the number, −4, repeat the number, −2, repeat the number.

PART A—NUMBER SERIES

TIME: 20 Minutes. 24 Questions.

Directions: Each number series question consists of a series of numbers which follows some definite order. The numbers progress from left to right according to some rule. One lettered pair of numbers comprises the next two numbers in the series. Study each series to try to find a pattern to the series and to figure out the rule which governs the progression. Choose the answer pair which continues the series according to the pattern established and mark its letter on your answer sheet. Correct answers are on page 150.

1. 13 12 8 11 10 8 9 .... (A) 8 7 (B) 6 8 (C) 8 6 (D) 8 8 (E) 7 8
2. 13 18 13 17 13 16 13 .... (A) 15 13 (B) 13 14 (C) 13 15 (D) 14 15 (E) 15 14
3. 13 13 10 12 12 10 11 .... (A) 10 10 (B) 10 9 (C) 11 9 (D) 9 11 (E) 11 10
4. 6 5 4 6 5 4 6 .... (A) 4 6 (B) 6 4 (C) 5 4 (D) 5 6 (E) 4 5
5. 10 10 9 8 8 7 6 .... (A) 5 5 (B) 5 4 (C) 6 5 (D) 6 4 (E) 5 3
6. 20 16 18 14 16 12 14 ...... (A) 16 12 (B) 10 12 (C) 16 18 (D) 12 12 (E) 12 10
7. 7 12 8 11 9 10 10 .... (A) 11 9 (B) 9 8 (C) 9 11 (D) 10 11 (E) 9 10
8. 13 13 12 15 15 14 17 ...... (A) 17 16 (B) 14 17 (C) 16 19 (D) 19 19 (E) 16 16
9. 65 59 53 51 49 43 37 35 .... (A) 29 27 (B) 33 29 (C) 27 24 (D) 33 27 (E) 32 25
10. 73 65 65 58 58 52 52 ...... (A) 52 46 (B) 52 47 (C) 47 47 (D) 46 46 (E) 45 45
11. 6 4 8 5 15 13 26 23 ..... (A) 69 67 (B) 37 33 (C) 29 44 (D) 75 78 (E) 46 49
12. 19 16 21 18 23 20 25 ..... (A) 30 33 (B) 22 27 (C) 28 22 (D) 22 24 (E) 30 27
13. 35 40 5 45 50 5 55 .... (A) 55 5 (B) 60 5 (C) 5 60 (D) 5 55 (E) 60 65
14. 22 20 18 18 16 14 14 ...... (A) 14 12 (B) 12 12 (C) 14 10 (D) 14 16 (E) 12 10
15. 11 22 23 13 26 27 17 ..... (A) 7 8 (B) 18 36 (C) 18 8 (D) 7 14 (E) 34 35
16. 9 1 10 1 11 1 12 .... (A) 13 14 (B) 13 1 (C) 1 13 (D) 12 1 (E) 12 13
17. 48 10 46 17 44 24 42 ..... (A) 31 40 (B) 27 28 (C) 40 38 (D) 28 38 (E) 30 40

18. 8 8 17 26 26 35 44 .... (A) 53 53 (B) 44 53 (C) 44 44 (D) 45 55 (E) 44 54

19. 71 68 62 59 53 50 44 ..... (A) 40 32 (B) 38 35 (C) 41 38 (D) 41 35 (E) 41 33

20. 1 7 8 2 7 8 3 .... (A) 4 7 (B) 7 8 (C) 4 5 (D) 7 4 (E) 2 8

21. 1 2 2 1 1 2 2 .... (A) 1 1 (B) 1 2 (C) 2 1 (D) 2 2 (E) 1 3

22. 14 25 37 48 60 71 83 ..... (A) 92 100 (B) 96 110 (C) 89 98 (D) 95 105 (E) 94 106

23. 35 43 45 53 55 63 65 ..... (A) 65 68 (B) 75 83 (C) 73 75 (D) 65 73 (E) 73 83

24. 3 6 12 12 24 48 48 .... (A) 48 96 (B) 96 96 (C) 60 96 (D) 96 192 (E) 60 60

END OF PART A

If you finish before time is up, check over your work on this part only. Do not turn the page until you are told to do so.

PART B—ADDRESS CODING

SAMPLE QUESTIONS

The seven sample questions for this part are based upon the addresses in the five boxes below. Your task is to mark on your answer sheet the letter of the box in which each address belongs. The instructions for Part B permit you to look at the boxes if you cannot remember in which box an address belongs. You may look at the boxes while answering these Part B sample questions. The questions in Part C of the exam will be based upon the same boxes as the questions in Part B, but in answering Part C you may NOT look at the boxes. There will be no sample questions before Part C.

A	B	C	D	E
9200-9899 Salem Hickory 3200-3499 Paine Kingwood 4000-4799 Lee	8500-8599 Salem Inverness 1200-3199 Paine Oxford 4800-5699 Lee	7800-8099 Salem Rutland 4500-4899 Paine Mohegan 3800-3999 Lee	9900-9999 Salem Moorland 3500-3799 Paine Wyndcliff 5700-5899 Lee	8100-8499 Salem Vaneck 3800-4499 Paine Stratton 5900-6199 Lee

1. 9200-9899 Salem
2. Stratton
3. 3500-3799 Paine
4. 4800-5699 Lee
5. Mohegan
6. Kingwood
7. 8100-8499 Salem

SAMPLE ANSWER SHEET

1. Ⓐ Ⓑ Ⓒ Ⓓ Ⓔ   5. Ⓐ Ⓑ Ⓒ Ⓓ Ⓔ
2. Ⓐ Ⓑ Ⓒ Ⓓ Ⓔ   6. Ⓐ Ⓑ Ⓒ Ⓓ Ⓔ
3. Ⓐ Ⓑ Ⓒ Ⓓ Ⓔ   7. Ⓐ Ⓑ Ⓒ Ⓓ Ⓔ
4. Ⓐ Ⓑ Ⓒ Ⓓ Ⓔ

CORRECT ANSWERS

1. A   5. C
2. E   6. A
3. D   7. E
4. B

PART B—ADDRESS CODING

Directions: There are five boxes labeled A, B, C, D, and E. In each box are five addresses, three of which include a number span and a name and two of which are names alone. You will have (5) minutes to memorize the locations of all twenty-five addresses. Then you will have three (3) minutes to mark your answer sheet with the letter of the box in which each address in the question list belongs. For Part B you may refer to the boxes while answering, though you will lose speed by doing so. For Part C you may NOT look at the boxes, so do your best to memorize in the five minutes allowed you now. Correct answers are on page 151.

MEMORIZING TIME: 5 Minutes.

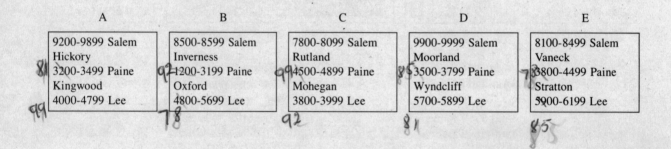

A	B	C	D	E
9200-9899 Salem Hickory 3200-3499 Paine Kingwood 4000-4799 Lee	8500-8599 Salem Inverness 1200-3199 Paine Oxford 4800-5699 Lee	7800-8099 Salem Rutland 4500-4899 Paine Mohegan 3800-3999 Lee	9900-9999 Salem Moorland 3500-3799 Paine Wyndcliff 5700-5899 Lee	8100-8499 Salem Vaneck 3800-4499 Paine Stratton 5900-6199 Lee

ANSWERING TIME: 3 Minutes. 88 Questions.

1. 9900-9999 Salem
2. 3800-4499 Paine
3. Stratton
4. 4000-4799 Lee
5. Inverness
6. Wyndcliff
7. 3800-3999 Lee
8. 3500-3799 Paine
9. 7800-8099 Salem
10. 9200-9899 Salem
11. 1200-3199 Paine
12. Hickory
13. Mohegan
14. Moorland
15. 3200-3499 Paine

16. 4800-5699 Lee
17. 5700-5899 Lee
18. 4500-4899 Paine
19. Vaneck
20. Kingwood
21. 8500-8599 Salem
22. 5900-6199 Lee
23. Rutland
24. Oxford
25. 8100-8499 Salem
26. 3500-3799 Paine
27. 8500-8599 Salem
28. Mohegan
29. 9200-9899 Salem
30. 4800-5699 Lee

31. 3800-3999 Lee
32. Inverness
33. Stratton
34. 3200-3499 Paine
35. 3500-3499 Paine
36. Wyndcliff
37. 4800-5699 Lee
38. 8100-8499 Salem
39. 9200-9899 Salem
40. Rutland
41. Moorland
42. 1200-3199 Paine
43. 4000-4799 Lee
44. Hickory
45. Vaneck
46. Oxford
47. 9900-9999 Salem
48. 8500-8599 Salem
49. 5700-5899 Lee
50. 4500-4899 Paine
51. 3800-4489 Paine
52. 5900-6199 Lee
53. Kingwood
54. Moorland
55. 1200-3199 Paine
56. 3800-3999 Lee
57. 9200-9899 Salem
58. Inverness
59. Wyndcliff

60. 9900-9999 Salem
61. 5700-5899 Lee
62. 3200-3499 Paine
63. Vaneck
64. Mohegan
65. 3800-4499 Paine
66. 7800-8099 Salem
67. 4800-5699 Lee
68. Oxford
69. Hickory
70. 5900-6199 Lee
71. 3500-3799 Paine
72. 8100-8499 Salem
73. Kingwood
74. Stratton
75. 4800-5699 Lee
76. 1200-3199 Paine
77. 7800-8099 Salem
78. Rutland
79. 4500-4899 Paine
80. Oxford
81. 3500-3799 Paine
82. 9900-9999 Salem
83. 4000-4799 Lee
84. 9200-9899 Salem
85. 3200–3499 Paine
86. Vaneck
87. Inverness
88. 5900-6199 Lee

END OF PART B

If you finish before time is up, use the remaining few seconds to continue memorizing locations for addresses. Do not turn the page until you are told to do so.

PART C—ADDRESS CODE MEMORY

TIME: 5 Minutes. 88 Questions.

Directions: *Relying entirely upon your memory, mark you answer sheet with the letter of the box in which each address belongs. Correct answers are on page 151.*

1. 1200-3199 Paine
2. 4800-5699 Lee
3. 9200-9899 Salem
4. 8100-8499 Salem
5. Wyndcliff
6. 5700-5899 Lee
7. 3200-3499 Paine
8. Rutland
9. Vaneck
10. Hickory
11. 3800-3999 Lee
12. 8500-8599 Salem
13. 4000-4799 Lee
14. 3800-4499 Paine
15. 4500-4899 Paine
16. Oxford
17. Mohegan
18. Stratton
19. 5900-6199 Lee
20. 9900-9999 Salem
21. 7800-8099 Salem
22. 3500-3799 Paine
23. Kingwood
24. Inverness
25. Moorland
26. 3200-3499 Paine
27. 5900-6199 Lee
28. 9200-9899 Salem
29. Oxford
30. 7800-8099 Salem
31. Mohegan
32. 4800-5699 Lee
33. 3500-3799 Paine
34. 5700-5899 Lee
35. 9900-9999 Salem

36. 8100-8499 Salem
37. Hickory
38. Stratton
39. Wyndcliff
40. 4000-4799 Lee
41. 8500-8599 Salem
42. Rutland
43. Vaneck
44. 5700-5899 Lee
45. 3800-4499 Paine
46. 4000-4799 Lee
47. 8500-8599 Salem
48. 9900-9999 Salem
49. Kingwood
50. Stratton
51. Moorland
52. 4500-4899 Paine
53. 8100-8499 Salem
54. 4800-5699 Lee
55. Rutland
56. Vaneck
57. 5700-5899 Lee
58. 5900-6199 Lee
59. 1200-3199 Paine
60. Inverness
61. Wyndcliff
62. Oxford
63. 3500-3799 Paine
64. 9200-9899 Salem
65. 3800-3999 Lee
66. Hickory
67. Stratton
68. 8100-8499 Salem
69. 4500-4899 Paine
70. 4000-4799 Lee

71. Inverness
72. Mohegan
73. 9200-9899 Salem
74. 3500-3799 Paine
75. 5700-5899 Lee
76. 3800-3999 Lee
77. Stratton
78. Hickory
79. Wyndcliff

80. 8500-8599 Salem
81. 1200-3199 Paine
82. 4800-5699 Lee
83. 9900-9999 Salem
84. Rutland
85. Vaneck
86. 5900-6199 Lee
87. 3200-3499 Paine
88. Moorland

END OF PART C

If you finish before time is up, check your answers on this part only. Do not turn the page until you are told to do so.

PART D—ADDRESS CHECKING TEST

SAMPLE QUESTIONS

You will be allowed three minutes to read the directions and answer the five sample questions which follow. On the actual test, however, you will have only six minutes to answer 95 questions, so see how quickly you can compare addresses and still get the correct answer.

Directions: Each question consists of two addresses. If the two addresses are alike in EVERY *way, mark Ⓐ on your answer sheet. If the two addresses are* different in ANY *way, mark Ⓓ on your answer sheet.*

1 . . .	Ft Collins CO 80523	Ft Collins CO 85023
2 . . .	3626 Pennsylvania Ave NE	3626 Pennsylvania Ave NE
3 . . .	2418 E 514th St	2418 E 515th St
4 . . .	4437 Continental Tpke	4437 Continental Tpke
5 . . .	682 Dunbarton Rd	682 Dunbarton Dr

SAMPLE ANSWER SHEET

1. ⒶⒹ	4. ⒶⒹ
2. ⒶⒹ	5. ⒶⒹ
3. ⒶⒹ	

CORRECT ANSWERS

1. D	4. A
2. A	5. D
3. D	

Fourth Model Exam / 147

PART D—ADDRESS CHECKING

TIME: 6 Minutes. 95 Questions.

Directions: Look carefully at the two addresses in each question. If the two addresses are alike in EVERY way, mark Ⓐ on your answer sheet. If the two addresses are different in ANY way, mark Ⓓ on your answer sheet. Correct answers are on page 152.

1	Lancaster PA 17604	Lancaster PA 17604
2	7845 Bluebonnet Blvd	7485 Bluebonnet Blvd
3	1418 W 279th Pl	1418 W 297th Pl
4	8316 S Conduit Ave	8316 S Conduit Ave
5	9063 Pipeline Rd	9063 Pipeline Rd
6	7412 Aqueduct Ave	7412 Aquaduct Ave
7	Atlanta GA 30332	Atlanta GA 30322
8	Washington DC 20057	Washington DG 20057
9	1373 Oakland Beach Ave	1373 Oakland Beach Rd
10	4812 Illinois Ave SE	4812 Illinois Ave SE
11	7412 Arcadian Pl	7412 Arcadia Pl
12	892 Chilmark Row N	892 Chilmark Row N
13	7415 Dalewood Dr	7415 Dalewood Rd
14	Athens GA 30602	Athens GA 30602
15	8563 W 199th Rd	8563 W 199th Rd
16	5168 Longview Dr	5168 Longview Dr
17	2281 Stewart Pl	2821 Steward Pl
18	Washington DC 20052	Washington DC 20025
19	7415 Soundview Ave	7451 Soundview Ave
20	1432 Chickamawga Crk	1432 Chickamauga Crk
21	Towson MD 21204	Towson MD 21240
22	8458 Oneida St	8458 Oneida St
23	9146 Oneonta Dr	9164 Oneonta Dr
24	8050 Castellano Way	8050 Castellanho Way
25	Atlanta GA 30303	Atlanta GA 30303
26	7416 Brockport Apts	7416 Brockport Apts
27	5179 Quincy Mkt	5179 Quincy Mkt
28	3784 Hingham Hall	3784 Hingham Hall
29	8136 Gennessee Sq	8163 Gennessee Sq
30	Grinnell IA 50112	Grinnell IA 50012
31	4162 W Kirkland St	4162 Kirkland St
32	3500 Hamilton Ave	3500 Hamilton Ave
33	666 Burr St	6666 Burr St
34	Clinton NY 13323	Clinton NY 13323
35	5505 Hampshire Hlw	5505 Hampshire Hlw
36	6416 Collegiate Wy	6146 Collegiate Wy

37 . . . Amherst MA 01002		Amherst MA 01022
38 . . . 2022 University Tpke		2022 University Tpke
39 . . . West Hartford CT 06117		West Hartford CT 06617
40 . . . Cambridge MA 02138		Cambridge ME 02138
41 . . . 3525 S Creighton Ave		3525 S Creighton Ave
42 . . . 7907 Adelphi Wy No		7907 Adelphi Wy No
43 . . . 1776 American Hwy		1776 American Hwy
44 . . . 7432 Antiochus Rd		7432 Antiochus Rd
45 . . . 1618 S 425th St		1618 S 425th St
46 . . . Haverford PA 19041		Haverfort PA 19041
47 . . . Geneva NY 14456		Geneva NY 14456
48 . . . 4562 California Ave NE		4562 California Ave NE
49 . . . 1404 Barnard Bridge		1404 Barnard Bridge
50 . . . 8305 Bowdoin Ave		8305 Bowdoin Ave
51 . . . 4106 Carmelita St		4106 Carmelite St
52 . . . Hempstead NY 11550		Hempstead NY 11500
53 . . . Hollins VA 24020		Hollins VA 24202
54 . . . 1986 W 314th St		1968 W 314th St
55 . . . 1556 LaSalle St		1556 Lasalle St
56 . . . 4593 Lesley La		4593 Lesley La
57 . . . Worcester MA 01610		Worcester MA 01610
58 . . . 8342 Macalester Ave		8342 Macalester Ave
59 . . . 6412 Nannyhagen Dr		6412 Nannahagen Dr
60 . . . 1762 SW North St		1762 SW North St
61 . . . 9034 Parkway Dr E		9034 Parkway Dr
62 . . . 1785 W Fourth Ave		1785 W Fourth Ave
63 . . . Houston TX 77004		Houston TX 77044
64 . . . Pocatello ID 83209		Pocatello ID 83209
65 . . . Normal IL 61761		Normal IL 61761
66 . . . 2154 Brandeis Apts		2154 Brandeis Apts
67 . . . 8416 The Colchester		8146 The Colchester
68 . . . 7412 N Hunter Mtn		7412 N Hunter Mtn
69 . . . 419 Kiamesha Ln		419 Kiamesha Ln
70 . . . 1790 Brigham St		1970 Brigham St
71 . . . 4163 Champaign Dr		4163 Champaign Rd
72 . . . Urbana IL 61801		Urbana OH 61801
73 . . . Bloomington IN 47401		Bloomingtown IN 47401
74 . . . 7417 W Pomona Hwy		7417 E Pomona Hwy
75 . . . 1901 Romero Rd		1901 Romero Rd
76 . . . 4186 S 174th St		4186 S 174th St
77 . . . 5183 Shakespeare Path		5183 Shakespeare Path
78 . . . 613 VanMeter Fenway		613 Vanmeter Fenway
79 . . . 9049 Hastings Hall		9409 Hastings Hall
80 . . . Ames IA 50011		Ames IA 50011
81 . . . 2436 Hoosier Hill		2436 Hoossier Hill
82 . . . 4165 New Mexico Ave NE		4156 New Mexico Ave NE
83 . . . 3514 W 256th St		3514 W 265th St
84 . . . 1783 Bucknell Blvd		1783 Bucknell Blvd
85 . . . Washington DC 20059		Washington DC 20095
86 . . . 8413 Howard Hwy		8413 Howard Hwy
87 . . . New York NY 10021		New York NY 10021

88 . . . 5163 Hunter Ave   5163 Hunter Ave
89 . . . Iowa City IA 52242   Iowa City IA 52422
90 . . . 7146 Friendship Pkwy   7146 Freindship Pkwy
91 . . . 1232 S Idlewild Alley   1232 S Idlewild Alley
92 . . . 4167 Kennedey Court   4167 Kennedy Court
93 . . . 3216 Greenridge Dr   3216 Greenridge Dr
94 . . . Ithaca NY 14850   Ithaca NY 18450
95 . . . 9041 Oriental Ave   9041 Orienta Ave

END OF EXAM

If you finish before time is up, check over your work on this part only. Do not return to any previous part.

CORRECT ANSWERS— FOURTH MODEL EXAM

PART A—NUMBER SERIES

1. D	4. C	7. C	10. C	13. B	16. C	19. D	22. E
2. A	5. C	8. A	11. A	14. E	17. A	20. B	23. C
3. E	6. B	9. D	12. B	15. E	18. B	21. A	24. D

EXPLANATIONS—NUMBER SERIES

1. **(D)** The series descends 13 12 11 10 9 8, with the number $\underline{8}$ appearing between each set of two numbers.

2. **(A)** Again the series descends. This time the number $\underline{13}$ appears between all numbers.

3. **(E)** This time the number repeats itself before descending. The number $\underline{10}$ appears between each set of descending numbers.

4. **(C)** The three number series repeats itself over and over.

5. **(C)** The series descends. The even numbers repeat.

6. **(B)** Mark the differences between numbers. The pattern that emerges is $-4, +2, -4, +2$ and so on.

7. **(C)** There are two alternating series. The first series begins with $\underline{7}$ and ascends by $+1$. The alternating series begins with $\underline{12}$ and descends one number at a time.

8. **(A)** One series, the odd numbers, repeats and ascends by $+2$. The alternating series, the even numbers, also ascends by $+2$, but does not repeat.

9. **(D)** The pattern is: $-6, -6, -2, -2; -6, -6, -2, -2 \ldots$

10. **(C)** The pattern is: -8, repeat the number; -7, repeat the number; -6, repeat the number, -5, repeat the number . . . .

11. **(A)** The pattern is: $-2, \times2, -3, \times3; -2, \times2, -3, \times3; -2, \times2, -3, \times3$.

12. **(B)** The easiest way to see this is to mark the pattern: $-3, +5; -3, +5$ and so on. If, however, you see two alternating series both ascending by $+2$, you will also get the correct answer.

13. **(B)** This is a $+5$ series with the number $\underline{5}$ appearing after each two numbers in the series.

14. **(E)** The pattern is: $-2, -2$, repeat the number; $-2, -2$, repeat the number . . . .

15. **(E)** The pattern is $\times2, +1, -10; \times2, +1, -10; \times2, +1, -10 \ldots$

16. **(C)** The series is simply 9 10 11 12 13 . . . with the number $\underline{1}$ appearing between each step of the series.

17. **(A)** There are two alternating series. The first series starts with 48 and descends at the rate of −2. The alternating series starts with 10 and ascends at the rate of +7.

18. **(B)** The pattern is: repeat the number, +9, +9, repeat the number, +9, +9 . . . .

19. **(D)** The pattern is: −3, −6; −3, −6 . . . .

20. **(B)** The pattern is a 1 2 3 . . . with the numbers 7 8 intervening between members of the series.

21. **(A)** The series consists of repetitions of the sequence 1 2 2 1, or, if you see it otherwise, repetitions of 1 1; 2 2; 1 1; 2 2; 1 1 beginning in the middle of a repetition of 1's.

22. **(E)** The pattern is: +11, +12; +11, +12 . . . .

23. **(C)** The pattern is: +8, +2; +8, +2 . . . .

24. **(D)** The pattern is: ×2, ×2, repeat the number, ×2, ×2, repeat the number . . . .

PART B—ADDRESS CODING

1. D	12. A	23. C	34. A	45. E	56. C	67. B	78. C
2. E	13. C	24. B	35. D	46. B	57. A	68. B	79. C
3. E	14. D	25. E	36. D	47. D	58. B	69. A	80. B
4. A	15. A	26. D	37. B	48. B	59. D	70. E	81. D
5. B	16. B	27. B	38. E	49. D	60. D	71. D	82. D
6. D	17. D	28. C	39. A	50. C	61. D	72. E	83. A
7. C	18. C	29. A	40. C	51. E	62. A	73. A	84. A
8. D	19. E	30. B	41. D	52. E	63. E	74. E	85. A
9. C	20. A	31. C	42. B	53. A	64. C	75. B	86. E
10. A	21. B	32. B	43. A	54. D	65. E	76. B	87. B
11. B	22. E	33. E	44. A	55. B	66. C	77. C	88. E

PART C—ADDRESS CODE MEMORY

1. B	12. B	23. A	34. D	45. E	56. E	67. E	78. A
2. B	13. A	24. B	35. D	46. A	57. D	68. E	79. D
3. A	14. E	25. D	36. E	47. B	58. E	69. C	80. B
4. E	15. C	26. A	37. A	48. D	59. B	70. A	81. B
5. D	16. B	27. E	38. E	49. A	60. B	71. B	82. B
6. D	17. C	28. A	39. D	50. E	61. D	72. C	83. D
7. A	18. E	29. B	40. A	51. D	62. B	73. A	84. C
8. C	19. E	30. C	41. B	52. C	63. D	74. D	85. E
9. E	20. D	31. C	42. C	53. E	64. A	75. D	86. E
10. A	21. C	32. B	43. E	54. B	65. C	76. C	87. A
11. C	22. D	33. D	44. D	55. C	66. A	77. E	88. D

PART D—ADDRESS CHECKING

1. A	13. D	25. A	37. D	49. A	61. D	73. D	85. D
2. D	14. A	26. A	38. A	50. A	62. A	74. D	86. A
3. D	15. A	27. A	39. D	51. D	63. D	75. A	87. A
4. A	16. A	28. A	40. D	52. D	64. A	76. A	88. A
5. A	17. D	29. D	41. A	53. D	65. A	77. A	89. D
6. D	18. D	30. D	42. A	54. D	66. A	78. D	90. D
7. D	19. D	31. D	43. A	55. D	67. D	79. D	91. A
8. D	20. D	32. A	44. A	56. A	68. A	80. A	92. D
9. D	21. D	33. D	45. A	57. A	69. A	81. D	93. A
10. A	22. A	34. A	46. D	58. A	70. D	82. D	94. D
11. D	23. D	35. A	47. A	59. D	71. D	83. D	95. D
12. A	24. D	36. D	48. A	60. A	72. D	84. A	

ADDRESS CHECKING ERROR ANALYSIS CHART

Type of Error	Tally	Total Number
Number of addresses that were alike and you incorrectly marked "different"		
Number of addresses that were different and you incorrectly marked "alike"		3
Number of addresses in which you missed a difference in NUMBERS	1	1
Number of addresses in which you missed a difference in ABBREVIATIONS		
Number of addresses in which you missed a difference in NAMES	1	2

SCORE SHEET FOR FOURTH MODEL EXAM

PART A—NUMBER SERIES

Number Right equals Score

_____ = _____

PART B—ADDRESS CODING

Number Right minus (Number Wrong ÷ 4) equals Score

_____ − _____ = _____

PART C—ADDRESS CODE MEMORY

Number Right minus (Number Wrong ÷ 4) equals Score

_____ − _____ = _____

PART D—ADDRESS CHECKING

Number Right minus Number Wrong equals Score

_____ − _____ = _____

SELF-EVALUATION CHART

Part	Excellent	Good	Average	Fair	Poor
Number Series	21–24	18–20	14–17	11–13	1–10
Address Coding	75–88	63–74	52–62	40–51	1–39
Address Code Memory	75–88	60–74	45–59	30–44	1–29
Address Checking	80–95	65–79	50–64	35–49	1–34

PROGRESS CHART

Blacken to the closest score to chart your progress.

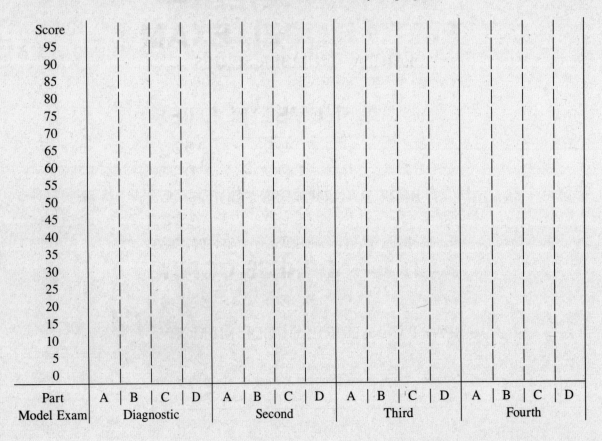

Score
95
90
85
80
75
70
65
60
55
50
45
40
35
30
25
20
15
10
5
0

Part	A	B	C	D	A	B	C	D	A	B	C	D	A	B	C	D
Model Exam	Diagnostic				Second				Third				Fourth			

ANSWER SHEET—
FIFTH MODEL EXAM

Tear out this Answer Sheet and use it to mark your answers for the exam that follows.

PART A—NUMBER SERIES

1. Ⓐ Ⓑ Ⓒ Ⓓ Ⓔ	6. Ⓐ Ⓑ Ⓒ Ⓓ Ⓔ	11. Ⓐ Ⓑ Ⓒ Ⓓ Ⓔ	16. Ⓐ Ⓑ Ⓒ Ⓓ Ⓔ	21. Ⓐ Ⓑ Ⓒ Ⓓ Ⓔ
2. Ⓐ Ⓑ Ⓒ Ⓓ Ⓔ	7. Ⓐ Ⓑ Ⓒ Ⓓ Ⓔ	12. Ⓐ Ⓑ Ⓒ Ⓓ Ⓔ	17. Ⓐ Ⓑ Ⓒ Ⓓ Ⓔ	22. Ⓐ Ⓑ Ⓒ Ⓓ Ⓔ
3. Ⓐ Ⓑ Ⓒ Ⓓ Ⓔ	8. Ⓐ Ⓑ Ⓒ Ⓓ Ⓔ	13. Ⓐ Ⓑ Ⓒ Ⓓ Ⓔ	18. Ⓐ Ⓑ Ⓒ Ⓓ Ⓔ	23. Ⓐ Ⓑ Ⓒ Ⓓ Ⓔ
4. Ⓐ Ⓑ Ⓒ Ⓓ Ⓔ	9. Ⓐ Ⓑ Ⓒ Ⓓ Ⓔ	14. Ⓐ Ⓑ Ⓒ Ⓓ Ⓔ	19. Ⓐ Ⓑ Ⓒ Ⓓ Ⓔ	24. Ⓐ Ⓑ Ⓒ Ⓓ Ⓔ
5. Ⓐ Ⓑ Ⓒ Ⓓ Ⓔ	10. Ⓐ Ⓑ Ⓒ Ⓓ Ⓔ	15. Ⓐ Ⓑ Ⓒ Ⓓ Ⓔ	20. Ⓐ Ⓑ Ⓒ Ⓓ Ⓔ	

PART B—ADDRESS CODING

1. Ⓐ Ⓑ Ⓒ Ⓓ Ⓔ	19. Ⓐ Ⓑ Ⓒ Ⓓ Ⓔ	37. Ⓐ Ⓑ Ⓒ Ⓓ Ⓔ	55. Ⓐ Ⓑ Ⓒ Ⓓ Ⓔ	73. Ⓐ Ⓑ Ⓒ Ⓓ Ⓔ
2. Ⓐ Ⓑ Ⓒ Ⓓ Ⓔ	20. Ⓐ Ⓑ Ⓒ Ⓓ Ⓔ	38. Ⓐ Ⓑ Ⓒ Ⓓ Ⓔ	56. Ⓐ Ⓑ Ⓒ Ⓓ Ⓔ	74. Ⓐ Ⓑ Ⓒ Ⓓ Ⓔ
3. Ⓐ Ⓑ Ⓒ Ⓓ Ⓔ	21. Ⓐ Ⓑ Ⓒ Ⓓ Ⓔ	39. Ⓐ Ⓑ Ⓒ Ⓓ Ⓔ	57. Ⓐ Ⓑ Ⓒ Ⓓ Ⓔ	75. Ⓐ Ⓑ Ⓒ Ⓓ Ⓔ
4. Ⓐ Ⓑ Ⓒ Ⓓ Ⓔ	22. Ⓐ Ⓑ Ⓒ Ⓓ Ⓔ	40. Ⓐ Ⓑ Ⓒ Ⓓ Ⓔ	58. Ⓐ Ⓑ Ⓒ Ⓓ Ⓔ	76. Ⓐ Ⓑ Ⓒ Ⓓ Ⓔ
5. Ⓐ Ⓑ Ⓒ Ⓓ Ⓔ	23. Ⓐ Ⓑ Ⓒ Ⓓ Ⓔ	41. Ⓐ Ⓑ Ⓒ Ⓓ Ⓔ	59. Ⓐ Ⓑ Ⓒ Ⓓ Ⓔ	77. Ⓐ Ⓑ Ⓒ Ⓓ Ⓔ
6. Ⓐ Ⓑ Ⓒ Ⓓ Ⓔ	24. Ⓐ Ⓑ Ⓒ Ⓓ Ⓔ	42. Ⓐ Ⓑ Ⓒ Ⓓ Ⓔ	60. Ⓐ Ⓑ Ⓒ Ⓓ Ⓔ	78. Ⓐ Ⓑ Ⓒ Ⓓ Ⓔ
7. Ⓐ Ⓑ Ⓒ Ⓓ Ⓔ	25. Ⓐ Ⓑ Ⓒ Ⓓ Ⓔ	43. Ⓐ Ⓑ Ⓒ Ⓓ Ⓔ	61. Ⓐ Ⓑ Ⓒ Ⓓ Ⓔ	79. Ⓐ Ⓑ Ⓒ Ⓓ Ⓔ
8. Ⓐ Ⓑ Ⓒ Ⓓ Ⓔ	26. Ⓐ Ⓑ Ⓒ Ⓓ Ⓔ	44. Ⓐ Ⓑ Ⓒ Ⓓ Ⓔ	62. Ⓐ Ⓑ Ⓒ Ⓓ Ⓔ	80. Ⓐ Ⓑ Ⓒ Ⓓ Ⓔ
9. Ⓐ Ⓑ Ⓒ Ⓓ Ⓔ	27. Ⓐ Ⓑ Ⓒ Ⓓ Ⓔ	45. Ⓐ Ⓑ Ⓒ Ⓓ Ⓔ	63. Ⓐ Ⓑ Ⓒ Ⓓ Ⓔ	81. Ⓐ Ⓑ Ⓒ Ⓓ Ⓔ
10. Ⓐ Ⓑ Ⓒ Ⓓ Ⓔ	28. Ⓐ Ⓑ Ⓒ Ⓓ Ⓔ	46. Ⓐ Ⓑ Ⓒ Ⓓ Ⓔ	64. Ⓐ Ⓑ Ⓒ Ⓓ Ⓔ	82. Ⓐ Ⓑ Ⓒ Ⓓ Ⓔ
11. Ⓐ Ⓑ Ⓒ Ⓓ Ⓔ	29. Ⓐ Ⓑ Ⓒ Ⓓ Ⓔ	47. Ⓐ Ⓑ Ⓒ Ⓓ Ⓔ	65. Ⓐ Ⓑ Ⓒ Ⓓ Ⓔ	83. Ⓐ Ⓑ Ⓒ Ⓓ Ⓔ
12. Ⓐ Ⓑ Ⓒ Ⓓ Ⓔ	30. Ⓐ Ⓑ Ⓒ Ⓓ Ⓔ	48. Ⓐ Ⓑ Ⓒ Ⓓ Ⓔ	66. Ⓐ Ⓑ Ⓒ Ⓓ Ⓔ	84. Ⓐ Ⓑ Ⓒ Ⓓ Ⓔ
13. Ⓐ Ⓑ Ⓒ Ⓓ Ⓔ	31. Ⓐ Ⓑ Ⓒ Ⓓ Ⓔ	49. Ⓐ Ⓑ Ⓒ Ⓓ Ⓔ	67. Ⓐ Ⓑ Ⓒ Ⓓ Ⓔ	85. Ⓐ Ⓑ Ⓒ Ⓓ Ⓔ
14. Ⓐ Ⓑ Ⓒ Ⓓ Ⓔ	32. Ⓐ Ⓑ Ⓒ Ⓓ Ⓔ	50. Ⓐ Ⓑ Ⓒ Ⓓ Ⓔ	68. Ⓐ Ⓑ Ⓒ Ⓓ Ⓔ	86. Ⓐ Ⓑ Ⓒ Ⓓ Ⓔ
15. Ⓐ Ⓑ Ⓒ Ⓓ Ⓔ	33. Ⓐ Ⓑ Ⓒ Ⓓ Ⓔ	51. Ⓐ Ⓑ Ⓒ Ⓓ Ⓔ	69. Ⓐ Ⓑ Ⓒ Ⓓ Ⓔ	87. Ⓐ Ⓑ Ⓒ Ⓓ Ⓔ
16. Ⓐ Ⓑ Ⓒ Ⓓ Ⓔ	34. Ⓐ Ⓑ Ⓒ Ⓓ Ⓔ	52. Ⓐ Ⓑ Ⓒ Ⓓ Ⓔ	70. Ⓐ Ⓑ Ⓒ Ⓓ Ⓔ	88. Ⓐ Ⓑ Ⓒ Ⓓ Ⓔ
17. Ⓐ Ⓑ Ⓒ Ⓓ Ⓔ	35. Ⓐ Ⓑ Ⓒ Ⓓ Ⓔ	53. Ⓐ Ⓑ Ⓒ Ⓓ Ⓔ	71. Ⓐ Ⓑ Ⓒ Ⓓ Ⓔ	
18. Ⓐ Ⓑ Ⓒ Ⓓ Ⓔ	36. Ⓐ Ⓑ Ⓒ Ⓓ Ⓔ	54. Ⓐ Ⓑ Ⓒ Ⓓ Ⓔ	72. Ⓐ Ⓑ Ⓒ Ⓓ Ⓔ	

PART C—ADDRESS CODE MEMORY

1. Ⓐ Ⓑ Ⓒ Ⓓ Ⓔ
2. Ⓐ Ⓑ Ⓒ Ⓓ Ⓔ
3. Ⓐ Ⓑ Ⓒ Ⓓ Ⓔ
4. Ⓐ Ⓑ Ⓒ Ⓓ Ⓔ
5. Ⓐ Ⓑ Ⓒ Ⓓ Ⓔ
6. Ⓐ Ⓑ Ⓒ Ⓓ Ⓔ
7. Ⓐ Ⓑ Ⓒ Ⓓ Ⓔ
8. Ⓐ Ⓑ Ⓒ Ⓓ Ⓔ
9. Ⓐ Ⓑ Ⓒ Ⓓ Ⓔ
10. Ⓐ Ⓑ Ⓒ Ⓓ Ⓔ
11. Ⓐ Ⓑ Ⓒ Ⓓ Ⓔ
12. Ⓐ Ⓑ Ⓒ Ⓓ Ⓔ
13. Ⓐ Ⓑ Ⓒ Ⓓ Ⓔ
14. Ⓐ Ⓑ Ⓒ Ⓓ Ⓔ
15. Ⓐ Ⓑ Ⓒ Ⓓ Ⓔ
16. Ⓐ Ⓑ Ⓒ Ⓓ Ⓔ
17. Ⓐ Ⓑ Ⓒ Ⓓ Ⓔ
18. Ⓐ Ⓑ Ⓒ Ⓓ Ⓔ

19. Ⓐ Ⓑ Ⓒ Ⓓ Ⓔ
20. Ⓐ Ⓑ Ⓒ Ⓓ Ⓔ
21. Ⓐ Ⓑ Ⓒ Ⓓ Ⓔ
22. Ⓐ Ⓑ Ⓒ Ⓓ Ⓔ
23. Ⓐ Ⓑ Ⓒ Ⓓ Ⓔ
24. Ⓐ Ⓑ Ⓒ Ⓓ Ⓔ
25. Ⓐ Ⓑ Ⓒ Ⓓ Ⓔ
26. Ⓐ Ⓑ Ⓒ Ⓓ Ⓔ
27. Ⓐ Ⓑ Ⓒ Ⓓ Ⓔ
28. Ⓐ Ⓑ Ⓒ Ⓓ Ⓔ
29. Ⓐ Ⓑ Ⓒ Ⓓ Ⓔ
30. Ⓐ Ⓑ Ⓒ Ⓓ Ⓔ
31. Ⓐ Ⓑ Ⓒ Ⓓ Ⓔ
32. Ⓐ Ⓑ Ⓒ Ⓓ Ⓔ
33. Ⓐ Ⓑ Ⓒ Ⓓ Ⓔ
34. Ⓐ Ⓑ Ⓒ Ⓓ Ⓔ
35. Ⓐ Ⓑ Ⓒ Ⓓ Ⓔ
36. Ⓐ Ⓑ Ⓒ Ⓓ Ⓔ

37. Ⓐ Ⓑ Ⓒ Ⓓ Ⓔ
38. Ⓐ Ⓑ Ⓒ Ⓓ Ⓔ
39. Ⓐ Ⓑ Ⓒ Ⓓ Ⓔ
40. Ⓐ Ⓑ Ⓒ Ⓓ Ⓔ
41. Ⓐ Ⓑ Ⓒ Ⓓ Ⓔ
42. Ⓐ Ⓑ Ⓒ Ⓓ Ⓔ
43. Ⓐ Ⓑ Ⓒ Ⓓ Ⓔ
44. Ⓐ Ⓑ Ⓒ Ⓓ Ⓔ
45. Ⓐ Ⓑ Ⓒ Ⓓ Ⓔ
46. Ⓐ Ⓑ Ⓒ Ⓓ Ⓔ
47. Ⓐ Ⓑ Ⓒ Ⓓ Ⓔ
48. Ⓐ Ⓑ Ⓒ Ⓓ Ⓔ
49. Ⓐ Ⓑ Ⓒ Ⓓ Ⓔ
50. Ⓐ Ⓑ Ⓒ Ⓓ Ⓔ
51. Ⓐ Ⓑ Ⓒ Ⓓ Ⓔ
52. Ⓐ Ⓑ Ⓒ Ⓓ Ⓔ
53. Ⓐ Ⓑ Ⓒ Ⓓ Ⓔ
54. Ⓐ Ⓑ Ⓒ Ⓓ Ⓔ

55. Ⓐ Ⓑ Ⓒ Ⓓ Ⓔ
56. Ⓐ Ⓑ Ⓒ Ⓓ Ⓔ
57. Ⓐ Ⓑ Ⓒ Ⓓ Ⓔ
58. Ⓐ Ⓑ Ⓒ Ⓓ Ⓔ
59. Ⓐ Ⓑ Ⓒ Ⓓ Ⓔ
60. Ⓐ Ⓑ Ⓒ Ⓓ Ⓔ
61. Ⓐ Ⓑ Ⓒ Ⓓ Ⓔ
62. Ⓐ Ⓑ Ⓒ Ⓓ Ⓔ
63. Ⓐ Ⓑ Ⓒ Ⓓ Ⓔ
64. Ⓐ Ⓑ Ⓒ Ⓓ Ⓔ
65. Ⓐ Ⓑ Ⓒ Ⓓ Ⓔ
66. Ⓐ Ⓑ Ⓒ Ⓓ Ⓔ
67. Ⓐ Ⓑ Ⓒ Ⓓ Ⓔ
68. Ⓐ Ⓑ Ⓒ Ⓓ Ⓔ
69. Ⓐ Ⓑ Ⓒ Ⓓ Ⓔ
70. Ⓐ Ⓑ Ⓒ Ⓓ Ⓔ
71. Ⓐ Ⓑ Ⓒ Ⓓ Ⓔ
72. Ⓐ Ⓑ Ⓒ Ⓓ Ⓔ

73. Ⓐ Ⓑ Ⓒ Ⓓ Ⓔ
74. Ⓐ Ⓑ Ⓒ Ⓓ Ⓔ
75. Ⓐ Ⓑ Ⓒ Ⓓ Ⓔ
76. Ⓐ Ⓑ Ⓒ Ⓓ Ⓔ
77. Ⓐ Ⓑ Ⓒ Ⓓ Ⓔ
78. Ⓐ Ⓑ Ⓒ Ⓓ Ⓔ
79. Ⓐ Ⓑ Ⓒ Ⓓ Ⓔ
80. Ⓐ Ⓑ Ⓒ Ⓓ Ⓔ
81. Ⓐ Ⓑ Ⓒ Ⓓ Ⓔ
82. Ⓐ Ⓑ Ⓒ Ⓓ Ⓔ
83. Ⓐ Ⓑ Ⓒ Ⓓ Ⓔ
84. Ⓐ Ⓑ Ⓒ Ⓓ Ⓔ
85. Ⓐ Ⓑ Ⓒ Ⓓ Ⓔ
86. Ⓐ Ⓑ Ⓒ Ⓓ Ⓔ
87. Ⓐ Ⓑ Ⓒ Ⓓ Ⓔ
88. Ⓐ Ⓑ Ⓒ Ⓓ Ⓔ

PART D—ADDRESS CHECKING

1. Ⓐ Ⓓ	20. Ⓐ Ⓓ	39. Ⓐ Ⓓ	58. Ⓐ Ⓓ	77. Ⓐ Ⓓ
2. Ⓐ Ⓓ	21. Ⓐ Ⓓ	40. Ⓐ Ⓓ	59. Ⓐ Ⓓ	78. Ⓐ Ⓓ
3. Ⓐ Ⓓ	22. Ⓐ Ⓓ	41. Ⓐ Ⓓ	60. Ⓐ Ⓓ	79. Ⓐ Ⓓ
4. Ⓐ Ⓓ	23. Ⓐ Ⓓ	42. Ⓐ Ⓓ	61. Ⓐ Ⓓ	80. Ⓐ Ⓓ
5. Ⓐ Ⓓ	24. Ⓐ Ⓓ	43. Ⓐ Ⓓ	62. Ⓐ Ⓓ	81. Ⓐ Ⓓ
6. Ⓐ Ⓓ	25. Ⓐ Ⓓ	44. Ⓐ Ⓓ	63. Ⓐ Ⓓ	82. Ⓐ Ⓓ
7. Ⓐ Ⓓ	26. Ⓐ Ⓓ	45. Ⓐ Ⓓ	64. Ⓐ Ⓓ	83. Ⓐ Ⓓ
8. Ⓐ Ⓓ	27. Ⓐ Ⓓ	46. Ⓐ Ⓓ	65. Ⓐ Ⓓ	84. Ⓐ Ⓓ
9. Ⓐ Ⓓ	28. Ⓐ Ⓓ	47. Ⓐ Ⓓ	66. Ⓐ Ⓓ	85. Ⓐ Ⓓ
10. Ⓐ Ⓓ	29. Ⓐ Ⓓ	48. Ⓐ Ⓓ	67. Ⓐ Ⓓ	86. Ⓐ Ⓓ
11. Ⓐ Ⓓ	30. Ⓐ Ⓓ	49. Ⓐ Ⓓ	68. Ⓐ Ⓓ	87. Ⓐ Ⓓ
12. Ⓐ Ⓓ	31. Ⓐ Ⓓ	50. Ⓐ Ⓓ	69. Ⓐ Ⓓ	88. Ⓐ Ⓓ
13. Ⓐ Ⓓ	32. Ⓐ Ⓓ	51. Ⓐ Ⓓ	70. Ⓐ Ⓓ	89. Ⓐ Ⓓ
14. Ⓐ Ⓓ	33. Ⓐ Ⓓ	52. Ⓐ Ⓓ	71. Ⓐ Ⓓ	90. Ⓐ Ⓓ
15. Ⓐ Ⓓ	34. Ⓐ Ⓓ	53. Ⓐ Ⓓ	72. Ⓐ Ⓓ	91. Ⓐ Ⓓ
16. Ⓐ Ⓓ	35. Ⓐ Ⓓ	54. Ⓐ Ⓓ	73. Ⓐ Ⓓ	92. Ⓐ Ⓓ
17. Ⓐ Ⓓ	36. Ⓐ Ⓓ	55. Ⓐ Ⓓ	74. Ⓐ Ⓓ	93. Ⓐ Ⓓ
18. Ⓐ Ⓓ	37. Ⓐ Ⓓ	56. Ⓐ Ⓓ	75. Ⓐ Ⓓ	94. Ⓐ Ⓓ
19. Ⓐ Ⓓ	38. Ⓐ Ⓓ	57. Ⓐ Ⓓ	76. Ⓐ Ⓓ	95. Ⓐ Ⓓ

FIFTH MODEL EXAM

PART A—NUMBER SERIES

SAMPLE QUESTIONS

The following sample questions show you the type of question that will be used in Part A. Since this type of question may be new and unfamiliar to you, the examiner will work through the first five questions with you. Once you understand the task, you will have five minutes to answer sample questions 6 to 14 on your own. Correct answers and explanations follow.

Directions: Each number series question consists of a series of numbers which follows some definite order. The numbers progress from left to right according to some rule. One pair of numbers to the right of the series comprises the next two numbers in the series. Study each series to try to find a pattern to the series and to figure out the rule which governs the progression. Choose the answer pair which continues the series according to the pattern established and mark its letter on your answer sheet.

1. 75   75   72   72   69   69   66   .....   (A) 66   66 (B) 66   68 (C) 63   63 (D) 66   63 (E) 63   60

    The pattern established in this series is: repeat the number, -3; repeat the number -3. . . .To continue the series, repeat 66, then subtract 3. The answer is **(D)**.

2. 12   16   21   27   31   36   42   .....   (A) 48   56 (B) 44   48 (C) 48   52 (D) 46   52 (E) 46   51

    By marking the amount and direction of change from one number of the series to the next, you can see that the pattern is: $+4, +5, +6; +4, +5, +6; +4, +5, +6$. Continuing the series: $42 + 4 = 46 + 5 = 51$. **(E)** is the correct answer.

3. 22   24   12   26   28   12   30   .....   (A) 12   32 (B) 32   34 (C) 32   12 (D) 12   12 (E) 32   36

    In this series the basic pattern is $+2$. The series may be read: 22 24 26 28 30 32. After each two numbers of the series we find the number 12 which serves no function except for repetition. To continue the series, add 2 to 30 to get 32. After 30 and 32, you must put in the number 12, so **(C)** is the correct answer.

4. 5 70 10 68 15 66 20 .... (A) 25 64 (B) 64 25 (C) 24 63 (D) 25 30 (E) 64 62

In this problem there are two distinct series alternating with one another. The first series is going up by a factor of +5. It reads: 10 15 20. The alternating series is going down by a factor of −2. It reads: 70 68 66. At the point where you must continue the series, the next number must be a member of the descending series, so it must be 64. Following that number must come the next number of the ascending series, which is 25. **(B)** is the answer.

5. 13 22 32 43 55 68 82 ..... (A) 97 113 (B) 100 115 (C) 96 110 (D) 95 105 (E) 99 112

The numbers are large, but the progression is simple. If you mark the differences between numbers, you can readily recognize: +9, +10, +11, +12, +13, +14. Continuing the series: 82 + 15 = 97 + 16 = 113. **(A)** is the correct answer.

You will now have five minutes to complete the remaining number series sample questions.

6. 33 40 34 41 35 42 36 ..... (A) 37 43 (B) 43 37 (C) 36 37 (D) 37 38 (E) 42 41

7. 12 10 8 8 6 7 4 .... (A) 2 2 (B) 6 4 (C) 6 2 (D) 4 6 (E) 2 6

8. 20 22 22 19 21 21 18 ..... (A) 22 22 (B) 19 19 (C) 20 20 (D) 20 17 (E) 19 17

9. 5 7 6 10 7 13 8 .... (A) 16 9 (B) 16 10 (C) 9 15 (D) 10 15 (E) 15 9

10. 3 0 6 0 0 12 0 0 0 ..... (A) 18 0 (B) 0 18 (C) 0 0 (D) 0 24 (E) 24 0

11. 64 64 32 32 16 16 8 .... (A) 4 4 (B) 8 8 (C) 8 4 (D) 4 2 (E) 8 2

12. 5 34 10 30 15 26 20 .... (A) 22 24 (B) 25 24 (C) 25 20 (D) 22 25 (E) 25 22

13. 9 11 15 21 23 27 33 .... (A) 37 43 (B) 35 39 (C) 37 39 (D) 35 41 (E) 39 42

14. 99 90 83 78 69 62 57 ..... (A) 57 50 (B) 50 45 (C) 48 41 (D) 57 48 (E) 49 43

SAMPLE ANSWER SHEET		CORRECT ANSWERS	
1. Ⓐ Ⓑ Ⓒ Ⓓ Ⓔ	8. Ⓐ Ⓑ Ⓒ Ⓓ Ⓔ	1. D	8. C
2. Ⓐ Ⓑ Ⓒ Ⓓ Ⓔ	9. Ⓐ Ⓑ Ⓒ Ⓓ Ⓔ	2. E	9. A
3. Ⓐ Ⓑ Ⓒ Ⓓ Ⓔ	10. Ⓐ Ⓑ Ⓒ Ⓓ Ⓔ	3. C	10. E
4. Ⓐ Ⓑ Ⓒ Ⓓ Ⓔ	11. Ⓐ Ⓑ Ⓒ Ⓓ Ⓔ	4. B	11. C
5. Ⓐ Ⓑ Ⓒ Ⓓ Ⓔ	12. Ⓐ Ⓑ Ⓒ Ⓓ Ⓔ	5. A	12. D
6. Ⓐ Ⓑ Ⓒ Ⓓ Ⓔ	13. Ⓐ Ⓑ Ⓒ Ⓓ Ⓔ	6. B	13. B
7. Ⓐ Ⓑ Ⓒ Ⓓ Ⓔ	14. Ⓐ Ⓑ Ⓒ Ⓓ Ⓔ	7. E	14. C

EXPLANATIONS

6. **(B)** There are two ways of looking at this series, both of which will give you the correct answer. You might mark differences between numbers. If you were to do this, you would come up with the pattern: +7, −6; +7, −6; +7 −6. . . . Or you might see alternating series, both ascending at the rate of +1. In such instance, you would see 33 34 35 36 37 alternating with 40 41 42 <u>43</u>.

7. **(E)** There are two series. Numbers of the first series appear two at a time, alternating with one number of the second series. The first series begins with <u>12</u> and descends by −2: 12 10 8 6 4 <u>2</u>. The second series begins with <u>8</u> and descends by −1: 8 7 <u>6</u>. Diagrammed, the problem looks like this:

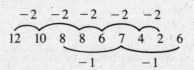

8. **(C)** There are two series. One series simply descends by −1, beginning with <u>20</u>. The other series repeats each number before descending.

9. **(A)** The first series increases by +1. The alternating series ascends by +3.

10. **(E)** There are two patterns. The first pattern is a simple ×2 pattern: 3 6 12 <u>24</u>. The intervening pattern consists of an ever-increasing number of <u>0</u>'s.

11. **(C)** The pattern is: repeat the number, ÷2; repeat the number ÷2 . . . .

12. **(D)** There are two alternating series. The first series ascends by +5. The alternating series descends by −4.

13. **(B)** The pattern is: +2, +4, +6; +2, +4, +6; +2, +4, +6.

14. **(C)** The pattern is: −9, −7, −5; −9, −7, −5; −9 −7; −5 . . . .

PART A—NUMBER SERIES

TIME: 20 Minutes. 24 Questions.

Directions: Each number series question consists of a series of numbers which follows some definite order. The numbers progress from left to right according to some rule. One lettered pair of numbers comprises the next two numbers in the series. Study each series to try to find a pattern to the series and to figure the rule which governs the progression. Choose the answer pair which continues the series according to the pattern established and mark its letter on your answer sheet. Correct answers are on page 174.

1. 3 8 4 9 5 10 6 .... (A) 7 11 (B) 7 8 (C) 11 8 (D) 12 7 (E) 11 7

2. 18 14 19 17 20 20 21 ...... (A) 22 24 (B) 14 19 (C) 24 21 (D) 21 23 (E) 23 22

3. 6 9 10 7 11 12 8 .... (A) 9 10 (B) 9 13 (C) 16 14 (D) 13 14 (E) 14 15

4. 7 5 3 9 7 5 11 .... (A) 13 12 (B) 7 5 (C) 9 7 (D) 13 7 (E) 9 9

5. 7 9 18 10 12 18 13 .... (A) 18 14 (B) 15 18 (C) 14 15 (D) 15 14 (E) 14 18

6. 2 6 4 8 6 10 8 .... (A) 12 10 (B) 6 10 (C) 10 12 (D) 12 16 (E) 6 4

7. 7 9 12 14 17 19 22 .... (A) 25 27 (B) 23 24 (C) 23 25 (D) 24 27 (E) 26 27

8. 3 23 5 25 7 27 9 .... (A) 10 11 (B) 27 29 (C) 29 11 (D) 11 28 (E) 28 10

9. 1 2 2 3 4 12 5 6 .... (A) 7 8 (B) 11 7 (C) 11 56 (D) 56 7 (E) 30 7

10. 1 2 3 6 4 5 6 6 7 ...... (A) 6 5 (B) 8 9 (C) 6 8 (D) 7 6 (E) 8 6

11. 1 3 40 5 7 37 9 .... (A) 11 39 (B) 9 11 (C) 34 11 (D) 11 34 (E) 11 35

12. 25 27 29 31 33 35 37 ..... (A) 39 41 (B) 38 39 (C) 37 39 (D) 37 38 (E) 39 40

13. 91 85 17 81 75 15 71 ..... (A) 74 14 (B) 61 51 (C) 65 13 (D) 65 10 (E) 66 33

14. 41 37 46 42 51 47 56 ..... (A) 51 70 (B) 52 61 (C) 49 60 (D) 60 43 (E) 55 65

15. 6 6 6 18 18 18 54 .... (A) 54 108 (B) 54 162 (C) 108 108 (D) 108 162 (E) 54 54

16. 13 23 14 22 15 21 16 ...... (A) 17 20 (B) 20 17 (C) 17 18 (D) 20 19 (E) 16 20

17. 52 10 48 20 44 30 40 ..... (A) 36 50 (B) 50 36 (C) 36 40 (D) 40 36 (E) 40 40

18. 94 84 75 67 60 54 49 ..... (A) 45 42 (B) 49 45 (C) 44 40 (D) 46 42 (E) 45 40

19. 76 38 38 48 24 24 34 ..... (A) 34 44 (B) 34 34 (C) 17 17 (D) 34 17 (E) 17 27

20. 83 38 84 48 85 58 86 ..... (A) 86 68 (B) 87 78 (C) 59 95 (D) 68 88 (E) 68 87

21. 19 21 21 24 24 24 28 ..... (A) 28 31 (B) 28 33 (C) 32 36 (D) 28 28 (E) 28 32

22. 52 45 38 32 26 21 16 ..... (A) 16 12 (B) 12 8 (C) 11 6 (D) 11 7 (E) 12 9

23. 100 81 64 49 36 25 16 .... (A) 12 10 (B) 8 4 (C) 8 2 (D) 9 4 (E) 9 2

24. 4 40 44 5 50 55 6 .... (A) 60 66 (B) 6 60 (C) 6 66 (D) 7 70 (E) 70 77

END OF PART A

If you finish before time is up, check over your work on this part only. Do not turn the page until you are told to do so.

PART B—ADDRESS CODING

SAMPLE QUESTIONS

The seven sample questions for this part are based upon the addresses in the five boxes below. Your task is to mark on your answer sheet the letter of the box in which each address belongs. The instructions for Part B permit you to look at the boxes if you cannot remember in which box an address belongs. You may look at the boxes while answering these Part B sample questions. The questions in Part C of the exam will be based upon the same boxes as the questions in Part B, but in answering Part C you may NOT look at the boxes. There will be no sample questions before Part C.

A	B	C	D	E
4300-4699 White Primrose 1300-1599 Parkway Andrea 8300-8399 Shawnee	3100-3899 White Barnaby 1900-2299 Parkway Rogers 7600-7999 Shawnee	5200-5299 White Brewster 2300-2899 Parkway Continental 8000-8299 Shawnee	4700-5199 White Dorchester 2900-2999 Parkway Oakland 5800-6299 Shawnee	3900-4299 White Magnolia 1600-1899 Parkway Lynwood 6300-7599 Shawnee

1. 1900-2299 Parkway
2. 6300-7599 Shawnee
3. Dorchester
4. 8000-8299 Shawnee
5. Barnaby
6. 3900-4299 White
7. Andrea

SAMPLE ANSWER SHEET		CORRECT ANSWERS	
1. Ⓐ Ⓑ Ⓒ Ⓓ Ⓔ	5. Ⓐ Ⓑ Ⓒ Ⓓ Ⓔ	1. B	5. B
2. Ⓐ Ⓑ Ⓒ Ⓓ Ⓔ	6. Ⓐ Ⓑ Ⓒ Ⓓ Ⓔ	2. E	6. E
3. Ⓐ Ⓑ Ⓒ Ⓓ Ⓔ	7. Ⓐ Ⓑ Ⓒ Ⓓ Ⓔ	3. D	7. A
4. Ⓐ Ⓑ Ⓒ Ⓓ Ⓔ		4. C	

PART B—ADDRESS CODING

Directions: There are five boxes labeled A, B, C, D, and E. In each box are five addresses, three of which include a number span and a name and two of which are names alone. You will have five (5) minutes to memorize the locations of all twenty-five addresses. Then you will have three (3) minutes to mark your answer sheet with the letter of the box in which each address in the question list belongs. For Part B you may refer to the boxes while answering, though you will lose speed by doing so. For Part C you may NOT look at the boxes, so do your best to memorize in the five minutes allowed you now. Correct answers are on page 175.

MEMORIZING TIME: 5 Minutes.

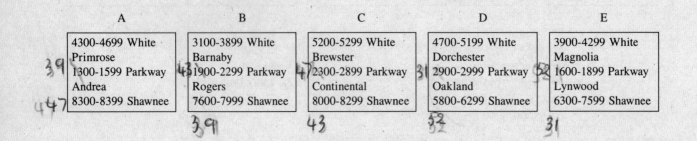

A	B	C	D	E
4300-4699 White	3100-3899 White	5200-5299 White	4700-5199 White	3900-4299 White
Primrose	Barnaby	Brewster	Dorchester	Magnolia
1300-1599 Parkway	1900-2299 Parkway	2300-2899 Parkway	2900-2999 Parkway	1600-1899 Parkway
Andrea	Rogers	Continental	Oakland	Lynwood
8300-8399 Shawnee	7600-7999 Shawnee	8000-8299 Shawnee	5800-6299 Shawnee	6300-7599 Shawnee

ANSWERING TIME: 3 Minutes. 88 Questions.

1. 2300-2899 Parkway
2. Andrea
3. 3900-4299 White
4. 5800-6299 Shawnee
5. Lynwood
6. 4300-4699 White
7. 1900-2299 Parkway
8. Rogers
9. Brewster
10. 8300-8399 Shawnee
11. Magnolia
12. Primrose
13. 6300-7599 Shawnee
14. 2900-2999 Parkway

15. Barnaby
16. 1600-1899 Parkway
17. 4700-5199 White
18. 3100-3899 White
19. 5200-5299 White
20. Continental
21. Dorchester
22. 1300-1599 Parkway
23. Oakland
24. 7600-7999 Shawnee
25. 8000-8299 Shawnee
26. 3900-4299 White
27. 2900-2999 Parkway
28. 3100-3899 White

29. Andrea
30. 8300-8399 Shawnee
31. Lynwood
32. 2900-2999 Parkway
33. 1300-1599 Parkway
34. 7600-7999 Shawnee
35. Barnaby
36. Continental
37. 5200-5299 White
38. 4700-5199 White
39. 2300-2899 Parkway
40. Magnolia
41. Brewster
42. Oakland
43. 1600-1899 Parkway
44. 5800-6299 Shawnee
45. 8000-8299 Shawnee
46. 1900-2299 Parkway
47. Dorchester
48. Magnolia
49. Rogers
50. 4300-4699 White
51. 3900-4299 White
52. 2300-2899 Parkway
53. 6300-7599 Shawnee
54. Primrose
55. Oakland
56. 1300-1599 Parkway
57. Andrea
58. 4700-5199 White

59. 6300-7599 Shawnee
60. 8000-8299 Shawnee
61. 3900-4299 White
62. Barnaby
63. Dorchester
64. Continental
65. 3100-3899 White
66. 7600-7999 Shawnee
67. 1900-2299 Parkway
68. Rogers
69. Magnolia
70. 8300-8399 Shawnee
71. 1600-1899 Parkway
72. 2900-2999 Parkway
73. 5200-5299 White
74. Lynwood
75. 3100-3899 White
76. 4300-4699 White
77. 1900-2299 Parkway
78. 5800-6299 Shawnee
79. Primrose
80. Andrea
81. Dorchester
82. 7600-7999 Shawnee
83. 1600-1899 Parkway
84. 1300-1599 Parkway
85. Lynwood
86. Oakland
87. Rogers
88. 2300-2899 Parkway

END OF PART B

If you finish before time is up, use the remaining few seconds to continue memorizing the address locations. Do not turn the page until you are told to do so.

PART C—ADDRESS CODE MEMORY

TIME: 5 Minutes. 88 Questions.

Directions: *Relying entirely upon your memory, mark your answer sheet with the letter of the box in which each address belongs. Correct answers are on page 176.*

1. 4300-4699 White
2. 8000-8299 Shawnee
3. Magnolia
4. Dorchester
5. 1900-2299 Parkway
6. 8300-8399 Shawnee
7. Barnaby
8. 3100-3899 White
9. 5800-6299 Shawnee
10. Primrose
11. Lynwood
12. Brewster
13. 3900-4299 White
14. 1600-1899 Parkway
15. 4700-5199 White
16. Continental
17. 7600-7999 Shawnee
18. 1300-1599 Parkway
19. Rogers
20. Oakland
21. 5200-5299 White
22. 6300-7599 Shawnee
23. 2900-2999 Parkway
24. 2300-2899 Parkway
25. Continental
26. Oakland
27. 1300-1599 Parkway
28. 5800-6299 Shawnee
29. 4300-4699 White
30. Lynwood
31. Magnolia
32. 4700-5199 White
33. 8300-8399 Shawnee
34. 5200-5299 White
35. Primrose

36. Barnaby
37. Andrea
38. 1900-2299 Parkway
39. 3100-3899 White
40. Rogers
41. 6300-7599 Shawnee
42. 8000-8299 Shawnee
43. Brewster
44. 7600-7999 Shawnee
45. 3900-4299 White
46. 1600-1899 Parkway
47. Dorchester
48. 3100-3899 White
49. 1600-1899 Parkway
50. Primrose
51. 8300-8399 Shawnee
52. 2300-2899 Parkway
53. 4700-5199 White
54. Barnaby
55. Magnolia
56. 5800-6299 Shawnee
57. 3900-4299 White
58. Andrea
59. Continental
60. Oakland
61. 1300-1599 Parkway
62. 4300-4699 White
63. 6300-7599 Shawnee
64. Brewster
65. Rogers
66. 5200-5299 White
67. 7600-7999 Shawnee
68. Lynwood
69. 3100-3899 White
70. Oakland

71. 4300-4699 White
72. 1600-1899 Parkway
73. 5800-6299 Shawnee
74. Andrea
75. Rogers
76. Magnolia
77. 6300-7599 Shawnee
78. 1300-1599 Parkway
79. 2900-2999 Parkway

80. 5200-5299 White
81. Dorchester
82. Continental
83. 8300-8399 Shawnee
84. 3100-3899 White
85. 3900-4299 White
86. Primrose
87. Barnaby
88. Brewster

END OF PART C

*If you finish before time is up, check your answers on this
part only. Do not turn the page until you are told to do so.*

PART D—ADDRESS CHECKING TEST

SAMPLE QUESTIONS

You will be allowed three minutes to read the directions and answer the five sample questions which follow. On the actual test, however, you will have only six minutes to answer 95 questions, so see how quickly you can compare addresses and still get the correct answer.

Directions: *Each question consists of two addresses. If the two addresses are* alike *in EVERY way, mark* Ⓐ *on your answer sheet. If the two addresses are* different *in ANY way, mark* Ⓓ *on your answer sheet.*

1 . . .	1706 Artillery La	1706 Artillery Ln
2 . . .	4464 Baroque Blvd	4644 Baroque Blvd
3 . . .	Santa Cruz CA 95064	Santa Cruz GA 95064
4 . . .	2859 SW 145th Dr	2859 SW 145th Dr
5 . . .	1984 Oregon Ave SE	1984 Oregon Ave SE

SAMPLE ANSWER SHEET	
1. ⒶⒹ	4. ⒶⒹ
2. ⒶⒹ	5. ⒶⒹ
3. ⒶⒹ	

CORRECT ANSWERS	
1. D	4. A
2. D	5. A
3. D	

Fifth Model Exam / 171

PART D—ADDRESS CHECKING

TIME: 6 Minutes. 95 Questions.

Directions: Look carefully at the two addresses in each question. If the two addresses are alike in EVERY way, mark Ⓐ on your answer sheet. If the two addresses are different in ANY way, mark Ⓓ on your answer sheet. Correct answers are on page 176.

1 . . . 3824 W Burgess Rd	3824 W Burgess Rd
2 . . . 1828 Stonewall Ln	1828 Stonewall Ln
3 . . . 7521 Wyoming Ave NE	7521 Wyoming Ave NE
4 . . . Ithaca NY 14850	Ithaca NY 14850
5 . . . 1377 Clarence Rd	1377 Clarence Rd
6 . . . 1918 Kings Highway S	1819 Kings Highway S
7 . . . Jacksonville FL 32211	Jacksonville FL 33211
8 . . . 8516 Reservoir Dr	8516 Reservoir Rd
9 . . . 1903 Highland Wy	1903 Highland Wy
10 . . . 5142 S 157th Pl	5142 S 157th Pl
11 . . . 6714 Mariposa Blvd	6174 Mariposa Blvd
12 . . . Baltimore MD 21218	Baltimore MO 21218
13 . . . 846 N Weymouth St	846 N Waymouth St
14 . . . 2164 N Broadway	2164 N Broadway
15 . . . 7456 Sheridan Plza	7456 Sheriden Plza
16 . . . 8518 W Garthwoods Apts	8518 W Garth Woods Apts
17 . . . Kalamazoo MI 49007	Kalamazoo MI 49007
18 . . . Manhattan KS 66506	Manhattan KS 65506
19 . . . 6405 Fraternity Row	6405 Fraternity Row W
20 . . . 5118 Carnegie Hall	518 Carnegie Hall
21 . . . 7413 S Hartt Hwy	7413 S Hartt Hwy
22 . . . Lawrence KS 66045	Laurence KS 66045
23 . . . 890 Boulder Ln	890 Boulder Ln
24 . . . 1141 Vernon Dr	1141 Vernon Dr
25 . . . 2136 Johnson St	2163 Johnson St
26 . . . 9016 Atherstone Ln	9016 Atherstone La
27 . . . 7415 Tintern Blvd	7145 Tintern Blvd
28 . . . Kent OH 44242	Kent OH 42242
29 . . . Lexington KY 40506	Lexington KY 40506
30 . . . 7189 Chavez Ravine	7198 Chavez Ravine
31 . . . 5181 SE Poplar St	5181 SE Popular St
32 . . . 4313 N 356th St	4313 N 365th St
33 . . . 9096 Washington Ave SW	9096 Washington Av SW
34 . . . Gambier OH 43022	Gambler OH 43022

35 . . . 7413 W Coliseum Pl	7413 W Coliseum Pl
36 . . . 1927 Kenyon Tpke	1927 Kenyon Tpke
37 . . . Galesburg IL 61401	Galesburg IN 61401
38 . . . 8906 Barcelona Blvd	8960 Barcelona Blvd
39 . . . 6170 Lafayette Hwy	6170 Lafayette Hwy
40 . . . 9684 Phillipsberg Pike	9684 Philipsberg Pike
41 . . . Easton PA 18042	Easton PA 18042
42 . . . 1862 Regional Circle	1862 Regional Circle
43 . . . 7412 Henkel Pl	7412 Henckel Pl
44 . . . 6519 W 384th St	6519 W 384th St
45 . . . 4178 Tanglewood Rd	4178 Tandlewood Dr
46 . . . Lake Forest IL 60045	Lake Forest IL 60445
47 . . . 9054 Symphony Sta	9504 Symphony Sta
48 . . . 1361 Romantic La	1361 Romantic La
49 . . . 4156 Livonia Ave	4156 Livonia Ave So
50 . . . Appleton WI 54911	Appleton WI 54911
51 . . . 6412 Lehigh Tpke	6412 Lehigh Tpke
52 . . . 416 Machiavelli Ave	416 Machiavelli Ave
53 . . . Bethlehem PA 18015	Bethlehem PN 18015
54 . . . 5238 Centenary Pl	5328 Centenary Pl
55 . . . 4196 Rosemary Hall	4169 Rosemary Hill
56 . . . 4519 Porsche Pkwy	4591 Porsche Pkwy
57 . . . Baton Rouge LA 70803	Baton Rouge LA 70803
58 . . . 8569 Freedom Hwy	8596 Freedom Hwy
59 . . . 7107 N Loyola St	7107 W Loyola St
60 . . . Louisville KY 40208	Louiseville KY 40208
61 . . . 7618 Coalition Hwy	7618 Coalition Hwy
62 . . . 5890 E 179th Ave	5890 E 179th Ave
63 . . . 7944 Seventh Ave	794 Seventh Ave
64 . . . Chicago IL 60611	Chicago IL 60611
65 . . . St Paul MI 55105	St Paul MN 55105
66 . . . 8904 Galveston Rd	8904 Galveston Rd
67 . . . 5693 Gravesend Bay	5693 Gravend Bay
68 . . . 9830 Oregon Ave SE	9380 Oregon Ave SE
69 . . . 8417 N 294th St	8417 N 295th St
70 . . . Orono ME 04473	Onono ME 04473
71 . . . 8415 Back Bay Sta	8415 Back Bay Sta
72 . . . 3519 Philharmonic Hwy	3519 Philharmonic Hwy
73 . . . 4711 Manhattanville Wy	4711 Manhattanville Wy
74 . . . Purchase NY 10577	Purchase NY 10557
75 . . . 1468 Dammann Hall	1468 Damann Hall
76 . . . 9809 Lancaster Pike	9909 Lancaster Pike
77 . . . Marlboro VT 05344	Marlboro VT 05344
78 . . . Milwaukee WI 53233	Milwaukee WI 52323
79 . . . 7819 W Marquette Ave	7819 W Marquette Ave
80 . . . 7621 Campustown St	7621 Campustown St
81 . . . 1692 Archambault Ave	1692 Archambault Ave
82 . . . 4768 Pinebrook Blvd	4768 Pinebrooks Blvd
83 . . . College Park MD 20742	College Park MD 20742
84 . . . Cambridge MA 02139	Cambridge MA 02319
85 . . . 9045 Framingham St	9045 Farmingham St

86	1876 Fitchburg Dr	1876 E Fitchburg Dr
87	4870 Bridgewater Blvd	4870 Bridgewater Blvd
88	9482 Lowell Row	9482 Lovell Row
89	1094 W Memorial Dr	1904 W Memorial Dr
90	4586 Simmons Ave	4596 Simmons Ave
91	6945 Bay State Blvd	6495 Bay State Blvd
92	Amherst MA 01002	Amherst MA 01002
93	7415 E Quebec Alley	7415 E Quebec Alley
94	8041 McLennan Ave	8401 McLennan Ave
95	7401 N 287th Row	7401 N 278th Row

END OF EXAM

If you finish before time is up, check over your answers on this part only. Do not return to any previous part.

CORRECT ANSWERS—FIFTH MODEL EXAM

PART A—NUMBER SERIES

1. E	4. C	7. D	10. B	13. C	16. B	19. C	22. B
2. E	5. B	8. C	11. D	14. B	17. D	20. E	23. D
3. D	6. A	9. E	12. A	15. E	18. A	21. D	24. A

EXPLANATIONS—NUMBER SERIES

1. **(E)** There are two alternating series, each ascending by $+1$. One series begins with 3, the other with 8.

2. **(E)** The two alternating series progress at different rates. The first, beginning with 18, moves up one number at a time. The alternating series, beginning with 14, increases by $+3$.

3. **(D)** There are two alternating series, but this time two numbers of one series interpose between steps of the other series. Thus, one series reads 6 7 8 while the other reads 9 10 11 12 13 14.

4. **(C)** Here we have a series of mini-series. The pattern in each mini-series is -2, -2. Then the pattern repeats with the first number of the next mini-series two numbers higher than the first number of the preceding mini-series.

5. **(B)** The series really is $+2$, $+1$ with the number 18 appearing between the two numbers at the $+1$ phase.

6. **(A)** Two series alternate, both ascending by $+2$.

7. **(D)** Here the progression is $+2$, $+3$; $+2$, $+3$, and so on.

8. **(C)** Both alternating series move up by $+2$.

9. **(E)** The series is essentially 1 2 3 4 5 6 7, but, after each two numbers in the series we find the product of the multiplication of those two numbers. $1 \times 2 = 2$; $3 \times 4 = 12$; $5 \times 6 = 30$; 7 . . . .

10. **(B)** The series is simply 1 2 3 4 5 6 7 8 9. After each three numbers of the series, we find the number 6.

11. **(D)** There are two series. The ascending series up by $+2$. The descending series intervenes after every two members of the ascending series. The descending series moves in steps of -3.

12. **(A)** Weren't you ready for an easy one? There is no catch. The series moves by $+2$.

13. **(C)** You may feel the rhythm of this series and spot the pattern without playing around with the numbers. If you cannot solve the problem by inspection, then you might see three parallel series. The first series descends by -10 (91 81 71); the second series, also descends by minus 10 (85 75 65); the third series descends by -2 (17 15 13). Or, you

might see a series of mini-series. Each mini-series begins with a number 10 lower than the first number of the previous mini-series. Within each mini-series the pattern is −6, ÷5.

14. **(B)** The pattern is −4, +9; −4, +9 . . . Or, there are two alternating series. The first series ascends at the rate of +5; the alternating series also ascends at the rate of +5.

15. **(E)** Each number appears three times then is multiplied by 3.

16. **(B)** There are two alternating series. One starts at 13 and moves up by +1 and the other starts at 23 and moves down by −1.

17. **(D)** There are two alternating series. The first series begins with 52 and descends at the rate of −4. The alternating series begins with 10 and ascends at the rate of +10.

18. **(A)** The pattern is: −10, −9, −8, −7, −6, −5, −4, −3.

19. **(C)** The pattern is: ÷2, repeat the number, +10; ÷2, repeat the number +10; ÷2, repeat the number, +10.

20. **(E)** You see a simple series, 83 84 85 86 . . . . After each number in this series you see its mirror image, that is, the mirror image of 83 is 38; the mirror image of 84 is 48 and so forth. Or you might see a series that increases by +1 alternating with a series that increases by +10.

21. **(D)** The pattern is: +2, repeat the number 2 times; +3, repeat the number 3 times; +4, repeat the number 4 times.

22. **(B)** The pattern is −7, −7, −6, −6, −5, −5, −4, −4.

23. **(D)** The series consists of the squares of the whole numbers in descending order.

24. **(A)** You can probably get this one by inspection. If not, notice the series of mini-series. In each mini-series the pattern is 10 times the first number, 11 times the first number.

PART B—ADDRESS CODING

1. C	12. A	23. D	34. B	45. C	56. A	67. B	78. D
2. A	13. E	24. B	35. B	46. B	57. A	68. B	79. A
3. E	14. D	25. C	36. C	47. D	58. D	69. E	80. A
4. D	15. B	26. E	37. C	48. E	59. E	70. A	81. D
5. E	16. E	27. D	38. D	49. B	60. C	71. E	82. B
6. A	17. D	28. B	39. C	50. A	61. E	72. D	83. E
7. B	18. B	29. A	40. E	51. E	62. B	73. C	84. A
8. B	19. C	30. A	41. C	52. C	63. D	74. E	85. E
9. C	20. C	31. E	42. D	53. E	64. C	75. B	86. D
10. A	21. D	32. D	43. E	54. A	65. B	76. A	87. B
11. E	22. A	33. A	44. D	55. D	66. B	77. B	88. C

176 *Distribution Clerk, Machine/U.S. Postal Service*

PART C—ADDRESS CODE MEMORY

1. A	12. C	23. D	34. C	45. E	56. D	67. B	78. A
2. C	13. E	24. C	35. A	46. E	57. E	68. E	79. D
3. E	14. E	25. C	36. B	47. D	58. A	69. B	80. C
4. D	15. D	26. D	37. A	48. B	59. C	70. D	81. D
5. B	16. C	27. A	38. B	49. E	60. D	71. A	82. C
6. A	17. B	28. D	39. B	50. A	61. A	72. E	83. A
7. B	18. A	29. A	40. B	51. A	62. A	73. D	84. B
8. B	19. B	30. E	41. E	52. C	63. E	74. A	85. E
9. D	20. D	31. E	42. C	53. D	64. C	75. B	86. A
10. A	21. C	32. D	43. C	54. B	65. B	76. E	87. B
11. E	22. E	33. A	44. B	55. E	66. C	77. E	88. C

PART D—ADDRESS CHECKING

1. A	13. D	25. D	37. D	49. D	61. A	73. A	85. D
2. A	14. A	26. D	38. D	50. A	62. A	74. D	86. D
3. A	15. D	27. D	39. A	51. A	63. D	75. D	87. A
4. A	16. D	28. D	40. D	52. A	64. A	76. D	88. D
5. A	17. A	29. A	41. A	53. D	65. D	77. A	89. D
6. D	18. D	30. D	42. A	54. D	66. D	78. D	90. D
7. D	19. D	31. D	43. D	55. D	67. D	79. A	91. D
8. D	20. D	32. D	44. A	56. D	68. D	80. A	92. A
9. A	21. A	33. D	45. D	57. A	69. D	81. A	93. A
10. A	22. D	34. D	46. D	58. D	70. D	82. D	94. D
11. D	23. A	35. A	47. D	59. D	71. A	83. A	95. D
12. D	24. A	36. A	48. A	60. D	72. A	84. D	

ADDRESS CHECKING ERROR ANALYSIS CHART

Type of Error	Tally	Total Number
Number of addresses that were alike and you incorrectly marked "different"		
Number of addresses that were different and you incorrectly marked "alike"		
Number of addresses in which you missed a difference in NUMBERS	2	2
Number of addresses in which you missed a difference in ABBREVIATIONS		
Number of addresses in which you missed a difference in NAMES		

SCORE SHEET FOR FIFTH MODEL EXAM

PART A—NUMBER SERIES

Number Right equals Score

_____ = _____

PART B—ADDRESS CODING

Number Right minus (Number Wrong ÷ 4) equals Score

_____ − _____ = _____

PART C—ADDRESS CODE MEMORY

Number Right minus (Number Wrong ÷ 4) equals Score

_____ − _____ = _____

PART D—ADDRESS CHECKING

Number Right minus Number Wrong equals Score

_____ − _____ = _____

SELF-EVALUATION CHART

Part	Excellent	Good	Average	Fair	Poor
Number Series	21–24	18–20	14–17	11–13	1–10
Address Coding	75–88	63–74	52–62	40–51	1–39
Address Code Memory	75–88	60–74	45–59	30–44	1–29
Address Checking	80–95	65–79	50–64	35–49	1–34

PROGRESS CHART

Blacken to the closest score to chart your progress.

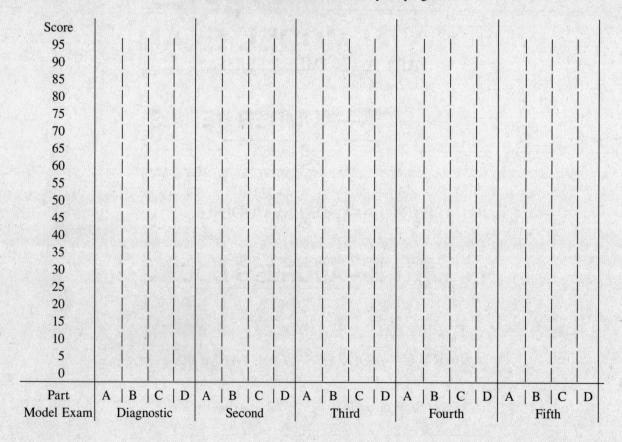

Score																				
95																				
90																				
85																				
80																				
75																				
70																				
65																				
60																				
55																				
50																				
45																				
40																				
35																				
30																				
25																				
20																				
15																				
10																				
5																				
0																				

Part	A	B	C	D	A	B	C	D	A	B	C	D	A	B	C	D	A	B	C	D
Model Exam	Diagnostic				Second				Third				Fourth				Fifth			

ANSWER SHEET— SIXTH MODEL EXAM

Tear out this Answer Sheet and use it to mark your answers for the exam that follows.

PART A—NUMBER SERIES

1. Ⓐ Ⓑ Ⓒ Ⓓ Ⓔ   6. Ⓐ Ⓑ Ⓒ Ⓓ Ⓔ   11. Ⓐ Ⓑ Ⓒ Ⓓ Ⓔ   16. Ⓐ Ⓑ Ⓒ Ⓓ Ⓔ   21. Ⓐ Ⓑ Ⓒ Ⓓ Ⓔ
2. Ⓐ Ⓑ Ⓒ Ⓓ Ⓔ   7. Ⓐ Ⓑ Ⓒ Ⓓ Ⓔ   12. Ⓐ Ⓑ Ⓒ Ⓓ Ⓔ   17. Ⓐ Ⓑ Ⓒ Ⓓ Ⓔ   22. Ⓐ Ⓑ Ⓒ Ⓓ Ⓔ
3. Ⓐ Ⓑ Ⓒ Ⓓ Ⓔ   8. Ⓐ Ⓑ Ⓒ Ⓓ Ⓔ   13. Ⓐ Ⓑ Ⓒ Ⓓ Ⓔ   18. Ⓐ Ⓑ Ⓒ Ⓓ Ⓔ   23. Ⓐ Ⓑ Ⓒ Ⓓ Ⓔ
4. Ⓐ Ⓑ Ⓒ Ⓓ Ⓔ   9. Ⓐ Ⓑ Ⓒ Ⓓ Ⓔ   14. Ⓐ Ⓑ Ⓒ Ⓓ Ⓔ   19. Ⓐ Ⓑ Ⓒ Ⓓ Ⓔ   24. Ⓐ Ⓑ Ⓒ Ⓓ Ⓔ
5. Ⓐ Ⓑ Ⓒ Ⓓ Ⓔ   10. Ⓐ Ⓑ Ⓒ Ⓓ Ⓔ   15. Ⓐ Ⓑ Ⓒ Ⓓ Ⓔ   20. Ⓐ Ⓑ Ⓒ Ⓓ Ⓔ

PART B—ADDRESS CODING

1. Ⓐ Ⓑ Ⓒ Ⓓ Ⓔ   19. Ⓐ Ⓑ Ⓒ Ⓓ Ⓔ   37. Ⓐ Ⓑ Ⓒ Ⓓ Ⓔ   55. Ⓐ Ⓑ Ⓒ Ⓓ Ⓔ   73. Ⓐ Ⓑ Ⓒ Ⓓ Ⓔ
2. Ⓐ Ⓑ Ⓒ Ⓓ Ⓔ   20. Ⓐ Ⓑ Ⓒ Ⓓ Ⓔ   38. Ⓐ Ⓑ Ⓒ Ⓓ Ⓔ   56. Ⓐ Ⓑ Ⓒ Ⓓ Ⓔ   74. Ⓐ Ⓑ Ⓒ Ⓓ Ⓔ
3. Ⓐ Ⓑ Ⓒ Ⓓ Ⓔ   21. Ⓐ Ⓑ Ⓒ Ⓓ Ⓔ   39. Ⓐ Ⓑ Ⓒ Ⓓ Ⓔ   57. Ⓐ Ⓑ Ⓒ Ⓓ Ⓔ   75. Ⓐ Ⓑ Ⓒ Ⓓ Ⓔ
4. Ⓐ Ⓑ Ⓒ Ⓓ Ⓔ   22. Ⓐ Ⓑ Ⓒ Ⓓ Ⓔ   40. Ⓐ Ⓑ Ⓒ Ⓓ Ⓔ   58. Ⓐ Ⓑ Ⓒ Ⓓ Ⓔ   76. Ⓐ Ⓑ Ⓒ Ⓓ Ⓔ
5. Ⓐ Ⓑ Ⓒ Ⓓ Ⓔ   23. Ⓐ Ⓑ Ⓒ Ⓓ Ⓔ   41. Ⓐ Ⓑ Ⓒ Ⓓ Ⓔ   59. Ⓐ Ⓑ Ⓒ Ⓓ Ⓔ   77. Ⓐ Ⓑ Ⓒ Ⓓ Ⓔ
6. Ⓐ Ⓑ Ⓒ Ⓓ Ⓔ   24. Ⓐ Ⓑ Ⓒ Ⓓ Ⓔ   42. Ⓐ Ⓑ Ⓒ Ⓓ Ⓔ   60. Ⓐ Ⓑ Ⓒ Ⓓ Ⓔ   78. Ⓐ Ⓑ Ⓒ Ⓓ Ⓔ
7. Ⓐ Ⓑ Ⓒ Ⓓ Ⓔ   25. Ⓐ Ⓑ Ⓒ Ⓓ Ⓔ   43. Ⓐ Ⓑ Ⓒ Ⓓ Ⓔ   61. Ⓐ Ⓑ Ⓒ Ⓓ Ⓔ   79. Ⓐ Ⓑ Ⓒ Ⓓ Ⓔ
8. Ⓐ Ⓑ Ⓒ Ⓓ Ⓔ   26. Ⓐ Ⓑ Ⓒ Ⓓ Ⓔ   44. Ⓐ Ⓑ Ⓒ Ⓓ Ⓔ   62. Ⓐ Ⓑ Ⓒ Ⓓ Ⓔ   80. Ⓐ Ⓑ Ⓒ Ⓓ Ⓔ
9. Ⓐ Ⓑ Ⓒ Ⓓ Ⓔ   27. Ⓐ Ⓑ Ⓒ Ⓓ Ⓔ   45. Ⓐ Ⓑ Ⓒ Ⓓ Ⓔ   63. Ⓐ Ⓑ Ⓒ Ⓓ Ⓔ   81. Ⓐ Ⓑ Ⓒ Ⓓ Ⓔ
10. Ⓐ Ⓑ Ⓒ Ⓓ Ⓔ   28. Ⓐ Ⓑ Ⓒ Ⓓ Ⓔ   46. Ⓐ Ⓑ Ⓒ Ⓓ Ⓔ   64. Ⓐ Ⓑ Ⓒ Ⓓ Ⓔ   82. Ⓐ Ⓑ Ⓒ Ⓓ Ⓔ
11. Ⓐ Ⓑ Ⓒ Ⓓ Ⓔ   29. Ⓐ Ⓑ Ⓒ Ⓓ Ⓔ   47. Ⓐ Ⓑ Ⓒ Ⓓ Ⓔ   65. Ⓐ Ⓑ Ⓒ Ⓓ Ⓔ   83. Ⓐ Ⓑ Ⓒ Ⓓ Ⓔ
12. Ⓐ Ⓑ Ⓒ Ⓓ Ⓔ   30. Ⓐ Ⓑ Ⓒ Ⓓ Ⓔ   48. Ⓐ Ⓑ Ⓒ Ⓓ Ⓔ   66. Ⓐ Ⓑ Ⓒ Ⓓ Ⓔ   84. Ⓐ Ⓑ Ⓒ Ⓓ Ⓔ
13. Ⓐ Ⓑ Ⓒ Ⓓ Ⓔ   31. Ⓐ Ⓑ Ⓒ Ⓓ Ⓔ   49. Ⓐ Ⓑ Ⓒ Ⓓ Ⓔ   67. Ⓐ Ⓑ Ⓒ Ⓓ Ⓔ   85. Ⓐ Ⓑ Ⓒ Ⓓ Ⓔ
14. Ⓐ Ⓑ Ⓒ Ⓓ Ⓔ   32. Ⓐ Ⓑ Ⓒ Ⓓ Ⓔ   50. Ⓐ Ⓑ Ⓒ Ⓓ Ⓔ   68. Ⓐ Ⓑ Ⓒ Ⓓ Ⓔ   86. Ⓐ Ⓑ Ⓒ Ⓓ Ⓔ
15. Ⓐ Ⓑ Ⓒ Ⓓ Ⓔ   33. Ⓐ Ⓑ Ⓒ Ⓓ Ⓔ   51. Ⓐ Ⓑ Ⓒ Ⓓ Ⓔ   69. Ⓐ Ⓑ Ⓒ Ⓓ Ⓔ   87. Ⓐ Ⓑ Ⓒ Ⓓ Ⓔ
16. Ⓐ Ⓑ Ⓒ Ⓓ Ⓔ   34. Ⓐ Ⓑ Ⓒ Ⓓ Ⓔ   52. Ⓐ Ⓑ Ⓒ Ⓓ Ⓔ   70. Ⓐ Ⓑ Ⓒ Ⓓ Ⓔ   88. Ⓐ Ⓑ Ⓒ Ⓓ Ⓔ
17. Ⓐ Ⓑ Ⓒ Ⓓ Ⓔ   35. Ⓐ Ⓑ Ⓒ Ⓓ Ⓔ   53. Ⓐ Ⓑ Ⓒ Ⓓ Ⓔ   71. Ⓐ Ⓑ Ⓒ Ⓓ Ⓔ
18. Ⓐ Ⓑ Ⓒ Ⓓ Ⓔ   36. Ⓐ Ⓑ Ⓒ Ⓓ Ⓔ   54. Ⓐ Ⓑ Ⓒ Ⓓ Ⓔ   72. Ⓐ Ⓑ Ⓒ Ⓓ Ⓔ

Tear here

PART C—ADDRESS CODE MEMORY

1. Ⓐ Ⓑ Ⓒ Ⓓ Ⓔ	19. Ⓐ Ⓑ Ⓒ Ⓓ Ⓔ	37. Ⓐ Ⓑ Ⓒ Ⓓ Ⓔ	55. Ⓐ Ⓑ Ⓒ Ⓓ Ⓔ	73. Ⓐ Ⓑ Ⓒ Ⓓ Ⓔ
2. Ⓐ Ⓑ Ⓒ Ⓓ Ⓔ	20. Ⓐ Ⓑ Ⓒ Ⓓ Ⓔ	38. Ⓐ Ⓑ Ⓒ Ⓓ Ⓔ	56. Ⓐ Ⓑ Ⓒ Ⓓ Ⓔ	74. Ⓐ Ⓑ Ⓒ Ⓓ Ⓔ
3. Ⓐ Ⓑ Ⓒ Ⓓ Ⓔ	21. Ⓐ Ⓑ Ⓒ Ⓓ Ⓔ	39. Ⓐ Ⓑ Ⓒ Ⓓ Ⓔ	57. Ⓐ Ⓑ Ⓒ Ⓓ Ⓔ	75. Ⓐ Ⓑ Ⓒ Ⓓ Ⓔ
4. Ⓐ Ⓑ Ⓒ Ⓓ Ⓔ	22. Ⓐ Ⓑ Ⓒ Ⓓ Ⓔ	40. Ⓐ Ⓑ Ⓒ Ⓓ Ⓔ	58. Ⓐ Ⓑ Ⓒ Ⓓ Ⓔ	76. Ⓐ Ⓑ Ⓒ Ⓓ Ⓔ
5. Ⓐ Ⓑ Ⓒ Ⓓ Ⓔ	23. Ⓐ Ⓑ Ⓒ Ⓓ Ⓔ	41. Ⓐ Ⓑ Ⓒ Ⓓ Ⓔ	59. Ⓐ Ⓑ Ⓒ Ⓓ Ⓔ	77. Ⓐ Ⓑ Ⓒ Ⓓ Ⓔ
6. Ⓐ Ⓑ Ⓒ Ⓓ Ⓔ	24. Ⓐ Ⓑ Ⓒ Ⓓ Ⓔ	42. Ⓐ Ⓑ Ⓒ Ⓓ Ⓔ	60. Ⓐ Ⓑ Ⓒ Ⓓ Ⓔ	78. Ⓐ Ⓑ Ⓒ Ⓓ Ⓔ
7. Ⓐ Ⓑ Ⓒ Ⓓ Ⓔ	25. Ⓐ Ⓑ Ⓒ Ⓓ Ⓔ	43. Ⓐ Ⓑ Ⓒ Ⓓ Ⓔ	61. Ⓐ Ⓑ Ⓒ Ⓓ Ⓔ	79. Ⓐ Ⓑ Ⓒ Ⓓ Ⓔ
8. Ⓐ Ⓑ Ⓒ Ⓓ Ⓔ	26. Ⓐ Ⓑ Ⓒ Ⓓ Ⓔ	44. Ⓐ Ⓑ Ⓒ Ⓓ Ⓔ	62. Ⓐ Ⓑ Ⓒ Ⓓ Ⓔ	80. Ⓐ Ⓑ Ⓒ Ⓓ Ⓔ
9. Ⓐ Ⓑ Ⓒ Ⓓ Ⓔ	27. Ⓐ Ⓑ Ⓒ Ⓓ Ⓔ	45. Ⓐ Ⓑ Ⓒ Ⓓ Ⓔ	63. Ⓐ Ⓑ Ⓒ Ⓓ Ⓔ	81. Ⓐ Ⓑ Ⓒ Ⓓ Ⓔ
10. Ⓐ Ⓑ Ⓒ Ⓓ Ⓔ	28. Ⓐ Ⓑ Ⓒ Ⓓ Ⓔ	46. Ⓐ Ⓑ Ⓒ Ⓓ Ⓔ	64. Ⓐ Ⓑ Ⓒ Ⓓ Ⓔ	82. Ⓐ Ⓑ Ⓒ Ⓓ Ⓔ
11. Ⓐ Ⓑ Ⓒ Ⓓ Ⓔ	29. Ⓐ Ⓑ Ⓒ Ⓓ Ⓔ	47. Ⓐ Ⓑ Ⓒ Ⓓ Ⓔ	65. Ⓐ Ⓑ Ⓒ Ⓓ Ⓔ	83. Ⓐ Ⓑ Ⓒ Ⓓ Ⓔ
12. Ⓐ Ⓑ Ⓒ Ⓓ Ⓔ	30. Ⓐ Ⓑ Ⓒ Ⓓ Ⓔ	48. Ⓐ Ⓑ Ⓒ Ⓓ Ⓔ	66. Ⓐ Ⓑ Ⓒ Ⓓ Ⓔ	84. Ⓐ Ⓑ Ⓒ Ⓓ Ⓔ
13. Ⓐ Ⓑ Ⓒ Ⓓ Ⓔ	31. Ⓐ Ⓑ Ⓒ Ⓓ Ⓔ	49. Ⓐ Ⓑ Ⓒ Ⓓ Ⓔ	67. Ⓐ Ⓑ Ⓒ Ⓓ Ⓔ	85. Ⓐ Ⓑ Ⓒ Ⓓ Ⓔ
14. Ⓐ Ⓑ Ⓒ Ⓓ Ⓔ	32. Ⓐ Ⓑ Ⓒ Ⓓ Ⓔ	50. Ⓐ Ⓑ Ⓒ Ⓓ Ⓔ	68. Ⓐ Ⓑ Ⓒ Ⓓ Ⓔ	86. Ⓐ Ⓑ Ⓒ Ⓓ Ⓔ
15. Ⓐ Ⓑ Ⓒ Ⓓ Ⓔ	33. Ⓐ Ⓑ Ⓒ Ⓓ Ⓔ	51. Ⓐ Ⓑ Ⓒ Ⓓ Ⓔ	69. Ⓐ Ⓑ Ⓒ Ⓓ Ⓔ	87. Ⓐ Ⓑ Ⓒ Ⓓ Ⓔ
16. Ⓐ Ⓑ Ⓒ Ⓓ Ⓔ	34. Ⓐ Ⓑ Ⓒ Ⓓ Ⓔ	52. Ⓐ Ⓑ Ⓒ Ⓓ Ⓔ	70. Ⓐ Ⓑ Ⓒ Ⓓ Ⓔ	88. Ⓐ Ⓑ Ⓒ Ⓓ Ⓔ
17. Ⓐ Ⓑ Ⓒ Ⓓ Ⓔ	35. Ⓐ Ⓑ Ⓒ Ⓓ Ⓔ	53. Ⓐ Ⓑ Ⓒ Ⓓ Ⓔ	71. Ⓐ Ⓑ Ⓒ Ⓓ Ⓔ	
18. Ⓐ Ⓑ Ⓒ Ⓓ Ⓔ	36. Ⓐ Ⓑ Ⓒ Ⓓ Ⓔ	54. Ⓐ Ⓑ Ⓒ Ⓓ Ⓔ	72. Ⓐ Ⓑ Ⓒ Ⓓ Ⓔ	

Tear here

PART D—ADDRESS CHECKING

1. ⒶⒹ	20. ⒶⒹ	39. ⒶⒹ	58. ⒶⒹ	77. ⒶⒹ
2. ⒶⒹ	21. ⒶⒹ	40. ⒶⒹ	59. ⒶⒹ	78. ⒶⒹ
3. ⒶⒹ	22. ⒶⒹ	41. ⒶⒹ	60. ⒶⒹ	79. ⒶⒹ
4. ⒶⒹ	23. ⒶⒹ	42. ⒶⒹ	61. ⒶⒹ	80. ⒶⒹ
5. ⒶⒹ	24. ⒶⒹ	43. ⒶⒹ	62. ⒶⒹ	81. ⒶⒹ
6. ⒶⒹ	25. ⒶⒹ	44. ⒶⒹ	63. ⒶⒹ	82. ⒶⒹ
7. ⒶⒹ	26. ⒶⒹ	45. ⒶⒹ	64. ⒶⒹ	83. ⒶⒹ
8. ⒶⒹ	27. ⒶⒹ	46. ⒶⒹ	65. ⒶⒹ	84. ⒶⒹ
9. ⒶⒹ	28. ⒶⒹ	47. ⒶⒹ	66. ⒶⒹ	85. ⒶⒹ
10. ⒶⒹ	29. ⒶⒹ	48. ⒶⒹ	67. ⒶⒹ	86. ⒶⒹ
11. ⒶⒹ	30. ⒶⒹ	49. ⒶⒹ	68. ⒶⒹ	87. ⒶⒹ
12. ⒶⒹ	31. ⒶⒹ	50. ⒶⒹ	69. ⒶⒹ	88. ⒶⒹ
13. ⒶⒹ	32. ⒶⒹ	51. ⒶⒹ	70. ⒶⒹ	89. ⒶⒹ
14. ⒶⒹ	33. ⒶⒹ	52. ⒶⒹ	71. ⒶⒹ	90. ⒶⒹ
15. ⒶⒹ	34. ⒶⒹ	53. ⒶⒹ	72. ⒶⒹ	91. ⒶⒹ
16. ⒶⒹ	35. ⒶⒹ	54. ⒶⒹ	73. ⒶⒹ	92. ⒶⒹ
17. ⒶⒹ	36. ⒶⒹ	55. ⒶⒹ	74. ⒶⒹ	93. ⒶⒹ
18. ⒶⒹ	37. ⒶⒹ	56. ⒶⒹ	75. ⒶⒹ	94. ⒶⒹ
19. ⒶⒹ	38. ⒶⒹ	57. ⒶⒹ	76. ⒶⒹ	95. ⒶⒹ

SIXTH MODEL EXAM

PART A—NUMBER SERIES

SAMPLE QUESTIONS

The following sample questions show you the type of questions that will be used in Part A. Since this type of question may be new and unfamiliar to you, the examiner will work through the first five questions with you. Once you understand the task, you will have five minutes to answer sample questions 6 to 14 on your own. Correct answers and explanations follow.

Directions: Each number series question consists of a series of numbers which follows some definite order. The numbers progress from left to right according to some rule. One pair of numbers to the right of the series comprises the next two numbers in the series. Study each series to try to find a pattern to the series and to figure out the rule which governs the progression. Choose the answer pair which continues the series according to the pattern established and mark its letter on your answer sheet.

1. 21 24 29 32 37 40 45 ..... (A) 50 55 (B) 48 51 (C) 50 53 (D) 48 53 (E) 48 55

   Write the direction and degree of change between the numbers of the series. The pattern that emerges is: $+3, +5; +3, +5; +3, +5$. Continue the series: $45 + 3 = 48 + 5 = 53$. **(D)** is the answer.

2. 51 51 30 47 47 30 43 ..... (A) 43 43 (B) 30 30 (C) 43 30 (D) 30 39 (E) 43 39

   If you look carefully, you realize that 30 is inserted after every two numbers. Ignoring 30 for a moment, the pattern for the remaining numbers is: repeat the number, -4; repeat the number, -4; repeat the number, -4. To continue the series, you must repeat the number 43; then, since the number 30 appears after each set of two numbers, you must insert the number 30. **(C)** is the correct answer. If the series were to continue, the next few numbers would be 39 39 30 35 . . . .

3. 8 16 9 18 11 22 15 .... (A) 30 23 (B) 12 25 (C) 25 13 (D) 12 44 (E) 30 20

   At first glance this problem looks impossible. You may need to try more than one approach before you can figure out the pattern. Do not allow yourself to be bound by the fact that most of the progressions advance by $+$ or $-$. The pattern is $\times 2, -7; \times 2, -7; \times 2, -7$. Continue the series: $15 - 2 = 30 - 7 = 23$. The answer is **(A)**.

4. 32   25   86   32   25   86   32 ..... (A) 32   25   (B) 32   86   (C) 86   25   (D) 26   87   (E) 25   86

This series follows no mathematical rule. The sequence 32 25 86 simply repeats itself over and over. The answer is **(E),** continuation of the sequence.

5. 75   65   56   48   41   35   30 ..... (A) 27   23   (B) 26   23   (C) 29   28   (D) 25   20   (E) 26   22

The pattern is: $-10, -9, -8, -7, -6, -5$. Continue with: $30 - 4 = 26 - 3 = 23$. **(B)** is the answer.

You will now have five minutes to complete the remaining numbers series sample questions.

6.   3   9   9   15   21   21   27 ..... (A) 27   27   (B) 27   33   (C) 33   39   (D) 33   33   (E) 39   39

7.   10   35   14   38   18   41   22 ...... (A) 26   29   (B) 45   48   (C) 44   26   (D) 45   25   (E) 26   44

8.   1   2   0   2   3   0   3 .... (A) 4   0   (B) 4   5   (C) 0   4   (D) 3   0   (E) 0   3

9.   12   14   16   20   24   30   36 ..... (A) 42   48   (B) 42   50   (C) 44   54   (D) 40   46   (E) 44   52

10.   84   76   68   60   52   44   36 ..... (A) 28   20   (B) 26   16   (C) 30   24   (D) 28   22   (E) 30   22

11.   63   18   61   23   59   28   57 ..... (A) 55   33   (B) 30   62   (C) 59   30   (D) 32   59   (E) 33   55

12.   1   5   1   2   6   2   3   7 .... (A) 4   3   (B) 7   3   (C) 3   4   (D) 4   5   (E) 6   5

13.   27   29   31   33   35   37   39 ..... (A) 40   41   (B) 41   43   (C) 43   45   (D) 41   45   (E) 39   41

14.   58   57   59   58   60   59   61 ..... (A) 62   63   (B) 59   62   (C) 62   60   (D) 60   62   (E) 63   60

SAMPLE ANSWER SHEET		CORRECT ANSWERS	
1. A B C D E	8. A B C D E	1. D	8. A
2. A B C D E	9. A B C D E	2. C	9. E
3. A B C D E	10. A B C D E	3. A	10. A
4. A B C D E	11. A B C D E	4. E	11. E
5. A B C D E	12. A B C D E	5. B	12. C
6. A B C D E	13. A B C D E	6. D	13. B
7. A B C D E	14. A B C D E	7. C	14. D

EXPLANATIONS

6. **(D)** The pattern is: +6, repeat the number, +6; +6, repeat the number, +6; +6, repeat the number, +6. 27 + 6 = 33; then repeat the number 33.

7. **(C)** There are two distinct, alternating series. One series, beginning with 10, increases by +4: 10 14 18 22 and the continuation number is 26. The alternating series begins with 35 and increases by +3: 35 38 41 and the continuation number is 44.

8. **(A)** You may be able to answer this problem without ever defining a pattern. You may feel a rhythm: 1, 2 0 2, 3 0 3, 4 0 4 . . . . Or you might see that the series progresses by +1 with the number 0 appearing after each set of two numbers and with the number that appears before the 0 repeating itself after the 0 before the series continues upwards.

9. **(E)** The pattern is: +2, +2, +4, +4, +6, +6. Logically, the pattern would extend to +8, +8. 36 + 8 = 44 + 8 = 52.

10. **(A)** This is a simple −8 series.

11. **(E)** In this series, two distinct and separate series alternate. The first series begins with 63 and decreases at the rate of −2: 63 61 59 57 55. The alternating series begins with 18 and increases at the rate of +5: 18 23 28 33.

12. **(C)** You can see this series as a collection of mini-series, each mini-series moving up one step from the previous one. Group the series: 1 5 1; 2 6 2; 3 7 3; 4 8 4. . . .

13. **(B)** Not all series are of equal complexity, and some of the later series may be less difficult for you than some of the earlier ones. This is a simple + 2 series.

14. **(D)** If you mark the direction and degree of change between the number, you see the pattern: −1, +2; −1, +2; −1, +2. You could also see two alternating series, one beginning with 58, the other beginning with 57 and both increasing at the rate of +1. Either interpretation yields the same correct answer.

PART A—NUMBER SERIES

TIME: 20 Minutes. 24 Questions.

Directions: *Each number series question consists of a series of numbers which follows some definite order. The numbers progress from left to right according to some rule. One lettered pair of numbers comprises the next two numbers in the series. Study each series to try to find a pattern to the series and to figure out the rule which governs the progression. Choose the answer pair which continues the series according to the pattern established and mark its letter on your answer sheet. Correct answers are on page 198.*

1. 5 7 30 9 11 30 13 .... (A) 15 16 (B) 15 17 (C) 14 17 (D) 15 30 (E) 30 17
2. 5 7 11 13 17 19 23 .... (A) 27 29 (B) 25 29 (C) 25 27 (D) 27 31 (E) 29 31
3. 9 15 10 17 12 19 15 21 19 .... (A) 23 24 (B) 25 23 (C) 17 23 (D) 23 31 (E) 21 24
4. 34 37 30 33 26 29 22 ..... (A) 17 8 (B) 18 11 (C) 25 28 (D) 25 20 (E) 25 18
5. 10 16 12 14 14 12 16 ...... (A) 14 12 (B) 10 18 (C) 10 14 (D) 14 18 (E) 14 16
6. 11 12 18 11 13 19 11 14 ..... (A) 18 11 (B) 16 11 (C) 20 11 (D) 11 21 (E) 17 11
7. 20 9 8 19 10 9 18 11 10 .... (A) 19 11 (B) 17 10 (C) 19 12 (D) 17 12 (E) 19 10
8. 28 27 26 31 30 29 34 ...... (A) 36 32 (B) 32 31 (C) 33 32 (D) 33 36 (E) 35 36
9. 12 24 15 30 21 42 33 ..... (A) 66 57 (B) 44 56 (C) 28 43 (D) 47 69 (E) 24 48
10. 46 76 51 70 56 64 61 ...... (A) 61 68 (B) 69 71 (C) 58 65 (D) 66 71 (E) 58 66
11. 37 28 28 19 19 10 10 ...... (A) 9 9 (B) 1 1 (C) 10 9 (D) 10 1 (E) 9 1
12. 1 2 3 6 4 5 6 15 7 ..... (A) 8 15 (B) 7 8 (C) 8 9 (D) 9 17 (E) 9 24
13. 55 51 12 56 52 12 57 ...... (A) 57 12 (B) 12 53 (C) 58 12 (D) 53 12 (E) 12 57
14. 75 75 8 50 50 9 25 .... (A) 25 25 (B) 25 10 (C) 10 25 (D) 25 12 (E) 10 10
15. 1 2 3 4 5 5 4 .... (A) 3 2 (B) 5 4 (C) 4 5 (D) 5 6 (E) 4 4
16. 3 6 9 4 7 10 5 .... (A) 8 9 (B) 9 6 (C) 8 11 (D) 9 12 (E) 11 8
17. 5 7 9 18 20 22 44 .... (A) 60 66 (B) 66 80 (C) 66 68 (D) 88 90 (E) 46 48

18. 94 82 72 64 58 54 .... (A) 52 50 (B) 54 52 (C) 50 46 (D) 52 52 (E) 54 50

19. 85 85 86 85 86 87 85 ..... (A) 85 86 (B) 86 87 (C) 87 89 (D) 87 86 (E) 84 83

20. 99 89 79 69 59 49 39 ..... (A) 29 19 (B) 39 29 (C) 38 37 (D) 39 38 (E) 19 9

21. 33 42 41 39 48 47 45 .... (A) 42 41 (B) 44 42 (C) 54 53 (D) 54 52 (E) 54 63

22. 85 89 89 84 88 88 83 ..... (A) 83 87 (B) 83 83 (C) 87 87 (D) 87 82 (E) 87 83

23. 1 2 3 3 4 5 5 6 7 ..... (A) 7 7 (B) 8 8 (C) 8 9 (D) 7 6 (E) 7 8

24. 5 10 15 15 20 15 25 ...... (A) 30 35 (B) 15 30 (C) 15 15 (D) 30 15 (E) 30 30

END OF PART A

*If you finish before time is up, check over your work on this
part only. Do not turn the page until you are told to do so.*

PART B—ADDRESS CODING

SAMPLE QUESTIONS

The seven sample questions for this part are based upon the addresses in the five boxes below. Your task is to mark on your answer sheet the letter of the box in which each address belongs. The instructions for Part B permit you to look at the boxes if you cannot remember in which box an address belongs. You may look at the boxes while answering these Part B sample questions. The questions in Part C of the exam will be based upon the same boxes as the questions in Part B, but in answering Part C you may NOT look at the boxes. There will be no sample questions before Part C.

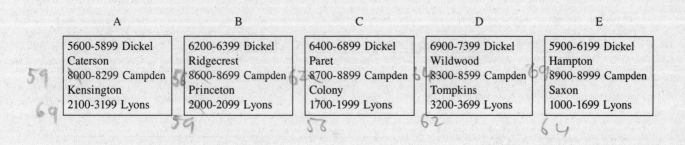

	A	B	C	D	E
	5600-5899 Dickel	6200-6399 Dickel	6400-6899 Dickel	6900-7399 Dickel	5900-6199 Dickel
	Caterson	Ridgecrest	Paret	Wildwood	Hampton
	8000-8299 Campden	8600-8699 Campden	8700-8899 Campden	8300-8599 Campden	8900-8999 Campden
	Kensington	Princeton	Colony	Tompkins	Saxon
	2100-3199 Lyons	2000-2099 Lyons	1700-1999 Lyons	3200-3699 Lyons	1000-1699 Lyons

1. 2100-3199 Lyons
2. Tompkins
3. 8600-8699 Campden
4. Hampton

5. 6400-6899 Dickel
6. Caterson
7. 2000-2099 Lyons

SAMPLE ANSWER SHEET		CORRECT ANSWERS	
1. Ⓐ Ⓑ Ⓒ Ⓓ Ⓔ	5. Ⓐ Ⓑ Ⓒ Ⓓ Ⓔ	1. A	5. C
2. Ⓐ Ⓑ Ⓒ Ⓓ Ⓔ	6. Ⓐ Ⓑ Ⓒ Ⓓ Ⓔ	2. D	6. A
3. Ⓐ Ⓑ Ⓒ Ⓓ Ⓔ	7. Ⓐ Ⓑ Ⓒ Ⓓ Ⓔ	3. B	7. B
4. Ⓐ Ⓑ Ⓒ Ⓓ Ⓔ		4. E	

PART B—ADDRESS CODING

Directions: *There are five boxes labeled A, B, C, D, and E. In each box are five addresses, three of which include a number span and a name and two of which are names alone. You will have five (5) minutes to memorize the locations of all twenty-five addresses. Then you will have three (3) minutes to mark your answer sheet with the letter of the box in which each address in the questions list belongs. For Part B you may refer to the boxes while answering, though you will lose speed by doing so. For Part C you may NOT look at the boxes, so do your best to memorize in the five minutes allowed you now. Correct answers are on page 199.*

MEMORIZING TIME: 5 Minutes.

A	B	C	D	E
5600-5899 Dickel	6200-6399 Dickel	6400-6899 Dickel	6900-7399 Dickel	5900-6199 Dickel
Caterson	Ridgecrest	Paret	Wildwood	Hampton
8000-8299 Campden	8600-8699 Campden	8700-8899 Campden	8300-8599 Campden	8900-8999 Campden
Kensington	Princeton	Colony	Tompkins	Saxon
2100-3199 Lyons	2000-2099 Lyons	1700-1999 Lyons	3200-3699 Lyons	1000-1699 Lyons

ANSWERING TIME: 3 Minutes. 88 Questions.

1. 2100-3199 Lyons
2. 3200-3699 Lyons
3. 6200-6399 Dickel
4. Colony
5. Wildwood
6. 8000-8299 Campden
7. 5900-6199 Dickel
8. Caterson
9. 8600-8699 Campden
10. 6900-7399 Dickel
11. Colony
12. Kensington
13. 1000-1699 Lyons
14. 8900-8999 Campden

15. 6400-6899 Dickel
16. Tompkins
17. Paret
18. Ridgecrest
19. 2000-2099 Lyons
20. 5600-5899 Dickel
21. 1700-1999 Lyons
22. 8300-8599 Campden
23. Princeton
24. 8700-8899 Campden
25. Saxon
26. Hampton
27. 6900-7399 Dickel
28. Kensington

29. 2000-2099 Lyons
30. 8700-8899 Campden
31. 6400-6899 Dickel
32. 5900-6199 Dickel
33. Ridgecrest
34. Tompkins
35. Hampton
36. 8300-8599 Campden
37. 1000-1699 Lyons
38. Caterson
39. Saxon
40. 5600-5899 Dickel
41. 1700-1999 Lyons
42. 8000-8299 Campden
43. 8900-8999 Campden
44. Princeton
45. Wildwood
46. 3200-3699 Lyons
47. 2100-3199 Lyons
48. 6200-6399 Dickel
49. 6900-7399 Dickel
50. Paret
51. Hampton
52. 8600-8699 Campden
53. Colony
54. 3200-3699 Lyons
55. 5600-5899 Dickel
56. 1000-1699 Lyons
57. Ridgecrest
58. 8300-8599 Campden

59. 6400-6899 Dickel
60. 8000-8299 Campden
61. Hampton
62. Princeton
63. 2100-3199 Lyons
64. 8900-8999 Campden
65. 6900-7399 Dickel
66. Paret
67. Saxon
68. 6200-6399 Dickel
69. 1700-1999 Lyons
70. Kensington
71. Wildwood
72. 5900-6199 Dickel
73. 3200-3699 Lyons
74. Colony
75. Caterson
76. 6200-6399 Dickel
77. 8700-8899 Campden
78. 6900-7399 Dickel
79. Saxon
80. Tompkins
81. 2000-2099 Lyons
82. 8600-8699 Campden
83. 1000-1699 Lyons
84. Wildwood
85. Ridgecrest
86. 8300-8599 Campden
87. 2100-3199 Lyons
88. 1700-1999 Lyons

END OF PART B

If you finish before time is up, use the remaining few seconds to continue memorizing the locations of the addresses. Do not turn the page until you are told to do so.

PART C—ADDRESS CODE MEMORY

TIME: 5 Minutes. 88 Questions.

Directions: Relying entirely upon your memory, mark your answer sheet with the letter of the box in which each address belongs. Correct answers are on page 200.

1. 8900-8999 Campden
2. 2100-3199 Lyons
3. 6900-7399 Dickel
4. Kensington
5. Saxon
6. 5600-5899 Dickel
7. 8600-8699 Campden
8. 1700-1999 Lyons
9. Princeton
10. Wildwood
11. 3200-3699 Lyons
12. 8000-8299 Campden
13. 6900-7399 Dickel
14. Tompkins
15. Colony
16. 8300-8599 Campden
17. 6200-6399 Dickel
18. 2000-2099 Lyons
19. Paret
20. Caterson
21. 6400-6899 Dickel
22. 1000-1699 Lyons
23. 8700-8899 Campden
24. Ridgecrest
25. Hampton
26. 8000-8299 Campden
27. Tompkins
28. 2100-3199 Lyons
29. 5900-6199 Dickel
30. Wildwood
31. Caterson
32. 8300-8599 Campden
33. Princeton
34. 5600-5899 Dickel
35. 6900-7399 Dickel

36. 6400-6899 Dickel
37. 1000-1699 Lyons
38. 8300-8599 Campden
39. Hampton
40. Kensington
41. Paret
42. Saxon
43. 3200-3699 Lyons
44. 2000-2099 Lyons
45. Tompkins
46. 6200-6399 Dickel
47. Caterson
48. 1700-1999 Lyons
49. 8600-8699 Campden
50. 8900-8999 Campden
51. Colony
52. 6400-6899 Dickel
53. 2100-3199 Lyons
54. 5600-5899 Dickel
55. 8000-8299 Campden
56. Kensington
57. 1000-1699 Lyons
58. Paret
59. Ridgecrest
60. 8300-8599 Campden
61. 2000-2099 Lyons
62. Wildwood
63. Tompkins
64. Saxon
65. 8600-8699 Campden
66. 6900-7399 Dickel
67. 1700-1999 Lyons
68. 8900-8999 Campden
69. 5600-5899 Dickel
70. Princeton

71. Hampton
72. 5900-6199 Dickel
73. 8300-8599 Campden
74. 2100-3199 Lyons
75. Caterson
76. Paret
77. 8000-8299 Campden
78. 2000-2099 Lyons
79. Kensington

80. Wildwood
81. 1000-1699 Lyons
82. 6400-6899 Dickel
83. 6900-7399 Dickel
84. 8600-8699 Campden
85. Saxon
86. Colony
87. 3200-3699 Lyons
88. 8700-8899 Campden

END OF PART C

If you finish before time is up, check your answers on this part only. Do not turn the page until you are told to do so.

PART D—ADDRESS CHECKING TEST

SAMPLE QUESTIONS

You will be allowed three minutes to read the directions and answer the five sample questions which follow. On the actual test, however, you will have only six minutes to answer 95 questions, so see how quickly you can compare addresses and still get the correct answer.

Directions: *Each question consists of two addresses. If the two addresses are* alike in EVERY *way, mark Ⓐ on your answer sheet. If the two addresses are* different in ANY *way, mark Ⓓ on your answer sheet.*

1 . . . 4240 SW 146th Rd	4240 NW 146th Rd
2 . . . 7019 Hutchinson Ave	7019 Hutchinson Ave
3 . . . 4212 Marsupial Pky	4312 Marsupial Pky
4 . . . Boulder CO 80302	Boulder CO 80302
5 . . . 8364 Barclay Blvd	8364 Barclays Blvd

SAMPLE ANSWER SHEET		CORRECT ANSWERS	
1. ⒶⒹ	4. ⒶⒹ	1. D	4. A
2. ⒶⒹ	5. ⒶⒹ	2. A	5. D
3. ⒶⒹ		3. D	

PART D—ADDRESS CHECKING

TIME: 6 Minutes. 95 Questions.

Directions: *Look carefully at the two addresses in each question. If the two addresses are* alike *in EVERY way, mark* Ⓐ *on your answer sheet. If the two addresses are* different *in ANY way, mark* Ⓓ *on your answer sheet. Correct answers are on page 200.*

1	2001 Spacecoast Hwy	2001 Spacecoast Hwy
2	7813 W Tamiment Terr	7813 W Tamamint Terr
3	4783 Clearview Expy	4873 Clearview Expy
4	Oxford OH 45056	Oxford OH 45056
5	9034 S Francis Lewis Blvd	9034 S Francis Lewis Blvd
6	Coral Gables FL 33124	Coral Gables FL 33124
7	8762 Juniata Dr	8762 Juniata Rd
8	5967 Pulaski Skywy E	5967 Pulaski Skywy E
9	4283 Old Army Rd	4823 Old Army Rd
10	East Lansing MI 48824	East Lansing MI 48224
11	7821 S Mill Run	7821 S Mills Run
12	4830 E 256th Ave	4830 E 265th Ave
13	7315 Capitol Hill	7315 Capital Hill
14	Ann Arbor MI 48104	Ann Arbor MI 48104
15	5032 Conservative Wy	5032 Conservative Wy
16	Middlebury VT 05753	Middlebury VT 07553
17	894 Monotony Hill	894 Monopoly Hill
18	9016 W Fordham Rd	9016 Fordham Rd
19	4612 Struthers St	4612 Struthers St
20	8417 Picadilly Sq	8417 Picadilly Sq
21	Oakland CA 94613	Oakland CA 94631
22	9416 Starkville Tpke	9416 Starkville Tpke
23	3206 Ridgecrest Terr W	3206 Ridgecrest Ter W
24	7852 Robbinhood Rd	7852 Robinhood Rd
25	5221 Ferry Pt	5521 Ferry Pt
26	Minneapolis MN 55455	Minneapolis MI 55455
27	4424 Walbrooke Close	4424 Walbrooke Close
28	7314 Tenafly Tpke S	7314 Tenafly Tpke So
29	University MS 38677	University MS 38677
30	814 W Maroon Ave	814 W Maroon Ave
31	7135 Administration Bldg	7135 Administrative Bldg
32	4963 Baronial Apts	4693 Baronial Apts
33	Columbia MO 65201	Columbus MO 65201
34	Missoula MT 59812	Missoula MT 59812
35	8314 Road 912	8314 Road 912
36	7583 Circumference Dr	7583 Circumferenee Dr

#		
37	4693 E Sycamore Blvd	4963 E Sycamore Blvd
38	6126 NE 178th Pl	6216 NE 178th Pl
39	5234 Minnesota Ave SW	5234 Minnesota Ave SW
40	8915 Sickle St	8915 Sickles St
41	1235 Cardiac Hill	1235 Cardiac Hill
42	8531 Terrapin Terr	8531 Terrapin Terr
43	Baltimore MD 21239	Baltimore MD 21239
44	7415 Morganville Ave	7415 Morganville Ave
45	9036 W Morningside Blvd	9063 W Morningside Blvd
46	South Hadley MA 01075	South Hadlay MA 01075
47	6213 Holyoke St	6213 Holyoke St
48	Lincoln NE 68508	Lincoln NE 68508
49	4872 LaBelle Hwy	4872 LaBelle Hwy
50	1582 Piedmont Pkwy	1582 Piedmont Pky
51	Reno NV 89557	Reno MN 98557
52	8327 VanWezel Ave	8327 VanWezel Ave
53	1483 Crimean Cres	1483 Crimean Cres
54	4836 Grinnell Hall	4836 Grinnell Hall
55	Sarasota FL 33580	Sarasota FL 33580
56	7142 E Hydrangea Wy	7142 E Hydrangea Wy
57	1932 W 486th St	1932 W 864th St
58	9032 Peter Cooper Vill So	9032 Peter Cooper Vill s
59	8361 Pawtucket Hwy	8361 Pawtucket Hwy
60	Durham NH 03824	Dunham NH 03824
61	Albuquerque NM 87131	Albuquerque NM 87131
62	7412 Playboy Apts	7412 Playboy Apts
63	4114 Tacitus Terr	414 Tacitus Terr
64	Albany NY 12222	Albany NY 12222
65	4682 Newcomb St	4682 Newcombe St
66	5834 E 179th Rd	5843 E 179th Rd
67	9090 South Carolina Ave SE	9090 South Carolina Ave SW
68	Stony Brook NY 11794	Stoney Brook NY 11794
69	6311 Setauket St	6311 Setauket St
70	4613 International Hse	4613 International Hse
71	7412 Rambling Cir	7412 Rambling Circ
72	9414 Titanic Rd	9414 Titanic Rd
73	New York NY 10003	New York NY 11003
74	4816 Southeast Pkwy	4816 Southeast Pkwy
75	3092 Repertory Hall	3092 Repertory Hill
76	4850 W Zoology Ridge	4850 W Zoology Ridge
77	Chapel Hill NC 27514	Chapel Hill NC 25714
78	Boston MA 02115	Boston MA 02115
79	Evanston IL 60201	Evanston IL 60201
80	5286 S Northwestern Blvd	5286 S Northwestern Blvd
81	1131 E Grecian Dr	1131 E Grecian Dr
82	5613 Perimeter Rd	5613 Perimeter Rd
83	Notre Dame IN 46556	Notre Dame IN 46556
84	1503 Springsteen St	1503 Springstien St
85	4160 Doobie Rd	4160 Doobie Dr
86	Oberlin OH 44074	–Oberlin OK 44074
87	5564 Conservatory Hill	5564 Conservatory Hill

88	8933 Arboretum Dr	8933 Arboretum Dr
89	Los Angeles CA 90041	Los Angeles CA 90014
90	1324 Occidental Ln	1324 Occidentel Ln
91	5903 W 293rd St	5903 W 293rd St
92	909 Dodger Dr	909 E Dodger Dr
93	8395 Eagle Rock St	8395 Eagle Rock St
94	5912 Copper Beech Ln	5912 Copper Beech Ln
95	4416 Bluebell Pl	4146 Bluebell Pl

END OF EXAM

If you finish before time is up, look over your answers on this part only. Do not return to any previous part.

CORRECT ANSWERS—SIXTH MODEL EXAM

PART A—NUMBER SERIES

1. D	4. E	7. D	10. E	13. D	16. C	19. B	22. C
2. B	5. B	8. C	11. B	14. B	17. E	20. A	23. E
3. A	6. C	9. A	12. C	15. A	18. D	21. C	24. D

EXPLANATIONS—NUMBER SERIES

1. **(D)** The series increases by $+2$. The number $\underline{30}$ appears after each two numbers in the series.

2. **(B)** The pattern is: $+2$, $+4$; $+2$, $+4$; $+2$, $+4$; etc.

3. **(A)** There are two alternating series which advance according to different rules. The first series begins with $\underline{9}$. The rule for this series is $+1$, $+2$, $+3$, $+4$, $+5$. The alternating series begins with $\underline{15}$ and advances in steady increments of $+2$.

4. **(E)** There are two alternating series, one series beginning with $\underline{34}$ and the other with $\underline{37}$. Both series decrease by subtracting 4 each time.

5. **(B)** The two series are moving in opposite directions. The first series begins with $\underline{10}$ and increases by $+2$. The alternating series begins with $\underline{16}$ and decreases by -2.

6. **(C)** You may be able to figure this one by reading it rhythmically. If not, consider that there are two series, one beginning with $\underline{12}$, the other with $\underline{18}$. Both series advance by $+1$. The number $\underline{11}$ separates each progression of the two series.

7. **(D)** There are two series alternating at the rate of 1 to 2. The first series decreases by -1—20 19 18 $\underline{17}$. The other series goes one step backward and two steps forward: or -1, $+2$. Read: $9 \overset{-1}{} 8 \overset{+2}{} 10 \overset{-1}{} 9 \overset{+2}{} 11 \overset{-1}{} 10 \overset{+2}{} \underline{12}$.

8. **(C)** The pattern is -1, -1, $+5$ and repeat -1, -1, $+5$ and repeat again.

9. **(A)** The pattern is: $\times 2$, -9; $\times 2$, -9 . . . .

10. **(E)** There are two alternating series. The first series increases by $+5$. The alternating series decreases at the rate of -6.

11. **(B)** The pattern is -9 and repeat the number; -9 and repeat the number; -9 and repeat the number.

12. **(C)** The series is: 1 2 3 4 5 6 7 8 . . . . After each three numbers in the series we find the sum of those three numbers. So: $1 + 2 + 3 = 6$; $4 + 5 + 6 = 15$; $7 + \underline{8} + \underline{9} = 24$; 10 . . . .

13. **(D)** The pattern is -4, $+5$, and the number $\underline{12}$; -4, $+5$, and the number $\underline{12}$ . . . .

14. **(B)** There are two series. One series proceeds: repeat the number, -25; repeat the number, -25. The other series simply advances by $+1$.

15. **(A)** The series proceeds upwards from 1 to 5, then turns around and descends, one number at a time.

16. **(C)** There are two interpretations for this series. You may see $+3, +3, -5; +3, +3, -5 \ldots$ Or, you might see a series of $+3, +3$ mini-series, each mini-series beginning at a number one higher than the beginning number of the previous mini-series.

17. **(E)** The pattern is: $+2, +2, \times 2; +2, +2, \times 2 \ldots$

18. **(D)** The pattern is: $-12, -10, -8, -6, -4, -2, -0 \ldots$

19. **(B)** Each mini-series begins with 85. With each cycle the series progresses to one more number. 85; 85 86; 85 86 87; 85 86 87 88 . . . .

20. **(A)** This is a simple -10 series.

21. **(C)** The pattern is: $+9, -1, -2; +9, -1, -2 \ldots$

22. **(C)** The pattern is $+4$, repeat the number, $-5; +4$, repeat the number, $-5; +4$ . . . . You might, instead have seen two descending series, one beginning with 85 and descending by -1, the other beginning with 89 and repeating itself before each descent.

23. **(E)** This is a deceptive series. Actually the series consists of a series of mini-series, each beginning with the last number of the previous mini-series. If you group the numbers, you can see: 1 2 3; 3 4 5; 5 6 7; 7 8 . . . .

24. **(D)** The series is a $+5$ series with the number 15 interposing after each two numbers of the series. If you substitute X for the interposing 15, you can see that the series reads: 5 10 X 15 20 X 25 30 X.

PART B—ADDRESS CODING

1. A	12. A	23. B	34. D	45. D	56. E	67. E	78. D
2. D	13. E	24. C	35. E	46. D	57. B	68. B	79. E
3. B	14. E	25. E	36. D	47. A	58. D	69. C	80. D
4. C	15. C	26. E	37. E	48. B	59. C	70. A	81. B
5. D	16. D	27. D	38. A	49. D	60. A	71. D	82. B
6. A	17. C	28. A	39. E	50. C	61. E	72. E	83. E
7. E	18. B	29. B	40. A	51. E	62. B	73. D	84. D
8. A	19. B	30. C	41. C	52. B	63. A	74. C	85. B
9. B	20. A	31. C	42. A	53. C	64. E	75. A	86. D
10. D	21. C	32. E	43. E	54. D	65. D	76. B	87. A
11. C	22. D	33. B	44. B	55. A	66. C	77. C	88. C

PART C—ADDRESS CODE MEMORY

1. E	12. A	23. C	34. A	45. D	56. A	67. C	78. B
2. A	13. D	24. B	35. D	46. B	57. E	68. E	79. A
3. D	14. D	25. E	36. C	47. A	58. C	69. A	80. D
4. A	15. C	26. A	37. E	48. C	59. B	70. B	81. E
5. E	16. D	27. D	38. D	49. B	60. D	71. E	82. C
6. A	17. B	28. A	39. E	50. E	61. B	72. E	83. D
7. B	18. B	29. E	40. A	51. C	62. D	73. D	84. B
8. C	19. C	30. D	41. C	52. C	63. D	74. A	85. E
9. B	20. A	31. A	42. E	53. A	64. E	75. A	86. C
10. D	21. C	32. D	43. D	54. A	65. B	76. C	87. D
11. D	22. E	33. B	44. B	55. A	66. D	77. A	88. C

PART D—ADDRESS CHECKING

1. A	13. D	25. D	37. D	49. A	61. A	73. D	85. D
2. D	14. A	26. D	38. D	50. D	62. A	74. A	86. D
3. D	15. A	27. A	39. A	51. D	63. D	75. D	87. A
4. A	16. D	28. D	40. D	52. A	64. A	76. A	88. A
5. A	17. D	29. A	41. A	53. A	65. D	77. D	89. D
6. A	18. D	30. A	42. A	54. D	66. D	78. A	90. D
7. D	19. A	31. D	43. A	55. A	67. D	79. A	91. A
8. A	20. A	32. D	44. A	56. A	68. D	80. A	92. D
9. D	21. D	33. D	45. D	57. D	69. D	81. A	93. A
10. D	22. A	34. D	46. D	58. D	70. A	82. A	94. A
11. D	23. D	35. A	47. A	59. A	71. D	83. A	95. D
12. D	24. D	36. A	48. A	60. D	72. A	84. D	

ADDRESS CHECKING ERROR ANALYSIS CHART

Type of Error	Tally	Total Number
Number of addresses that were alike and you incorrectly marked "different"		
Number of addresses that were different and you incorrectly marked "alike"		
Number of addresses in which you missed a difference in NUMBERS		
Number of addresses in which you missed a difference in ABBREVIATIONS		
Number of addresses in which you missed a difference in NAMES		

SCORE SHEET FOR SIXTH MODEL EXAM

PART A—NUMBER SERIES

Number Right equals Score

_____ = _____

PART B—ADDRESS CODING

Number Right minus (Number Wrong ÷ 4) equals Score

_____ – _____ = _____

PART C—ADDRESS CODE MEMORY

Number Right minus (Number Wrong ÷ 4) equals Score

_____ – _____ = _____

PART D—ADDRESS CHECKING

Number Right minus Number Wrong equals Score

_____ – _____ = _____

SELF-EVALUATION CHART

Part	Excellent	Good	Average	Fair	Poor
Number Series	21–24	18–20	14–17	11–13	1–10
Address Coding	75–88	63–74	52–62	40–51	1–39
Address Code Memory	75–88	60–74	45–59	30–44	1–29
Address Checking	80–95	65–79	50–64	35–49	1–34

PROGRESS CHART

Blacken to the closest score to chart your progress.

Score
95
90
85
80
75
70
65
60
55
50
45
40
35
30
25
20
15
10
5
0

Part	A	B	C	D	A	B	C	D	A	B	C	D	A	B	C	D	A	B	C	D	A	B	C	D
Model Exam	Diagnostic				Second				Third				Fourth				Fifth				Sixth			

ANSWER SHEET—
SEVENTH MODEL EXAM

Tear out this Answer Sheet and use it to mark your answers for the exam that follows.

PART A—NUMBER SERIES

1. Ⓐ Ⓑ Ⓒ Ⓓ Ⓔ	6. Ⓐ Ⓑ Ⓒ Ⓓ Ⓔ	11. Ⓐ Ⓑ Ⓒ Ⓓ Ⓔ	16. Ⓐ Ⓑ Ⓒ Ⓓ Ⓔ	21. Ⓐ Ⓑ Ⓒ Ⓓ Ⓔ
2. Ⓐ Ⓑ Ⓒ Ⓓ Ⓔ	7. Ⓐ Ⓑ Ⓒ Ⓓ Ⓔ	12. Ⓐ Ⓑ Ⓒ Ⓓ Ⓔ	17. Ⓐ Ⓑ Ⓒ Ⓓ Ⓔ	22. Ⓐ Ⓑ Ⓒ Ⓓ Ⓔ
3. Ⓐ Ⓑ Ⓒ Ⓓ Ⓔ	8. Ⓐ Ⓑ Ⓒ Ⓓ Ⓔ	13. Ⓐ Ⓑ Ⓒ Ⓓ Ⓔ	18. Ⓐ Ⓑ Ⓒ Ⓓ Ⓔ	23. Ⓐ Ⓑ Ⓒ Ⓓ Ⓔ
4. Ⓐ Ⓑ Ⓒ Ⓓ Ⓔ	9. Ⓐ Ⓑ Ⓒ Ⓓ Ⓔ	14. Ⓐ Ⓑ Ⓒ Ⓓ Ⓔ	19. Ⓐ Ⓑ Ⓒ Ⓓ Ⓔ	24. Ⓐ Ⓑ Ⓒ Ⓓ Ⓔ
5. Ⓐ Ⓑ Ⓒ Ⓓ Ⓔ	10. Ⓐ Ⓑ Ⓒ Ⓓ Ⓔ	15. Ⓐ Ⓑ Ⓒ Ⓓ Ⓔ	20. Ⓐ Ⓑ Ⓒ Ⓓ Ⓔ	

PART B—ADDRESS CODING

1. Ⓐ Ⓑ Ⓒ Ⓓ Ⓔ	19. Ⓐ Ⓑ Ⓒ Ⓓ Ⓔ	37. Ⓐ Ⓑ Ⓒ Ⓓ Ⓔ	55. Ⓐ Ⓑ Ⓒ Ⓓ Ⓔ	73. Ⓐ Ⓑ Ⓒ Ⓓ Ⓔ
2. Ⓐ Ⓑ Ⓒ Ⓓ Ⓔ	20. Ⓐ Ⓑ Ⓒ Ⓓ Ⓔ	38. Ⓐ Ⓑ Ⓒ Ⓓ Ⓔ	56. Ⓐ Ⓑ Ⓒ Ⓓ Ⓔ	74. Ⓐ Ⓑ Ⓒ Ⓓ Ⓔ
3. Ⓐ Ⓑ Ⓒ Ⓓ Ⓔ	21. Ⓐ Ⓑ Ⓒ Ⓓ Ⓔ	39. Ⓐ Ⓑ Ⓒ Ⓓ Ⓔ	57. Ⓐ Ⓑ Ⓒ Ⓓ Ⓔ	75. Ⓐ Ⓑ Ⓒ Ⓓ Ⓔ
4. Ⓐ Ⓑ Ⓒ Ⓓ Ⓔ	22. Ⓐ Ⓑ Ⓒ Ⓓ Ⓔ	40. Ⓐ Ⓑ Ⓒ Ⓓ Ⓔ	58. Ⓐ Ⓑ Ⓒ Ⓓ Ⓔ	76. Ⓐ Ⓑ Ⓒ Ⓓ Ⓔ
5. Ⓐ Ⓑ Ⓒ Ⓓ Ⓔ	23. Ⓐ Ⓑ Ⓒ Ⓓ Ⓔ	41. Ⓐ Ⓑ Ⓒ Ⓓ Ⓔ	59. Ⓐ Ⓑ Ⓒ Ⓓ Ⓔ	77. Ⓐ Ⓑ Ⓒ Ⓓ Ⓔ
6. Ⓐ Ⓑ Ⓒ Ⓓ Ⓔ	24. Ⓐ Ⓑ Ⓒ Ⓓ Ⓔ	42. Ⓐ Ⓑ Ⓒ Ⓓ Ⓔ	60. Ⓐ Ⓑ Ⓒ Ⓓ Ⓔ	78. Ⓐ Ⓑ Ⓒ Ⓓ Ⓔ
7. Ⓐ Ⓑ Ⓒ Ⓓ Ⓔ	25. Ⓐ Ⓑ Ⓒ Ⓓ Ⓔ	43. Ⓐ Ⓑ Ⓒ Ⓓ Ⓔ	61. Ⓐ Ⓑ Ⓒ Ⓓ Ⓔ	79. Ⓐ Ⓑ Ⓒ Ⓓ Ⓔ
8. Ⓐ Ⓑ Ⓒ Ⓓ Ⓔ	26. Ⓐ Ⓑ Ⓒ Ⓓ Ⓔ	44. Ⓐ Ⓑ Ⓒ Ⓓ Ⓔ	62. Ⓐ Ⓑ Ⓒ Ⓓ Ⓔ	80. Ⓐ Ⓑ Ⓒ Ⓓ Ⓔ
9. Ⓐ Ⓑ Ⓒ Ⓓ Ⓔ	27. Ⓐ Ⓑ Ⓒ Ⓓ Ⓔ	45. Ⓐ Ⓑ Ⓒ Ⓓ Ⓔ	63. Ⓐ Ⓑ Ⓒ Ⓓ Ⓔ	81. Ⓐ Ⓑ Ⓒ Ⓓ Ⓔ
10. Ⓐ Ⓑ Ⓒ Ⓓ Ⓔ	28. Ⓐ Ⓑ Ⓒ Ⓓ Ⓔ	46. Ⓐ Ⓑ Ⓒ Ⓓ Ⓔ	64. Ⓐ Ⓑ Ⓒ Ⓓ Ⓔ	82. Ⓐ Ⓑ Ⓒ Ⓓ Ⓔ
11. Ⓐ Ⓑ Ⓒ Ⓓ Ⓔ	29. Ⓐ Ⓑ Ⓒ Ⓓ Ⓔ	47. Ⓐ Ⓑ Ⓒ Ⓓ Ⓔ	65. Ⓐ Ⓑ Ⓒ Ⓓ Ⓔ	83. Ⓐ Ⓑ Ⓒ Ⓓ Ⓔ
12. Ⓐ Ⓑ Ⓒ Ⓓ Ⓔ	30. Ⓐ Ⓑ Ⓒ Ⓓ Ⓔ	48. Ⓐ Ⓑ Ⓒ Ⓓ Ⓔ	66. Ⓐ Ⓑ Ⓒ Ⓓ Ⓔ	84. Ⓐ Ⓑ Ⓒ Ⓓ Ⓔ
13. Ⓐ Ⓑ Ⓒ Ⓓ Ⓔ	31. Ⓐ Ⓑ Ⓒ Ⓓ Ⓔ	49. Ⓐ Ⓑ Ⓒ Ⓓ Ⓔ	67. Ⓐ Ⓑ Ⓒ Ⓓ Ⓔ	85. Ⓐ Ⓑ Ⓒ Ⓓ Ⓔ
14. Ⓐ Ⓑ Ⓒ Ⓓ Ⓔ	32. Ⓐ Ⓑ Ⓒ Ⓓ Ⓔ	50. Ⓐ Ⓑ Ⓒ Ⓓ Ⓔ	68. Ⓐ Ⓑ Ⓒ Ⓓ Ⓔ	86. Ⓐ Ⓑ Ⓒ Ⓓ Ⓔ
15. Ⓐ Ⓑ Ⓒ Ⓓ Ⓔ	33. Ⓐ Ⓑ Ⓒ Ⓓ Ⓔ	51. Ⓐ Ⓑ Ⓒ Ⓓ Ⓔ	69. Ⓐ Ⓑ Ⓒ Ⓓ Ⓔ	87. Ⓐ Ⓑ Ⓒ Ⓓ Ⓔ
16. Ⓐ Ⓑ Ⓒ Ⓓ Ⓔ	34. Ⓐ Ⓑ Ⓒ Ⓓ Ⓔ	52. Ⓐ Ⓑ Ⓒ Ⓓ Ⓔ	70. Ⓐ Ⓑ Ⓒ Ⓓ Ⓔ	88. Ⓐ Ⓑ Ⓒ Ⓓ Ⓔ
17. Ⓐ Ⓑ Ⓒ Ⓓ Ⓔ	35. Ⓐ Ⓑ Ⓒ Ⓓ Ⓔ	53. Ⓐ Ⓑ Ⓒ Ⓓ Ⓔ	71. Ⓐ Ⓑ Ⓒ Ⓓ Ⓔ	
18. Ⓐ Ⓑ Ⓒ Ⓓ Ⓔ	36. Ⓐ Ⓑ Ⓒ Ⓓ Ⓔ	54. Ⓐ Ⓑ Ⓒ Ⓓ Ⓔ	72. Ⓐ Ⓑ Ⓒ Ⓓ Ⓔ	

PART C—ADDRESS CODE MEMORY

1. Ⓐ Ⓑ Ⓒ Ⓓ Ⓔ   19. Ⓐ Ⓑ Ⓒ Ⓓ Ⓔ   37. Ⓐ Ⓑ Ⓒ Ⓓ Ⓔ   55. Ⓐ Ⓑ Ⓒ Ⓓ Ⓔ   73. Ⓐ Ⓑ Ⓒ Ⓓ Ⓔ

2. Ⓐ Ⓑ Ⓒ Ⓓ Ⓔ   20. Ⓐ Ⓑ Ⓒ Ⓓ Ⓔ   38. Ⓐ Ⓑ Ⓒ Ⓓ Ⓔ   56. Ⓐ Ⓑ Ⓒ Ⓓ Ⓔ   74. Ⓐ Ⓑ Ⓒ Ⓓ Ⓔ

3. Ⓐ Ⓑ Ⓒ Ⓓ Ⓔ   21. Ⓐ Ⓑ Ⓒ Ⓓ Ⓔ   39. Ⓐ Ⓑ Ⓒ Ⓓ Ⓔ   57. Ⓐ Ⓑ Ⓒ Ⓓ Ⓔ   75. Ⓐ Ⓑ Ⓒ Ⓓ Ⓔ

4. Ⓐ Ⓑ Ⓒ Ⓓ Ⓔ   22. Ⓐ Ⓑ Ⓒ Ⓓ Ⓔ   40. Ⓐ Ⓑ Ⓒ Ⓓ Ⓔ   58. Ⓐ Ⓑ Ⓒ Ⓓ Ⓔ   76. Ⓐ Ⓑ Ⓒ Ⓓ Ⓔ

5. Ⓐ Ⓑ Ⓒ Ⓓ Ⓔ   23. Ⓐ Ⓑ Ⓒ Ⓓ Ⓔ   41. Ⓐ Ⓑ Ⓒ Ⓓ Ⓔ   59. Ⓐ Ⓑ Ⓒ Ⓓ Ⓔ   77. Ⓐ Ⓑ Ⓒ Ⓓ Ⓔ

6. Ⓐ Ⓑ Ⓒ Ⓓ Ⓔ   24. Ⓐ Ⓑ Ⓒ Ⓓ Ⓔ   42. Ⓐ Ⓑ Ⓒ Ⓓ Ⓔ   60. Ⓐ Ⓑ Ⓒ Ⓓ Ⓔ   78. Ⓐ Ⓑ Ⓒ Ⓓ Ⓔ

7. Ⓐ Ⓑ Ⓒ Ⓓ Ⓔ   25. Ⓐ Ⓑ Ⓒ Ⓓ Ⓔ   43. Ⓐ Ⓑ Ⓒ Ⓓ Ⓔ   61. Ⓐ Ⓑ Ⓒ Ⓓ Ⓔ   79. Ⓐ Ⓑ Ⓒ Ⓓ Ⓔ

8. Ⓐ Ⓑ Ⓒ Ⓓ Ⓔ   26. Ⓐ Ⓑ Ⓒ Ⓓ Ⓔ   44. Ⓐ Ⓑ Ⓒ Ⓓ Ⓔ   62. Ⓐ Ⓑ Ⓒ Ⓓ Ⓔ   80. Ⓐ Ⓑ Ⓒ Ⓓ Ⓔ

9. Ⓐ Ⓑ Ⓒ Ⓓ Ⓔ   27. Ⓐ Ⓑ Ⓒ Ⓓ Ⓔ   45. Ⓐ Ⓑ Ⓒ Ⓓ Ⓔ   63. Ⓐ Ⓑ Ⓒ Ⓓ Ⓔ   81. Ⓐ Ⓑ Ⓒ Ⓓ Ⓔ

10. Ⓐ Ⓑ Ⓒ Ⓓ Ⓔ   28. Ⓐ Ⓑ Ⓒ Ⓓ Ⓔ   46. Ⓐ Ⓑ Ⓒ Ⓓ Ⓔ   64. Ⓐ Ⓑ Ⓒ Ⓓ Ⓔ   82. Ⓐ Ⓑ Ⓒ Ⓓ Ⓔ

11. Ⓐ Ⓑ Ⓒ Ⓓ Ⓔ   29. Ⓐ Ⓑ Ⓒ Ⓓ Ⓔ   47. Ⓐ Ⓑ Ⓒ Ⓓ Ⓔ   65. Ⓐ Ⓑ Ⓒ Ⓓ Ⓔ   83. Ⓐ Ⓑ Ⓒ Ⓓ Ⓔ

12. Ⓐ Ⓑ Ⓒ Ⓓ Ⓔ   30. Ⓐ Ⓑ Ⓒ Ⓓ Ⓔ   48. Ⓐ Ⓑ Ⓒ Ⓓ Ⓔ   66. Ⓐ Ⓑ Ⓒ Ⓓ Ⓔ   84. Ⓐ Ⓑ Ⓒ Ⓓ Ⓔ

13. Ⓐ Ⓑ Ⓒ Ⓓ Ⓔ   31. Ⓐ Ⓑ Ⓒ Ⓓ Ⓔ   49. Ⓐ Ⓑ Ⓒ Ⓓ Ⓔ   67. Ⓐ Ⓑ Ⓒ Ⓓ Ⓔ   85. Ⓐ Ⓑ Ⓒ Ⓓ Ⓔ

14. Ⓐ Ⓑ Ⓒ Ⓓ Ⓔ   32. Ⓐ Ⓑ Ⓒ Ⓓ Ⓔ   50. Ⓐ Ⓑ Ⓒ Ⓓ Ⓔ   68. Ⓐ Ⓑ Ⓒ Ⓓ Ⓔ   86. Ⓐ Ⓑ Ⓒ Ⓓ Ⓔ

15. Ⓐ Ⓑ Ⓒ Ⓓ Ⓔ   33. Ⓐ Ⓑ Ⓒ Ⓓ Ⓔ   51. Ⓐ Ⓑ Ⓒ Ⓓ Ⓔ   69. Ⓐ Ⓑ Ⓒ Ⓓ Ⓔ   87. Ⓐ Ⓑ Ⓒ Ⓓ Ⓔ

16. Ⓐ Ⓑ Ⓒ Ⓓ Ⓔ   34. Ⓐ Ⓑ Ⓒ Ⓓ Ⓔ   52. Ⓐ Ⓑ Ⓒ Ⓓ Ⓔ   70. Ⓐ Ⓑ Ⓒ Ⓓ Ⓔ   88. Ⓐ Ⓑ Ⓒ Ⓓ Ⓔ

17. Ⓐ Ⓑ Ⓒ Ⓓ Ⓔ   35. Ⓐ Ⓑ Ⓒ Ⓓ Ⓔ   53. Ⓐ Ⓑ Ⓒ Ⓓ Ⓔ   71. Ⓐ Ⓑ Ⓒ Ⓓ Ⓔ

18. Ⓐ Ⓑ Ⓒ Ⓓ Ⓔ   36. Ⓐ Ⓑ Ⓒ Ⓓ Ⓔ   54. Ⓐ Ⓑ Ⓒ Ⓓ Ⓔ   72. Ⓐ Ⓑ Ⓒ Ⓓ Ⓔ

Tear here

PART D—ADDRESS CHECKING

1. Ⓐ Ⓓ	20. Ⓐ Ⓓ	39. Ⓐ Ⓓ	58. Ⓐ Ⓓ	77. Ⓐ Ⓓ
2. Ⓐ Ⓓ	21. Ⓐ Ⓓ	40. Ⓐ Ⓓ	59. Ⓐ Ⓓ	78. Ⓐ Ⓓ
3. Ⓐ Ⓓ	22. Ⓐ Ⓓ	41. Ⓐ Ⓓ	60. Ⓐ Ⓓ	79. Ⓐ Ⓓ
4. Ⓐ Ⓓ	23. Ⓐ Ⓓ	42. Ⓐ Ⓓ	61. Ⓐ Ⓓ	80. Ⓐ Ⓓ
5. Ⓐ Ⓓ	24. Ⓐ Ⓓ	43. Ⓐ Ⓓ	62. Ⓐ Ⓓ	81. Ⓐ Ⓓ
6. Ⓐ Ⓓ	25. Ⓐ Ⓓ	44. Ⓐ Ⓓ	63. Ⓐ Ⓓ	82. Ⓐ Ⓓ
7. Ⓐ Ⓓ	26. Ⓐ Ⓓ	45. Ⓐ Ⓓ	64. Ⓐ Ⓓ	83. Ⓐ Ⓓ
8. Ⓐ Ⓓ	27. Ⓐ Ⓓ	46. Ⓐ Ⓓ	65. Ⓐ Ⓓ	84. Ⓐ Ⓓ
9. Ⓐ Ⓓ	28. Ⓐ Ⓓ	47. Ⓐ Ⓓ	66. Ⓐ Ⓓ	85. Ⓐ Ⓓ
10. Ⓐ Ⓓ	29. Ⓐ Ⓓ	48. Ⓐ Ⓓ	67. Ⓐ Ⓓ	86. Ⓐ Ⓓ
11. Ⓐ Ⓓ	30. Ⓐ Ⓓ	49. Ⓐ Ⓓ	68. Ⓐ Ⓓ	87. Ⓐ Ⓓ
12. Ⓐ Ⓓ	31. Ⓐ Ⓓ	50. Ⓐ Ⓓ	69. Ⓐ Ⓓ	88. Ⓐ Ⓓ
13. Ⓐ Ⓓ	32. Ⓐ Ⓓ	51. Ⓐ Ⓓ	70. Ⓐ Ⓓ	89. Ⓐ Ⓓ
14. Ⓐ Ⓓ	33. Ⓐ Ⓓ	52. Ⓐ Ⓓ	71. Ⓐ Ⓓ	90. Ⓐ Ⓓ
15. Ⓐ Ⓓ	34. Ⓐ Ⓓ	53. Ⓐ Ⓓ	72. Ⓐ Ⓓ	91. Ⓐ Ⓓ
16. Ⓐ Ⓓ	35. Ⓐ Ⓓ	54. Ⓐ Ⓓ	73. Ⓐ Ⓓ	92. Ⓐ Ⓓ
17. Ⓐ Ⓓ	36. Ⓐ Ⓓ	55. Ⓐ Ⓓ	74. Ⓐ Ⓓ	93. Ⓐ Ⓓ
18. Ⓐ Ⓓ	37. Ⓐ Ⓓ	56. Ⓐ Ⓓ	75. Ⓐ Ⓓ	94. Ⓐ Ⓓ
19. Ⓐ Ⓓ	38. Ⓐ Ⓓ	57. Ⓐ Ⓓ	76. Ⓐ Ⓓ	95. Ⓐ Ⓓ

Tear here

SEVENTH MODEL EXAM

PART A—NUMBER SERIES

SAMPLE QUESTIONS

The following sample questions show you the type of question that will be used in Part A. Since this type of question may be new and unfamiliar to you, the examiner will work through the first five questions with you. Once you understand the task, you will have five minutes to answer sample questions 6 to 14 on your own. Correct answers and explanations follow.

> *Directions: Each number series question consists of a series of numbers which follows some definite order. The numbers progress from left to right according to some rule. One pair of numbers to the right of the series comprises the next two numbers in the series. Study each series to try to find a pattern to the series and to figure out the rule which governs the progression. Choose the answer pair which continues the series according to the pattern established and mark its letter on your answer sheet.*

1. 23   23   25   23   28   23   32   ..... (A) 32   37 (B) 23   37 (C) 32   23 (D) 37   23 (E) 23   36

   The pattern of this series is $+2$, $+3$, $+4$, $+5$ with the number $\underline{23}$ intervening after each number in the main series. Do not be confused by what appears to be an initial repetition of the number $\underline{23}$. It is coincidental that the series happens to begin with the same number which then intervenes during the series. The answer is **(B)**: intervening $\underline{23}$, then $32 + 5 = \underline{37}$.

2. 40   35   31   30   25   21   20   15   ... (A) 10   6   (B) 14   9   (C) 14   10 (D) 11   7   (E) 11   10

   The pattern is: -5, -4, -1; -5, -4, -1; -5, -4, -1. The answer is **(E)** because $15 - 4 = \underline{11} - 1 = \underline{10}$.

3. 98   24   92   28   86   32   80   ..... (A) 74   36 (B) 26   84 (C) 38   84 (D) 36   75 (E) 36   74

   There are two separate and distinct alternating series within this series. The first series progresses at the rate of -6: 98   92   86   80 $\underline{74}$. The alternating series progresses at the rate of $+4$: 24   28   32 $\underline{36}$. The correct answer is **(E)**.

4. 17   17   28   28   40   40   53   .....   (A) 53   66   (B) 53   53   (C) 66   66   (D) 53   67   (E) 67   67

The pattern being established is: repeat the number, +11, repeat the number, +12, repeat the number, +13, repeat the number, +14. The answer is **(D)**: repeat the <u>53</u>, then 53 + 14 = <u>67</u>.

5. 19   15   10   19   15   10   19   ......   (A) 15   10   (B) 10   15   (C) 19   15   (D) 19   10   (E) 15   19

The sequence 19 15 10 repeats itself over and over again. The answer is **(A).**

You will now have five minutes to complete the remaining number series sample questions.

6. 1   1   1   3   2   2   2   6   3   ......   (A) 2   1   (B) 6   6   (C) 3   3   (D) 3   6   (E) 6   9

7. 53   50   46   41   35   28   20   ......   (A) 10   2   (B) 11   1   (C) 12   4   (D) 10   1   (E) 20   11

8. 36   51   64   75   84   91   96   .....   (A) 101   106 (B) 100   104 (C) 100   103 (D) 99   100 (E) 98   101

9. 88   88   85   82   82   79   76   .....   (A) 76   76   (B) 73   73   (C) 73   76   (D) 76   73   (E) 76   79

10. 2   8   12   13   22   18   32   ....   (A) 23   42 (B) 42   47 (C) 42   23 (D) 28   37 (E) 37   47

11. 78   69   60   60   51   60   42   .....   (A) 42   60   (B) 60   60   (C) 33   24   (D) 60   33   (E) 33   60

12. 3   3   6   6   12   12   24   ....   (A) 24   24   (B) 24   48   (C) 24   36   (D) 36   48   (E) 48   48

13. 15   5   5   9   3   3   12   ....   (A) 15   5   (B) 12   4   (C) 12   6   (D) 4   4   (E) 6   6

14. 55   49   49   44   44   40   40   .....   (A) 40   37   (B) 37   36   (C) 37   37   (D) 37   34   (E) 37   33

SAMPLE ANSWER SHEET		CORRECT ANSWERS	
1. Ⓐ Ⓑ © Ⓓ Ⓔ	8. Ⓐ Ⓑ © Ⓓ Ⓔ	1. B	8. D
2. Ⓐ Ⓑ © Ⓓ Ⓔ	9. Ⓐ Ⓑ © Ⓓ Ⓔ	2. E	9. D
3. Ⓐ Ⓑ © Ⓓ Ⓔ	10. Ⓐ Ⓑ © Ⓓ Ⓔ	3. E	10. A
4. Ⓐ Ⓑ © Ⓓ Ⓔ	11. Ⓐ Ⓑ © Ⓓ Ⓔ	4. D	11. E
5. Ⓐ Ⓑ © Ⓓ Ⓔ	12. Ⓐ Ⓑ © Ⓓ Ⓔ	5. A	12. B
6. Ⓐ Ⓑ © Ⓓ Ⓔ	13. Ⓐ Ⓑ © Ⓓ Ⓔ	6. C	13. D
7. Ⓐ Ⓑ © Ⓓ Ⓔ	14. Ⓐ Ⓑ © Ⓓ Ⓔ	7. B	14. C

EXPLANATIONS

6. **(C)** The developing pattern consists of three identical numbers followed by their sum; up one step, then again three identical numbers and their sum. Continuing the progression, up one step, then three identical numbers again.

7. **(B)** This is not a difficult pattern: $-3, -4, -5, -6, -7, -8, -9, -10 \ldots$

8. **(D)** You probably had to write the changes between the numbers in this series. If you did, then you had no trouble recognizing $+15, +13, +11, +9, +7, +5$ and then continuing with $+3, +1$.

9. **(D)** The pattern is: repeat the number, $-3, -3$; repeat the number, $-3, -3$; repeat the number, $-3, -3$.

10. **(A)** Here there are two alternating series. The first series is a $+10$ series: 2 12 22 32 <u>42</u>. The alternating series is a $+5$ series: 8 13 18 <u>23</u>.

11. **(E)** This series is difficult because of the coincidence of numbers falling together. The main series is a -9 series: 78 69 60 51 42 <u>33</u>. The number <u>60</u> appears after each two numbers of the main series. The two 60's back to back are not a repetition.

12. **(B)** The pattern is: repeat the number, $\times 2$; repeat the number, $\times 2$; repeat the number, $\times 2$.

13. **(D)** The pattern is: repeat the number, $\div 3$; repeat the number, $+3$; and so on.

14. **(C)** The pattern is: -6, repeat the number, -5, repeat the number, -4, repeat the number, -3, repeat the number.

PART A—NUMBER SERIES

TIME: 20 Minutes. 24 Questions.

Directions: Each number series question consists of a series of numbers which follows some definite order. The numbers progress from left to right according to some rule. One lettered pair of numbers comprises the next two numbers in the series. Study each series to try to find a pattern to the series and to figure the rule which governs the progression. Choose the answer pair which continues the series according to the pattern established and mark its letter on your answer sheet. Correct answers are on page 222.

1. 19 18 12 17 16 13 15 ...... (A) 16 12 (B) 14 14 (C) 12 14 (D) 14 12 (E) 12 16

2. 7 15 12 8 16 13 9 .... (A) 17 14 (B) 17 10 (C) 14 10 (D) 14 17 (E) 10 14

3. 18 15 6 16 14 6 14 .... (A) 12 6 (B) 14 13 (C) 6 12 (D) 13 12 (E) 33 6

4. 6 6 5 8 8 7 10 10 .... (A) 8 12 (B) 9 12 (C) 22 12 (D) 12 9 (E) 9 9

5. 17 20 23 26 29 32 35 ..... (A) 37 40 (B) 41 44 (C) 38 41 (D) 38 42 (E) 36 39

6. 15 5 7 16 9 11 17 .... (A) 18 13 (B) 15 17 (C) 12 19 (D) 13 15 (E) 12 13

7. 19 17 16 16 13 15 10 ..... (A) 14 7 (B) 12 9 (C) 14 9 (D) 7 12 (E) 10 14

8. 11 1 16 10 6 21 9 .... (A) 12 26 (B) 26 8 (C) 11 26 (D) 11 8 (E) 8 11

9. 15 22 19 26 23 30 27 ...... (A) 28 34 (B) 27 35 (C) 31 34 (D) 29 33 (E) 34 31

10. 99 9 88 8 77 7 66 .... (A) 55 5 (B) 6 55 (C) 66 5 (D) 55 6 (E) 55 44

11. 25 29 29 33 37 37 41 ..... (A) 41 41 (B) 41 45 (C) 45 49 (D) 45 45 (E) 49 49

12. 81 71 61 52 43 35 27 ..... (A) 27 20 (B) 21 14 (C) 20 14 (D) 21 15 (E) 20 13

13. 12 14 16 48 50 52 156 .... (A) 468 470 (B) 158 316 (C) 158 474 (D) 158 160 (E) 158 158

14. 47 42 38 35 30 26 23 ..... (A) 18 14 (B) 21 19 (C) 23 18 (D) 19 14 (E) 19 13

15. 84 84 91 91 97 97 102 .... (A) 102 102 (B) 102 104 (C) 104 106 (D) 106 106 (E) 102 106

16. 66 13 62 21 58 29 54 ..... (A) 50 48 (B) 62 66 (C) 34 42 (D) 37 50 (E) 58 21

17. 14 12 10 10 20 18 16 16 . (A) 32 32 (B) 32 30 (C) 30 28 (D) 16 32 (E) 16 14

18. 25 30 35 30 25 30 35 ..... (A) 30 40 (B) 25 30 (C) 25 20 (D) 35 30 (E) 30 25

19. 19 19 19 57 57 57 171 .... (A) 171 513 (B) 513 513 (C) 171 171 (D) 171 57 (E) 57 18

20. 75 69 63 57 51 45 39 ..... (A) 36 33 (B) 39 36 (C) 39 33 (D) 33 27 (E) 33 33

21. 6 15 23 30 36 41 45 .... (A) 48 50 (B) 49 53 (C) 45 41 (D) 46 47 (E) 47 49

22. 12 58 25 51 38 44 51 ..... (A) 64 37 (B) 37 64 (C) 51 51 (D) 51 64 (E) 51 37

23. 1 2 4 8 16 32 64 .... (A) 64 32 (B) 64 64 (C) 64 128 (D) 128 256 (E) 128 128

24. 5 86 7 81 10 77 14 .... (A) 16 80 (B) 70 25 (C) 79 13 (D) 19 74 (E) 74 19

END OF PART A

If you finish before time is up, check over your work on this part only. Do not turn the page until you are told to do so.

PART B—ADDRESS CODING

SAMPLE QUESTIONS

The seven sample questions for this part are based upon the addresses in the five boxes below. Your task is to mark on your answer sheet the letter of the box in which each address belongs. The instructions for Part B permit you to look at the boxes if you cannot remember in which box an address belongs. You may look at the boxes while answering these Part B sample questions. The questions in Part C of the exam will be based upon the same boxes as the questions in Part B, but in answering Part C you may NOT look at the boxes. There will be no sample questions before Part C.

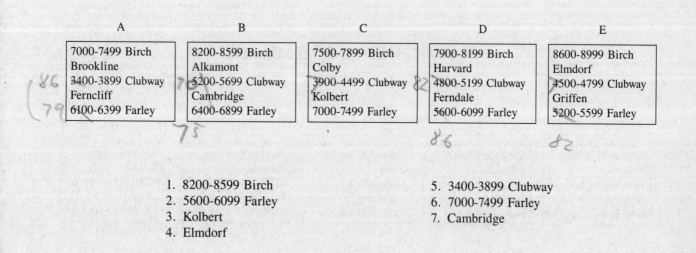

1. 8200-8599 Birch
2. 5600-6099 Farley
3. Kolbert
4. Elmdorf
5. 3400-3899 Clubway
6. 7000-7499 Farley
7. Cambridge

SAMPLE ANSWER SHEET

1. Ⓐ Ⓑ Ⓒ Ⓓ Ⓔ
2. Ⓐ Ⓑ Ⓒ Ⓓ Ⓔ
3. Ⓐ Ⓑ Ⓒ Ⓓ Ⓔ
4. Ⓐ Ⓑ Ⓒ Ⓓ Ⓔ
5. Ⓐ Ⓑ Ⓒ Ⓓ Ⓔ
6. Ⓐ Ⓑ Ⓒ Ⓓ Ⓔ
7. Ⓐ Ⓑ Ⓒ Ⓓ Ⓔ

CORRECT ANSWERS

1. B
2. D
3. C
4. E
5. A
6. C
7. B

PART B—ADDRESS CODING

Directions: There are five boxes labeled A, B, C, D, and E. In each box are five addresses, three of which include a number span and a name and two of which are names alone. You will have five (5) minutes to memorize the locations of all twenty-five addresses. Then you will have three (3) minutes to mark your answer sheet with the letter of the box in which each address in the question list belongs. For Part B you may refer to the boxes while answering, though you will lose speed by doing so. For Part C you may NOT look at the boxes, so do your best to memorize in the five minutes allowed you now. Correct answers are on page 223.

MEMORIZING TIME: 5 Minutes.

A	B	C	D	E
7000-7499 Birch Brookline 3400-3899 Clubway Ferncliff 6100-6399 Farley	8200-8599 Birch Alkamont 5200-5699 Clubway Cambridge 6400-6899 Farley	7500-7899 Birch Colby 3900-4499 Clubway Kolbert 7000-7499 Farley	7900-8199 Birch Harvard 4800-5199 Clubway Ferndale 5600-6099 Farley	8600-8999 Birch Elmdorf 4500-4799 Clubway Griffen 5200-5599 Farley

ANSWERING TIME: 3 Minutes. 88 Questions.

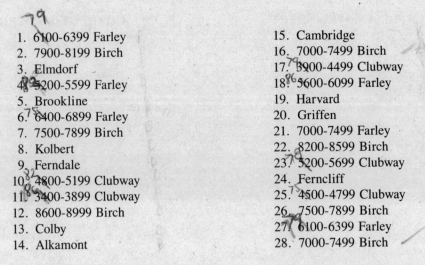

1. 6100-6399 Farley
2. 7900-8199 Birch
3. Elmdorf
4. 5200-5599 Farley
5. Brookline
6. 6400-6899 Farley
7. 7500-7899 Birch
8. Kolbert
9. Ferndale
10. 4800-5199 Clubway
11. 3400-3899 Clubway
12. 8600-8999 Birch
13. Colby
14. Alkamont
15. Cambridge
16. 7000-7499 Birch
17. 3900-4499 Clubway
18. 5600-6099 Farley
19. Harvard
20. Griffen
21. 7000-7499 Farley
22. 8200-8599 Birch
23. 5200-5699 Clubway
24. Ferncliff
25. 4500-4799 Clubway
26. 7500-7899 Birch
27. 6100-6399 Farley
28. 7000-7499 Birch

29. Alkamont
30. Griffen
31. 4800-5199 Clubway
32. 6400-6899 Farley
33. 3400-3899 Clubway
34. 8600-8999 Birch
35. 7000-7499 Farley
36. Brookline
37. Cambridge
38. Harvard
39. 4500-4799 Clubway
40. 8200-8599 Birch
41. 7900-8199 Birch
42. Kolbert
43. Colby
44. 6100-6399 Farley
45. 5200-5599 Farley
46. Elmdorf
47. 5200-5699 Clubway
48. 7500-7899 Birch
49. 3900-4499 Clubway
50. Ferncliff
51. Ferndale
52. 5600-6099 Farley
53. 7000-7499 Birch
54. 5200-5599 Farley
55. 3400-3899 Clubway
56. Griffen
57. 7000-7499 Farley
58. 5200-5699 Clubway

59. Kolbert
60. 8200-8599 Birch
61. 5600-6099 Farley
62. Brookline
63. Elmdorf
64. 7900-8199 Birch
65. 4500-4799 Clubway
66. Colby
67. Ferncliff
68. 8600-8999 Birch
69. 6400-6899 Farley
70. 7000-7499 Farley
71. Cambridge
72. 6100-6399 Farley
73. 8200-8599 Birch
74. Alkamont
75. Griffen
76. 5600-6099 Farley
77. 3400-3899 Clubway
78. 7900-8199 Birch
79. Ferncliff
80. Harvard
81. 8600-8999 Birch
82. 3900-4499 Clubway
83. Elmdorf
84. 7000-7499 Birch
85. 7000-7499 Farley
86. Cambridge
87. Ferndale
88. 4800-5199 Clubway

END OF PART B

If you finish before time is up, use the remaining few seconds to continue memorizing the locations of the addresses. Do not turn the page until you are told to do so.

PART C—ADDRESS CODE MEMORY

TIME: 5 Minutes. 88 Questions.

Directions: *Relying entirely upon your memory, mark your answer sheet with the letter of the box in which each address belongs. Correct answers are on page 224.*

1. 7000-7499 Birch
2. 5200-5599 Farley
3. 3900-4499 Clubway
4. Cambridge
5. Ferndale
6. 6400-6899 Farley
7. 7900-8199 Birch
8. 4500-4799 Clubway
9. Brookline
10. Griffen
11. 8600-8999 Birch
12. 3400-3899 Clubway
13. 6100-6399 Farley
14. Kolbert
15. Harvard
16. 5200-5699 Clubway
17. 5600-6099 Farley
18. 8200-8599 Birch
19. Alkamont
20. Colby
21. 7000-7499 Farley
22. 7500-7899 Birch
23. 4800-5199 Clubway
24. Elmdorf
25. Harvard
26. 6100-6399 Farley
27. Ferncliff
28. 5200-5699 Clubway
29. 3400-3899 Clubway
30. 7000-7499 Farley
31. 7000-7499 Birch
32. Brookline
33. Kolbert
34. 5600-6099 Farley
35. 4500-4799 Clubway

36. 6400-6899 Farley
37. Alkamont
38. Ferndale
39. Colby
40. 8600-8999 Birch
41. 7500-7899 Birch
42. Cambridge
43. 7900-8199 Birch
44. 5200-5699 Clubway
45. 8200-8599 Birch
46. 5600-6099 Farley
47. 5200-5699 Clubway
48. 4500-4799 Clubway
49. Brookline
50. Harvard
51. Griffen
52. Alkamont
53. 7900-8199 Birch
54. 7500-7899 Birch
55. 8600-8999 Birch
56. 6100-6399 Farley
57. Elmdorf
58. Cambridge
59. Kolbert
60. 4800-5199 Clubway
61. 7000-7499 Farley
62. 3900-4499 Clubway
63. Colby
64. Ferndale
65. 6400-6899 Farley
66. 5200-5599 Farley
67. Ferncliff
68. 5200-5699 Clubway
69. 7900-8199 Birch
70. Cambridge

71. 7500-7899 Birch
72. 4800-5199 Clubway
73. 6100-6399 Farley
74. Ferndale
75. Kolbert
76. 6400-6899 Farley
77. 7000-7499 Birch
78. Alkamont
79. Elmdorf

80. 8600-8999 Birch
81. 4500-4799 Clubway
82. 5200-5599 Farley
83. Colby
84. 7000-7499 Farley
85. 3900-4499 Clubway
86. 8200-8599 Birch
87. Griffen
88. Harvard

END OF PART C

If you finish before time is up, check your answers on this part only. Do not turn the page until you are told to do so.

PART D—ADDRESS CHECKING TEST

SAMPLE QUESTIONS

You will be allowed three minutes to read the directions and answer the five sample questions which follow. On the actual test, however, you will have only six minutes to answer 95 questions, so see how quickly you can compare addresses and still get the correct answer.

Directions: Each question consists of two addresses. If the two addresses are alike in EVERY way, *mark* Ⓐ *on your answer sheet. If the two addresses are* different in ANY way, *mark* Ⓓ *on your answer sheet.*

1 . . . 4836 Mineola Blvd	4386 Mineola Blvd
2 . . . 3062 W 197th St	3062 W 197th Rd
3 . . . Columbus OH 43210	Columbus OH 43210
4 . . . 9413 Alcan Hwy So	9413 Alcan Hwy So
5 . . . 4186 Carrier Ln	4186 Carreer Ln

SAMPLE ANSWER SHEET	
1. Ⓐ Ⓓ	4. Ⓐ Ⓓ
2. Ⓐ Ⓓ	5. Ⓐ Ⓓ
3. Ⓐ Ⓓ	

CORRECT ANSWERS	
1. D	4. A
2. D	5. D
3. A	

Seventh Model Exam / 219

PART D—ADDRESS CHECKING

TIME: 6 Minutes. 95 Questions.

Directions: Look carefully at the two addresses in each question. If the two addresses are alike *in EVERY way, mark* Ⓐ *on your answer sheet. If the two addresses are* different *in ANY way, mark* Ⓓ *on your answer sheet. Correct answers are on page 224.*

1	8132 W Buckeye Blvd	8132 W Buckeye Blvd
2	9286 SE 296th St	9286 SE 269th St
3	3177 Haitian St	3177 Haitian St
4	Athens OH 45701	Athena OH 45701
5	8945 Miramar Hwy	9845 Miramar Hwy
6	3432 Wesleyan Walk	3432 Wesleyan Walk
7	7106 Algonquin St	7106 Algonquin St
8	Delaware OH 43015	Delaware OK 43015
9	4516 W Bromley Wy	4516 W Bromley Wy
10	Stillwater OK 74704	Stillwater OK 74704
11	8415 Sergeant Dr	8415 Seargant Dr
12	4413 W Scarswold Apts	4413 W Scarswold Apts
13	9305 Barthelson Rd	9305 Barthelson Rd
14	3182 Hofbrau House	3182 Hofbrau Houses
15	Norman OK 73069	Norman OK 73609
16	5583 Psychedelic Pkwy	5583 E Psychedelic Pkwy
17	909 Brambly Terr	909 Brambly Terr
18	4831 Ridgecrest N	4831 Ridgecrest N
19	4596 Plymouth Pt	4596 Plymouth Pt
20	Corvallis OR 97331	Corvallis OR 97331
21	3473 S Healy Ave	3473 S Healy Ave
22	5512 Principia Dr	5512 Principia Rd
23	8780 Arkansas Ave SE	7808 Arkansas Ave SE
24	4017 E 523rd Wy	4017 E 523rd Way
25	4863 Fairbanks St	4863 Fairbanks St
26	University Park PA 16802	University Park PN 16802
27	4316 Suicide Rdge	4316 Suicide Rdge
28	Greenvale NY 11548	Greenville NY 11548
29	9005 Edgewater Dr	905 Edgewater Dr
30	4511 Bayridge Pl	4511 BayRidge Pl
31	2384 N 175th Wy	2384 N 175th Wy
32	Princeton NJ 08540	Princeton NY 08540
33	1123 Country Club Ln	1123 Country Club La
34	7518 Pumpkin Pkwy	7518 Pumpkin Pkwy
35	8798 Friedman Tpke	8798 Freedman Tpke

36	. . . Lynchburg VA 24503	Lynchburg VA 24503
37	. . . 1234 Grand Boulevard	1234 Grande Boulevard
38	. . . 4167 Rubicks Ct	4167 Rubiks Ct
39	. . . 4816 E Hutchinson Ave	4816 E Hutchinson Ave
40	. . . 5613 Rensselaer St	5631 Rensselaer St
41	. . . 7622 Russell Sage Blvd	762 Russell Sage Blvd
42	. . . Troy NY 12180	Troy NY 12180
43	. . . 4832 Median Pkwy	4382 Median Pkwy
44	. . . 6873 Barbera Ave	6873 Barbara Ave
45	. . . 7514 S Delano Dr	7514 S Delano Dr
46	. . . 9804 Polytechnic Pkwy	9804 Polytechnic Pky
47	. . . Kingston RI 02881	Kingston RI 02811
48	. . . 1972 Amendment Artery	1972 Amendment Artery
49	. . . 3385 N Giovanni Rd	3385 N Giovanni Rd
50	. . . Houston TX 77001	Houston TX 77001
51	. . . 8516 Cooley Ave No	8516 Cooley Ave No
52	. . . 5583 Galveston Blvd	5583 Galveston Blvd
53	. . . 1386 Blackbird Hollow	1386 Blackbird Hollow
54	. . . 9035 Copper Beech Rd	9035 Cooper Beech Rd
55	. . . Rochester NY 14627	Rochester NY 16427
56	. . . 7513 Cyclotron Hill	7531 Cyclotron Hill
57	. . . 6683 W 256th Ave	6683 W 265th Ave
58	. . . 482 Scylla St	4822 Scylla St
59	. . . 3333 Heraldic Hwy	3333 Heraldic Hwy
60	. . . 5184 Dewey Thrwy	5184 Dewey Thrwy
61	. . . New Brunswick NJ 08903	New Brunswick NJ 09803
62	. . . St Bonaventure NY 14778	St Bonaventure NY 14778
63	. . . 7413 Stringfellow St	7413 Stringfellow St
64	. . . 4596 S Einstein Ave	4596 S Einstein Ave
65	. . . 5734 Enchanted Cor	5734 Enchanted Cor
66	. . . Annapolis MD 21404	Annapollis MD 21404
67	. . . 5562 Amorphous Hall	5562 Amorphous Hall
68	. . . 4367 McDonald Close	4367 MacDonald Close
69	. . . 8462 StLawrence Wy	8462 StLawrence Wy
70	. . . Canton NY 13617	Canton NY 13617
71	. . . 8512 N Mohawk Trail	8512 N Mohawk Trail
72	. . . 4617 Pothole Hwy	4617 Pothole Hwy
73	. . . St Louis MO 63103	St Louis MO 63103
74	. . . 8415 Babson Brdge	8451 Babson Brdge
75	. . . 8457 SE GAR Blvd	8547 SE GAR Blvd
76	. . . San Francisco CA 94117	San Francisco CA 94117
77	. . . 4459 Debenture Ave	4459 Debenture Av
78	. . . 3814 W 384th St	3841 W 384th St
79	. . . Bronxville NY 10708	Bronxvalle NY 10708
80	. . . 8914 Skidmore Row	8914 Skidmore Row
81	. . . 5316 W Simmons St	5316 E Simmons St
82	. . . Saratoga Springs NY 12866	Saratoga Spring NY 12866
83	. . . 8593 Greenwich Hwy	8593 Greenwich Hwy
84	. . . Northampton MA 01063	Northampton MA 01063
85	. . . 1331 E Holyoke Dr	1331 E Holyoke Dr
86	. . . 5831 Monadnock Apts	5831 Monadnock Apts

87 . . . 3649 St Helens Hill	3469 St Helens Hill
88 . . . Columbia SC 29208	Colombia SC 29208
89 . . . 693 SE 497th Ave	693 SE 497th Ave
90 . . . 3900 Legislative Hill	3900 Legislative Hall
91 . . . Vermillion SD 57069	Vermillion SD 57096
92 . . . 4497 Edwardsville Hwy	4497 Edwardsville Hwy
93 . . . 6343 S Seventeenth Ave	6343 S Seventeenth Ave
94 . . . Carbondale IL 62901	Carbondale IL 69201
95 . . . 8506 Highland Park	8506 Highland Park

END OF EXAM

If you finish before time is up, check over your answers on this part only. Do not return to any previous part.

CORRECT ANSWERS—SEVENTH MODEL EXAM

PART A—NUMBER SERIES

1. B	4. B	7. A	10. B	13. D	16. D	19. C	22. B
2. A	5. C	8. C	11. D	14. A	17. B	20. D	23. D
3. E	6. D	9. E	12. E	15. E	18. E	21. A	24. E

EXPLANATIONS—NUMBER SERIES

1. **(B)** There are two series. The first series descends one number at a time, beginning with 19. The second series enters between each two numbers of the first series. The second series increases by $+1$. Thus, the series are: 19 18 17 16 15 14 and 12 13 14.

2. **(A)** The repeating pattern is $+8$, -3, -5.

3. **(E)** This is a difficult problem. The first series begins with 18 and decreases by -2: 18 16 14 . . . . The second series begins with 15 and descends by -1: 15 14 13 . . . . The number 6 separates each pair of descending numbers.

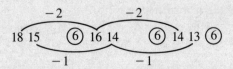

4. **(B)** The even numbers repeat themselves as they increase; the odd numbers simply increase by $+2$, alternating with the evens.

5. **(C)** Just add three to each number to get the next number.

6. **(D)** One series increases by $+1$: 15 16 17 18. The other series, which intervenes with two numbers to the first series' one, increases by $+2$: 5 7 9 11 13.

7. **(A)** The rule for the first series is -3. The rule for the alternating series is -1.

8. **(C)** There are two series here. The first reads 11 10 9. The second series starts at 1 and follows the rule $+15$, -10, $+15$, -10. The second series takes two steps to the first series' one. The solution to this problem is best seen by diagramming.

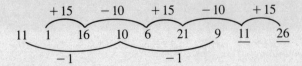

9. **(E)** The pattern is: $+7$, -3; $+7$, -3; . . . . Or, you might see alternating series, both increasing by $+4$.

222

10. **(B)** You might see two series. One series decreases at the rate of −11; the other decreases at the rate of −1. Or, you might see a series of the multiples of 11 each divided by 11.

11. **(D)** The pattern is +4, repeat the number, +4; +4, repeat the number, +4; +4, repeat the number +4 . . . .

12. **(E)** The pattern is: −10, −10, −9, −9, −8, −8, −7, −7, −6 . . . .

13. **(D)** The pattern is: +2, +2, ×3; +2, +2, ×3 . . . .

14. **(A)** The pattern is: −5, −4, −3; −5, −4, −3; −5 . . . .

15. **(E)** The pattern is: repeat the number, +7, repeat the number, +6, repeat the number, +5, repeat the number, +4 . . . .

16. **(D)** There are two alternating series. The first series descends at the rate of −4. The alternating series ascends at the rate of +8.

17. **(B)** The pattern is: −2, −2, repeat the number, ×2; −2, −2, repeat the number, ×2; −2 . . . .

18. **(E)** The pattern is: +5, +5, −5, −5; +5, +5, −5, −5; +5 . . . . Or you might see the repeat of the 4 numbers 25 30 35 30.

19. **(C)** The pattern is: repeat the number three times, ×3; repeat the number three times, ×3; repeat the number three times, ×3.

20. **(D)** The pattern is simply: −6, −6, −6 . . . .

21. **(A)** The pattern is: +9, +8, +7, +6, +5, +4, +3, +2, +1.

22. **(B)** There are two alternating series. The first series increases at the rate of +13. The alternating series decreases at the rate of −7.

23. **(D)** The pattern is: ×2, ×2, ×2 . . . .

24. **(E)** There are two alternating series. The pattern of the first series is: +2, +3, +4, +5. The pattern of the alternating series is: −5, −4, −3, −2.

PART B—ADDRESS CODING

1. A	12. E	23. B	34. E	45. E	56. E	67. A	78. D
2. D	13. C	24. A	35. C	46. E	57. C	68. E	79. A
3. E	14. B	25. E	36. A	47. B	58. B	69. B	80. D
4. E	15. B	26. C	37. B	48. C	59. C	70. C	81. E
5. A	16. A	27. A	38. D	49. C	60. B	71. B	82. C
6. B	17. C	28. A	39. E	50. A	61. D	72. A	83. E
7. C	18. D	29. B	40. B	51. D	62. A	73. B	84. A
8. C	19. D	30. E	41. D	52. D	63. E	74. B	85. C
9. D	20. E	31. D	42. C	53. A	64. D	75. E	86. B
10. D	21. C	32. B	43. C	54. E	65. E	76. D	87. D
11. A	22. B	33. A	44. A	55. A	66. C	77. A	88. D

PART C—ADDRESS CODE MEMORY

1. A	12. A	23. D	34. D	45. B	56. A	67. A	78. B
2. E	13. A	24. E	35. E	46. D	57. E	68. B	79. E
3. C	14. C	25. D	36. B	47. B	58. B	69. D	80. E
4. B	15. D	26. A	37. B	48. E	59. C	70. B	81. E
5. D	16. B	27. A	38. D	49. A	60. D	71. C	82. E
6. B	17. D	28. B	39. C	50. D	61. C	72. D	83. C
7. D	18. B	29. A	40. E	51. E	62. C	73. A	84. C
8. E	19. B	30. C	41. C	52. B	63. C	74. D	85. C
9. A	20. C	31. A	42. B	53. D	64. D	75. C	86. B
10. E	21. C	32. A	43. D	54. C	65. B	76. B	87. E
11. E	22. C	33. C	44. B	55. E	66. E	77. A	88. D

PART D—ADDRESS CHECKING

1. A	13. A	25. A	37. D	49. A	61. D	73. A	85. A
2. D	14. D	26. D	38. D	50. A	62. A	74. D	86. A
3. A	15. D	27. A	39. A	51. A	63. A	75. D	87. D
4. D	16. D	28. D	40. D	52. A	64. A	76. A	88. D
5. D	17. A	29. D	41. D	53. A	65. A	77. D	89. A
6. A	18. A	30. D	42. A	54. D	66. D	78. D	90. D
7. A	19. A	31. A	43. D	55. D	67. A	79. D	91. D
8. D	20. A	32. D	44. D	56. D	68. D	80. A	92. A
9. A	21. A	33. D	45. A	57. D	69. A	81. D	93. A
10. A	22. D	34. A	46. D	58. D	70. A	82. D	94. D
11. D	23. D	35. D	47. D	59. A	71. A	83. A	95. A
12. A	24. D	36. A	48. A	60. A	72. A	84. D	

ADDRESS CHECKING ERROR ANALYSIS CHART

Type of Error	Tally	Total Number
Number of addresses that were alike and you incorrectly marked "different"		
Number of addresses that were different and you incorrectly marked "alike"		
Number of addresses in which you missed a difference in NUMBERS		
Number of addresses in which you missed a difference in ABBREVIATIONS		
Number of addresses in which you missed a difference in NAMES		

SCORE SHEET FOR SEVENTH MODEL EXAM

PART A—NUMBER SERIES

Number Right equals Score

_____ = _____

PART B—ADDRESS CODING

Number Right minus (Number Wrong ÷ 4) equals Score

_____ - _____ = _____

PART C—ADDRESS CODE MEMORY

Number Right minus (Number Wrong ÷ 4) equals Score

_____ - _____ = _____

PART D—ADDRESS CHECKING

Number Right minus Number Wrong equals Score

_____ - _____ = _____

SELF-EVALUATION CHART

Part	Excellent	Good	Average	Fair	Poor
Number Series	21–24	18–20	14–17	11–13	1–10
Address Coding	75–88	63–74	52–62	40–51	1–39
Address Code Memory	75–88	60–74	45–59	30–44	1–29
Address Checking	80–95	65–79	50–64	35–49	1–34

PROGRESS CHART

Blacken to the closest score to chart your progress.

Score																												
95																												
90																												
85																												
80																												
75																												
70																												
65																												
60																												
55																												
50																												
45																												
40																												
35																												
30																												
25																												
20																												
15																												
10																												
5																												
0																												

Part	A	B	C	D	A	B	C	D	A	B	C	D	A	B	C	D	A	B	C	D	A	B	C	D	A	B	C	D
Model Exam	Diagnostic				Second				Third				Fourth				Fifth				Sixth				Seventh			

ANSWER SHEET— FINAL MODEL EXAM

Tear out this Answer Sheet and use it to mark your answers for the exam that follows.

PART A—NUMBER SERIES

1. Ⓐ Ⓑ Ⓒ Ⓓ Ⓔ   6. Ⓐ Ⓑ Ⓒ Ⓓ Ⓔ   11. Ⓐ Ⓑ Ⓒ Ⓓ Ⓔ   16. Ⓐ Ⓑ Ⓒ Ⓓ Ⓔ   21. Ⓐ Ⓑ Ⓒ Ⓓ Ⓔ
2. Ⓐ Ⓑ Ⓒ Ⓓ Ⓔ   7. Ⓐ Ⓑ Ⓒ Ⓓ Ⓔ   12. Ⓐ Ⓑ Ⓒ Ⓓ Ⓔ   17. Ⓐ Ⓑ Ⓒ Ⓓ Ⓔ   22. Ⓐ Ⓑ Ⓒ Ⓓ Ⓔ
3. Ⓐ Ⓑ Ⓒ Ⓓ Ⓔ   8. Ⓐ Ⓑ Ⓒ Ⓓ Ⓔ   13. Ⓐ Ⓑ Ⓒ Ⓓ Ⓔ   18. Ⓐ Ⓑ Ⓒ Ⓓ Ⓔ   23. Ⓐ Ⓑ Ⓒ Ⓓ Ⓔ
4. Ⓐ Ⓑ Ⓒ Ⓓ Ⓔ   9. Ⓐ Ⓑ Ⓒ Ⓓ Ⓔ   14. Ⓐ Ⓑ Ⓒ Ⓓ Ⓔ   19. Ⓐ Ⓑ Ⓒ Ⓓ Ⓔ   24. Ⓐ Ⓑ Ⓒ Ⓓ Ⓔ
5. Ⓐ Ⓑ Ⓒ Ⓓ Ⓔ   10. Ⓐ Ⓑ Ⓒ Ⓓ Ⓔ   15. Ⓐ Ⓑ Ⓒ Ⓓ Ⓔ   20. Ⓐ Ⓑ Ⓒ Ⓓ Ⓔ

PART B—ADDRESS CODING

1. Ⓐ Ⓑ Ⓒ Ⓓ Ⓔ   19. Ⓐ Ⓑ Ⓒ Ⓓ Ⓔ   37. Ⓐ Ⓑ Ⓒ Ⓓ Ⓔ   55. Ⓐ Ⓑ Ⓒ Ⓓ Ⓔ   73. Ⓐ Ⓑ Ⓒ Ⓓ Ⓔ
2. Ⓐ Ⓑ Ⓒ Ⓓ Ⓔ   20. Ⓐ Ⓑ Ⓒ Ⓓ Ⓔ   38. Ⓐ Ⓑ Ⓒ Ⓓ Ⓔ   56. Ⓐ Ⓑ Ⓒ Ⓓ Ⓔ   74. Ⓐ Ⓑ Ⓒ Ⓓ Ⓔ
3. Ⓐ Ⓑ Ⓒ Ⓓ Ⓔ   21. Ⓐ Ⓑ Ⓒ Ⓓ Ⓔ   39. Ⓐ Ⓑ Ⓒ Ⓓ Ⓔ   57. Ⓐ Ⓑ Ⓒ Ⓓ Ⓔ   75. Ⓐ Ⓑ Ⓒ Ⓓ Ⓔ
4. Ⓐ Ⓑ Ⓒ Ⓓ Ⓔ   22. Ⓐ Ⓑ Ⓒ Ⓓ Ⓔ   40. Ⓐ Ⓑ Ⓒ Ⓓ Ⓔ   58. Ⓐ Ⓑ Ⓒ Ⓓ Ⓔ   76. Ⓐ Ⓑ Ⓒ Ⓓ Ⓔ
5. Ⓐ Ⓑ Ⓒ Ⓓ Ⓔ   23. Ⓐ Ⓑ Ⓒ Ⓓ Ⓔ   41. Ⓐ Ⓑ Ⓒ Ⓓ Ⓔ   59. Ⓐ Ⓑ Ⓒ Ⓓ Ⓔ   77. Ⓐ Ⓑ Ⓒ Ⓓ Ⓔ
6. Ⓐ Ⓑ Ⓒ Ⓓ Ⓔ   24. Ⓐ Ⓑ Ⓒ Ⓓ Ⓔ   42. Ⓐ Ⓑ Ⓒ Ⓓ Ⓔ   60. Ⓐ Ⓑ Ⓒ Ⓓ Ⓔ   78. Ⓐ Ⓑ Ⓒ Ⓓ Ⓔ
7. Ⓐ Ⓑ Ⓒ Ⓓ Ⓔ   25. Ⓐ Ⓑ Ⓒ Ⓓ Ⓔ   43. Ⓐ Ⓑ Ⓒ Ⓓ Ⓔ   61. Ⓐ Ⓑ Ⓒ Ⓓ Ⓔ   79. Ⓐ Ⓑ Ⓒ Ⓓ Ⓔ
8. Ⓐ Ⓑ Ⓒ Ⓓ Ⓔ   26. Ⓐ Ⓑ Ⓒ Ⓓ Ⓔ   44. Ⓐ Ⓑ Ⓒ Ⓓ Ⓔ   62. Ⓐ Ⓑ Ⓒ Ⓓ Ⓔ   80. Ⓐ Ⓑ Ⓒ Ⓓ Ⓔ
9. Ⓐ Ⓑ Ⓒ Ⓓ Ⓔ   27. Ⓐ Ⓑ Ⓒ Ⓓ Ⓔ   45. Ⓐ Ⓑ Ⓒ Ⓓ Ⓔ   63. Ⓐ Ⓑ Ⓒ Ⓓ Ⓔ   81. Ⓐ Ⓑ Ⓒ Ⓓ Ⓔ
10. Ⓐ Ⓑ Ⓒ Ⓓ Ⓔ   28. Ⓐ Ⓑ Ⓒ Ⓓ Ⓔ   46. Ⓐ Ⓑ Ⓒ Ⓓ Ⓔ   64. Ⓐ Ⓑ Ⓒ Ⓓ Ⓔ   82. Ⓐ Ⓑ Ⓒ Ⓓ Ⓔ
11. Ⓐ Ⓑ Ⓒ Ⓓ Ⓔ   29. Ⓐ Ⓑ Ⓒ Ⓓ Ⓔ   47. Ⓐ Ⓑ Ⓒ Ⓓ Ⓔ   65. Ⓐ Ⓑ Ⓒ Ⓓ Ⓔ   83. Ⓐ Ⓑ Ⓒ Ⓓ Ⓔ
12. Ⓐ Ⓑ Ⓒ Ⓓ Ⓔ   30. Ⓐ Ⓑ Ⓒ Ⓓ Ⓔ   48. Ⓐ Ⓑ Ⓒ Ⓓ Ⓔ   66. Ⓐ Ⓑ Ⓒ Ⓓ Ⓔ   84. Ⓐ Ⓑ Ⓒ Ⓓ Ⓔ
13. Ⓐ Ⓑ Ⓒ Ⓓ Ⓔ   31. Ⓐ Ⓑ Ⓒ Ⓓ Ⓔ   49. Ⓐ Ⓑ Ⓒ Ⓓ Ⓔ   67. Ⓐ Ⓑ Ⓒ Ⓓ Ⓔ   85. Ⓐ Ⓑ Ⓒ Ⓓ Ⓔ
14. Ⓐ Ⓑ Ⓒ Ⓓ Ⓔ   32. Ⓐ Ⓑ Ⓒ Ⓓ Ⓔ   50. Ⓐ Ⓑ Ⓒ Ⓓ Ⓔ   68. Ⓐ Ⓑ Ⓒ Ⓓ Ⓔ   86. Ⓐ Ⓑ Ⓒ Ⓓ Ⓔ
15. Ⓐ Ⓑ Ⓒ Ⓓ Ⓔ   33. Ⓐ Ⓑ Ⓒ Ⓓ Ⓔ   51. Ⓐ Ⓑ Ⓒ Ⓓ Ⓔ   69. Ⓐ Ⓑ Ⓒ Ⓓ Ⓔ   87. Ⓐ Ⓑ Ⓒ Ⓓ Ⓔ
16. Ⓐ Ⓑ Ⓒ Ⓓ Ⓔ   34. Ⓐ Ⓑ Ⓒ Ⓓ Ⓔ   52. Ⓐ Ⓑ Ⓒ Ⓓ Ⓔ   70. Ⓐ Ⓑ Ⓒ Ⓓ Ⓔ   88. Ⓐ Ⓑ Ⓒ Ⓓ Ⓔ
17. Ⓐ Ⓑ Ⓒ Ⓓ Ⓔ   35. Ⓐ Ⓑ Ⓒ Ⓓ Ⓔ   53. Ⓐ Ⓑ Ⓒ Ⓓ Ⓔ   71. Ⓐ Ⓑ Ⓒ Ⓓ Ⓔ
18. Ⓐ Ⓑ Ⓒ Ⓓ Ⓔ   36. Ⓐ Ⓑ Ⓒ Ⓓ Ⓔ   54. Ⓐ Ⓑ Ⓒ Ⓓ Ⓔ   72. Ⓐ Ⓑ Ⓒ Ⓓ Ⓔ

Tear here

PART C—ADDRESS CODE MEMORY

1. Ⓐ Ⓑ Ⓒ Ⓓ Ⓔ
2. Ⓐ Ⓑ Ⓒ Ⓓ Ⓔ
3. Ⓐ Ⓑ Ⓒ Ⓓ Ⓔ
4. Ⓐ Ⓑ Ⓒ Ⓓ Ⓔ
5. Ⓐ Ⓑ Ⓒ Ⓓ Ⓔ
6. Ⓐ Ⓑ Ⓒ Ⓓ Ⓔ
7. Ⓐ Ⓑ Ⓒ Ⓓ Ⓔ
8. Ⓐ Ⓑ Ⓒ Ⓓ Ⓔ
9. Ⓐ Ⓑ Ⓒ Ⓓ Ⓔ
10. Ⓐ Ⓑ Ⓒ Ⓓ Ⓔ
11. Ⓐ Ⓑ Ⓒ Ⓓ Ⓔ
12. Ⓐ Ⓑ Ⓒ Ⓓ Ⓔ
13. Ⓐ Ⓑ Ⓒ Ⓓ Ⓔ
14. Ⓐ Ⓑ Ⓒ Ⓓ Ⓔ
15. Ⓐ Ⓑ Ⓒ Ⓓ Ⓔ
16. Ⓐ Ⓑ Ⓒ Ⓓ Ⓔ
17. Ⓐ Ⓑ Ⓒ Ⓓ Ⓔ
18. Ⓐ Ⓑ Ⓒ Ⓓ Ⓔ

19. Ⓐ Ⓑ Ⓒ Ⓓ Ⓔ
20. Ⓐ Ⓑ Ⓒ Ⓓ Ⓔ
21. Ⓐ Ⓑ Ⓒ Ⓓ Ⓔ
22. Ⓐ Ⓑ Ⓒ Ⓓ Ⓔ
23. Ⓐ Ⓑ Ⓒ Ⓓ Ⓔ
24. Ⓐ Ⓑ Ⓒ Ⓓ Ⓔ
25. Ⓐ Ⓑ Ⓒ Ⓓ Ⓔ
26. Ⓐ Ⓑ Ⓒ Ⓓ Ⓔ
27. Ⓐ Ⓑ Ⓒ Ⓓ Ⓔ
28. Ⓐ Ⓑ Ⓒ Ⓓ Ⓔ
29. Ⓐ Ⓑ Ⓒ Ⓓ Ⓔ
30. Ⓐ Ⓑ Ⓒ Ⓓ Ⓔ
31. Ⓐ Ⓑ Ⓒ Ⓓ Ⓔ
32. Ⓐ Ⓑ Ⓒ Ⓓ Ⓔ
33. Ⓐ Ⓑ Ⓒ Ⓓ Ⓔ
34. Ⓐ Ⓑ Ⓒ Ⓓ Ⓔ
35. Ⓐ Ⓑ Ⓒ Ⓓ Ⓔ
36. Ⓐ Ⓑ Ⓒ Ⓓ Ⓔ

37. Ⓐ Ⓑ Ⓒ Ⓓ Ⓔ
38. Ⓐ Ⓑ Ⓒ Ⓓ Ⓔ
39. Ⓐ Ⓑ Ⓒ Ⓓ Ⓔ
40. Ⓐ Ⓑ Ⓒ Ⓓ Ⓔ
41. Ⓐ Ⓑ Ⓒ Ⓓ Ⓔ
42. Ⓐ Ⓑ Ⓒ Ⓓ Ⓔ
43. Ⓐ Ⓑ Ⓒ Ⓓ Ⓔ
44. Ⓐ Ⓑ Ⓒ Ⓓ Ⓔ
45. Ⓐ Ⓑ Ⓒ Ⓓ Ⓔ
46. Ⓐ Ⓑ Ⓒ Ⓓ Ⓔ
47. Ⓐ Ⓑ Ⓒ Ⓓ Ⓔ
48. Ⓐ Ⓑ Ⓒ Ⓓ Ⓔ
49. Ⓐ Ⓑ Ⓒ Ⓓ Ⓔ
50. Ⓐ Ⓑ Ⓒ Ⓓ Ⓔ
51. Ⓐ Ⓑ Ⓒ Ⓓ Ⓔ
52. Ⓐ Ⓑ Ⓒ Ⓓ Ⓔ
53. Ⓐ Ⓑ Ⓒ Ⓓ Ⓔ
54. Ⓐ Ⓑ Ⓒ Ⓓ Ⓔ

55. Ⓐ Ⓑ Ⓒ Ⓓ Ⓔ
56. Ⓐ Ⓑ Ⓒ Ⓓ Ⓔ
57. Ⓐ Ⓑ Ⓒ Ⓓ Ⓔ
58. Ⓐ Ⓑ Ⓒ Ⓓ Ⓔ
59. Ⓐ Ⓑ Ⓒ Ⓓ Ⓔ
60. Ⓐ Ⓑ Ⓒ Ⓓ Ⓔ
61. Ⓐ Ⓑ Ⓒ Ⓓ Ⓔ
62. Ⓐ Ⓑ Ⓒ Ⓓ Ⓔ
63. Ⓐ Ⓑ Ⓒ Ⓓ Ⓔ
64. Ⓐ Ⓑ Ⓒ Ⓓ Ⓔ
65. Ⓐ Ⓑ Ⓒ Ⓓ Ⓔ
66. Ⓐ Ⓑ Ⓒ Ⓓ Ⓔ
67. Ⓐ Ⓑ Ⓒ Ⓓ Ⓔ
68. Ⓐ Ⓑ Ⓒ Ⓓ Ⓔ
69. Ⓐ Ⓑ Ⓒ Ⓓ Ⓔ
70. Ⓐ Ⓑ Ⓒ Ⓓ Ⓔ
71. Ⓐ Ⓑ Ⓒ Ⓓ Ⓔ
72. Ⓐ Ⓑ Ⓒ Ⓓ Ⓔ

73. Ⓐ Ⓑ Ⓒ Ⓓ Ⓔ
74. Ⓐ Ⓑ Ⓒ Ⓓ Ⓔ
75. Ⓐ Ⓑ Ⓒ Ⓓ Ⓔ
76. Ⓐ Ⓑ Ⓒ Ⓓ Ⓔ
77. Ⓐ Ⓑ Ⓒ Ⓓ Ⓔ
78. Ⓐ Ⓑ Ⓒ Ⓓ Ⓔ
79. Ⓐ Ⓑ Ⓒ Ⓓ Ⓔ
80. Ⓐ Ⓑ Ⓒ Ⓓ Ⓔ
81. Ⓐ Ⓑ Ⓒ Ⓓ Ⓔ
82. Ⓐ Ⓑ Ⓒ Ⓓ Ⓔ
83. Ⓐ Ⓑ Ⓒ Ⓓ Ⓔ
84. Ⓐ Ⓑ Ⓒ Ⓓ Ⓔ
85. Ⓐ Ⓑ Ⓒ Ⓓ Ⓔ
86. Ⓐ Ⓑ Ⓒ Ⓓ Ⓔ
87. Ⓐ Ⓑ Ⓒ Ⓓ Ⓔ
88. Ⓐ Ⓑ Ⓒ Ⓓ Ⓔ

Tear here

PART D—ADDRESS CHECKING

1. ⒶⒹ
2. Ⓐ Ⓓ
3. Ⓐ Ⓓ
4. Ⓐ Ⓓ
5. Ⓐ Ⓓ
6. Ⓐ Ⓓ
7. Ⓐ Ⓓ
8. Ⓐ Ⓓ
9. Ⓐ Ⓓ
10. Ⓐ Ⓓ
11. Ⓐ Ⓓ
12. Ⓐ Ⓓ
13. Ⓐ Ⓓ
14. Ⓐ Ⓓ
15. Ⓐ Ⓓ
16. Ⓐ Ⓓ
17. Ⓐ Ⓓ
18. Ⓐ Ⓓ
19. Ⓐ Ⓓ

20. Ⓐ Ⓓ
21. Ⓐ Ⓓ
22. Ⓐ Ⓓ
23. Ⓐ Ⓓ
24. Ⓐ Ⓓ
25. Ⓐ Ⓓ
26. Ⓐ Ⓓ
27. Ⓐ Ⓓ
28. Ⓐ Ⓓ
29. Ⓐ Ⓓ
30. Ⓐ Ⓓ
31. Ⓐ Ⓓ
32. Ⓐ Ⓓ
33. Ⓐ Ⓓ
34. Ⓐ Ⓓ
35. Ⓐ Ⓓ
36. Ⓐ Ⓓ
37. Ⓐ Ⓓ
38. Ⓐ Ⓓ

39. Ⓐ Ⓓ
40. Ⓐ Ⓓ
41. Ⓐ Ⓓ
42. Ⓐ Ⓓ
43. Ⓐ Ⓓ
44. Ⓐ Ⓓ
45. Ⓐ Ⓓ
46. Ⓐ Ⓓ
47. Ⓐ Ⓓ
48. Ⓐ Ⓓ
49. Ⓐ Ⓓ
50. Ⓐ Ⓓ
51. Ⓐ Ⓓ
52. Ⓐ Ⓓ
53. Ⓐ Ⓓ
54. Ⓐ Ⓓ
55. Ⓐ Ⓓ
56. Ⓐ Ⓓ
57. Ⓐ Ⓓ

58. Ⓐ Ⓓ
59. Ⓐ Ⓓ
60. Ⓐ Ⓓ
61. Ⓐ Ⓓ
62. Ⓐ Ⓓ
63. Ⓐ Ⓓ
64. Ⓐ Ⓓ
65. Ⓐ Ⓓ
66. Ⓐ Ⓓ
67. Ⓐ Ⓓ
68. Ⓐ Ⓓ
69. Ⓐ Ⓓ
70. Ⓐ Ⓓ
71. Ⓐ Ⓓ
72. Ⓐ Ⓓ
73. Ⓐ Ⓓ
74. Ⓐ Ⓓ
75. Ⓐ Ⓓ
76. Ⓐ Ⓓ

77. Ⓐ Ⓓ
78. Ⓐ Ⓓ
79. Ⓐ Ⓓ
80. Ⓐ Ⓓ
81. Ⓐ Ⓓ
82. Ⓐ Ⓓ
83. Ⓐ Ⓓ
84. Ⓐ Ⓓ
85. Ⓐ Ⓓ
86. Ⓐ Ⓓ
87. Ⓐ Ⓓ
88. Ⓐ Ⓓ
89. Ⓐ Ⓓ
90. Ⓐ Ⓓ
91. Ⓐ Ⓓ
92. Ⓐ Ⓓ
93. Ⓐ Ⓓ
94. Ⓐ Ⓓ
95. Ⓐ Ⓓ

Tear here

FINAL MODEL EXAM

PART A—NUMBER SERIES

SAMPLE QUESTIONS

The following sample questions show you the type of question that will be used in Part A. Since this type of question may be new and unfamiliar to you, the examiner will work through the first five questions with you. Once you understand the task, you will have five minutes to answer sample questions 6 to 14 on your own. Correct answers and explanations follow.

Directions: Each number series question consists of a series of numbers which follows some definite order. The numbers progress from left to right according to some rule. One pair of numbers to the right of the series comprises the next two numbers in the series. Study each series to try to find a pattern to the series and to figure out the rule which governs the progression. Choose the answer pair which continues the series according to the pattern established and mark its letter on your answer sheet.

1. 6   7   8   10   12   15   18   .... (A) 19   20 (B) 21   24 (C) 21   25 (D) 22   26 (E) 23   28

Look at the progression of numbers. The series moves at the rate of $+1$, $+1$, $+2$, $+2$, $+3$, $+3$; logically what should come next is $+4$, $+4$. $18 + 4 = 22 + 4 = 26$, which makes **(D)** the correct answer.

2. 80   78   76   76   74   72   72   ..... (A) 72   70 (B) 72   74 (C) 70   68 (D) 74   72 (E) 68   68

The pattern is: -2, -2, repeat; -2, -2, repeat. Now continue with -2, -2. In other words, $72 - 2 = 70 - 2 = 68$, and **(C)** is the correct answer.

3. 30   60   58   30   60   58   30   ..... (A) 60   58 (B) 30   58 (C) 58   60 (D) 60   30 (E) 58   30

This is a simple repetitive series. The three numbers 30 60 58 repeat themselves, in order, over and over again. Choice **(A)** is the correct answer.

4. 10   10   20   10   30   10   40   ..... (A) 10   10 (B) 10   50 (C) 40   10 (D) 40   50 (E) 50   10

Do not be fooled by the seeming repeat at the beginning of this series. The series is a simple $+10$ series with the number 10 interposing itself between members of the series. The series continues with the static number 10 and then the next regular member 50 ($40 + 10$). The answer is **(B)**.

5. 75 41 73 43 71 45 69 ..... (A) 47 72 (B) 43 69 (C) 47 71 (D) 67 47 (E) 47 67

This series is, in reality, two alternating series. The first series begins with the number 75 and progresses by a factor of −2. The alternating series begins with 41 and progresses by a factor of +2. The next number in the total series should be a member of the +2 series. 45 + 2 = 47. It should be followed by the next member of the −2 series; 69 −2 = 67. The correct answer is **(E)**.

You will now have five minutes to complete the remaining number series sample questions.

6. 2 2 6 6 18 18 54 .... (A) 54 54 (B) 18 18 (C) 54 162 (D) 54 72 (E) 72 162

7. 5 15 24 32 39 84 89 .... (A) 94 99 (B) 93 96 (C) 93 97 (D) 92 95 (E) 92 94

8. 36 46 43 41 36 46 43 ..... (A) 46 36 (B) 46 56 (C) 36 56 (D) 41 36 (E) 53 56

9. 15 76 19 70 23 64 27 ..... (A) 58 31 (B) 31 35 (C) 35 60 (D) 31 58 (E) 59 32

10. 24 25 23 24 21 22 18 ..... (A) 19 20 (B) 20 19 (C) 19 14 (D) 25 20 (E) 22 12

11. 21 21 22 23 23 24 25 ..... (A) 24 25 (B) 25 25 (C) 25 24 (D) 24 23 (E) 25 26

12. 15 8 22 8 29 8 36 .... (A) 8 30 (B) 8 44 (C) 43 8 (D) 8 43 (E) 8 42

13. 72 65 65 66 66 60 60 ..... (A) 60 59 (B) 59 59 (C) 59 58 (D) 58 58 (E) 57 57

14. 62 59 55 50 47 43 38 ..... (A) 33 29 (B) 32 25 (C) 34 31 (D) 35 30 (E) 35 31

SAMPLE ANSWER SHEET		CORRECT ANSWERS	
1. Ⓐ Ⓑ Ⓒ Ⓓ Ⓔ	8. Ⓐ Ⓑ Ⓒ Ⓓ Ⓔ	1. D	8. D
2. Ⓐ Ⓑ Ⓒ Ⓓ Ⓔ	9. Ⓐ Ⓑ Ⓒ Ⓓ Ⓔ	2. C	9. A
3. Ⓐ Ⓑ Ⓒ Ⓓ Ⓔ	10. Ⓐ Ⓑ Ⓒ Ⓓ Ⓔ	3. A	10. C
4. Ⓐ Ⓑ Ⓒ Ⓓ Ⓔ	11. Ⓐ Ⓑ Ⓒ Ⓓ Ⓔ	4. B	11. E
5. Ⓐ Ⓑ Ⓒ Ⓓ Ⓔ	12. Ⓐ Ⓑ Ⓒ Ⓓ Ⓔ	5. E	12. D
6. Ⓐ Ⓑ Ⓒ Ⓓ Ⓔ	13. Ⓐ Ⓑ Ⓒ Ⓓ Ⓔ	6. C	13. B
7. Ⓐ Ⓑ Ⓒ Ⓓ Ⓔ	14. Ⓐ Ⓑ Ⓒ Ⓓ Ⓔ	7. B	14. E

EXPLANATIONS

6. **(C)** The pattern is: repeat the number, multiply the number by 3; repeat the number, multiply the number 3, etc. At the point at which you must continue the series, you must repeat the 54, then multiply 54 by 3 to get 162.

7. **(B)** The numbers in the series increase at a steadily decreasing rate. If you mark the differences between numbers in the series, you will see that the rate of increase is + 10, +9, +8, +7, +6, +5. Continue the series by increasing first by +4, then by +3. 89 + 4 = 93 + 3 = 96.

8. **(D)** This series consists simply of the sequence 46   43   41 being repeated over and over with the number 36 appearing between sequences. The fact that the series begins with the periodically repeating number makes this a difficult series to solve at first glance. However, the pattern of numbers on either side of the second intervening 36 makes it evident that this is the only solution.

9. **(A)** Here are two alternating series. One series increases at the rate of +4, the other decreases at the rate of −6.

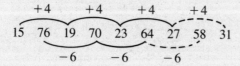

10. **(C)** This pattern is not complicated, but you must write direction and degree of change between members of the series in order to solve the question. The pattern is: +1, −2, +1, −3, +1, −4; continue with +1, −5. Thus, 18 + 1 = 19 − 5 = 14.

11. **(E)** The pattern is: repeat the number, +1, +1; repeat the number, +1, +1; continue by repeating 25 and adding 1 = 26.

12. **(D)** This is a simple +7 series with the number 8 appearing regularly between members of the series. Diagramming, you can see:

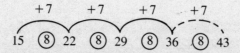

13. **(B)** This is a difficult series. Basically, the numbers of the series repeat before decreasing. The series begins with the second number of a repeat. You must visualize that the series began with an additional 72 before the printed one. Then, the series decreases at a decreasing rate, each amount of decrease being two smaller than the one before it. Thus, the pattern reads: −7, repeat, −5, repeat, −3, repeat. Continue with −1 and repeat. 60 − 1 = 59 and repeat 59.

14. **(E)** Once you have written the direction and degree of change, this pattern is not difficult. −3, −4, −5; −3 −4 −5. Continue with −3, −4. 38 − 3 = 35 − 4 = 31.

PART A—NUMBER SERIES

TIME: 20 Minutes. 24 Questions.

Directions: Each number series question consists of a series of numbers which follows some definite order. The numbers progress from left to right according to some rule. One lettered pair of numbers comprises the next two numbers in the series. Study each series to try to find a pattern to the series and to figure the rule which governs the progression. Choose the answer pair which continues the series according to the pattern established and mark its letter on your answer sheet. Correct answers are on page 246.

1. 12 16 12 16 12 16 12 .... (A) 12 12 (B) 16 16 (C) 12 16 (D) 16 12 (E) 14 16

2. 31 32 33 32 33 34 33 ..... (A) 33 34 (B) 34 35 (C) 34 33 (D) 32 32 (E) 34 36

3. 52 54 56 42 44 46 32 ..... (A) 22 12 (B) 42 52 (C) 34 36 (D) 33 34 (E) 36 38

4. 75 66 57 48 39 30 21 ..... (A) 12 3 (B) 13 6 (C) 15 5 (D) 10 1 (E) 11 4

5. 11 11 13 26 26 28 56 ..... (A) 56 56 (B) 56 28 (C) 56 112 (D) 58 58 (E) 56 58

6. 3 5 35 6 3 63 4 .... (A) 4 42 (B) 2 4 (C) 2 42 (D) 4 4 (E) 2 44

7. 83 81 79 76 73 69 65 ..... (A) 60 54 (B) 59 52 (C) 59 53 (D) 60 55 (E) 61 57

8. 46 18 25 44 16 23 42 ..... (A) 20 12 (B) 16 23 (C) 22 10 (D) 14 20 (E) 14 21

9. 10 100 9 81 8 64 7 .... (A) 36 6 (B) 49 6 (C) 49 7 (D) 49 36 (E) 42 6

10. 53 17 49 20 45 23 41 ..... (A) 26 37 (B) 37 26 (C) 26 44 (D) 27 38 (E) 38 27

11. 84 84 7 72 72 6 60 .... (A) 5 48 (B) 50 5 (C) 60 5 (D) 5 60 (E) 48 4

12. 17 21 28 25 29 36 33 ..... (A) 30 37 (B) 40 37 (C) 40 44 (D) 34 39 (E) 37 44

13. 23 56 25 54 29 50 35 ..... (A) 44 43 (B) 43 44 (C) 42 45 (D) 41 39 (E) 39 41

14. 71 25 63 25 56 25 50 ..... (A) 44 25 (B) 25 45 (C) 45 25 (D) 25 46 (E) 25 44

15. 5 5 25 6 6 36 7 .... (A) 7 14 (B) 49 8 (C) 49 7 (D) 7 49 (E) 7 7

16. 12 24 14 28 18 36 26 ..... (A) 26 6 (B) 24 4 (C) 6 12 (D) 12 6 (E) 52 42

17. 6 54 15 18 27 6 42 .... (A) 2 60 (B) 3 84 (C) 4 62 (D) 2 57 (E) 3 60

18. 21 21 24 42 42 24 84 ..... (A) 24 168 (B) 84 168 (C) 84 42 (D) 84 24 (E) 42 24

19. 6 0 0 6 1 1 6 .... (A) 6 1 (B) 1 0 (C) 2 2 (D) 6 6 (E) 1 2

20. 32 32 32 39 39 39 46 ..... (A) 53 53 (B) 46 53 (C) 52 52 (D) 39 32 (E) 46 46

21. 40 57 43 60 47 64 52 ..... (A) 68 58 (B) 69 58 (C) 59 69 (D) 58 69 (E) 68 57

22. 16 19 22 17 12 15 18 ...... (A) 13 16 (B) 21 16 (C) 21 24 (D) 21 26 (E) 13 8

23. 50 4 10 10 10 4 2 .... (A) 2 2 (B) 2 4 (C) 10 4 (D) 2 10 (E) 50 50

24. 11 13 15 17 19 17 15 ...... (A) 15 16 (B) 14 13 (C) 17 19 (D) 13 11 (E) 19 17

END OF PART A

If you complete this part before time is up, go over your work on this part only. Do not turn the page until you are told to do so.

PART B—ADDRESS CODING

SAMPLE QUESTIONS

The seven sample questions for this part are based upon the addresses in the five boxes below. Your task is to mark on your answer sheet the letter of the box in which each address belongs. The instructions for Part B permit you to look at the boxes if you cannot remember in which box an address belongs. You may look at the boxes while answering these Part B sample questions. The questions in Part C of the exam will be based upon the same boxes as the questions in Part B, but in answering Part C you may NOT look at the boxes. There will be no sample questions before Part C.

A	B	C	D	E
5600-5899 Weber	9400-9799 Weber	1200-1799 Weber	2600-2899 Weber	1800-1899 Weber
Ridge	Lockwood	Richbell	Bethel	Glantz
3400-4099 Heath	4400-4499 Heath	7500-7699 Heath	6200-7199 Heath	8400-9199 Heath
Anderson	Kingston	Garth	Alperson	Pound
8300-8399 Brite	3000-3399 Brite	2100-3099 Brite	9000-9299 Brite	4500-6199 Brite

1. 4400-4499 Heath
2. 2100-3099 Brite
3. Alperson
4. Ridge

5. 1800-1899 Weber
6. 8300-8399 Brite
7. 9400-9799 Weber

SAMPLE ANSWER SHEET		CORRECT ANSWERS	
1. Ⓐ Ⓑ Ⓒ Ⓓ Ⓔ	5. Ⓐ Ⓑ Ⓒ Ⓓ Ⓔ	1. B	5. E
2. Ⓐ Ⓑ Ⓒ Ⓓ Ⓔ	6. Ⓐ Ⓑ Ⓒ Ⓓ Ⓔ	2. C	6. A
3. Ⓐ Ⓑ Ⓒ Ⓓ Ⓔ	7. Ⓐ Ⓑ Ⓒ Ⓓ Ⓔ	3. D	7. B
4. Ⓐ Ⓑ Ⓒ Ⓓ Ⓔ		4. A	

PART B—ADDRESS CODING

Directions: There are five boxes labeled A, B, C, D, and E. In each box are five addresses, three of which include a number span and a name and two of which are names alone. You will have five (5) minutes to memorize the locations of all twenty-five addresses. Then you will have three (3) minutes to mark your answer sheet with the letter of the box in which each address in the question list belongs. For Part B you may refer to the boxes while answering, though you will lose speed by doing so. For Part C you may NOT look at the boxes, so do your best to memorize in the five minutes allowed you now. Correct answers are on page 248.

MEMORIZING TIME: 5 Minutes.

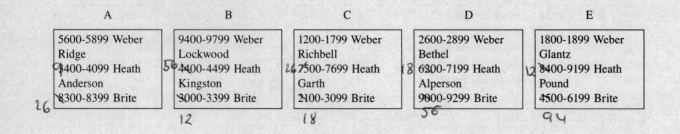

A	B	C	D	E
5600-5899 Weber Ridge	9400-9799 Weber Lockwood	1200-1799 Weber Richbell	2600-2899 Weber Bethel	1800-1899 Weber Glantz
3400-4099 Heath Anderson	4400-4499 Heath Kingston	7500-7699 Heath Garth	6200-7199 Heath Alperson	8400-9199 Heath Pound
8300-8399 Brite	3000-3399 Brite	2100-3099 Brite	9000-9299 Brite	4500-6199 Brite

ANSWERING TIME: 3 Minutes. 88 Questions.

1. 2100-3099 Brite
2. 4400-4499 Heath
3. Pound
4. 2600-2899 Weber
5. 8300-8399 Brite
6. Lockwood
7. Alperson
8. 9400-9799 Weber
9. 8400-9199 Heath
10. 9000-9299 Brite
11. Kingston
12. Glantz
13. Richbell
14. 3400-4099 Heath

15. 4500-6199 Brite
16. 2600-2899 Weber
17. 7500-7699 Heath
18. 4500-6199 Brite
19. Anderson
20. Pound
21. 5600-5899 Weber
22. 1800-1899 Weber
23. 3000-3399 Brite
24. 8400-9199 Heath
25. Bethel
26. 3400-4099 Heath
27. 2600-2899 Weber
28. 4400-4499 Heath

29. 2100-3099 Brite
30. Garth
31. Kingston
32. Lockwood
33. 9400-9799 Weber
34. 6200-7199 Heath
35. 8300-8399 Brite
36. 4500-6199 Brite
37. Ridge
38. Alperson
39. 3000-3399 Brite
40. 7500-7699 Heath
41. 5600-5899 Weber
42. Richbell
43. Glantz
44. 8400-9199 Heath
45. 9000-9299 Brite
46. Bethel
47. Pound
48. Anderson
49. 1200-1799 Weber
50. 1800-1899 Weber
51. 3400-4099 Heath
52. 4500-6199 Brite
53. 2600-2899 Weber
54. Kingston
55. Pound
56. 5600-5899 Weber
57. 6200-7199 Heath
58. 9000-9299 Brite

59. 8400-9199 Heath
60. Richbell
61. Glantz
62. 8300-8399 Brite
63. 7500-7699 Heath
64. 4400-4499 Heath
65. 8400-9199 Heath
66. 4500-6199 Brite
67. Bethel
68. Ridge
69. Lockwood
70. 2100-3099 Brite
71. 3000-3399 Brite
72. Alperson
73. Garth
74. 1200-1799 Weber
75. 2600-2899 Weber
76. 2100-3099 Brite
77. 1800-1899 Weber
78. Bethel
79. Anderson
80. Glantz
81. 2600-2899 Weber
82. 9000-9299 Brite
83. 3400-4099 Heath
84. 6200-7199 Heath
85. 5600-5899 Weber
86. 4400-4499 Heath
87. Ridge
88. Kingston

END OF PART B

If you finish before time is up, use the remaining few seconds to continue memorizing the locations of the addresses. Do not turn the page until you are told to do so.

PART C—ADDRESS CODE MEMORY

TIME: 5 Minutes. 88 Questions.

Directions: *Relying entirely upon your memory, mark your answer sheet with the letter of the box in which each address belongs. Correct answers are on page 249.*

1. Kingston
2. 8400-9199 Heath
3. 9000-9299 Brite
4. 2600-2899 Weber
5. 3400-4099 Heath
6. Richbell
7. Alperson
8. 4500-6199 Brite
9. 9400-9799 Weber
10. 7500-7699 Heath
11. 5600-5899 Weber
12. 4500-6199 Brite
13. Anderson
14. Glantz
15. Lockwood
16. 8300-8399 Brite
17. 1200-1799 Weber
18. 1800-1899 Weber
19. 8400-9199 Heath
20. 4500-6199 Brite
21. Bethel
22. Richbell
23. 9400-9799 Weber
24. 2100-3099 Brite
25. 2600-2899 Weber
26. 3400-4099 Heath
27. Ridge
28. Kingston
29. 7500-7699 Heath
30. 9000-9299 Brite
31. 6200-7199 Heath
32. Lockwood
33. Glantz
34. Pound
35. 5600-5899 Weber

36. 4400-4499 Heath
37. 2100-3099 Brite
38. Bethel
39. Garth
40. 9000-9299 Brite
41. 8400-9199 Heath
42. 1800-1899 Weber
43. 3400-4099 Heath
44. 9400-9799 Weber
45. 7500-7699 Heath
46. Richbell
47. Bethel
48. 1800-1899 Weber
49. 3400-4099 Heath
50. 3000-3399 Brite
51. 2100-3099 Brite
52. 1800-1899 Weber
53. Anderson
54. Alperson
55. 5600-5899 Weber
56. 4400-4499 Heath
57. 9000-9299 Brite
58. 8400-9199 Heath
59. Glantz
60. 7500-7699 Heath
61. Garth
62. Pound
63. 2600-2899 Weber
64. 7500-7699 Heath
65. 3000-3399 Brite
66. 6200-7199 Heath
67. 2600-2899 Weber
68. 8400-9199 Heath
69. 3000-3399 Brite
70. 7500-7699 Heath

71. Ridge
72. Bethel
73. 5600-5899 Weber
74. 6200-7199 Heath
75. 9000-9299 Brite
76. Lockwood
77. Richbell
78. 2600-2899 Weber
79. 4400-4499 Heath

80. 9400-9799 Weber
81. 2100-3099 Brite
82. Glantz
83. Anderson
84. 9400-9799 Weber
85. 4500-6199 Brite
86. 3400-4099 Heath
87. 1200-1799 Weber
88. Pound

END OF PART C

If you finish before time is up, check your answers on this part only. Do not turn the page until you are told to do so.

PART D—ADDRESS CHECKING TEST

SAMPLE QUESTIONS

You will be allowed three minutes to read the directions and answer the five sample questions which follow. On the actual test, however, you will have only six minutes to answer 95 questions, so see how quickly you can compare addresses and still get the correct answer.

Directions: *Each question consists of two addresses. If the two addresses are* alike in EVERY way, *mark* Ⓐ *on your answer sheet. If the two addresses are* different in ANY way, *mark* Ⓓ *on your answer sheet.*

1 . . . 3290 Rugby Road   3290 Rugby Rd
2 . . . 3336 Nonantum St   3363 Nonantum St
3 . . . Ridgefield NJ 07657   Ridgeville NJ 07657
4 . . . 341 N State St   341 N State St
5 . . . 3063 Mark Lane   3063 Mark Ln

SAMPLE ANSWER SHEET	
1. ⒶⒹ	4. ⒶⒹ
2. ⒶⒹ	5. ⒶⒹ
3. ⒶⒹ	

CORRECT ANSWERS	
1. A	4. A
2. D	5. D
3. D	

PART D—ADDRESS CHECKING

TIME: 6 Minutes. 95 Questions.

Directions: Look carefully at the two addresses in each question. If the two addresses are alike *in EVERY way, mark Ⓐ on your answer sheet. If the two addresses are different in ANY way, mark Ⓓ on your answer sheet. Correct answers are on page 249.*

1	3192 Brookline Rd	3192 Brookline Rd
2	4815 Baraud Rd	4815 Baurad Rd
3	4925 Correll Rd	4925 Corell Rd
4	Lewisburg PA 17837	Lewisburg PA 17837
5	6591 Dobbs Terr	6591 Dobbs Terr
6	381 NE 135th St	381 NE 135th St
7	1416 Dimsdale Rd	1416 Dimsdale Dr
8	Pasadena CA 91125	Pasadena CA 91225
9	3753 Chesterfield Rd	3753 Chesterfield Rd
10	6941 Catherine Rd	6491 Catherine Rd
11	Northfield MN 55057	Northfield MN 55057
12	6403 Massachusetts Ave NW	6403 Massachusetts Ave NW
13	2521 Cotswold Wy	2512 Cotswold Wy
14	2232 E 193rd St	2232 E 193rd St
15	Long Beach CA 90840	Long Branch CA 90840
16	Pittsburgh PA 15213	Pittsburgh PA 12513
17	3540 Herkimer St	3540 Herkimer Rd
18	2509 S Evandale Rd	2509 N Evandale Rd
19	411 Gatehouse Ln	4111 Gatehouse Ln
20	3206 Greenville Blvd	3206 Greenville Blvd
21	2792 Interlaken Pkwy	2972 Interlaken Pkwy
22	San Francisco CA 94132	San Francisco CA 94132
23	1255 Mohican Path	1255 Mohican Path
24	1245 Moore St	1245 Morse St
25	San Jose CA 95192	San Jose CA 95912
26	9927 Lamesa Ave	9927 LaMesa Ave
27	1152 Lakeland Hwy	1152 Lakeland Hwy
28	5937 Thorneycroft	5937 Thornycroft
29	2836 Woodford Rd	2836 Woodruff Rd
30	Cleveland OH 44106	Cleveland OH 44106
31	8624 Alabama Ave SE	8624 Alabama Ave SE
32	Washington DC 20064	Washington DC 20064
33	Chicago IL 60637	Chicago IL 60637
34	1159 Lake Shore Dr	1159 Lakeshore Dr
35	3776 Paxford Ave	3667 Paxford Ave

36 . . . 2838 Checkerboard Sq	2838 Checkerboard Sq
37 . . . 9374 Saunders Hwy	9374 Saunders Hwy
38 . . . 951 Pondfield Rd	951 Pondfield Rd
39 . . . 5301 Jerome Ave	5301 Jerome Ave
40 . . . Berkeley CA 94720	Berkeley CA 94720
41 . . . 2495 Sprain Valley Rd	2495 Sprain Valley Dr
42 . . . 7983 Sunrise Hwy	7893 Sunrise Hwy
43 . . . 5231 Springdale Pkwy	5231 Springdell Pkwy
44 . . . 7986 Colonial Hts	7968 Colonial Hts
45 . . . Cincinnati OH 45221	Cincinatti OH 45221
46 . . . Davis CA 95616	Davis CO 95616
47 . . . 1589 Waverly Pl	1589 Waverly Pl
48 . . . 1151 Oberdan Dr	1151 Oberdan Dr
49 . . . 3361 Putah Crk	3316 Putah Crk
50 . . . New York NY 10031	New York NY 10031
51 . . . 7826 SE 148th Wy	7826 SE 148th Way
52 . . . 683 Shubert Alley	683 Sherbert Alley
53 . . . 2020 Tudor Ln	2020 Tudor La
54 . . . Claremont CA 91711	Claremount CA 91711
55 . . . 9321 Shawnee Rd	9321 Shawnee Rd
56 . . . 1067 Weaver St	1067 Weaver St
57 . . . 1201 Post Rd	1201 Post St
58 . . . 9549 Parkway Cl	9549 Parkway Cl
59 . . . 6905 Salem Dr	6905 Salem Dr
60 . . . Worcester MA 01610	Worcester ME 01610
61 . . . 836 Trimmingham St	836 Trimmingham St
62 . . . 7841 W 357th St	7841 W 375th St
63 . . . 1616 Atherstone Rd	1616 Atherstone Rd
64 . . . 845 Tintern La	845 Tintern La
65 . . . Irvine CA 92717	Irvine CA 92717
66 . . . 7501 Rockingchair Rd	7051 Rochingchair Rd
67 . . . 9316 Severn Rd	9316 Severn Dr
68 . . . 3012 Brayton Blvd	2013 Brayton Blvd
69 . . . 2333 Poe St	233 E Poe St
70 . . . Waterville ME 04901	Waterville ME 04901
71 . . . Los Angeles CA 90024	Los Angeles CA 90024
72 . . . 9812 E Madison St	9812 E Madison St
73 . . . 5094 Tewkesbury Rd	5049 Tewkesbury Rd
74 . . . 1535 Plymouth Dr	1535 Plymouth Dr
75 . . . 9169 Bruckner Blvd	9169 Bruckner Blvd
76 . . . 8751 S Industrial Hwy	9571 S Industrial Hwy
77 . . . 8714 Graham Tpke	8714 Graham Tpke
78 . . . Riverside CA 92502	Riverside CA 92502
79 . . . Hamilton NY 13346	Hamilton NJ 13346
80 . . . 7227 Rock Creek Ln	7227 Rock Creek Ln
81 . . . 1181 Popham Rd	1181 Popham Rd
82 . . . 9999 Kings Hwy S	999 Kings Hwy S
83 . . . 1624 Butler Rd	1624 Butter Rd
84 . . . Colorado Springs CO 80903	Colorado Springs CO 80903
85 . . . 9753 Old Colony Rd	9573 Old Colony Rd
86 . . . 8523 Rogers Dr	8523 Rodgers Dr

87 . . . LaJolla CA 92093   LaJolla CA 90293
88 . . . 2295 Ross Rd   2295 Russ Rd
89 . . . 3262 W 418th Rd   3262 W 418th Dr
90 . . . 1095 Ridge St   1095 Bridge St
91 . . . 7796 Delaware Ave SW   7796 Delaware Ave SW
92 . . . 1472 Morningside Hts   1472 Morningside Hts
93 . . . 3409 Toonerville Apts   3049 Toonerville Apts
94 . . . 1259 Webster Rd   1259 Webster Rd
95 . . . 7542 Claremont Circle   7542 Claremont Circle

END OF EXAM

If you finish before time is up, check over your answers on this part only. Do not return to any previous part.

CORRECT ANSWERS—FINAL MODEL EXAM

PART A—NUMBER SERIES

1. D	4. A	7. D	10. A	13. A	16. E	19. C	22. E
2. B	5. E	8. E	11. C	14. B	17. A	20. E	23. A
3. C	6. C	9. B	12. E	15. D	18. D	21. B	24. D

EXPLANATIONS—NUMBER SERIES

1. **(D)** This is the simplest type of series, and you should be able to solve it by inspection as a repetitive 12, 16, 12, 16. If you have gotten into the habit of solving all series mathematically, this one is $+4$, -4. This method is fine, too.

2. **(B)** You might solve this series by grouping into threes and reading rythmically with the accent on the third number. If you have done this, you know that each mini-series is a plus one series and that each successive mini-series is one step above the previous one. You can also solve this series as $+1$, $+1$, -1.

3. **(C)** This is another series question that may be seen either as a series of mini-series or can be solved arithmetically. The mini-series are $+2$ series and each successive mini-series begins 10 below its predecessor. You might find it simpler to read the questions as $+2$, $+2$, -10; $+2$, $+2$, -10.

4. **(A)** This is a straightforward -9 series.

5. **(E)** If you marked the spaces between the numbers accurately, you know that the pattern is: repeat the number $+2$, $\times 2$; repeat the number, $+2$, $\times 2$. Continue by repeating the number and adding 2.

6. **(C)** This is a nontraditional series. The first two numbers combine, physically not arithmetically, to form the third. The series then continues with two more numbers that combine to form a third. There is no particular relationship between numbers in the parts of the series. To solve this series, you must first determine the pattern that was just described. Then look at the second number in each pair of answer choices. That number must be made up of the final given number in the series placed before the first number in the answer choice. In choice (C), the 42 is made up of the 4 at the end of the given series and the 2 which begins choice (C).

7. **(D)** The pattern is: -2, -2, -3, -3, -4, -4. It is reasonable to continue with -5, -5.

8. **(E)** Each mini-series is two steps down from the previous mini-series, and this relationship is consistent even though the numbers within a mini-series have no meaningful relationship to each other. If you don't see the mini-series, you might consider that there are three alternating -2 series, the first beginning with 46, the second with 18 and the third with 25.

9. **(B)** In descending order, the pattern is numbers beginning with 10 followed by their squares.

10. **(A)** There are two alternating series. The series beginning with 53 is a −4 series. The series beginning with 17 is a +3 series. Once you have determined that you are dealing with alternating series, it is easy to figure the direction and degree of change within each. Be alert to which series determines the first number of the answer and which series determines the second number.

11. **(C)** There is a lot happening in this series. First the number is repeated. Then the number is divided by 12 and the answer follows that number. Furthermore, 12 is subtracted from the number to create the next number to be repeated. The diagram is complicated but not difficult.

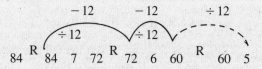

$$-12 \qquad -12 \qquad \div 12$$
$$\div 12 \qquad \div 12$$
$$84 \quad ^R 84 \quad 7 \quad 72 \quad ^R 72 \quad 6 \quad 60 \quad ^R \quad 60 \quad 5$$

12. **(E)** The pattern is: +4, +7, −3; +4, +7, −3.

13. **(A)** This is a difficult problem. There are two alternating patterns, one increasing at an ever-increasing rate and the other decreasing by an equally increasing rate. The diagram explains it best.

$$+2 \qquad +4 \qquad +6 \qquad +8$$
$$23 \quad 56 \quad 25 \quad 54 \quad 29 \quad 50 \quad 35 \quad 44 \quad 43$$
$$-2 \qquad -4 \qquad -6$$

14. **(B)** The series decreases at a steadily decreasing rate while the number 25 interposes itself between members of the series. The main series' pattern is: −8, −7, −6, and can be continued with −5.

15. **(D)** Solve this one by inspection. $5 \times 5 = 25$; $6 \times 6 = 36$; $7 \times 7 = 49$.

16. **(E)** The pattern is: ×2, −10; ×2, −10; ×2, −10.

17. **(A)** Some number series questions really are harder than others. This is a hard one. First you must determine that there are two alternating series. The pattern of the series beginning with 6 is: +9, +12, +15. Obviously, as the series progresses, the additive number increases by 3. In continuing the series, the number to be added to 42 is 15 + 3 or 18. 42 + 18 = 60. The other series, that beginning with 54 is a ÷3 series. The diagram looks like this:

$$+9 \qquad +12 \qquad +15 \qquad +18$$
$$6 \quad 54 \quad 15 \quad 18 \quad 27 \quad 6 \quad 42 \quad 2 \quad 60$$
$$\div 3 \qquad \div 3 \qquad \div 3$$

18. **(D)** The main pattern is repeat the number, ×2; repeat the number ×2. The extraneous number 24 appears between the number being multiplied by 2 and its product.

$$R \qquad \times 2 \qquad R \qquad \times 2 \qquad R$$
$$21 \quad 21 \quad \textcircled{24} \quad 42 \quad 42 \quad \textcircled{24} \quad 84 \quad 84 \quad \textcircled{24}$$

19. **(C)** Some series are easier to answer than to explain. By inspection, you can see that the number <u>6</u> appears between pairs and that the series is 0 0, 1 1, 2 2.

20. **(E)** This is a +7 series with double repeats. That is: repeat, repeat, +7; repeat, repeat, +7.

21. **(B)** There are two alternating series, both progressing at the same increasing rate, that is, +3, +4, +5, +6.

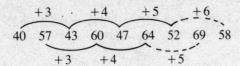

22. **(E)** The pattern is: +3, +3, −5, −5; +3, +3, −5, −5.

23. **(A)** You won't find many questions as difficult as this one. If you figured this out, have no fears about your exam. You can answer anything. If you missed this one, do not be discouraged. Very few people can figure a question at this level, especially under time pressure. This question combines double repeats, division, and a regularly recurring extraneous number. Consider that the initial <u>50</u> is the third number of a double repeat. It is divided by 5 to yield <u>10</u> which is repeated twice and itself divided by 5 yielding <u>2</u>, which must be repeated twice as your answer. The number <u>4</u> recurs between the number being divided by 5 and its quotient.

$$
\begin{array}{ccccccc}
\text{R} & \div 5 & \text{R} & \text{R} & \div 5 & \text{R} & \text{R} \\
50 & ④ & 10 & 10 & 10 & ④ \ 2 & 2 & 2
\end{array}
$$

24. **(D)** This series increases by +2 until it reaches its peak at <u>19</u>, then turns around and decreases by −2. When completed, the series is symmetrical.

$$11 \;^{+2}\; 13 \;^{+2}\; 15 \;^{+2}\; 17 \;^{+2}\; 19 \;^{-2}\; 17 \;^{-2}\; 15 \;^{-2}\; 13 \;^{-2}\; 11$$

PART B—ADDRESS CODING

1. C	12. E	23. B	34. D	45. D	56. A	67. D	78. D
2. B	13. C	24. E	35. A	46. D	57. D	68. A	79. A
3. E	14. A	25. D	36. E	47. E	58. D	69. B	80. E
4. D	15. E	26. A	37. A	48. A	59. E	70. C	81. D
5. A	16. D	27. D	38. D	49. C	60. C	71. B	82. D
6. B	17. C	28. B	39. B	50. E	61. E	72. D	83. A
7. D	18. E	29. C	40. C	51. A	62. A	73. C	84. D
8. B	19. A	30. C	41. A	52. E	63. C	74. C	85. A
9. E	20. E	31. B	42. C	53. D	64. B	75. D	86. B
10. D	21. A	32. B	43. E	54. B	65. E	76. C	87. A
11. B	22. E	33. B	44. E	55. E	66. E	77. E	88. B

PART C—ADDRESS CODE MEMORY

1. B	12. E	23. B	34. E	45. C	56. B	67. D	78. D
2. E	13. A	24. C	35. A	46. C	57. D	68. E	79. B
3. D	14. E	25. D	36. B	47. D	58. E	69. B	80. B
4. D	15. B	26. A	37. C	48. E	59. E	70. C	81. C
5. A	16. A	27. A	38. D	49. A	60. C	71. A	82. E
6. C	17. C	28. B	39. C	50. B	61. C	72. D	83. A
7. D	18. E	29. C	40. D	51. C	62. E	73. A	84. B
8. E	19. E	30. D	41. E	52. E	63. D	74. D	85. E
9. B	20. E	31. D	42. E	53. A	64. C	75. D	86. A
10. C	21. D	32. B	43. A	54. D	65. B	76. B	87. C
11. A	22. C	33. E	44. B	55. A	66. D	77. C	88. E

PART D—ADDRESS CHECKING

1. A	13. D	25. D	37. A	49. D	61. A	73. D	85. D
2. D	14. A	26. D	38. A	50. A	62. D	74. A	86. D
3. D	15. D	27. A	39. A	51. D	63. A	75. A	87. D
4. A	16. D	28. D	40. A	52. D	64. A	76. D	88. D
5. A	17. D	29. D	41. D	53. D	65. A	77. A	89. D
6. A	18. D	30. A	42. D	54. D	66. D	78. A	90. D
7. D	19. D	31. A	43. D	55. A	67. D	79. D	91. A
8. D	20. A	32. A	44. D	56. A	68. D	80. A	92. A
9. A	21. D	33. A	45. D	57. D	69. D	81. A	93. D
10. D	22. A	34. D	46. D	58. A	70. A	82. D	94. A
11. A	23. A	35. D	47. A	59. A	71. A	83. D	95. A
12. A	24. D	36. A	48. A	60. D	72. A	84. A	

ADDRESS CHECKING ERROR ANALYSIS CHART

Type of Error	Tally	Total Number
Number of addresses that were alike and you incorrectly marked "different"		
Number of addresses that were different and you incorrectly marked "alike"		
Number of addresses in which you missed a difference in NUMBERS		
Number of addresses in which you missed a difference in ABBREVIATIONS		
Number of addresses in which you missed a difference in NAMES		

SCORE SHEET FOR FINAL MODEL EXAM

PART A—NUMBER SERIES

Number Right equals Score

_____ = _____

PART B—ADDRESS CODING

Number Right minus (Number Wrong ÷ 4) equals Score

_____ − _____ = _____

PART C—ADDRESS CODE MEMORY

Number Right minus (Number Wrong ÷ 4) equals Score

_____ − _____ = _____

PART D—ADDRESS CHECKING

Number Right minus Number Wrong equals Score

_____ − _____ = _____

SELF-EVALUATION CHART

Part	Excellent	Good	Average	Fair	Poor
Number Series	21–24	18–20	14–17	11–13	1–10
Address Coding	75–88	63–74	52–62	40–51	1–39
Address Code Memory	75–88	60–74	45–59	30–44	1–29
Address Checking	80–95	65–79	50–64	35–49	1–34

PROGRESS CHART

Blacken to the closest score to chart your progress.

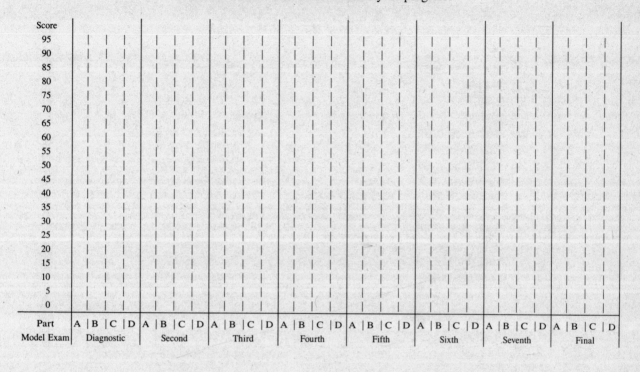

Score
95
90
85
80
75
70
65
60
55
50
45
40
35
30
25
20
15
10
5
0

Part	A B C D	A B C D	A B C D	A B C D	A B C D	A B C D	A B C D	A B C D
Model Exam	Diagnostic	Second	Third	Fourth	Fifth	Sixth	Seventh	Final